EMERGENCY
PROPAGANDA

EMERGENCY PROPAGANDA

The Winning of Malayan Hearts and Minds 1948–1958

Kumar Ramakrishna

CURZON

First Published in 2002
by Curzon Press
Richmond, Surrey
http://www.curzonpress.co.uk

© 2002 Kumar Ramakrishna

Typeset in Sabon by LaserScript Ltd, Mitcham, Surrey
Printed and bound in Great Britain by
TJ International, Padstow, Cornwall

British Library Cataloguing in Publication Data
A catalogue record of this book is available from the British Library

Library of Congress Cataloguing in Publication Data
A catalogue record for this book has been requested

ISBN 0–7007–1510–X

Contents

Acknowledgements   ix
List of Abbreviations   xi
Map   xiv

1   Propaganda in the Malayan Emergency: The Missing Dimension   1

     The Malayan Emergency: History and Historiography   4

     Defining 'Hearts and Minds'   11

     Understanding 'Propaganda'   12

     The Antecedents of British Propaganda in the Malayan
         Emergency I: Propaganda of Words   17

     The Antecedents of British Propaganda in the Malayan
         Emergency II: Propaganda of the Deed   21

     Approach   25

**2   The Malayan Communist Party and its Impact on Terrorist
and Rural Chinese Confidence**   26

     The Malayan Communist Party, the Rural Chinese and the
         'Rank and File'   27

     Central's Intellectual and Doctrinal Problems   31

     The MCP, the Terrorists and the Tension between Education
         and Coercion   36

     The MCP, the Masses and the Tension between Education and
         Terror   40

     Admission of Doctrinal Mistakes: The October 1951 Directives
         and the Aftermath   47

     Conclusion   52

3 **Propaganda in Disarray: The Mistakes of the Gurney Years,**
   June 1948–May 1950   54
   Introduction   54
   Gurney, MacDonald and the Rural Chinese   55
   The Consequences of the Loss of the Chinese Protectorate   58
   The Propaganda Implications of Government and Security Force
     Behaviour   61
   Detention, Deportation and Rehabilitation   64
   Government 'Deeds' and Terrorist Confidence   68
   The Disorganisation of Government Word-Propaganda   72
   Problems with Government Propaganda to the Rural Chinese
     Public   78
   Government Propaganda and the Terrorists   80
   Conclusion   84

4 **Propaganda on the Mend: The Impact of Briggs and Greene,**
   May 1950–February 1952   87
   Introduction   87
   Briggs, His Plan and the Rural Chinese   88
   The Limitations of Briggs as Leader-Propagandist and the
     Consequences   89
   The Propaganda Impact of Flawed Resettlement   92
   Detention, Deportation and Collective Punishment   97
   The Propaganda Consequences of Security Force Behaviour   100
   Government Measures and Terrorist Confidence   102
   Briggs, Greene and Government Propaganda of Words   104
   Government Psychological Warfare and the Terrorists   113
   Conclusion   118

5 **Propaganda Turning Point: Templer, February 1952–May 1954**   120
   Introduction   120
   The Man, the Plan, and the Rural Chinese   120
   The Propaganda Impact of the New Villages   126
   Operation Service and the Agents of Government   130
   From Collective Detention to White Areas   136
   The Improving Attack on Terrorist Confidence   140
   A.D.C. Peterson and the Birth of 'Information Services'   144
   Government Psychological Warfare and Terrorist Confidence   153
   Conclusion   159

**6 Propaganda Most Optimal: Tunku Abdul Rahman and the
    Collapse of the Communist Terrorist Organisation,
    June 1954–December 1958**   160

   Introduction   160

   Tunku Abdul Rahman: The Last Man for the Plan   161

   The New Villages under Tunku   167

   The Security Forces and Chinese Confidence   171

   Government's Increasingly 'Propaganda-Minded' Policies   174

   Government Deeds and the Steady Erosion of Terrorist
      Confidence   177

   Government Propaganda of Words in the Final Phase   180

   The Return of C.C. Too and the State of Government
      Psychological Warfare   187

   Propaganda Endgame: January 1955–December 1958   190

   Conclusion   201

Conclusion   204

Notes   216
Bibliography   283
Index   296

Acknowledgements

I would like to express my heartfelt thanks to my supervisor, Tony Stockwell, for his incisive comments and unstinting support throughout the preparation of the thesis on which this book is based. I have learned a great deal from him. I am also grateful to many other people for their help, advice and encouragement, in particular W.P. Coughlan, J.L.M. Gorrie, John Gullick, Datin Jean Marshall, Tony Short, Richard Stubbs, C.M. Turnbull and Dato Khoo Kay Kim. I would also like to record my appreciation for the help afforded me by three scholars who have since passed on: Ralph Smith, Richard Clutterbuck, and O.W. Wolters. Many have contributed positively to this book; any mistakes or omissions therein are entirely my own.

I must also thank Ian Pringle and Malcolm Campbell for giving me the confidence that my thesis on propaganda in the Emergency could become a useful book. Thanks also go out to Rachel Saunders and David McCarthy for expertly and gently shepherding the manuscript towards publication and to Rachel Choo for providing a useful index. I would also like to record my gratitude to Frank Cass Publishers for permission to use material from my article 'Content, Credibility and Context: Propaganda, Government Surrender Policy and the Malayan Communist Terrorist Mass Surrenders of 1958', published in *Intelligence and National Security*, Vol. 14, No. 4 (Winter 1999). In addition, I would like to acknowledge the Malaysian Branch of the Royal Asiatic Society for permission to cite from my article entitled 'The Making of a Malayan Propagandist: The Communists, the British and C.C. Too', which appears in *Journal of the Malaysian Branch of the Royal Asiatic Society*, published in June 2000. Finally, I would also like to thank the *Journal of Southeast Asian Studies* for permission to cite from my article "Transmogrifying" Malaya: the impact of Sir Gerald Templer (1952-54)', which was published in February 2001. I am also grateful to the Trustees of the Liddell Hart Centre for Military Archives, King's College London, for permission to cite from documents lodged in their excellent collection.

I would also like to record my appreciation for the valuable help provided by the librarians and archivists at the Public Record Office, Arkib Negara Malaysia, Rhodes House Library (Oxford), Liddell Hart Centre for Military Archives, National Army Museum, Imperial War Museum, the Institute of Southeast Asian Studies Library, the School of Oriental and African Studies Library, Royal Holloway College Bedford Library, Senate House Library, the Colindale Newspaper Library, the National Archives of Singapore, the National Library of Singapore and the SAFTI Military Institute Library. Particular thanks also go to Mr S.R. Nathan, President of the Republic of Singapore, for much-needed assistance in gaining access to documents on the late C.C. Too, and for his more general encouragement and support. I would also like to thank the Ministry of Defence, Singapore for graciously funding my studies in the United Kingdom, as well as Ong Chit Chung, Kwa Chong Guan and Sng Seow Lian for helping make my sponsorship possible. I am also grateful to Ang Cheng Guan, Khong Yuen Foong and Barry Desker, for encouraging and motivating me to continue with my research work.

I extend my enduring thanks to Edwin Thumboo and Lau Teik Soon for their advice and support at a crucial time in my career, as well as to my family and close friends for their love and encouragement down the years. To my dear wife Rosemary and sons Joshua and Jonathan, I dedicate this piece of work. Last but by no means least, I give thanks to God, who has always kept me steadfast in times of trial.

List of Abbreviations

AEBUS	Anti-Enemy Backing Up Society
AIO	Area Information Officer
ANM	Arkib Negara Malaysia (National Archives of Malaysia)
ARO	Assistant Resettlement Officer
ACAO	Assistant Chinese Affairs Officer
BBC	British Broadcasting Corporation
BMA	British Military Administration
CAO	Chinese Affairs Officer
CCM	Central Committee Member
CDW	Colonial Development and Welfare
CCP	Chinese Communist Party
CEP	Captured Enemy Personnel
CFO	Chinese Field Officer (Mobile Unit)
DCM	District Committee Member
DGIS	Director-General Information Services
DIS	Director Information Services/Department of Information Services
DO	District Officer
DOR	Director of Operations Review
DPR	Department of Public Relations
DWEC	District War Executive Committee
EEP	'End of Empire' Papers, Rhodes House Library, Oxford
EIS	Emergency Information Services
EOC	Emergency Operations Council
FEO	Federal Establishment Office
FMS	Federated Malay States
FO	Field Officer (Mobile Unit)
GCC	Good Citizens' Committee
HEIS	Head Emergency Information Services

HPWS	Head Psychological Warfare Section
IWM	Imperial War Museum
JIPC	Joint Information and Propaganda Committee
KMT	Kuomintang
LHCMA	Liddell Hart Centre for Military Archives, King's College London
MCA	Malayan Chinese Association
MCP	Malayan Communist Party
MCS	Malayan Civil Service
MOI	Ministry of Information, United Kingdom
MPABA	Malayan People's Anti-British Army
MPAJA	Malayan People's Anti-Japanese Army
MFU	Malayan Film Unit
MRLA	Malayan Races Liberation Army
NAM	National Army Museum
NAS	National Archives of Singapore
PMFTU	Pan-Malayan Federation of Trade Unions
PP	Private Papers, C.C. Too
PRS	Public Relations Secretary, Singapore
PSC	Public Service Commission
PWS	Psychological Warfare Section
RHO	Rhodes House Library, Oxford
RO	Resettlement Officer
SCA	Secretary for Chinese Affairs
SCM	State Committee Member
SEIO	State Emergency Information Officer
SEP	Surrendered Enemy Personnel
SIO	State Information Officer
SWEC	State War Executive Committee
TCLP-ISEAS	Tan Cheng Lock Papers, Institute of Southeast Asian Studies, Singapore
UMNO	United Malays National Organisation
VAC	Voice Aircraft Committee
WINSUM	'Security Forces' Weekly Intelligence Summary'
WNS	'Department of Information Weekly News Summary'

Federation of Malaya, 1948

CHAPTER ONE

Propaganda in the Malayan Emergency

The Missing Dimension

The Malayan Emergency is one of the few post-war insurgencies which the insurgents did not win, and this fact has generated much interest in the reasons as to why the Government of the Federation of Malaya was eventually able to overcome the revolt led by the Malayan Communist Party (MCP). The conventional view holds that Government succeeded because of its effectiveness in the administrative, military and political spheres. Administratively, by constructing New Villages that provided 'supplies of clean water, schools, community centres, basic medical care, some agricultural land' and some other basic essentials, Government is said to have secured the all-important 'hearts and minds' of the Malayan Chinese, who were the MCP's support base.[1] Complementing hearts-and-minds tactics were the 'severe penalties' of 'mass detention, deportations and resettlement', which, by removing the Chinese from the jungle fringes, disrupted the MCP's supply line and effectively broke the back of the Emergency.[2] Militarily, it is suggested that Government beat the MCP because it had an overall plan which co-ordinated administrative, Police and Army measures at all levels and sought to secure its own base areas before embarking on a military campaign against the terrorists. Moreover, the Security Forces were eventually able to secure better intelligence on the terrorists and mount effective food control operations which deprived the terrorists of their essential supplies. Furthermore, by adhering to the time-honoured 'principles' of small-unit operations instead of large scale ones and importantly, the use of minimum force in operations in support of the civil power, Government was able to function within the law and defeat the terrorists without alienating the public.[3] Finally, the conventional view posits that Government, because it was committed to a 'clear political aim' – granting the non-Malays, especially the Chinese, a political stake in the country as a prelude to *Merdeka* or independence – was able to steal the MCP's thunder, as the latter was supposedly fighting for that very outcome.

Hence, political reforms in the form of elections at not only the State and Federal but particularly the New Village level, were necessary to the defeat of the Insurrection.[4]

The fundamental problem with the conventional perspective outlined above is that it conflates the political and military dimensions of the Emergency. Essentially, it suggests that the defeat of the military insurgency was contingent on the attainment of political security for the Malayan Chinese: once the Chinese were assured of a political stake in an independent Malaya, they deprived the MCP of their support and the insurgency collapsed. As we shall see, however, while progress in the insurgency certainly contributed to the pace of advance toward *Merdeka*, the converse was not true: mere political reforms did not *ipso facto* confer on Government the initiative in the shooting war. This is because the resolution of the military insurgency did not depend on securing the hearts and minds of those Chinese interested in political, constitutional questions, but rather those who were the least enamoured of such issues: the rural Chinese. In essence, there were really two Emergencies. First, a political one in which the British strove to create an anti-Communist, friendly, united Malayan nation governed by a multiracial Government. The key to this political Emergency was the Malay and Chinese elites represented by the United Malays National Organisation (UMNO) and the Malayan Chinese Association (MCA). The second Emergency embraced the military insurgency in the rural areas of Malaya, and the key to the resolution of this campaign lay as we shall see, with the rural Chinese. This crucial distinction has been obscured in the conventional view, which essentially asserts that it was political advance toward *Merdeka* which won the hearts and minds of the rural Chinese. In fact a recurring theme in this study will be that Government's ability to win over the rural Chinese depended not so much on whether the latter were provided the opportunity to become Federal citizens and to shape their political destiny, but rather if their basic needs for physical and socio-economic security were met. Securing these less abstract, more concrete needs was the real key to rural Chinese hearts and minds.

The issue of 'hearts and minds' brings us to a second problem with the conventional analysis: the absence of conceptual rigour as to what 'hearts and minds' refers to in the Emergency. While Cloake and Stubbs for instance take the meaning of the phrase as self-evident and instead seek to identify when the term was first used during the Emergency, Carruthers merely suggests that the hearts and minds of not only colonial, but also metropolitan, peoples were an important objective for the British to secure.[5] Moreover, while Mockaitis gives the impression that the hearts and minds of the public were most important,[6] Hack distinguishes between 'civilian' and 'military' hearts and minds, and places political concessions, schools and piped water under the 'civilian' category, and propaganda, rewards for information, surrender policies and limiting collateral damage, under 'military'. He, however, makes no attempt to explain this distinction.[7] A third shortcoming with the received wisdom exists: although the psychological connotation of the phrase 'hearts and minds' is apparent, analysts pay relatively little attention to the psychological dimension of the Emergency. The emphasis has been on the functional aspects of counter-insurgency methods and techniques such as resettlement, food control, intelligence, civil-military co-operation and small unit operations. The ways in which such measures also generated mental pressures on the public and the terrorists — with operational consequences — have been far less noticed. Those few writers who do recognise the significance of psychological elements focus separately — and in a piecemeal fashion — on their effect on different groups in Malaya: the Malayan public, the MCP terrorists, and British troops. No work systematically examines the impact of psychological pressures on the key players in the rural insurrection: the MCP rank and file and the rural Chinese public.[8]

The final problem with the prevailing view derives directly from the general neglect of the psychological dimension: the relative marginalisation of the role of Government propaganda in the Emergency, despite acknowledgement that it was very effective.[9] This marginalisation has taken two forms: at one level, 'propaganda' has been narrowly conceived as Government's spoken, printed and broadcast output: leaflets and posters, mobile cinema shows, roving lectures by Surrendered Enemy Personnel, rewards for information, Voice Aircraft broadcasts and Civics Courses for instance. Such a limited perspective has meant that previous analysts have ignored the propaganda implications of certain Government policies as well as the behaviour of senior officials and the Security Forces amongst the public, and the ways in which Security Force pressure and food denial schemes also constituted 'propaganda' to harassed and starving terrorists. In addition, even with respect to Government spoken, printed and broadcast output — propaganda as conventionally understood — past works have opted for a descriptive rather than an analytical approach, failing to explain the philosophy underlying the usage of such propaganda media in Malaya and where it came from. Furthermore, there is disagreement on the relative contributions of Hugh Carleton Greene, Head Emergency Information Services (1950–1951) and A.D.C. Peterson, Director-General Information Services (1952–1954). While some writers highlight only Peterson,[10] others focus on Greene.[11] Very few have attempted to assess in detail the contributions of both.[12] Moreover, because most analyses treat Templer's departure from Malaya in mid-1954 as the virtual end of the Emergency and regard the remaining years as a long 'mopping up' process,[13] there has been little attention paid to the contributions of Yaacob Latiff, Director of Information Services from July 1954, and C.C. Too, Head Psychological Warfare Section from 1956, to Government propaganda in the decisive period January 1955 to December 1958. As we shall see, the actual collapse of terrorist morale compelling the MCP to demobilise occurred during this period, and Government propaganda played a decisive role.[14]

In light of these omissions in the literature, this study will show that fundamentally, Government was able to defeat the MCP's rural insurgency because it was gradually able, despite an inauspicious beginning, to secure the 'hearts and minds' – or more accurately the 'confidence' of not only the rural Chinese public but also that of the terrorist rank and file. We shall see that Government was able to achieve these outcomes through the propaganda of not merely its 'words', but even more importantly 'deeds' which promoted the physical and socio-economic security of the rural Chinese and ultimately even the terrorists. At the same time, we shall note that the MCP inadvertently contributed to Government's eventual success through serious doctrinal errors; mistakes constituting in themselves 'propaganda' which completely alienated the mass of the rural Chinese as well as the bulk of its own rank and file. Within this overarching framework, the study will also pursue five supplemental aims: it will examine the origins and evolution of certain Government attitudes and practices which had considerable propaganda implications in Malaya; analyse the origins and evolution of the media, organisation and philosophy of Government spoken, printed and broadcast propaganda in Malaya; evaluate the respective contributions of the key propagandists Hugh Greene and Alec Peterson to the development of Government propaganda; analyse the contributions of Yaacob Latiff and C.C. Too to Government propaganda during the final phase of the Insurrection between 1955 and the end of 1958; and finally show, from a propaganda perspective, that 21 December 1957 was the date which marked the beginning of the collapse in MCP morale, culminating in the mass surrenders of 1958. In line with these aims, this introductory chapter will briefly sketch out the historical and historiographical context of the Emergency, develop a model of propaganda applicable to the conflict, and identify the imperial and wartime antecedents of British propaganda in the Emergency.

THE MALAYAN EMERGENCY: HISTORY AND HISTORIOGRAPHY

In order to defend the eastern flank of the Indian Empire on the one hand and the security of the China trade route on the other, the British East India Company recognised that control of the Straits of Malacca was essential. Beginning in 1786, therefore, the Company established Settlements at Penang, Singapore, and Malacca, which were united formally in 1826 as the Straits Settlements. Control of the Settlements passed directly to the Colonial Office in 1867, when the Settlements became a Crown Colony.

Between 1874 and 1895, moreover, British power was further extended into the interior, encompassing the Malay States of Perak, Selangor, Negri Sembilan and Pahang. In these States, Malay Rulers allowed British Residents to tacitly assume effective administrative control over all matters except those pertaining to Malay religion and custom. In 1896, these Protected States were unified in the interests of administrative efficiency and referred to henceforth as the Federated Malay States. The Governor of the Straits Settlements became concurrently High Commissioner to the Federated Malay States. Furthermore, in 1909, the four northern States of Kedah, Perlis, Trengganu and Kelantan passed to British control from Siam, and in 1914, Johore was added. These five States were known collectively as the Unfederated Malay States, and accepted British Advisers with remits similar to those of the Residents in the Federated States. Hence, between 1874 and 1914, British control of the internal administration and foreign policy of the Malay States was consolidated.[15]

British intervention involved developing the resources of Malaya, principally tin and rubber, and this in turn demanded a labour force. The indigenous Malays – and the migrants from the surrounding archipelago who assimilated with them – lived in villages located near coasts and river estuaries, were primarily farmers and fishermen, and demonstrably unenthusiastic about working a fixed number of hours each day for wages.[16] This meant that immigrant labour was needed. The British thus encouraged Chinese and Indian immigration into Malaya, thereby shaping the country's demographic destiny. Indian immigration – mainly Madrasi Tamils from south India – tended to match the expansion of the Malayan rubber industry. Hence when the total acreage under rubber grew from 50,000 acres in 1900 to 3,272,000 acres by 1938 – making Malaya the world's largest producer of natural rubber – the Indian population – only 30,000 in 1870 – shot up to 625,000 in 1931. Plantation labour proved the most important economic activity of the Malayan Indians, employing 53 percent of the Indian population as late as 1947. By this date, however, other sectors were employing other Indians as well. These included English-educated Jaffna or Ceylon Tamils who had been brought in from the 1890s to staff clerical posts in the Railway, Postal Services, Accounts and Treasury Departments in particular; Sikhs, Punjabis and north Indians who filled jobs in the Police and other Government departments; Tamil professionals and south Indian Muslim retailers who filled the private sector; and the wealthy Chettyar Tamils who were principally money-lenders.[17]

Matching the diversity of Indian immigration, eclipsing it in terms of scale and crucially important to our understanding of the Emergency was Chinese immigration. The earliest Chinese immigrants, from the 1500s, had been Hokkiens from Fukien in south China who settled in Malacca, many of whom intermarrying with the Malays and producing the progeny that became known as the Straits Chinese or *Babas*. It was however the growth in European, especially British, demand for Straits tin from the 1850s and 1860s that led to a massive increase in Chinese coolie immigration into the tin-rich States of Perak, Selangor and Sungei Ujong (later part of Negri Sembilan). Thus by 1901 65 percent of the population of Selangor was Chinese. However, because these immigrant Chinese considered Malaya as a temporary abode, a place to make money before returning, there was considerable ebb and flow in migration between Malaya and China in the first decades of the 20th century. Nevertheless, up to the late 1920s, there was a considerable migrational gain to Malaya. However, following the worldwide tin and rubber slump in 1930, serious unemployment prompted thousands of Chinese to return to China. In addition, the Federated Malay States (FMS) Government passed the Immigration Restriction Ordinance in 1930 which sharply curtailed Chinese male immigration into Malaya. Hence while there had been 192,809 Chinese arriving in 1928, by 1933 the number had declined to 13,535. While the 1933 Aliens Ordinance also imposed a quota on male immigration, very significantly, it imposed none on female immigration. Thus between 1933 and 1938 190,000 Chinese females arrived in the Federated Malay States. This had the effect of improving the sex ratio: while there had been 5 females to every 10 Chinese males in 1931, by 1947, there were 8 females to every 10 males. These women were aged between 18 and 40, were mainly peasants and entered the rubber, tin and building industries as well as factories. They married the male coolies and settled in Malaya. Furthermore, indentured workers who had worked off their debts returned to China, married and brought their wives back to Malaya. These developments in the 1930s facilitated the transformation of the immigrant male Chinese from a temporary sojourner into a settled family man, and the immigrant Chinese in Malaya became a more stable community. Hence by the end of the Japanese Occupation, while the Malays formed 44 percent of the approximately 5 million population, the Chinese formed a significant 38.5 percent.[18]

These increasingly settled Chinese immigrants were largely from the southern Chinese provinces of Kwangtung, Kwangsi and Fukien, and comprised five main groups: Cantonese and Hakkas, who were cultivators and rubber tappers but mainly miners; Tiechius who were essentially agriculturalists in Penang/Province Wellesley; Hailams from Hainan island; and Hokkiens. While the Hokkiens were concentrated in Penang as traders, Hokkien sub-groups like the Hokchius, Hokchias and Hinghwas were mainly labourers. Of particular salience were the Chinese concentrated in the rural sector – the tappers, miners and agriculturalists. Although the coolie Chinese had been brought in principally to provide a labour pool for the exploitation of Malaya's tin and rubber, during times of food shortages and economic slumps, as in 1920–21, 1930–32, and 1938, the FMS Government established Food Production Reserves and issued the rural Chinese with Temporary Occupation Licences (TOLs) to encourage them to grow crops like rice, vegetables and even cash crops like tapioca and groundnuts to keep them occupied and earning a living. Although the tin and rubber industries, once recovered, re-employed these rural Chinese and Government withdrew the TOLs, many rural Chinese did not give up cash cropping as they had found it more stable and profitable than working on estates or mines. Hence by the time the Japanese invaded Malaya in December 1941, 150,000 rural Chinese remained on land without TOLs and were technically considered squatters. Furthermore, by the end of the Japanese Occupation in September 1945, the number of squatters had risen to about 300,000. Three factors contributed to this increase: first, thousands of urban Chinese had escaped from the towns because of Japanese persecution; second, urban food shortages, inflation of food prices and rationing had also acted as a push factor; and third, the Japanese, like the FMS Government in the 1920s and 1930s, had also tried to alleviate food shortages by resettling urban Chinese on rural estates, mines, State Land, Forest Reserves and even Malay Reservations. In addition, immediately after the war, because wages in the rubber and tin industries were insufficient to support families, many Chinese, even if working on estates and mines, continued to squat illegally, engaging in food cultivation to supplement their incomes. It was these rural, squatter Chinese who were to be the focus of the propaganda war between Government and the MCP during the Emergency.[19]

It was conscious British policy to maintain ethnic barriers in this plural society of Malays, Chinese and Indians. From the 1870s, realising that the large numbers of immigrants entering the country could conceivably threaten the future position of the Malays, the British pursued a declared policy of 'Malaya for the Malays', actively endeavouring to build up a Malay elite capable of assisting them in maintaining the Malay identity of the country. Hence in 1905 a Malay College was opened in Kuala Kangsar, while a Malayan Administrative Service was also started to absorb graduates of the College. The better Malay civil servants were then promoted to the British-dominated Malayan Civil Service (MCS). By the 1930s, about 10 percent of MCS officers were Malay.[20] These consciously maintained pre-war ethnic barriers were reinforced by the Occupation. While Malay Rulers, civil servants and ordinary people collaborated with the Japanese, 40,000 Chinese perished as part of the so-called *sook ching* campaign mounted by the Japanese Army. Furthermore, it was during the Occupation that the Malayan Communist Party (MCP) developed into a major political force on the peninsula. Formed originally in 1925 by mainland Chinese Communists, it was revamped on Comintern instructions in 1930 so as to establish more multiracial credentials. Throughout the 1930s, however, repeated disruptions of its communications links with the Comintern, internal schisms – and because it was illegal – Police repression, hampered its efforts. However, its fortunes began to improve from 1936, when it successfully mounted strikes and demonstrations exploiting worker distress during the slump caused by the global depression. A year later, moreover, following the Japanese invasion of China in July 1937, the Party enjoyed considerable success in setting up anti-Japanese fronts in Malaya to mobilise the local Chinese in decrying Japanese aggression, the most important being the Anti-Enemy Backing Up Society (AEBUS). During the Occupation, the MCP – now styling itself the Malayan People's Anti-Japanese Army (MPAJA) – built very close ties with the squatter Chinese mentioned earlier. As these Chinese generally bore the brunt of Japanese brutality, they welcomed the MPAJA's attempts to strike back on their behalf. Hence they not only joined the MPAJA fighting units but also supplied the Communists through the secret organisation called MPAJU (Malayan People's Anti-Japanese Union). So significant did the MPAJA become that by 1943 the British had recognised it as a force to be reckoned with and supplied it with instructors and arms. By the end of the war, the MPAJA boasted 7,000–8,000 men under arms with thousands more in the cells of the MPAJU. Significantly, in the three weeks between the Japanese surrender and the arrival of British forces, the MPAJA emerged from the jungle to dispense summary justice to collaborators with the Japanese. This resulted in large scale Sino-Malay clashes in Johore. Not only did these and later clashes have a lasting effect on Sino-Malay relations, they added credence to the perception that the MCP remained very much a Chinese Party, something which was to have fateful consequences during the Emergency.[21]

The end of the Occupation also saw British moves to effect a fundamental transformation in the political landscape of Malaya. Wartime British planners had recognised that change was overdue for several reasons: the existence of the politically separate Settlements and Malay States was administratively unwieldy; a unified Malayan State was desirable if the country's natural resources were to be efficiently harnessed to assist in Britain's economic rehabilitation after the war; a common citizenship embracing not only Malays but also the immigrants, especially the Chinese, was just reward for their assistance in helping defend British interests in Malaya, and such a scheme needed direct British sovereignty over Malaya – bypassing the Rulers – in order to succeed; and finally direct rule of Malaya leading to the imposition of a uniform political structure on Malaya and a common citizenship were necessary prerequisites to the long-term goal of self-government, an outcome calculated to appease Britain's American allies. Accordingly, the Malayan Union was promulgated on 1 April 1946, unifying the Settlements of Malacca and Penang (but not Singapore) and all nine Malay States under a Governor acting as the direct representative of the British King, and depriving the Malay Rulers of their sovereignty. However, Malay opposition to the scheme coalesced around Dato Onn bin Jaafar, the *Mentri Besar* (chief minister) of Johore, and the United Malays

National Organisation (UMNO) was formed in May 1946 to protest against the Union. The British, taken aback at this vociferous Malay opposition, backtracked and after several months of negotiations, and despite opposition from the educated non-Malays, the Union was replaced on 1 February 1948 by the Federation Agreement. While the latter restored the sovereignty of the Rulers and recognised State autonomy once more, the core ideas of the Malayan Union: a strong central Government and common citizenship, were retained, although they would henceforth be achieved through a more circuitous route.[22]

These political convulsions aside, post-war Malaya was also racked by socio-economic unrest. The British Military Administration (BMA) which re-occupied the country from September 1945 to March 1946, as well as the civil administration which took over from April, were unable to shield the suffering population from endemic shortages: for instance, official rice rations were insufficient to feed the people while black market rice was very expensive, and housing was in short supply as well as characterised by high rents and overcrowding. Meanwhile the cost of living in November 1945 was estimated to be 300–400 percent higher than in pre-war days, and yet basic wages were still paid according to pre-war scales. Little wonder that labour unrest broke out in urban areas in the peninsula from the very month the BMA was set up. Meanwhile the MCP, which had demobilised the MPAJA in December 1945, but was no longer proscribed, fully exploited the economic distress of Malayan workers through its vehicle, the Pan-Malayan General Labour Union (PMGLU – later split into the Pan-Malayan Federation of Trade Unions and the Singapore Federation of Trade Unions). PMGLU demands were pegged at the socio-economic level: large wage increases, free medical services, better housing, paid sick leave and paid holidays, for instance. Because the militant PMGLU met the real needs of workers, it gained a large measure of support which it translated into public demonstrations against the BMA, which peaked in January/February 1946 in Singapore and the peninsula. Because the BMA belatedly responded firmly with arrests of key Communist officials, however, from February 1946 onward the MCP withdrew from overt confrontation with Government. Instead until June 1948 it focused its energies at three levels: first, the Party intensified its labour agitation through its cadres in the unions, a strategy so successful that by March 1947, the PMFTU had branches in every industry and craft in Malaya. Second, the Communists set up front organisations like the New Democratic Youth League, the Ex-Servicemen's Association for former MPAJA guerrillas and even a Chinese Women's Association, to penetrate all sectors of the public. Finally, the MCP participated in the Malayan political arena by infiltrating the Malayan Democratic Union (MDU) which had been formed by English-educated intellectuals in December 1945, as well as radical Malay organisations and the pro-Indonesia Malay Nationalist Party. Hence the

MCP was able, through the MDU-led All-Malayan Council for Joint Action (AMCJA) and PUTERA (a coalition of radical Malay parties), to take part in fomenting opposition to the proposed Federation Agreement. In sum, between 1946 and 1948, the MCP sought to dominate Malaya by capturing and controlling industrial, social and political bodies.[23]

Nevertheless, despite its success in extending its influence through its 'open and legal struggle', in mid-June 1948 the MCP switched strategy: its members left the urban areas of Malaya, reactivated the wartime rural support organisation amongst the squatters and from the recesses of the Malayan jungle launched an armed revolt against the Federation Government. The origins of this Insurrection have been shrouded in controversy. One perspective posits that international factors were crucial in determining the timing of the Malayan uprising. Proponents of this view argue that in September 1947 in Poland the Soviet leader Andrei Zhdanov formally declared that wartime co-operation was at an end and the world was divided into two irreconcilably opposed camps, Imperialism and Anti-Imperialism. The Zhdanov line was emphasised again in February/March 1948 in Calcutta, at the Second Congress of the Communist Party of India and the Southeast Asian Youth Conference. According to this argument, therefore, it was no coincidence that revolts broke out in Malaya, Indonesia and Burma in 1948. On the other hand, another argument suggests that the change of MCP tack came about because of factors internal to Malaya: the assumption of the Secretary-Generalship by Chin Peng, who was inclined to a more militant line than his predecessor Lai Tek; the restlessness of MCP members who had been unhappy with the earlier decision to demobilise the MPAJA; the erosion of the MCP's ability to influence the masses due to the recovering economy; and the failure of the AMCJA-PUTERA strategy to help the MCP secure power. A further view posits that labour unrest on estates between 1946 and 1948 prompted a growing pattern of Government repression in the form of Police action against striking workers and banishment of Communist unionists, culminating in the swift passage of restrictive union legislation at the end of May 1948 which rendered the PMFTU illegal. Taken aback by the swiftness and ferocity of Government action, the MCP was forced to the jungle prematurely as a defensive reaction to Government measures.[24] Interestingly, in June 1998, Chin Peng surfaced in London and revealed that the MCP revolt was never directed from Moscow, and that while the Party from March 1948 had foreseen its possible proscription, this development had been expected to occur by September. Hence Government's clampdown following the murders of three planters in Sungei Siput, Perak on 16 June caught it utterly off-balance.[25] At any rate, by June 1948, the first shots in the Malayan Emergency had been fired, and it would be 12 long years before Government officially declared it at an end.

DEFINING 'HEARTS AND MINDS'

Having described the historical and historiographical context of the Emergency, we may now attempt a rigorous definition of 'hearts and minds' and 'propaganda'. To do so adequately however requires an understanding as to where these concepts fit into the very fabric of war, and there is no better guide to this subject than Clausewitz, the nineteenth-century Prussian philosopher. There exists an unfortunate modern misperception that Clausewitz was never interested in conflicts other than conventional wars. For instance Thomas K. Adams claims that because Clausewitz has no interest in 'psycho-social' means of statecraft, the Prussian has nothing useful to say about insurgencies.[26] In actual fact, Clausewitz starts off by arguing that 'psycho-social' or moral factors 'form the spirit which permeates the whole being of War', including not merely conventional wars but also what he calls 'popular uprisings'. Clausewitz's idea of the intrinsic psychological dynamic of all types of war is clearly expressed in the 'Trinity of War' concept – ignored by Adams – which posits that war in real life is waged when the basic *passions* of the People are harnessed by Government and translated into policies as well as military strategies which the Army pursues. It follows that the People are the well-spring – in not only the physical but also the moral sense – of the capacity of Government and the Army to wage war.[27] To Clausewitz, therefore, the People represents the ultimate 'centre of gravity' – the 'hub of all power and movement on which everything depends' – of a country at war.[28] If this is true of conventional wars, it is arguably even more so in insurgencies, where the support of the People is the *sine qua non* of success in counterinsurgency efforts. Hence Clausewitz emphasises that the centre of gravity in 'popular uprisings' is 'public opinion'.[29] Clausewitz therefore provides a theoretical 'nest' for the much-bandied phrase 'hearts and minds': in the context of an insurgency like the Emergency it refers to 'public opinion'. Of course, retaining the Clausewitzian framework does not *ipso facto* require us to adhere to his peculiar terminology. We might use other terms in preference to 'hearts and minds': for instance the student of propaganda Lasswell prefers the phrase 'moral',[30] while in the context of the Emergency, Short has referred to public 'confidence'.[31]

The People are the centre of gravity in an insurgency not only because Government and the Army need their support in implementing counter-insurgency measures but also because the insurgents emerge from the People as well. Hence if Government wins the support of the People, the flow of recruits to the insurgent cause would be cut off. This is not to say, however, that insurgent 'hearts and minds' are unimportant in relation to that of the wider People. After all, should the insurgents be persuaded at some point to lay down arms, the insurgency – and the need for an expensive counterinsurgency – would end immediately. Now persuading insurgents, or indeed any enemy forces, to lay down arms requires, as Clausewitz observes, not merely the destruction of their physical but especially their 'will' or 'psychic forces'.[32] Insurgents' 'psychic forces' are thus a legitimate target of Government efforts, and in modern parlance, is referred to as 'morale'. Rundquist and Sletto define morale as 'one's confidence in one's ability to cope with whatever the future may bring',[33] while Frezza argues that morale involves the 'conviction of having some resource adequate to meet the threat'.[34] A more rigorous definition of 'morale' has been provided by General William Slim, the charismatic commander of the Fourteenth Army in Burma during World War Two.[35] He defines 'morale' as a positive 'state of mind' that has three components: 'spiritual' confidence that the cause is just; 'intellectual' confidence that the goal can be attained; and 'material' confidence that the means of attaining the goal (good leadership, sufficient provisions and good working and living conditions), are available.[36]

In fact, throughout this study, we shall see that the terms 'confidence' and 'morale', rather than 'hearts and minds' – surprising as it may seem – were used more often by contemporary participants and observers to describe fluctuations in the state of mind of the public and the terrorists. By June 1951 for instance, both High Commissioner Gurney and Director of Operations Briggs reported that 'success depends on the morale of and the help given by the population and the breaking of communist morale and organisation'.[37] Hence in this study, instead of 'hearts and minds', we will adopt the term 'confidence' and generate working definitions based on this concept. Thus, if we accept that an integral aspect of 'confidence' is a sense of assurance and certainty, then in the specific context of the Emergency, we could consider 'public confidence' as the assurance enjoyed by members of the public that Government was willing and able to provide security and welfare despite the Communist Insurrection. Moreover, by 'terrorist confidence' we mean the assurance on the part of Communist terrorists, that the MCP was willing and able to fulfil its promises to them. We shall also observe that in the context of Government's surrender policy, terrorist confidence meant the assurance that Government promises of fair treatment would be kept.

UNDERSTANDING 'PROPAGANDA'

If the confidence of the People and the terrorists are important objectives to target in an insurgency, then what *means* could Government use to do so? This is where propaganda comes into the picture. 'Propaganda' (variously known as 'psychological warfare', 'psychological operations' and 'political warfare') represents 'a suspect word and a suspect activity', an exercise in making 'people do things against their will', utilising 'deceit' and 'trickery'.[38] Moreover, there is no shortage of definitions. For instance,

Lasswell argues that propaganda is concerned with 'the management of opinions and attitudes by the direct manipulation of social suggestion',[39] while Taylor opines that propaganda refers to the 'organisation of methods designed to persuade people to think and behave in a certain way'.[40] In addition, Linebarger has provided a well-known definition of propaganda: the 'planned use of any form of communication designed to affect the minds, emotions, and action of a given group for a specific purpose'.[41] These definitions certainly accommodate the use of public speeches, leaflets, film shows, radio broadcasts and other conventionally accepted media of propaganda. However, we argue here that a definition of propaganda limited merely to the content of various instruments of communication would be overly restrictive. Clausewitz helps us understand why.

To recapitulate, because moral factors permeate the entire being of war, Clausewitz's trinity – the Government, the Army and the People – live in not merely a physical but simultaneously a moral (or psychological) milieu as well. Moreover:[42]

> The effects of physical and psychological factors form an organic whole which, unlike a metal alloy, is inseparable by chemical processes.

The implication is that in war, every physical act has an inescapable psychological by-product. Hence, when Government forces shell an enemy position, they subject the opposing troops not merely to physical but also psychological pressure. 'Physical factors' do not only mean firepower. When Government officials build a clinic in a village, they not only meet the villagers' physical needs, they at the same time influence the villagers' *feelings* toward Government. This notion of the moral effects of physical action is not at all confined to Clausewitz. The Italian anarchist Carlo Pisacane argues that ideas always emanate from 'deeds', and Pisacane's thoughts subsequently influenced the French anti-parliamentarian Paule Brousse, who coined the famous phrase 'propaganda of the deed'.[43] Although 'propaganda of the deed' has traditionally been a pejorative phrase given its association with the underground activity of nineteenth-century Russian anarchists and social revolutionaries, it is nevertheless entirely relevant in helping us develop a more rounded appreciation of 'propaganda'. After all, even the noted student of propaganda Harold Lasswell accepts that physical deeds are simply another type of 'mass communication', because *like words, deeds can communicate a message*. Hence, not merely 'spoken or printed' words and pictures, but also 'physical acts' such as the assassination of a key figure, can communicate futility and 'destroy the enemy's will to fight'.[44] More recently, moreover, Saunders avers that 'carefully constructed images and words', as well as 'bullets, shells and bombs' can communicate power and 'reduce the enemy's will to win'.[45]

Because of the communicative characteristic of deeds, Watson argues that political, economic and military actions have as much 'psychological impact' on the target group as leaflets and broadcasts.[46] Thus 'civic action' – those attempts by Government to make 'real, lasting improvements to the social, economic and political environment', like building a school or a medical clinic; 'community relations' – activities such as organising a picnic for the villagers in a district; and 'troop behaviour' – the basic attitude of Government forces toward the local population – represent deeds with profound psychological effects and can be considered as propaganda.[47] In sum, because not only Government leaflets and other media but also Government 'deeds' communicate messages to an audience, Askenasy argues that 'propaganda' should be conceived as 'a co-ordinated approach' embracing both words and deeds to 'influence' the audience's 'way of thinking and acting'.[48] In other words, to ensure that its leaflets, films and radio broadcasts – its 'words' – are credible, Government must *co-ordinate its words and deeds so as to project the same message to the target audience*. If Government's words convey one thing but its actual deeds suggest something else, the audience will dismiss Government's words and lose confidence in its good faith. The need to synchronise all Government mass communications to a specific audience is the point of Luttwak's sardonic criticism of the American counterinsurgency approach in South Vietnam:[49]

> The [Agency for International Development] people would come to a village in Vietnam and help it out... The next day the air force would bomb the village. Then a special-forces team would go in to work with the survivors to rebuild the village and train them in self-defense [sic]. Next the artillery would barrage the village. Then a psychological operations unit would pass around leaflets and explain the importance of fighting the Vietcong. Then the navy would flatten the place with its gunfire.

In short, Vietnamese villagers could not consider as credible the message in Government leaflets that Government was their friend, when Government deeds suggested the opposite idea. It must be emphasised: to ensure the credibility of one's propaganda requires synchronising the pronouncements and actions of Government officials and troops. Askenasy thus argues that 'personnel should be sensitized [sic] to the psychological implications of potential actions', while 'sensitizing [sic] training' should be given not only to 'explicitly labeled [sic] psychological operations officers but also to commanders who make important decisions and to troops who are in daily contact' with the local population.[50]

Related to the need to ensure that one's words and deeds project the same message is the issue of their relative importance in one's overall propaganda. The anarchists felt that deeds were far more important.

Pisacane argues that 'intellectual propaganda' is 'an empty gesture', and Kropotkin avers that in dealing with largely uneducated people, physical 'deeds that attract general attention' can achieve 'more propagandizing in a few days than do thousands of leaflets'.[51] On the other hand, Most opines that words can be very helpful if closely co-ordinated with physical actions so as to exploit and amplify the message generated by the latter. This means that immediately after an action is carried out, pamphlets should be circulated 'setting out the reasons for the action in such a way as to draw from them the best possible benefit'.[52] In short, the psychological impact of a deed can be enhanced by the use of printed propaganda drawing the attention of the public to the act. However, while the psychological impact of a specific deed alone might be highly effective – as Kropotkin suggests – the psychological impact of words alone cannot. As Most suggests, printed or spoken propaganda needs to draw attention to – or 'exploit'- something tangible. If propaganda of words proclaims something which has no basis in reality, the audience will ignore it. Hence effective spoken, printed and even broadcast propaganda presupposes concrete deeds. Little wonder that more recently Katz observes that if political, social and economic programmes – concrete deeds – are 'seriously deficient', then 'no amount' of words 'will persuade the people that the programmes are worth while'.[53] In the case of the Emergency, moreover, Clutterbuck and Thompson have admitted that the work of Information Services simply had to be complemented by concrete progress in security and development in Malaya.[54] In sum, while the propagandist could conceivably persuade an audience through deeds alone, he cannot do so with words only. Words cannot persuade without concomitant deeds; the message conveyed by words must match that simultaneously communicated by real deeds.

It is now apposite to sum up this section by formulating a comprehensive understanding of 'propaganda': we may define 'propaganda' as *those relevant mass communications which influence the attitudes and behaviour of a specific audience*. The following points should be noted. First, the term 'mass communications' refers to both the conventional media of propaganda in addition to 'deeds' such as the behaviour of Government officials and the Security Forces, as well as certain Government policies. For propaganda to be credible both words and deeds have to be closely co-ordinated to ensure that they project the same message. If the propagandist's spoken, printed and broadcast output project one message but his actions convey a contradictory idea, the audience will reject his words and lose confidence in him. Furthermore, while the propagandist could influence an audience with deeds alone, he cannot do so with only words. Words have to exploit and amplify the message suggested by actual deeds.

The immediate objection to any definition of propaganda which encompasses 'deeds' is that *every* conceivable action or policy might be construed to have some impact on an audience, rendering the definition too broad to be tenable. This however, brings us to the next point: it is only those mass communications which are 'relevant' to a 'specific' audience that constitute propaganda to the latter. This is because the peculiar interests of a specific audience delimit the nature of the deeds (and for that matter the words) capable of influencing it. In short, propaganda is always audience-specific, and what constitutes propaganda for one group may not be for another. To use an analogy from the related field of advertising: a man who wants to buy a car naturally skips those newspaper classifieds which advertise vacuum cleaners. The advertisements about vacuum cleaners may be smartly-crafted and eye catching, but the man ignores them because they are not *relevant to his specific needs*. Similarly, the man would be less attentive toward a neighbour who shows up eager to show off his new vacuum cleaner than another who turns up in his new car which seems to be well-engineered. To reiterate: it is only those mass communications which address the real needs of a specific audience which translate into propaganda capable of influencing that audience. In the case of the Insurrection, therefore, Government's much-trumpeted moves to liberalise Federal citizenship conditions and introduce elections at all levels prompted a positive response mainly from the educated, wealthy urban Chinese. The rural Chinese however were largely unimpressed, judging from voter turnout at New Village elections. Grassroots democracy failed as propaganda to the rural Chinese because as it did not *ipso facto* improve their physical and socio-economic well-being, it was simply irrelevant from their point of view. Instead, what proved the most effective propaganda, contributing materially to increased rural Chinese confidence in Government, was effective Security Force protection from MCP terror, economic opportunities and welfare in the form of well-equipped New Villages.[55] Conversely, early Government indifference to the rural Chinese and harsh Security Force behaviour were highly relevant to rural Chinese interests and hence powerful but negative propaganda.[56]

A final point should be noted. Despite the assertion by some theorists of propaganda that the concept refers to mass communication that is not accidental but planned,[57] this is too restrictive. After all, as Askenasy argues in the context of insurgency campaigns, 'all military actions can have psychological effects on [villager] perception and behaviour whether or not the commander intended such effects'. He adds that 'such unintentional aspects of military operations may have a greater influence ... than do calculated schemes'.[58] Thus in Malaya, for instance, when a Royal West Kent mortar crew accidentally shelled and killed some people in a Chinese Resettlement Area in Selangor in November 1951,[59] although it was purely unplanned and accidental, it was highly *relevant* as it adversely undermined the rural Chinese sense of security and hence confidence. This reinforces our point: what makes a particular mass communication propaganda is not whether it is planned but whether it is *relevant* to a specific audience.

Having developed a theoretical understanding of how 'propaganda' properly conceived affects public and terrorist confidence in an insurgency context, it is now necessary to see how British imperial and wartime experience generated antecedents which profoundly affected British propaganda during the Emergency.

THE ANTECEDENTS OF BRITISH PROPAGANDA IN THE MALAYAN EMERGENCY I: PROPAGANDA OF WORDS

To be sure, most of the instruments of propaganda used in Malaya had already been introduced elsewhere. The leaflet for instance, had been widely used by the Royal Air Force during World War One as well as in the imperial pacification campaigns of the 1920s and 1930s in the Middle East and the Northwest Frontier of India, while rewards for information and amnesties had earlier been used to entice Boer guerrillas to give up.[60] In addition, in March 1929 the Colonial Film Committee drew attention to the propaganda value of British feature films,[61] while newsreels and documentaries were also perceived as useful in impressing upon colonial peoples the benefits of metropolitan rule. For instance, the Colonial Film Unit, formed by the British Ministry of Information (MOI) in 1939, produced *Katsina Tank* and *Comforts from Uganda* to show Africans how their financial contributions were being used for their benefit.[62] The Second World War, moreover, suggested that there had to be some means by which films could actually reach audiences in rural areas. Thus MOI provided African colonies with a limited number of mobile cinema vans which did good work. A small number of mobile vans were also used in Malaya just before the Japanese invasion.[63] Closely associated with film exhibitions by mobile vans was the roving song and drama troupe. In Nigeria, for instance, in addition to mobile cinema film shows, famous battles of the Second World War were enacted in the village marketplace, in conjunction with anti-Nazi sketches and songs like 'Hitler, causer of the war'.[64]

Radio also came of age in the inter-war years, and by the start of the Second World War, West African broadcasting had been fairly well established, and in Nairobi and Lusaka, radio stations transmitted war news, talks and entertainment programmes in English and selected local languages. A particularly important inter-war innovation in radio was Community Listening. This referred to the provision of low-cost public wireless receivers which would enable large groups of people to listen to broadcasts at any time. In Africa, for instance, community wireless receivers were set up at district headquarters, mission stations, and listening points in towns and farms. Where such receivers were unavailable, programmes were broadcast over loudspeakers. Hence in Nigeria, there were over 700 privately hired loudspeakers and seven public street loudspeakers.[65] In Malaya in 1941, moreover, scores of towns and villages were allocated loudspeakers with amplifiers.[66]

Instruments of 'word-propaganda' aside, a far more important legacy to Malayan propagandists was the well-articulated *philosophy* of spoken, printed and broadcast propaganda which had been forged by the end of the Second World War. Of the principles truly germane to our understanding of the later Emergency, the foremost was the need for establishing credibility. Richard H.S. Crossman, the leading wartime Allied propagandist,[67] argued that the first thing a propagandist should do was to ensure that his target audience believed him. This meant that the propagandist had to be prepared to tell the truth to the audience, even if the truth was not flattering to his cause.[68] If the propagandist lied to the audience and was found out, then his future output would be disregarded by his audience and he would therefore be unable to influence its thinking. Similarly, Leslie Glass, who served with the Far Eastern Bureau of the MOI, and later in the Burma section of the Psychological Warfare Division of Southeast Asia Command, pointed out that if his team had promised 'early victories' that proved 'hollow', the Burmese would have dismissed everything else the British put out.[69] Likewise, the British Broadcasting Corporation (BBC) was prepared to tell the truth about British defeats especially during the initial stages of the war, and won for itself a reputation for honesty which attracted audiences in Occupied Europe.[70] Crossman therefore emphasised that to preserve his credibility, the propagandist must remember that the 'central substance of propaganda is hard, correct information'.[71] Telling the truth is of course another way of saying that the message conveyed by one's words must be consistent with that emanating from one's actual deeds or achievements.

Since the stuff of propaganda was hard, correct information, it followed that the propagandist also had to have access to first-class intelligence on the enemy. What was needed was not merely an 'intimate knowledge of the background of the audience – its language, history, myths, institutions, practices, social composition and politics', but also a 'detailed knowledge of the current developments among the audience', in terms of 'current grievances'.[72] Thus, effective propaganda presupposed an efficient and 'large propaganda intelligence department', tasked with undertaking painstaking 'market research' into the psyche of the audience and thinking 'itself into the mind of the Communist, soaking itself in his phrases and his clichés until it writes and thinks them naturally'.[73] The last statement provides a link to the next precept of British propaganda philosophy: the propagandist must enjoy an 'empathy' with the audience, expressing himself in ways familiar to them.[74] Glass in Burma was very conscious of this need and was therefore of the opinion that 'propaganda aimed at a foreign people can be effective only if it is channelled through nationals of their own country'.[75] Other British propagandists, however, like Sir Robert

Bruce Lockhart, wartime head of the Political Warfare Executive, opined that British officers with 'first-hand experience of a country' could also do the job.[76] Thus in Europe, British propagandists charged with waging the radio war against Germany like Crossman, the noted black propagandist Sefton Delmer and Hugh Carleton Greene of the BBC's German Section, were extremely well acquainted with German politics, language and culture.[77]

Yet another precept was the need to respect the sensitivities of the audience. This was especially important in framing surrender appeals. First, it was important to avoid threats in leaflets directed at the enemy soldier, in case they frightened him into staying put and not surrendering. Second, it was also necessary to convince him that he would not lose face if he gave himself up. Thus Crossman argued that the whole 'art of the leaflet is to appear as a simple, honourable offer by one honourable soldier to another, saying, "You have fought very gallantly; now is the time when you have a perfectly good reason for giving in a little earlier"'.[78] Hence in Burma, in order to take into account the pride of the all but defeated Japanese troops, safe conduct passes substituted the phrase 'I cease resistance' for the potentially humiliating and hence offensive 'I surrender'.[79] Another principle of British propaganda of words was the need to provide the audience with information that was really attractive to them. Whether it was radio broadcasts or leaflets, the audience, especially if listening or living under 'risk and physical inconvenience', had 'every incentive to switch off the radio and not to pick up the leaflet'.[80] Hence, to attract attention, the propagandist had to give his readers what they really wanted: 'impersonal and unemotional news', about 'some big, vitally important, extremely interesting event whose general character is widely known and whose significance and probable consequences are of wide interest'.[81] Crossman in fact believed that 'news must take priority over views', and 'facts over preaching'.[82] A further precept was the recognition that entertainment had a place in propaganda. During the war it was found that music items interspersed in between news and talks helped to attract listeners. Crossman noted that 'entertainment is a valuable narcotic for dulling the sensibilities of a propaganda-conscious mind', and that German troops on the Atlantic Wall for instance were keen listeners to radio programmes chiefly but not completely devoted to light music. Significantly, they often passed on bits of information broadcast in between music items.[83] In Burma, furthermore, Japanese troops never once shot at Allied mobile units playing music.[84]

The final principle of British propaganda philosophy recapitulated the basic notion that the message expressed by one's words must be consistent with that projected by one's deeds. Thus Lockhart held that propaganda could never work in a vacuum, and it had to be always 'the handmaid of official policy and strategy'.[85] Crossman added that propaganda was 'not an independent arm' and could never achieve 'miracles on its own'.[86] This idea that the message communicated by one's words had to match that emanating from one's deeds was amply demonstrated by the fiasco of the so-called V Campaign of 1941. That year the BBC European Service launched an anti-Nazi radio campaign, urging the populations of Occupied Europe to write, wherever they could, the letter 'V' as the first letter of the French word for 'victory' and the Flemish word for freedom. When this proved successful in many towns, the BBC extended the scope of the Campaign to promote active civil defiance of the Germans. Hence Europeans were urged for example to hoard copper and nickel coins as these metals were vital to the German war effort.[87] To be sure, the V- sign proved to be an 'ingenious propaganda gimmick', raising morale both at home and in Occupied Europe.[88] However, because the BBC had acted on its own initiative, propaganda was out of step with both policy and strategy. Hence, while the V Campaign encouraged the European publics, it also conveyed the mistaken idea that the invasion of Europe was imminent when it was not, and led many people to take undue risks for which they paid the penalty.[89] The V Campaign thus turned into a propaganda disaster for the British.[90]

Apart from being very sensitive to the general strategic context, it was also necessary to seek the specific 'psychological moment' for transmitting propaganda to an audience. Crossman insisted that this was 'not a trite phrase but a precise description of what we had to aim at'.[91] That is, the propagandist had to act when the message emanating from the physical environment of the audience was particularly intense.[92] Thus the psychological moment for launching the V Campaign should have been the onset of an actual Allied invasion. In addition, the concept had applications at the tactical level as well, for instance during the Allied counteroffensive in the Ardennes in the winter of 1944. By 'keeping a curve on the morale of freshly taken prisoners on various sections of the front', Allied propagandists carefully *timed* the release of 'tactical' leaflets to German units cut off by the Allies. Crossman explained that if Allied leaflets had been dropped before the worsening military situation had demoralised the German Army, the latter would not have been affected. However, if leaflets had been released too late, that is, after demoralisation had set in, then 'propaganda would have been nugatory'.[93] In short, if surrender propaganda was to be effective, it had to be transmitted to the soldiers at the *correct moment,* in order to reinforce the notion of hopelessness generated by their immediate tactical plight.[94] Furthermore, in order for propagandists to ascertain the correct psychological moment to release propaganda at enemy troops in particular, it was essential that they were based close to the front line. Thus Crossman noted that during the war Psychological Warfare Divisions were set up not only at Supreme Headquarters but at the lowest level – Army headquarters – as well. In fact, the latter body was in charge of prisoner interrogation and the despatch of tactical leaflets.[95] In sum, imperial and wartime experience bequeathed not only various propaganda media, but also an explicit philosophy governing their usage. This emphasised the importance of credibility; the need for propaganda intelligence and trained propagandists; the necessity for respecting the sensitivities of the audience; the primacy of straight news; the utility of interspersing one's propaganda with entertainment items, and finally, the importance of the 'psychological moment' and more generally the need for ensuring that the ideas communicated by propaganda matched those suggested by actual policy.

THE ANTECEDENTS OF BRITISH PROPAGANDA IN THE MALAYAN EMERGENCY II: PROPAGANDA OF THE DEED

In line with the principle that credible propaganda requires that one's words and deeds communicate the same message, a key argument running through this study is that rural Chinese confidence in Government was enhanced not when Government leaflets projected the message that Government was their 'Provider', but when in addition to these media, the leadership style of senior political figures; the attitudes and behaviour of Government officials and the Security Forces as well as certain Government policies also projected the same message. Similarly, terrorists surrendered not when Government leaflets told them that further struggle was hopeless but only when Security Force pressure and food denial generated the same idea. On the role of leadership style, we shall see that General Templer's high-visibility campaigning made a tangible contribution to the winning of rural Chinese and even terrorist confidence.[96] But Templer was himself heavily influenced by the British Army's Second World War tradition of generalship as exemplified by his mentors Montgomery and Alexander.[97] The latter two commanders were fully cognisant of the propaganda value of a high personal profile in raising the confidence of the people around them. Hence while 'Monty' deliberately exuded 'an aura of self-confidence and calm, however depressing the news',[98] Alexander projected a 'modest, calm and confident' personality and was said to be able to win men's confidence 'at first sight'.[99] Even Churchill remarked that 'confidence spread around' Alexander, while Templer himself significantly argued that Montgomery's 'greatest contribution to modern warfare' was not 'tactical technique' but 'moral inspiration'.[100]

While British wartime leadership style when transplanted in Malaya was in itself to generate the idea that Government was Provider of the needs of the rural Chinese in particular, certain other habits of Empire were to instead suggest the notion that Government was Tormentor rather than Provider. In this connection, a basic tendency which was pronounced following the Indian Mutiny of May 1857 to July 1858 was the widespread negative stereotyping of colonial subjects.[101] Hence, 'Africans were perceived as dirty, immoral, untruthful, devious, and instinctively idle';[102] the Indian was 'tricky, devious, untruthful, sensuous and easily corrupted';[103] while the Irish were 'ignorant, unstable, indolent, superstitious, lying, dirty, vengeful and so forth'.[104] The upshot of this approach was that British administrators felt that 'a strong hand' was needed to keep the subject races in check.[105] Maj-General Younghusband of the Indian Army (1878–1918) thus advised:[106]

> It is never wise to stand studied impertinence, or even the semblance of it, from any Oriental ... the moment there is sign of revolt, mutiny, or treachery, of which the symptoms not unusually are a swollen head, and a tendency to incivility, it is wise to hit the Oriental straight between the eyes, and to keep on hitting him thus, till he appreciates exactly what he is, and who is who.

The 'strong hand' was expressed one way through *collective punishment* – the imposition of punitive sanctions not only on the perpetrators of a crime per se, but also the community of which they were a part. Central to the concept of collective punishment was the idea of collective responsibility, as evinced in the British attitude to the Amritsar unrest of April 1919. Because British officers saw Indians as generally devious, it followed that *all* of them were potential enemies, because after all, although most of them might not have actually done anything yet, they could well be 'planning to attack tomorrow'.[107] This perception of the general Indian community as a gang of troublemakers in waiting actually explains Brigadier-General Reginald Dyer's decision to open fire on the crowd at the Jallianwala Bagh in Amritsar on 13 April 1919. He wanted to produce a 'moral effect' throughout the Punjab to deter other potential malcontents.[108] Following the Jallianwalla Bagh incident, the 'strong hand' was further applied in the form of collective punishment: for instance, a Crawling Order was promulgated, requiring all Indians venturing out into the street between 0600 and 2200 hours to crawl along on all fours.[109] Other forms of collective punishment were also used in Ireland (1919–1921), the Arab Revolt (1936–1939) and the Jewish Insurgency (1939–1947). These included demolition of those houses whose occupants had been suspected of aiding terrorists;[110] the collective fine, slapped on any locality where there had been a disturbance and whose inhabitants had refused to provide information as to who the perpetrators were;[111] mass detentions;[112] and the ultimate collective punishment: martial law.[113] In the cases of Ireland and the Jewish insurgency, especially, the possibility that ordinary people had been too frightened of terrorist reprisals to provide the Security Forces with information was ignored by the British authorities. Collective punishment thus generated the image of an uncaring Government – which only alienated the public.[114]

Yet another form of collective punishment was more implicitly enshrined in the dubious strategy of 'air control'. This was the elaborate doctrine that guided the fledgling Royal Air Force in policing the large tracts of desert country in the Middle East, which came under British control following the break-up of the Ottoman Empire at the end of the First World War.[115] Air control was supposed to police rebels through what the Air Staff called the 'moral effect' of air bombardment. As early as 1924, senior air officers had examined the psychological effects of air bombardment on 'semi-civilised peoples' and concluded that 'intensive and continuous bombardment' could 'enforce surrender by insidious moral effect'.[116] Despite early successes, by the 1930s, it became increasingly clear that rebellious tribes were becoming less frightened of bombing, moving in the open even when aircraft were plainly visible and scattering only when attacked.[117] But a more serious problem with air control resided at the level of basic assumptions. The preferred RAF practice was to bomb the *village* from which a tribal force had been drawn, as actually locating rebel bands moving over broken and difficult country at night was difficult.[118] The Air Staff justified village bombing by averring that it was 'well-understood by tribesmen', and furthermore, it had been 'emphatically stated' by 'experienced administrators' that it caused 'no more resentment than any other form of punitive action'.[119] In fact, it is arguable that because the Air Staff perceived that it was dealing with 'semi-civilised people', the villagers *were* the rebels – either actual or potential. Hence the principle of collective responsibility was at work and air control was simply another form of collective punishment. It was only by the end of the Palestine Mandate in 1948 that the assumption of collective responsibility inherent in air control began to be regarded as untenable in the context of intricate communal insurgencies.[120] While it cannot be said that the air control doctrine was exported wholesale to Malaya, certain of its underlying assumptions, principally concerning the 'moral effect' of bombing, were to resurface in a Malayan setting.

Collective punishment aside, the 'strong hand' was also exercised over 'recalcitrant' colonial subjects directly through the agents of Empire. In this respect, British Police and soldiers were said to have had an attitude toward the indigenous people that was 'far more brutal than that of the officials or businessmen'.[121] In fact physical force was very much an integral aspect of the armoury of Police control, and George Orwell, an Imperial Policeman in Burma, admitted that striking the Burmese was 'routine', as 'everyone does these things in the East'.[122] This hard-line attitude toward the subject people on the part of the Imperial Police was reinforced by the fact that the latter tended to be recruited from the ranks of soldiers, and thus 'had no mental habituation to the methods and restraints of a [common-law] civil police force, and no affinity with the population amongst whom they now found themselves'.[123] This description was especially true of the militarised

Royal Irish Constabulary (RIC), which 'bristling with arms', could not 'have failed to induce terror rather than confidence into Irish hearts'.[124] In fact, through personnel transfers, the Irish paramilitary model of policing was gradually transmitted to Palestine and thence to other colonies like Malaya.[125] Another significant aspect of the Irish model was the idea of auxiliary Police, 'quasi-military forces' assembled to assist the regular Police in maintaining order.[126] The main problem with such forces was that they lacked discipline and were prone to using excessive force in securing public order. The most notorious example of these auxiliary Police were the so-called 'Black and Tans', or the Auxiliary Division of the RIC, which resorted to unauthorised reprisals against the Irish public.[127] As we shall see, in the early years of the Emergency, the problematic Special Constables would exemplify the image of Government as Tormentor.

While the Empire suggested some 'lessons' which were greatly to complicate Government's relations with the rural Chinese during the Emergency, other ideas were to help in the jungle war against the terrorists. The need to police the Empire and quash 'small wars' involving the warlike tribes on the Northwest Frontier of India, the Boers of South Africa and the Arab and Jewish bands in Palestine, compelled British soldiers to devise techniques of fighting that were well-suited to countering insurgencies as in Malaya. In particular, whether by design or accident, such counterinsurgency practices also had a 'moral effect' on rebels. Certainly, Orde Wingate was one officer who deliberately sought 'to produce in the minds of the rebels the conviction that the armed forces are able to move at night as freely and as dispersed as themselves' and that 'even when [the rebels] move across country by the most isolated tracks, they are liable suddenly to be attacked'.[128] The whole idea was to *worry* the rebels. In this regard, the major counterinsurgency technique, Wingate felt, that truly troubled guerrillas was small unit patrolling rather than large scale sweeps.[129] In fact, imperial campaigns taught the British Army 'that warfare against irregulars requires the breakup of conventional units into their smaller more mobile components'.[130] The Boer War of 1899 to 1902, moreover, had crystallised a further principle, which when coupled with intensive patrolling, put further psychological pressure on rebels: cutting the insurgent off from his sources of food and supply.[131] This was done in the Boer conflict by isolating behind barbed-wire and block-house defences the Boer homeland, systematically destroying within it the 'safe bases' of farms and homesteads, burning crops, and reconcentrating the families of Boer guerrillas.[132] The basic pattern of small-unit operations combined with the food-denying strategy of resettlement, was resorted to again during the Burma Revolt of 1932–33, as well as the Greek insurgency which erupted immediately after the Second World War.[133]

The Boer War also demonstrated to British commanders the utility of using captured Boer commandos as guides in special mounted units against

their former comrades. This improved the chances of the Army
the mobile mounted Boer commandos, while the idea that tl
comrades were coming after them also played upon Boer mi
another significant innovation was national registration. In
national registration was introduced on a voluntary basis during ... Arab
Revolt and made compulsory during the Jewish Insurgency.[135] This exercise
enabled the Police and Army to pick out rebels from the ranks of the public
and added to rebel anxieties about capture and elimination In short, as we
shall note, small unit patrolling, resettlement, national registration and to a
certain extent, the use of captured guerrillas in operations against their
former comrades, were to constitute potent propaganda when employed in
Malaya against the Communist terrorists, undermining their morale. To
sum up: the British were to bring into Malaya not only certain well-
articulated ideas on propaganda of words, they were to inadvertently
import attitudes, behaviour and policies which constituted propaganda – of
the deed. As we shall see, until Government was able consciously to
co-ordinate and synchronise word and deed to both the rural Chinese
public and the terrorists, its propaganda would lack credibility.

APPROACH

In this chapter we have established the aims and set the scene for the study,
developed a theoretical understanding of how propaganda affects public
and terrorist confidence in an insurgency context as well as examined those
imperial and wartime antecedents of British propaganda of word – and
deed – in the Emergency. We shall see that Government propaganda of
word and deed was to pass through four phases: starting from a state
of disarray from June 1948 until May 1950; to being on the mend from
then till February 1952; reaching a turning point between February 1952 to
May 1954; and then functioning optimally until December 1958. This
account would in fact be incomplete if we neglected the role of the MCP in
inadvertently creating the conditions for Government propaganda to
exploit. Hence, it is to the subject of the psychological consequences –
and propaganda implications – of the MCP's attitudinal and policy errors,
that we now turn.

CHAPTER TWO

The Malayan Communist Party and its Impact on Terrorist and Rural Chinese Confidence

As there have been various explanations highlighting how Government actions contributed to eventual victory over the Communists, there have also been analyses purporting to explain how Communist weaknesses themselves shaped the final outcome: first, it is held that the Malayan Communist Party (MCP),[1] unlike for instance the National Liberation Front in South Vietnam, never benefited from the relatively easy cross-border access to a powerful and friendly Communist sponsor like China; second, the MCP was never able to command the support of the majority Malay community, a tremendous handicap; third, it was deprived of its key means of resupply, the Chinese squatters, by the Government resettlement programme; and fourth, given its logistics problems and the resulting critical lack of heavy weapons, explosives and wireless communications, it was never a credible opponent for the Security Forces. In this connection, the MCP's reliance on a primitive system of couriers for internal communications in lieu of radio not only represented a grave vulnerability, the inherent inefficiency of the system also deprived its military operations of any strategic focus and reduced them to the level of uncoordinated terrorist attacks.[2] Once again, however, what is missing in these explanations is a proper regard for the psychological dimension; while the argument has been put forth that the MCP's terror policy alienated the masses, this has by no means been developed fully.[3] Moreover, the effect of Communist leaders' misdemeanours on the morale of the terrorist rank and file has been all but ignored.

This chapter will argue that in fact a key reason for the MCP's failure in Malaya accrued from the psychological consequences of its 'deeds': the actual attitudes and behaviour of the Communists demonstrated an appalling lack of respect for the rank and file terrorists and the wider rural Chinese public. Specifically, the failure of the Party leadership at all levels to provide promised material benefits to its rank and file; the harshness of life in the jungle and the imposition of draconian internal discipline all constituted negative propaganda of the deed – communicating the idea that the Party was not the benefactor or 'Provider' it had claimed to be – and this severely undermined terrorist confidence. Similarly, the reliance of the Party on terror to secure compliance amongst the rural Chinese public created the impression that the MCP was patently incapable of being the Provider of the benefits of physical and socio-economic security. We shall see that although the MCP made a conscious effort to emulate Mao Tse-Tung's success on the mainland, their approach in Malaya actually ran counter to that advocated by Mao, who clearly preached that unity between the officers and the men and between the Party and the people were vital ingredients of revolutionary success – and that showing a basic respect for both groups was essential to creating the two unities. Moreover, while Mao saw that political education was absolutely necessary in eradicating backward bourgeois tendencies amongst the rank and file and wider public, to the MCP, political education was regarded more as a strategy for imposing tight control amongst the rank and file, while it seriously neglected it with respect to the wider masses. In this context, it will be suggested that the failure of the Malayan Communists to recognise and apply these key elements of Maoist thought, was due to the dearth of sufficient intellectual capital at the Central Committee level by June 1948. Hence, quite apart from Government propaganda efforts, the MCP's own errors directly undermined the faith of its rank and file and the wider rural Chinese public in the Communist cause.

THE MALAYAN COMMUNIST PARTY, THE RURAL CHINESE AND THE 'RANK AND FILE'

It is first necessary to examine in more detail the nature of the MCP's relationship with the strategic rural Chinese community, the main source of its supplies and recruits. To be sure, three forces had traditionally competed for influence amongst Malayan Chinese: the Triads or secret societies, the Kuomintang (KMT) and the MCP. It was the Triads which exerted the greatest control at first: newly arrived Chinese immigrants were met at Penang or Singapore by representatives of one of two main societies: either the *Gi Hin* or the *Hai San*. These Triads financed the new arrivals, found work for them in the tin mines, protected them from rival gangs and redressed any wrongs on their behalf. In return the immigrant Chinese swore a complete oath of allegiance to the Triad. Government by Triad societies usually spelt 'trouble', and Malayan secret society rivalry, fuelled by the lucrative tin industry, erupted into riots with much loss of life in the 1850s and 1860s. This prompted the British, increasingly involved in peninsular affairs from 1874 onward, to declare them illegal in 1889. Government repression moreover meant that by the 1920s, the *Gi Hin* and

Hai San societies had split into smaller gangs and were much reduced in influence until after the Second World War.[4] The decline of the Triads coincided with the emergence of the MCP and the KMT. As noted the MCP began to enhance its stature amongst Malayan Chinese during the late 1930s by taking up the cause of anti-Japanese Chinese nationalism, a strategy it maintained into the Japanese Occupation by transmuting AEBUS work into MPAJA activities. Immediately after the surrender of the Japanese, moreover, the Party emerged from the jungle to set up headquarters in every village and town as well as the various front organisations mentioned in the previous chapter. However, during the British Military Administration, the KMT – which had predated the MCP in Malaya and also fought the Japanese during the Occupation as the Malayan Overseas Chinese Self Defence Army (MOCSDA) – capitalised on Republican China's new-found prestige as a World War Two victor: it moved aggressively amongst young Malayan Chinese, setting up the *San Min Chu Yi* Youth Corps as a direct competitor with the Communist New Democratic Youth League. In addition, in every town and large village, KMT headquarters were set up as near as possible to their MCP counterparts. Ideological tensions soon boiled over into clashes between the Communist and Republican youth organisations. To be sure, the spoils of the post-war MCP-KMT ideological struggle were shared: the KMT, with the help of mainland Republican emissaries, made greater inroads than the MCP amongst the better-off Chinese: wealthy businessmen, shopkeepers and some students. The MCP, meanwhile, fared better amongst the Chinese it had traditionally attracted since the late 1930s: Middle School students and teachers, and working class Chinese in the urban and rural sectors in such diverse occupations as *inter alia*, rattan workers, coffee shop employees, Singapore dockyard tradesmen, rubber and pineapple factory workers, coal and tin miners and rubber tappers. In fact the only potential competitor with the MCP for the allegiance of the rural and urban labourers were the Triads, which enjoyed a resurgence immediately after Liberation – thanks to the tolerant attitude of the BMA. Thus huge initiation ceremonies were held in Penang and Singapore and in Penang alone the *Ang Bin Hoay* society built up a membership of 10,000. Moreover, the Triads, avowedly anti-Communist, joined forces with the KMT in clashes throughout north Malaya with the MCP. However, renewed Government repression in 1946 and 1947 quashed Triad activity. Consequently, between 1946 and 1948, it was the MCP, not the KMT or the Triads, which dominated the immediate environment of ambitious, disaffected Chinese urban and rural workers.[5] MCP agents would thus mingle amongst workers at coffee shops, unions and labour lines, developing a 'very, very thorough knowledge of all the people on the ground level'.[6] The working class Chinese, who generally suffered from a low standard of education and in some cases even 'educational retardation', were relatively soft targets for the shrewd and seemingly knowledgeable MCP evangelists.[7]

Furthermore, when the onset of the Insurrection forced the MCP into the Malayan jungle, its links with the rural Chinese assumed greater urgency. The Party itself commented on this in a 1949 document entitled *The Present Day Situation and Duties of the Malayan Communist Party,* which was captured by the Security Forces. The document revealed that because the MCP had failed to make headway with the 'city population', it had to rely for its supplies on the 'Chinese rural population'.[8] The latter basically encompassed the tin miners, rubber workers on plantations and in factories, unskilled and semi-skilled workers in various crafts, coal miners and in particular, the 'genuine squatters': those Chinese who engaged in full-time farming. These rural folk were the 'most important group of all' from the point of view of the insurgency, because being situated on the fringes of the Malayan jungle, they were in closest contact with Communist cadres lurking nearby – hence the MCP naturally drew the bulk of its rank and file and its supporters from this community.[9] Little wonder then that a June 1954 Government study found that 61 percent of the surrendered terrorists (Surrendered Enemy Personnel or SEPs) in the sample interrogated had been rubber tappers, who were 'readily accessible to MCP influence'.[10] Moreover a 1956 study of a sample of 58 SEPs found that 46 of them had been unskilled labourers, mainly tappers, while interrogation of 25 SEPs in 1953 similarly discovered that 19 had been farmers, labourers, carpenters, tinkers and mainly tappers, all of whose 'geographical location' had increased their exposure to the Communists.[11]

Geographical propinquity aside, what forces compelled the rural Chinese to nail their colours to the Communist mast? As it turns out, there were different factors motivating different groups of individuals, and there is such considerable overlap that precise delineation of categories is not possible. Nevertheless, it could be said that about 10 percent of the rank and file were very much 'hard core', 'fanatics' who were utterly committed to the Party leadership and its quest for power.[12] These disaffected individuals, perceiving that they had been 'bullied' by 'Government', 'police' and 'robbers' – had jumped at the MCP's offer of a 'short cut to power'. As C.C. Too, the Government Psychological Warfare expert whom we shall encounter again later – and who never minced his words – observed, any notion that these Chinese joined the MCP to fight for 'equality' or 'democracy' or 'the poor' was quite simply, 'bullshit'.[13] In addition, another 20 percent of the rank and file was made up of former MPAJA guerrillas who had been recalled to service but given less important work than the hard core terrorists, while a 'good proportion' also included 'congenital thugs' out for 'plunder and rapine for its own sake'.[14]

Nevertheless, the overriding impulse of the mass of the willing rural Chinese recruits was 'material'.[15] They had been deeply frustrated in the

Malaya of the immediate post-war years, a country characterised by poverty, the breakdown of family relationships due to the dislocation of the Occupation and importantly, the lack of opportunities to improve one's lot in life. In these circumstances, they saw in the MCP a potential way out of their predicament. It must be noted, however, that these factors were not quite enough to compel the Chinese to take the final plunge into the jungle. As one study put it, many an SEP was like a swimmer who found himself drawn by circumstances to the edge of the pool. What compelled him to actually jump in was fear – of MCP reprisal if he failed to join, as well as of arrest by the Police if he lingered outside the jungle.[16] Thus a 1956 study found that 38 out of 58 SEPs from Pahang and 20 out of 54 SEPs from other States had taken the final step of joining the terrorists simply because of fear of arrest by Government.[17] One estimate even suggested that as many as 70 percent of the terrorist rank and file took the final plunge into the jungle because of Government repression.[18]

But what about political motivations? Were the mass of willing MCP recruits motivated by any desire to free Malaya from British Imperialism? Perhaps surprisingly, the answer is no. Government Chinese Affairs officers who observed the rural Chinese at close hand concluded that they as a whole consisted of people who wished 'to be left alone to earn their living' and did 'not want their lives complicated by politics either Chinese or Malayan'.[19] Likewise the terrorists who after all emerged from this community were equally devoid of political aspirations. For example, interrogation of 25 SEPs who had entered the jungle in 1948 and 1949 determined that they had had little interest in the political future of Malaya, and had not believed in the ideals of Communism either. Rather they had joined the MCP because of 'personal reasons': the belief that life in the jungle as the MCP suggested would be attractive; they would 'belong' to a disciplined, progressive organisation, and importantly, they would enjoy opportunities for material accumulation and personal advancement. In sum, their main pre-occupation had been a 'short-sighted' one: a concern with the making ends meet and improving their standard of living.[20] Other studies confirmed the predominance of 'felt economic needs'. These rendered the rural Chinese susceptible to MCP promises that jungle life would be replete with better food and clothes – and even women, cinema, sports and games – while after the Revolution, the standard of living would be higher, with better education and work for all. Hence for most willing rural Chinese recruits, Communism was not so much an ideal to be actualised as a 'vehicle' to realise their material aspirations.[21]

How then did these Chinese fit into the MCP framework? The rank and file were distributed between the actual combatants and the supply organisation with links to the wider rural community – the Min Yuen Organisation.[22] The combatants were initially organised into the Malayan People's Anti-British Army (MPABA) which in February 1949 was re-designated the

Malayan Races Liberation Army (MRLA). As the MCP and the old MPAJA had merged prior to the outbreak of the Insurrection, the political and military wings of the Communist organisation were by now better integrated than they had been during the Occupation. Hence the Party maintained political control through its political commissars of the various levels of MRLA formations: the State Committees supervised the Regiments, the District Committees the Companies and the Branch Committees the Platoons. Chin Peng recently confirmed that at its peak the MRLA numbered 8,000 men. The Min Yuen Organisation on the other hand was set up around the MCP District as the basic unit of administration. While there was variation between States, generally the District Committee Secretary oversaw, through his various Branch Committee Members, the work of several armed and sometimes uniformed Min Yuen workers. The latter, who were at times Party members, supervised the very important Masses Executives: these were not Party members, but were ordinary tappers for instance, whose job was to organise the rural Chinese into Cells. The Cells procured supplies, intelligence and funds and transmitted these to the Masses Executives, who passed them back up the chain to the District Committee Secretary, who in turn funnelled these to the local MRLA unit and State Committee. Protecting the Min Yuen network in the early years were two types of militia. One was a full-time Defence Corps of six to eight men and the other, a part-time Self-Defence Corps, composed of youth who could later be promoted to the MRLA. Following the October 1951 Directives however (see below), small parties of MRLA and Min Yuen were combined into Armed Work Forces to carry out terrorist and supply work. In sum, the 'terrorist rank and file' comprised the District and Branch Committee Members of the MCP; the Min Yuen workers, Masses Executives and their Cell members, the Min Yuen Defence and Self Defence Corps; the Armed Work Forces; ordinary MRLA combatants as well as MRLA commanders at Company level and below.[23]

CENTRAL'S INTELLECTUAL AND DOCTRINAL PROBLEMS

Having examined at length why and how the rural Chinese supplied the life force of the MCP, we now need to examine the reasons why the Party leadership inadvertently dried up this strategic well-spring. We shall argue that it was essentially a failure of interpreting Communist, in particular Maoist, doctrine. The doctrinal orientation of the MCP has received some attention: Short notes that for the MCP, 'true, or ideological north was in Russia. Magnetic, or affinitive north was in China'. He elsewhere adds that Communism in Malaya was subject to 'alternating phases of Chinese and Comintern influence': to 'Trotskyist or left-wing adventurist deviationism; and the rigid formalism which sought a proletarian oasis in the ideological desert of Asian peasantry'.[24] Brimmell, for his part, opines that the MCP was trying to follow the Chinese model, 'although more in its military than in its political aspect'.[25] Our argument here is that Central's basic doctrinal problem was its failure to fully apprehend the importance of the Maoist injunction to educate as well as 'respect' the masses – and the rank and file which sprang from the masses. To try to understand how this failure came about, it is first necessary to examine more closely the composition of Central itself by the outbreak of the Insurrection.

Following the KMT-CCP split in April 1927 and Chiang Kai Shek's subsequent persecution of members of the Chinese Communist Party (CCP), thousands of Hainanese Communists fled to Malaya. These dominated and provided leadership to the fledgling local Communist movement which had first emerged in 1921. In fact, most of the first 11-member Central Committee of the Party formed in April 1930 were experienced, able CCP members.[26] However, by the end of the Japanese Occupation, Central and the State level organs had been virtually denuded of this mainland Chinese leavening principally because of one man: the Annamite Lai Tek, who had first joined the MCP in 1934. He was elected to the Central Committee in September 1936 and, remarkably, was Secretary-General by April 1938. Lai Tek managed rapidly to secure control of the Party partly on the strength of his powerful personality, administrative acumen, and the reputation – actually concocted – of having been a founder member of the Indochina Communist Party and representative of the Comintern. But the key reason for his ability to outmanoeuvre his competitors was that he had also been an agent of the Special Branch since his arrival from the hands of the French secret police in Saigon in about 1934. During the Occupation moreover, Lai Tek switched allegiance to the Japanese, and he helped them eliminate over 60 senior Party members. So serious was this attrition of the MCP leadership that by April 1943, there was neither a 'proper' Central Committee or the supreme policy organ, the Politburo. It was this leadership void which accelerated the emergence, discernible since 1939, of younger Malayan-born Communist leaders like Chin Peng and Yeong Kwo. Towards the end of the war Lai Tek inducted Chin and Yeong into a Provisional Standing Committee which became the new Central Committee after the Occupation. Then when Lai Tek, realising that his ties with the Japanese and the British were about to be discovered, absconded with Party funds in March 1947, Central was left very much in the hands of a young, inexperienced Malayan Chinese leadership.[27] This was dominated by Chin Peng, the new Secretary-General, Yeong Kwo, the Deputy Secretary General, and Lau Lee, the Propaganda Bureau chief.[28]

To be sure, these younger leaders belonged to a post-war generation of Malayan-born Chinese who were more self-confident, militant, single-minded and less compliant than their forefathers. They possessed what Richard Broome[29] called the 'courage of the fanatic', adhering to 'one standard of value' – 'the interest of the Party' – and there was consequently 'no appeal which [could] reach them and no infamy to which they [would] not stoop'.[30] Fanatical dedication, however, could not compensate for the reality that while the pre-war MCP leadership had included people with post-secondary and university education and were relatively sophisticated intellectuals, the post-war MCP leaders were on the whole not similarly intellectually accomplished. They comprised mainly Chinese-educated barbers, factory workers and shop assistants, while the better educated men were no more than students, Chinese school teachers and secretaries to Chinese Associations or wealthy businessmen.[31] Chin Peng himself, for instance, attended a Chinese school up to Senior Middle 2 when he had to stop because the school ran out of funds in January 1940. He then moved to Anglo-Chinese Continuation School – for mature students – where he picked up some English. He only lasted there for seven months however, leaving hurriedly on hearing that Government was 'after' him for his Communist activities. Not only did Chin Peng not go to university, therefore, he never even had a complete school education. Thus, while he claimed to have read Maoist and Marxist-Leninist works between 1938 and 1941, it must be recognised that he was a teenager at the time. Short is surely correct therefore in asserting that despite his other qualities, Chin Peng's 'age and comparative inexperience' would have told against him. Chin Peng himself conceded this point at a workshop held in Canberra in February 1999.[32]

Exacerbating the diminished fund of intellectual capital within the post-war MCP leadership was a severe shortage of English-educated members.[33] The reason why there were not more English and university-educated men in Central was because the latter was deeply suspicious of the potential pro-British sympathies of English-educated university graduates. Central moreover worried that such intellectuals were soft-headed daydreamers instead of hard-core revolutionaries willing to sacrifice for the cause. However, because Central recognised that it needed the 'brain power' of the English-educated intellectuals to decipher some of the more obscure Communist scriptures, some English-speaking recruits like Gerald de Cruz and Osman China were brought in. Nevertheless, these men were never allowed into the highest echelons of the MCP.[34] In sum, the MCP's top leadership going into the Insurrection comprised impatient, arrogant young men with limited intellectual ability to cope with the intricacies of Communist theory. Hence C.C. Too, who fraternised closely with the MCP leadership during the BMA period, dismissed them as 'a gang of half-educated, swollen-headed, power-mad adolescent demagogues trying to take over the country', who, though well-capable of 'shouting loud slogans and making considerable trouble', had not 'the faintest idea' of how to form a government or carry out basic governmental functions.[35] Too also noted that because Central somehow considered the Chinese to be the majority ethnic group in Malaya, it reckoned that 'what was effective in China would also be effective in Malaya'. Hence with

> pseudo-scientific zeal, it carried out meticulous observation and analysis of the socio-economics [sic] and political conditions in this country, selectively picking up points to prove its preconceived conclusions, trying to identify such local conditions which bore some resemblance to the local conditions of a particular period in China, and making use of CCP's policy and methodology of that period in China to deal with supposedly similar conditions in Malaya.[36]

While Too thus considered Central 'too naïve', and of 'low calibre', other contemporary observers likewise felt that the Communist leaders lacked 'brains' and were 'amateur revolutionists'. Crozier also feels that Chin Peng 'contributed nothing' to Communist theory.[37] This basic intellectual deficit explains why Central, as we shall see, failed successfully to adapt Maoist theory to Malaya,[38] instead promulgating policies that alienated the bulk of its rank and file and the rural Chinese. This is not to suggest, however, that the MCP would have succeeded in establishing a Communist State if it had correctly understood and applied Maoist ideas in Malaya. The lack of support from the majority Malays, the geography of the country, the absence of external sponsors and poor internal communications were all formidable obstacles. At best, therefore, if the Party could have secured the willing support of the mass of the rural Chinese, it could have proved a longer term 'thorn in the flesh' of Government, and would have indefinitely delayed the transfer of power from the British.[39] In the event, Chin Peng and his clique could not even achieve this more modest objective, and doctrine was the nub of the problem.

Central's main theoretical blunder comprised the failure to heed Mao's injunction to preserve at all costs the unity between Communist leaders and the rank and file, and between the Party and the people – both unities were necessary if Revolutionary success was to be assured. Essentially, Mao's starting premise was that the peasant masses were backward and unsophisticated. He thus argued that the 'scattered and unsystematic ideas' of the masses concerning the material conditions of their existence must be concentrated, systematised and propagated back to them until they were aware of why they needed to revolt.[40] Mao thus placed great stock by political education of the people. Moreover, because the Party rank and file themselves emerged from the 'backward' masses, it was no surprise that fresh recruits brought 'petty bourgeois individualism' into the Party's inner sancta, which was manifested, for instance, when 'comrades' considered 'only the interests of their own small group' and not 'the general interest'; when they revealed a lack of determination whenever things went wrong, and when they evinced a desire for 'pleasure-seeking' and an avoidance of 'material privation'. To combat the threat of individualism amongst the rank and file, therefore, Mao insisted that the Party must 'strengthen education' so as to create a 'new socialist man', animated by a 'scientific spirit' which pervaded his 'thinking' and 'Party life'. Mao also advocated the use of regular self and mutual criticism sessions aimed at rectifying defects, strengthening the Party organisation and increasing its 'fighting capacity'.[41]

Furthermore, precisely because Mao recognised that bourgeois tendencies amongst the public and the Party rank and file *were to be expected*, he was extremely cautious in his attitude to coercion both inside and outside the Party: the lack of enthusiasm for the cause did not *ipso facto* imply the presence of class enemies to be exterminated but rather 'backward' elements to be educated. This is not to say that Mao ignored the need for strict discipline; he agreed with Lenin that it was necessary for creating an organised rank and file and public.[42] Mao's point was that because the Party needed the support of both the people and the rank and file for success in the Revolution, it was very important that relations with them should always be tempered by respect. Respect was integral to the 'unity between officers and men' and 'unity between the army and the people' which he advocated:[43]

> Many people think that it is wrong methods that make for strained relations between officers and men and between the army and the people, but I always tell them that it is a question of *basic attitude* (or basic principle), of *having respect for the soldiers and the people*. It is from this attitude that the various policies, methods and forms ensue. If we depart from this attitude, then the policies, methods and forms will certainly be wrong, and the *relations between officers and men and between the army and the people* are bound to be unsatisfactory (emp. mine).

The importance of respecting the rank and file and the public so as to retain their confidence in the Party also prompted Mao to emphasise that the Communists must back up their words with concrete achievements:[44]

> Our job is not to recite our political programme to the people, for nobody will listen to such recitations; *we must link the political mobilisation for the war with developments in the war and with the life of the soldiers and the people...* This is a matter of immense importance on which our victory in the war primarily depends (emp. mine).

In sum, to Mao, the success of the Revolution depended on actively persuading the rank and file and the public that they needed the Party as their Provider. To this end the Communists had to pursue methods and policies which showed respect for these two groups, and certainly one key way to do this was to back up promises with concrete deeds. Only through the propaganda of the 'deeds' of kept promises, and other 'methods' and 'policies' which revealed a basic respect for the rank and file and the public, could the Communists secure the confidence of these two key groups and achieve victory in the Revolution. As we shall now see, however, Chin Peng and Central chose 'methods' and 'policies' which showed anything but respect for the rank and file and the public. Moreover, Central's attitude toward the political education of both audiences was seriously deficient.

THE MCP, THE TERRORISTS AND THE TENSION BETWEEN EDUCATION AND COERCION

Central purposefully sought to adapt Mao's theory of protracted revolutionary war to Malaya.[45] To this end, it fully recognised the need for an organised, disciplined vanguard – in which lower organs, acknowledging that 'obedience' was 'all-important', determinedly executed 'the decisions and orders of higher organs' like the 'Party Congress' and the 'Central Executive Committee'.[46] Moreover, the MCP accepted that political education would eradicate individualism and replace it with 'party discipline'.[47] The importance of political education in Central's thinking was evinced by the fact that one of the three-man Politiburo, Lau Lee, was put in charge of the Party Education Committee, while every MRLA unit had simple printing facilities.[48] This Committee produced booklets and other reading material for the edification of Party members and the indoctrination of recruits. Moreover, the political commissar who was assigned to each level of the MRLA conducted lectures, quizzes, political theory examinations and study groups.[49] It was at this juncture however that Central began inadvertently to adulterate the Maoist emphasis on education. Implicit in Mao's emphasis on respect for the 'soldiers' or rank and file was the idea that nothing could replace a genuine bonding between the leaders and the led. But in Central's case, respect took a back seat and indoctrination subtly became a cynical weapon to manipulate the rank and file. Lucien Pye in this connection observes that the continuous loading of recruits with large amounts of Communist literature basically amounted to brainwashing. One SEP later admitted that after a point he could do nothing but merely accept what he was being told to read:[50]

> Before long, you just learn a lot of words and the more you read, the more you become acquainted with the words, and you think you understand them. But actually you don't understand any more than you did at the beginning.

The impact of this intensive indoctrination was that the lowly educated MCP recruits were soon less able to exercise sound judgement as to the veracity of MCP pronouncements and propaganda.[51] Not that Central actually permitted the rank and file much time to reflect. One man recalled:[52]

[The] busier you are, the more time you have to spend on your tasks, your duties, and the many problems you have to solve. There is little or no time left to consider your own position; to reflect critically, on your own situation; or on Party policy. Your job is to obey orders, not to consider what the policy is, or what it should be, or whether it is right or wrong. And you have no time even to begin to think about these things, because you are kept so busy.

The MCP's careful emphasis on rituals and ceremonies also created a somewhat surrealistic environment which impaired further the judgement of new recruits. One SEP recalled:[53]

I used to like best to take part [sic] in singing the Communist songs. When a group of us got up in front of our audience and sang some of them, I always got very excited and knew that we would conquer all. Nobody else had songs as fierce or as brave as the Communist ones. After you had heard them, how could you not believe that Communism would win?

Moreover, Central also corrupted the mutual and self criticism sessions which Mao had advocated. In form at least, each session followed the Maoist model: they required each comrade to analyse his personal strengths and weaknesses and share how he intended to 'improve the good and banish the bad aspects' of his character.[54] To this end, each comrade criticised the quality of his own work and personal behaviour (self-criticism). This was followed by the other members of the group adding their comments (mutual criticism). As to be expected, it was not easy owning up to the various errors of individualism, *inter alia*: 'disobedience, or resentment at orders previously given', 'quarrelling' with other comrades, 'decadent habits', not studying Communist ideology 'diligently', 'telling lies, or half-truths' and of 'being impatient or rude'. It was even worse when the others would point out – 'strongly and critically' – those errors that one had missed out either by mistake or out of shame.[55] Still, Mao's point was that some pain was acceptable as long as the spirit of the sessions was right, concerned with improving fighting capacity.[56] However, in the byzantine environment created by Central, mutual criticism degenerated into nothing more than a cynical mechanism for tightening Party control and weeding out potential traitors: instead of inspiring and motivating higher standards of behaviour, therefore, the sessions only generated fear. SEPs thus admitted that criticism sessions were so 'traumatic' they made them 'shake' because they never knew when they would be denounced and punished for 'wavering' or 'incorrect thoughts'. Consequently, they gradually ritualised the sessions, learning when to confess a major fault and at other times confessing to stock sins like 'laziness' and 'lack of industry'.[57]

While the corruption of the education process was evidence that Central had completely missed Mao's emphasis on respect for the rank and file, its insistence on draconian discipline evinced the same shortcoming and something more: a paranoid tendency to assume that traitors rather than 'backward' elements lurked in its midst. Thus, despite a 1940 injunction to Party leaders at all levels to adopt the Maoist approach of 'persuasion and education'[58] in dealing with recalcitrant terrorists, throughout the Emergency, there seemed to be greater emphasis on the stick rather than the carrot: the *milder* sanctions included being whipped 36 times with a length of split bamboo or being tied to a tree and exposed to the sun for hours without food and drink. The ultimate sanction was of course death. Miller noted that the customary form of execution was strangulation with rope or rattan, 'stabbing, bayoneting, or shooting', and even being buried alive.[59] Central's preference for uncompromising solutions to the problem of internal discipline thus violated Mao's injunction not to hastily 'label' members of the rank and file as 'opportunists' and wage 'struggles' against them.[60]

At the same time, Communist leaders at all levels utterly failed to support its rhetoric to the rank and file with concrete deeds. In hindsight it is not easy to understand why this happened when Central must have been cognisant of how its agents had actually secured willing recruits in the first place. Rather than riding the crest of a supposed 'groundswell' in support of the Party, cadres as noted had had to resort to a *quid pro quo* arrangement with the rural Chinese: join us and you will get status, material benefits and power. In other words, the rank and file had joined up not because they accepted that the Party was indeed their vanguard against the Imperialists but because they had expected to get something in return. Mao, whom C.C. Too considered far more 'practical' than the MCP leaders, would have recognised this – which is precisely why the Chinese leader emphasised the need to respect the rank and file by keeping promises made to them.[61] Similarly, Central and its middle level executives should have recognised that it was plain common sense, if the terrorists were to be kept happy, to deliver on promises. When Central therefore defaulted on this obligation to provide its recruits with promised security and material benefits, it undermined terrorist confidence. This notion of a betrayal of trust comes out in a May 1952 leaflet written by SEP Ching Kien, former Deputy Platoon Leader of the 11th Independent Platoon of the 5th MRLA Regiment. Ching Kien first drew attention to the material privations of life in the jungle:

> Comrades! You can see that we never have full meals, warm clothing, or secure accommodation in the jungle. When we get sick there is no medicine.

He then directed a scathing attack on the leaders for failing to provide opportunities for gratification of the very desires which had attracted the recruits in the first place:

Comrades! You can see how the Political Commissar of our Independent Platoon keeps all the new watches, plastic cloth and fountain pens for himself and only lets us have what he does not want any more. At the same time, is there any of you who has ever tasted the nutritive food he keeps for his own consumption? Are Political Commissars and upper ranks the only human beings, are we not human beings too?

He also decried the inconsiderate attitude of the leaders toward the legitimate needs of the rank and file:

When the lower ranks fall sick and ask for assistance, they will be regarded as being unable to bear hardships, as being too argumentative, in short, as exhibiting 'bad manifestations'.

Finally, Ching Kien touched on an extremely raw nerve:

Comrades! The upper ranks can make love in their secret huts, but if you want to find a lady friend, then you will have to wait until there is any left over from the upper ranks.[62]

This letter may have contributed to four further surrenders from the same unit.[63] Another SEP, Chai Soo, formerly Commander of the 36th Platoon of the MRLA 8th Company in Perak, shed further light on Central's abject failure to match its words with deeds. He complained that 'many actions ordered were inconsistent' with official Party policy, and instead of the promised status and material rewards, he had witnessed and experienced personally 'preferential treatment, unfairness, brutality and untrustworthiness'. In sum, 'Communism is not in fact what they taught us to believe'.[64] The theme of upper ranks not displaying congruence between their words and actual deeds is further captured in a 1953 study of 58 SEPs:[65]

The selfishness of the leaders, their failure to keep promises, their complete callousness and indifference to the lower ranks and their "bluffing lectures and propaganda" are all mentioned as causes of discontent or disgust, together with the inequality and irksome restrictions imposed on the rank and file in the jungle.

Finally, a 1954 interrogation of 343 Chinese SEPs found that until 1954, the most common reason given for surrender was tellingly, 'dislike of leaders'.[66] The MCP's own broken promises, irksome internal policies and insensitive behaviour thus constituted disastrous propaganda which in no way helped the Party secure the hearts and minds – or confidence – of its terrorist rank and file. As the MCP continued to ignore its obligations created by the patron-client relationship that it itself had offered the rank and file, it created opportunities for Government to step in as the new patron for the intensely pragmatic rural Chinese.[67] It was in this context, as we shall see, that Government propaganda was to be effective in undermining the 'unity between officers and men' that Mao had argued was so essential.

THE MCP, THE MASSES AND THE TENSION BETWEEN EDUCATION AND TERROR

Central's failure to infuse its efforts at education and discipline of its rank and file with fundamental respect, were repeated, *mutatis mutandis*, in its approach toward the rural Chinese public. This explains why the MCP was never able to create the all-important base areas identified by Mao as critical to revolutionary success. Base areas were regions, secure from Government encroachment, in which the Communist guerrillas could preserve themselves, recruit and train. The progressive expansion of base areas in fact represented the core of Mao's famous Theory of Protracted War, which unfolded in three stages: briefly, in the first, strategic defensive stage, the Communist guerrillas would engage in political education and mobilisation of the public in remote regions so as to create secure base areas. The main emphasis in this stage was to build up a power base and avoid major clashes with superior Government forces. In the second, strategic stalemate stage, the Communists, having remained undefeated, would step up guerrilla raids against weak Government forces in regions contiguous to the initial base areas, demoralise them, force their withdrawal and thereby expand the base areas. In the final strategic offensive stage, Communist forces, increasingly well supported by the public, better equipped through the capture of heavy weapons, and operating from ever larger base areas encircling the last urban strongholds, would engage and defeat Government forces in conventional operations, liberating the entire country.[68]

In particular, Mao was fully cognisant that base areas were not formed simply when the guerrillas moved into a District evacuated by Government forces. If the locality was not to become contested, continually changing hands between the Communists and Government – it was necessary for the Communists to sink roots amongst the population. It was in this context that Mao insisted that the Red Army had to win and hold the confidence of the people by the exemplary behaviour expressed in his 'Three Main Rules of Discipline and Eight Points for Attention'.[69] In this connection, because National Liberation Front (NLF) cadres in South Vietnam in the 1960s adhered closely to the very similar 'Twelve Points of Discipline for the People's Liberation Army' and behaved correctly in public, the villagers in response 'loved them, protected them [and] fed them'.[70] In other words, a true base area was created only when the Party had secured the confidence of the people living in that area, and the means to achieve this outcome were political education and correct behaviour of Party cadres.

On the one hand, between 1946 and 1948, the MCP, in good Maoist fashion, did ensure that the working class Chinese, both in the towns and villages, were given political education, and by all accounts, MCP propagandists were formidable showmen. One SEP recounted how he had been swayed by the power of the MCP propaganda meetings:[71]

> I got very excited at the meetings. They would put on plays, give lectures, and there was a lot of singing and shouting, and I would lose track of the time. The speaker would get very excited the words poured out of his mouth and it was wonderful to watch. He would ask us if we wanted to suffer for the capitalists and we would shout "No!" Then he would ask if we were ready to suffer for the revolution and we would all say "Yes!" When I went home from these meetings, I used to think that the Communist Party was an extremely powerful thing.

However, once the Insurrection broke out in June 1948, Chin Peng withdrew all the cadres involved in clandestine political education in the towns and villages into the jungle, virtually abandoning 'mass work'.[72] In place of direct word-of-mouth propaganda by MCP cadres, a prodigious amount of newssheets – usually stencilled on the back of old Government forms or other paper – were circulated amongst the rural Chinese. *Red Star* in Johore, for example, informed readers of MRLA successes and provided news of Soviet achievements and emerging China while urging that Malayans should see themselves as part of a worldwide working class movement. The general thrust of MCP literature plugged the main theme that it was fortunate that the Party was available to help the masses after the latter had 'spontaneously decided to revolt'.[73] Thus one leaflet exhorted 'All Brothers employed in estates, mines, factories or work-fields of the European or other reactionary Capitalists, to rise in unity with haste'.[74] Clearly, as the rural Chinese were perceived as 'the spirit of the revolution', Central fully expected them to rise in support of the Insurrection. Chin Peng himself admitted recently that as the Party was calling upon 'more or less the same people' who had helped it during the Occupation, it expected their support.[75] However, the relatively rapid recovery of the rubber and tin industries by 1948[76] had markedly dulled whatever 'revolutionary fervour' those 'same people' may have had. As Stenson points out, while many ordinary Chinese may have been willing to revolt in the 'socially disordered and economically disrupted atmosphere of 1945 or 1946', by 1948, the time for revolt had passed.[77] In these changed circumstances, therefore, there was a need for more mass work and political education of the masses, not less. Furthermore, not only did Central de-emphasise political education at the outset of the Insurrection, until October 1951, it failed to underscore to its cadres the overriding importance of being on their best behaviour when dealing with the public. Hence some observers wryly note that the only 'mass work' Central undertook during this period was coercing the masses to support the Party.[78]

That Central had got it wrong, however, was evident from the very beginning of the Insurrection. Instead of being 'willing, dedicated volunteers', many rural Chinese had to be press-ganged into the jungle by MCP terror squads.[79] Moreover, by mid-1949, captured documents revealed that the Party was in a 'state of perplexity' as to why the rural Chinese had yet to 'rise spontaneously in support', despite persuasion and even terrorism.[80] In addition, during the first six months after the start of the Insurrection, Central found it impossible to create secure base areas: terrorists were always being forced to 'move off elsewhere' when the Security Forces moved in, and an ambitious attempt to create three liberated areas met with failure as the Communists were swept out by the Security Forces. By late 1949, there were still no base areas in Malaya.[81] Central's response to its lack of success involved strengthening internal discipline and training while posting more political commissars to MRLA units. There was a lull in terrorist activity from April 1949 as this reorganisation was effected and the revolt was then resumed with greater vigour from October.[82] Critically, however, in November 1949 Central conceded that instead of Mao's permanent bases, it could only set up 'temporary bases' throughout the country. The reason why these bases were 'temporary' was because there was 'practically no such thing as an isolated spot in Malaya'. The good communications of the country meant that Security Forces could converge on practically any spot where the Party operated.[83] It has to be said that this was the lamest of excuses. Even if the Security Forces could converge on any area in Malaya, if the common Chinese were on the side of the Communists, they would have tried to 'protect' the latter, as the villagers in South Vietnam were to do in the case of the NLF.[84] As we shall see, however, once it was clear that there was little chance of reprisal, the rural Chinese in general had no qualms in providing information to Security Forces on Communist whereabouts. In sum, if the MCP had actually sunk roots amongst the Chinese in the rural Districts and won their trust and affection, many Districts would have had every chance to become permanent base areas, even if they were accessible to the Security Forces. Little wonder then that the November 1949 Directive conceded that it had been a mistake to have abandoned masses work, and warned against isolation from the people.[85] In the event, the Party by late 1953 was only able to set up a relatively small number of clandestine 'temporary bases' in the Cameron Highlands in Pahang; Kuala Lumpur in Selangor; Raub/Bentong in Pahang; Penang/Province Wellesley; Betong in southern Thailand; and Kluang in Johore.[86]

Certainly, some MCP leaders saw that Central's critical failure to establish permanent base areas was symptomatic of a larger problem: an adherence to unrealistic assumptions about the readiness of the masses to revolt and the degree of effort needed to create such a scenario. Of particular importance was Siew Lau, the top Party Commissar in Malacca, and someone who was, in an exception to the rule, genuinely grounded in Maoist thinking.[87] As early as 1949, he expressed disagreement with Central's policy of armed revolt, arguing that, while it was necessary to force British Imperialism to quit Malaya ultimately, the Insurrection had been launched prematurely. In line with Mao, he argued that guerrillas without bases were like fish without water, and it was thus simply essential to build up such bases through patient political work. Siew Lau therefore pushed strongly for the revolt to be called off until a strong United Front 'founded on the mutual economic interests of the three main races, the Chinese, Malays and Indians', had been built.[88] Siew Lau thus emphasised patience coupled with more education. Central, however, promptly branded Siew Lau a traitor and on 15 May 1951, executed him, his wife and some of his supporters.[89] In the cruellest of ironies, however, within five months, Siew Lau's views on the necessity for rejuvenating political education would become Party orthodoxy.

While the lack of extensive political education between June 1948 and October 1951 hampered the Party's ability to preserve 'unity' between itself and the public, the use of terror by the Communists was another key reason for the Party's failure to close ranks with the mass of the rural Chinese. Terror may be defined as the use of extreme violence to influence the thinking and behaviour of a specific audience.[90] This means that terror is in fact a form of propaganda – of the deed.[91] In anarchist theory, terror had the function of 'propagandizing for the insurgent movement'.[92] As Schmid and de Graaf explain:[93]

> [Terror], by using violence against one victim, seeks to persuade others. The immediate victim is merely instrumental, the skin on a drum beaten to achieve a calculated impact on a wider audience. As such, an act of [terror] is in reality an act of communication. For the terrorist the message matters, not the victim.

Furthermore, to ensure that this message was seared into the consciousness of the 'wider audience', it was essential that specific acts of terror involved the application of extreme violence. Such violence not only attracted attention, the accompanying shock effect impelled people to lose faith in the capacity of the existing support structures like the Police and Army to provide security.[94] In sum, the real target of terror was not the immediate victims but the spectators, and terror aimed to break the will of the latter through the psychological shock of extreme violence directed at the immediate victims. However, and this is important, although terror aimed to influence the minds of the watching audience, anarchists held that terror had to be directed only at a precise targets within this wider assembly. Indiscriminate terror would only alienate everyone and deprive the rebels of support. Hence precise terror was practised in 19th century Russia by the terrorist group *Narodnaya Volya,* which scrupulously targeted only Government officials and not members of the public. By avoiding the creation of an atmosphere of arbitrary murder, the *Narodniks* effectively projected themselves as the vanguard of public antipathy towards the Tsar.[95] The *Narodniks* influenced the Russian Communists; thus while Lenin and Trotsky were all for terror, they were clear that it had to be applied against certain discriminate targets: 'landlords, capitalists and generals striving to restore the capitalist order'.[96] Similarly, because Mao argued that 'every military action' had psychological and hence 'political consequences', he insisted on careful discrimination in the application of terror.[97] This was of course consistent with his overriding concern that the Communists must 'respect' the public and employ 'methods' reflecting that respect.[98] But how far did the MCP grasp all this? To be sure, Central was clearly spoiling for a savage fight:[99]

> In order to consolidate their colonial rule and protect their plundering interests, the British Imperialists have resorted to the waging of a colonial war aimed at *slaughtering the people.* They are, consequently, destined to become *even more extremist, employing political, economic, and military violence in their continued all-out assault upon the masses* ... they are certain to *employ every means, adopting the most ... brutal tactics, in their attempt at speedy annihilation of the forces of the revolution* (emp. mine).

Since the class enemy was by its very nature prepared to use any means whatsoever to strangle the revolution, the document warned that 'by nature the anti-British national revolutionary war will be protracted, uphill and violent'.[100] This analysis of the situation influenced Central's approach to the indoctrination of its own rank and file:[101]

> Gradually the Party builds inside you the conviction that you and the Party are "at war" with the rest of society. What happens when we are at war? ... The law "Thou shalt not kill" is changed into "Thou shalt kill – and kill and kill once more" until the enemy is destroyed.

The militancy of the top MCP leadership thus found expression on the ground. By the end of 1949, terrorists had killed 655, abducted 250 and wounded 360 civilians.[102] There were 4,300 terrorist-inspired incidents in 1950, 6,100 in 1951 and 4,700 in 1952.[103] Moreover, Central was fully aware that terror was propaganda. This was attested to by its deliberate amplification of physical acts of terror by propaganda leaflets distributed nearby.[104] For instance, in Bahau, Negri Sembilan, in mid-October 1951, the MCP used both propaganda of word and deed to cripple the rubber-tapping industry. In terms of acts, the terrorists among other things, dragged two Chinese tappers from an estate lorry and in front of their horrified fellow workers, shot them dead. Three gang foremen also suffered the same fate. Simultaneously, for three nights in a row, pamphlets were distributed amongst the terrified tappers, warning them that if they did not stop work they would be punished as well. In the absence of adequate Government protection at the time, Communist terror had the desired effect: a mere 15 terrorists dominated 6,000–7,000 tappers and brought to a complete standstill the tapping of rubber trees over 50,000 acres.[105] An early Government study of Communist propaganda admitted that 'this use of propaganda by the bandits as ancillary to, and specifically prepared for and related to, operational action, is effective'.[106]

While Central may have implicitly understood the propaganda value of terror, however, it committed a fatal error: it failed to use terror *selectively*. Certainly, Central identified its class enemies in the Malayan context: the 'British Imperialists', and 'the feudal elements in Malaya [who] have neither the right to rule nor any political status or economic power'.[107] Furthermore, one SEP revealed that the 'whole idea' behind terrorism was to keep 'harassing the Government forces and people sympathetic to Government'.[108] The problem was that the MCP suffered from a predilection to see 'people sympathetic to Government' *everywhere*. Thus rural Chinese workers and squatters bore the brunt of the MCP terror, 'presumably because they presented both the greatest hope and the greatest danger'.[109] Hence for instance, when a Masses Executive appearing on the jungle fringe encountered tappers who were unwilling to spare funds for the Revolution, rather than labelling them as unenlightened friends in need of further political education, they were all too often regarded instead as traitorous 'running dogs' of the Imperialists. The practical consequences of the MCP's propensity to hastily label uncooperative Chinese as 'lackeys' were horrifying, especially since Central resorted to extreme violence for maximum propaganda effect. Hence, in the Plentong District of Johore, terrorists shot dead a Chinese squatter and hacked his wife to death with a *parang*; furthermore, they set alight their hut and threw their eight-year old daughter into the flames. In Kampar, Perak, terrorists butchered a Chinese girl by hammering a nail through her head. At Pantai Seremban, two young men were forced to their knees, had their arms strapped behind their backs, and were battered to death by terrorists wielding *changkuls*. At Tapah, near Cameron Highlands, the terrorists raided a *Sakai* (aboriginal) settlement, massacred the men in cold blood and carried off the women into the jungle. At Kampar, a lone terrorist flung a grenade into a crowd watching a wayside circus, killing five people, including a woman and a child. A Police report prepared in late 1952 emphasised that this 'senseless cruelty' was not at all 'isolated' but typical of 'hundreds of similar incidents' throughout the country. Even captured terrorists balked at the methods used by the Party, one confessing that the 'tortures are too horrible for description'.[110] Central's tendency quickly to regard any sign of equivocation as evidence of class enmity found expression in its leaflet propaganda as well. Hence, instead of heeding Mao's insistence on respecting the people, Central found itself threatening them instead:[111]

> Comrade Sookoo Ling Nam, do not be misled when you hear that many shopkeepers have been robbed of their property and even that some of them were killed by us. This does not mean that we want their property, but it was due to their uncooperativeness and siding with the British Imperialists, so we take them to be our enemies. Now let us together drive away the British Imperialist from Malaya. We hope to get a sum of $1,000 from you as a start. We also hope to get a sum of $200 every month from you. We have informed you about this previously, and we hope that you will consider it carefully. Otherwise we do not guarantee your safety and the safety of your property.

Another example of Central's uncompromising attitude toward uncommitted members of the public was manifested by the leaflet 'Exterminated – a Traitor to the People':[112]

> Fellow Countrymen! Open up your eyes and see! Open your ears and hear! To-night this Conductor Maniam has been shot dead with a gun of the People. Everyone of you, Brothers and Sisters! Think deeply for what reason he has been shot dead.
>
> The Conductor Maniam was a Traitor. He was approached on several occasions by People's Volunteers who warned him and advised him, but he never ceased from deceiving the people... Brethren! Remember! The fate of Conductor Maniam will befall everyone who deceives the People and their Army by reporting to the Imperialists! Those who were hangers-on of this Conductor Maniam should improve their behaviour, otherwise they can be sure that they too will one day be shot dead.

Again, implicit in this passage is Central's clear assumption: anyone who did not support the Party was by definition a 'traitor'. The question of 'backwardness' requiring education did not arise. Such thinking thus enabled Central to adopt an 'elastic' definition of 'treachery'[113] and the MCP terror campaign, instead of being selective, appeared indiscriminate and constituted highly destructive propaganda. Central's carelessness up to October 1951 contrasted sharply with the later NLF practice of carefully surveying villages and classifying the villagers according to degree of allegiance to the Communists. This classification determined how the NLF actually treated each villager. In addition, the NLF imposed strict controls on the use of terror, preferring 'political re-education rather than violence as its principal means of dealing with hostile people'.[114] In fact, in the years following the October 1951 Directive, the Party did order its Branch Committees to make detailed situation reports of new areas, possibly to determine how the people therein ought to be treated.[115] However, it was a case of too little too late, as the unrestricted terror campaign from June 1948 to October 1951 had generated a deep reservoir of 'mass aversion' to the Party.[116] In sum, if Central had failed to adopt methods which promoted 'unity' between its leaders and the rank and file, its terror campaign even more seriously destroyed any hope of forging a basic 'unity between the army and the people'. This was to prove a tremendous boon to Government's propaganda efforts.

ADMISSION OF DOCTRINAL MISTAKES: THE OCTOBER 1951 DIRECTIVES AND THE AFTERMATH

A captured MCP document dated June 1951 declared that the Briggs Plan[117] was a failure, the Security Forces had created more foes among the masses by its 'rigorous action', and the latter had become better organised. Meanwhile the Min Yuen had augmented its presence in the Resettlement Camps, while the MRLA had increased in strength and technique, had captured many arms and was able to 'hit harder'. Thus, despite difficulties compelling the Party to continue in 'uncoordinated guerrilla warfare' for the foreseeable future, final victory was still possible. Hence, the MRLA in 1952 would be expected to mount 'constant ambushes to capture arms', develop more Min Yuen organisations, and create as many incidents as possible.[118] The upbeat optimism of this document, however, masked growing internal disquiet. Eight months earlier, Hoong Poh, Chairman of the Central Selangor District Committee, had sent a letter to Central, warning that the terror policy was not working:[119]

> If we insist on continuing our present policy, we will cause the enemy no disadvantage but create unpleasantness for the general public who will gradually withdraw from us.

Furthermore, questioning Central's assumption that most of the rural Chinese shared an identity of interests with the Party, Hoong Poh drew attention to the national registration exercise, in which Government had issued Malayans with identity cards in an effort to separate the terrorists from the public:[120]

> The enemy effectively carried out the Registration Scheme throughout Malaya within the short space of only a few months. Is this not sufficient demonstration of the willingness of the masses? If the masses have no desire to surrender their cards and we insist on taking them away then it will be a question of taking by force... If we attempt to carry out our resolution by force throughout Malaya, then we would be committing something against the will of the public. I think that public opinion is against us.

Then, perhaps in an effort to preserve his own skin, Hoong Poh suggested carefully that after all, was it not Stalin himself who had argued that 'methods must be changed according to different conditions'?[121] Even the CCP, which emphasised army-people unity, were unhappy with Central's terror policy, and Chin Peng was urged to change tactics in September 1951.[122] Possibly as a result of these internal and external pressures, the following month, Central issued new directives setting forth important changes in policy. These fell into the hands of the Security Forces exactly a year later,[123] and in December, were being studied in the Colonial Office.[124] The documents excited interest in both London and Kuala Lumpur, and were leaked controversially to the *Times*, which published an article tellingly entitled: 'Changed Policy of Terrorists: More Discrimination in Choosing Malayan Victims'.[125] It reported that the Party had admitted the error of past policy, and suggested that this rethink might have explained the 'almost complete absence of terrorist activity in every state except Johore, Perak and Pahang'.[126] The October 1951 Directives emphasised the importance of 'avoiding violent tactics which have antagonised peasants and workers.' It stipulated that the comrades must:[127]

> (i) stop seizing identity and ration cards (ii) stop burning new villages and coolie lines (iii) stop attacking post offices, reservoirs, power stations, and other public services; (iv) refrain from derailing civilian trains with high explosives (v) stop throwing grenades and take great care, when shooting running dogs found mixing with the masses, to prevent stray shots from hurting the masses; and (vi) stop burning religious buildings, sanitary trucks, Red Cross vehicles, and ambulances.

In addition, '[rubber] trees, tin mines, and factories must not be destroyed', because – as if this was something new – 'the workers' would 'lose their employment'. However, conceding that some form of terrorism had to be carried out at the *properly-identified* class enemy, it was advised that

> limited destruction can be carried out with the permission of the workers. The motive must be carefully explained to them and alternative employment must be found.[128]

In short, considerable restraints were to be imposed on violence-prone terrorists. Furthermore, Central ordered comrades not only to avoid killing ordinary people, but to take care not to even 'frighten' them. Hence, in advising terrorists not to shoot at trucks, it was explained that such an action would 'seriously frighten the drivers and civilians taking the same vehicles, and even wound them accidentally'. Furthermore, in a revealing commentary on how the Party had only belatedly grasped the Maoist injunction to respect the masses, the document explained that wounding the civilians 'accidentally' would cause them 'to harbour the misunderstanding that we had no consideration for their lives, or even that we deliberately aimed at them'. So seriously did the Party feel the need to inject an attitudinal sea-change into the rank and file that it even painstakingly prescribed how discrimination should be introduced into actual operations:[129]

> When striking at the military and police who escort the trains with passengers, one should first consider whether one could reduce the likelihood of inflicting casualties on the masses to a small degree before taking action, but explosives and other methods shall not be used to capsise [sic] the relevant trains, for in doing so it might inflict casualties on the masses, and even if casualties were not inflicted on the masses, they would be thus adversely effected [sic].

It was further advised that when considering hurling grenades at a clearly-identified class enemy, terrorists must carefully ensure that 'family members, shop employees, and servants of the object to be hurled at' were unhurt by the blast. In sum, the general refrain was that 'as much care as possible must be taken to avoid inflicting casualties on the masses'.[130] In conjunction with the de-emphasising of terror, Central announced that the primary task was now 'to expand and consolidate the organisation of the masses'. The latter was – in an echo of Siew Lau – to take the form of a united front of all communities and classes by acquiring the support of the bourgeoisie and capitalists. In addition, Central directed that '[political] activity and education' should be increased in 'large towns'. Subversion was to be intensified, with cadres exhorted to penetrate unions and the MCA. In line with Mao's emphasis on respecting the masses, moreover, Central reiterated that a more patient approach should also be taken with the masses; there should be 'no killing or thrashing; only advice, criticism, fines [and] education'.[131] The general thrust was to avoid treating the rural Chinese as reactionaries, because if they were treated as reactionaries, they would indeed behave as such.[132] However, the issue of how to combine the use of terror with the Maoist injunction to respect the people proved to be a circle which Central could not quite square. This was evinced in an extremely revealing section of the documents called 'On the Question of Compulsion in the Mass Movement'. On the one hand, it was decreed that the Party's relations with the masses should henceforth be geared toward

> educating and convincing the masses, and leading them to launch struggles so as to raise their level of cognition and consciousness. Our Party cannot compel the masses in the least, for compelling the masses would be a violation of our proletarian mass line.

But did this mean that any form of intimidation could not at all be used? Central's position was yes, it could, as long as the masses themselves used these methods to deal with recalcitrants in their number. The Party itself could not, and could not be seen, to compel the masses:

On a definite basis and under certain circumstances compulsion might be enforced within a definite degree. This is to say that through the self-consciousness and self-willingness of all the masses in a specific locality or through the resolution of the majority of the masses in a meeting, compulsion might be enforced. Such compulsion springs forth from the masses themselves, and is not the Party's compulsion on them.

But what to do if the masses did not spontaneously exercise self-regulation? This is where the doctrinal bankruptcy of Central revealed itself, for the proffered solution was: consult with higher authorities:

> Submit a detailed report on the actual circumstances to the organs at higher levels and wait for the further opinions of the organs at higher level. To act in this manner is not failure to carry out the resolutions of the organs at higher levels, for it is a question of the Party's relation with the masses, and if we obdulately [sic] compelled the masses to act accordingly then we would have violated the mass line of the Party.

Again, what is emphasised is that on no account must coercion be used on the masses. Moreover, 'leading organs', in dealing with particularly apathetic masses, were advised by Central to

> take care to make investigations and studies [sic] grasp the concrete state of affairs, and frequently check upon the mass work cadres [sic] link with the masses and the masse's [sic] sentiments and their demands etc. so as to enable the resolutions promulgated by the leading organs to entirely correspond with the demands and interests of the masses.[133]

Two points stand out: first, 'leading organs' must ensure that political education ('mass work cadres link with the masses') was being carried out. Second, Party policy must be made to reflect 'the demands and interest of the masses'. Central was hence betraying a belated appreciation of the Maoist position that political education was not so much a control mechanism as an important means of building a consensus, a 'unity' between the Party and the people.

In sum, the fundamental doctrinal shift enshrined in the October 1951 Directives from what might be termed 'much coercion, little education' to 'little coercion, much education', may have prompted C.C. Too to aver that the MCP was trying to transit 'from the European form of Marxism-Leninism to the Asian form of Maoism'.[134] It must be added, however, that the basic injunction in the documents to step up education and hence discipline of the increasingly unsettled terrorist rank and file, without any balancing emphasis on the need for leaders to respect the sensitivities of their charges, suggests that there were limits to the MCP's belated apprehension of Maoist dogma.[135] At any rate, the MCP henceforth devoted increasing attention to the political education and subversion of 'factories and schools in urban areas, and fishing villages, farms and small townships in rural areas'.[136] The new emphasis on political education meant that the Party had to make the effort to conserve the 'lives of the maximum number of trained Communists for furthering the work of subversion'.[137] In April 1952, therefore, at a meeting in Bentong, Pahang, Chin Peng decided to withdraw part of Central to South Thailand, and this was carried out in 1953. Other MRLA units also moved into south Thailand from 1952 onwards.[138] In 1955, moreover, to coincide with the switch to a 'political offensive' (see Chapter Six), Central formally adopted the policy of conserving its strength 'while waiting for an opportune moment when it would resume its armed struggle'.[139]

This policy of conserving strength while resorting to subversion did not mean that the MCP completely abandoned terror, however. A year after the October Directives, Central recognised that infiltration and subversion tactics were not as successful as hoped: the rural Chinese, instead of attributing the fall in terrorist incidents to a more caring MCP and increasing co-operation, chose to withhold assistance, judging that the 'rebellion was losing its impetus'.[140] In particular, the fall in rubber and tin prices were making the public less willing to pay Party subscriptions. Central thus issued a 1952 Directive calling for more terrorism to support infiltration and subversion.[141] However, the second wave of terror was 'feebler and far less effectual' than the first: the steep decline in monthly Security Force and civilian casualties that started around October 1951 (188 a month) continued throughout 1953, hovered at about 36 in March 1954, and then dropped to 20 in February 1956.[142] This decline in MCP terror, quite apart from the effect of the October Directives and the decision to conserve strength, was also due to the diminishing fighting potential of the MCP: between 1952 and 1954 the MRLA lost two-thirds of its rank and file and worse, between 1951 and 1953, the rate of replacement of terrorist losses declined sharply. Thus, while the loss of every 100 terrorists in 1951 represented a net loss of 13 terrorists after taking into account fresh recruitment, in 1953 the net loss had jumped to 69.[143]

In effect, between late 1951 and 1953, the Party not only lost the physical capacity to create a Communist State by force of arms, it found itself trapped in a no-win situation: needing the support of the mass of the rural Chinese to survive, let alone take the initiative against Government, it was unable to secure such support in most areas except through terror. And yet the resort to terror only damaged its own prospects of securing that same support. The MCP thus found itself a 'prisoner of terrorism', neither able to give up terror nor use it satisfactorily.[144] While Alec Peterson, Director-General of Information Services in Templer's time, told the American researcher Riley Sunderland in 1962 that the question of terror was a problem the MCP never solved,[145] C.C. Too added:[146]

The CPM was totally unable to reconcile the dichotomy of claiming to liberate the people from imperialism on the one hand, and slaughtering the people and destroying their livelihood and property on the other.

The entrapment of the MCP by its own terror policy compelled the more reflective of the rank and file to give up. As Osman China, who surrendered after the resumption of the terror policy in 1953 complained bitterly:[147]

They said they wanted to win over the masses, but what were they doing? They were frightening the tappers, they were burning the buses, they were doing all kinds of things to make the people become our enemies. It didn't make sense.

CONCLUSION

In this chapter we have argued that the key to the military insurgency was the rural Chinese community, as this group provided the numbers that formed the terrorist rank and file as well as food, funds and other material support to the Party. We have shown that even before the intervention of Government propaganda, terrorist and rural Chinese confidence were already being undermined by the actions of the Communist leaders themselves. Specifically, we have argued that Central's post-war leaders lacked the intellectual capacity and judgement to successfully adapt Maoist theory to the Malayan context. Basically, Central failed to give sufficient weight to Mao's realistic appreciation of the Chinese peasant as essentially backward and unsophisticated. Because the latter could consequently be expected to display petty bourgeois tendencies, the Communist Party had to be patient and resort to political education of the masses – and of the rank and file which emerged from the masses – in order to raise their consciousness to the required level. Without political education, the insurrection would be unsuccessful. In addition, Mao emphasised that because the masses and the rank and file were crucial to the success of the Revolution, he insisted that the Party simply had to adopt methods and policies which showed a basic respect for both groups. One manifestation of respect was the keeping of promises, of backing rhetoric with concrete improvements in the lives of the people and the rank and file.

We saw instead that the MCP view of political education of the rank and file did not quite coincide with Mao's essentially instrumentalist conception. Rather, political education the MCP way was a means of control, and its fruit was not so much the increase of 'fighting capacity' as Mao had projected but rather fear and alienation of the rank and file; moreover, Communist leaders ignored their promises to act as Provider of material benefits to its recruits and imposed jungle discipline instead. These 'deeds' alienated the bulk of the terrorists, rendering them, as we shall see, vulnerable to Government surrender appeals. In addition, Central between June 1948 and October 1951 ignored 'mass work', an omission which hampered relations with the all-important rural Chinese public. Greatly exacerbating matters was the general Communist tendency to label uncommitted Chinese as traitors rather than backward elements in need of education, and the resulting terror campaign which utterly destroyed the Party's credibility amongst the ordinary Chinese. Although the October 1951 Directives signalled a shift to a Maoist attitude of more education, persuasion and less terror, it was too late to win back the mass of the rural Chinese. Moreover, as noted, the Directives were virtually silent on the need for proper respect for the rank and file.

From 1953, therefore, losses, a fall in recruitment, the desire to husband limited resources and its inadvertent entrapment by the policy of terror meant that the MCP no longer tried to create a Communist State by force of arms. Rather it pursued the defensive objective of preserving organisational integrity and coherence in the face of Security Force pressure and propaganda, whilst seeking opportunities for subversion. This, however, did not automatically mean that Government had overcome the Insurrection. If Hack, in asserting that the 'back of the Emergency' was 'decisively broken between summer 1951 and summer 1952',[148] implies that the war was won in that time, he is mistaken. While the threat of an MCP military victory certainly receded subsequent to that period, this in itself was not a sufficient indication that Government had won. The greater long-term threat was clandestine political education – in a word, subversion. Hence the MCP could afford to be denuded of the bulk of its rank and file – as it was by 1954 – but as long as it retained a small but critical mass of hard core rank and file terrorists, like the mythical hydra it could still regenerate itself through surreptitious proselytising in the Chinese middle schools, unions and political parties.[149] This hard core therefore represented a 'residual threat' which had to be eliminated before the Emergency could be said to have been won.[150] In this respect we shall see that Government was gradually to find that rather than a physical solution to the terrorist threat, over the long term a psychological approach was the better option. Given the excellent sanctuary afforded by the Malayan jungle to ever-decreasing numbers of terrorists as the Emergency progressed, it was slowly recognised that it was easier to persuade insurgents to lay down arms than actually find and kill them. Persuasion implied winning the trust of not only the terrorists but also the rural Chinese community from which they drew their sustenance: both groups had to trust that Government was a better Provider of their material needs than the MCP. Indeed, Government would find that projecting the idea that it was a superior Provider simply had to involve synchronising the messages sent out by its pronouncements and its actions. That it by no means found this a straightforward task is the subject of the following chapters.

CHAPTER THREE

～∾～

Propaganda in Disarray
The Mistakes of the Gurney Years,
June 1948–May 1950

INTRODUCTION

The first three years of the Insurrection found Government very much on the back foot in the face of the Communist assault. Certainly Government and the European planters and miners in particular did well to stem the initial Communist onslaught in the first six months of the Emergency, with the happy consequence that the country's key industries remained viable. On the other hand, however, Government's response to the Insurrection largely undermined rural Chinese confidence while scarcely affecting that of the terrorists. The lack of visible, forceful leadership at the top, the tough Emergency Regulations and the insensitive behaviour of some Police and Army units represented propaganda which, rather than communicating to the rural Chinese the idea that Government was their Provider, suggested instead that Government was at best irrelevant and at worst, a Tormentor. In addition, the inept performance of the Security Forces shaped terrorist perceptions that Government was not about to win the war, and to remain with the MCP was to back the winning horse; thus the surrender rate during these years was low. On the spoken, printed and broadcast propaganda front, meanwhile, the three main agencies struggled with problems of organisation and co-ordination, as well as with the content and timing of propaganda. In any case, mere exhortations meant nothing to either the Chinese or the terrorists as long as Government was manifestly unable to back them up with concrete deeds. In short, the confidence of the rural Chinese and ultimately the terrorist rank and file was not going to be secured until Government, through not merely words but even more so, deeds, was able unequivocally to project the message that it was indeed a trustworthy Provider of their needs and wants. That this was to prove difficult at this stage is the subject of this chapter.

GURNEY, MACDONALD AND THE RURAL CHINESE

That Government's fundamental task in the face of the Communist uprising was the restoration and maintenance of public confidence, was made forcefully apparent as early as 22 June 1948, four days after the declaration of a Federation-wide State of Emergency. An irate delegation of European business interests based in Malaya met Colonial Secretary Creech Jones in London to complain that High Commissioner Edward Gent's inept response to the lawlessness afflicting Malaya had endangered the 'safety and future' of that country.[1] Although Creech Jones publicly defended High Commissioner Gent before the delegation, it was apparent to both the Colonial Office and Kuala Lumpur that if the decline in public confidence in Malaya was to be arrested, drastic measures had to be taken. Gent was thus recalled.[2] Meanwhile, in Malaya, Government tried hard to project the impression that it was on top of the situation. In a feverish burst of activity, it passed supplementary Emergency legislation during the Legislative Council meeting of 7 July, and further legislation before the year was up. Under these Emergency Regulations, Government arrogated to itself considerable licence to infringe personal liberties. These included the right to impose the death penalty for the carrying of firearms; detain persons without trial for up to two years; search persons and buildings without warrant; occupy properties; impose curfews and control movement of people and vehicles.[3]

Moreover, to ensure it had the muscle to enforce these Regulations, Government took measures to increase the strength of the Police Force. At the outbreak of the revolt there were about 9,000 Police in the Federation. These were immediately augmented by the raising of Special Constables for guard duty on the many scattered and exposed estates and mines throughout the country.[4] Hence by December 1948, 30,000 mainly Malay Special Constables had been recruited, while 16,966 part-time Auxiliary Police had been raised to relieve the regular Police of static duties and enable the latter to pursue the terrorists.[5] In addition, about 500 ex-Palestine Police constables and officers were recruited after the termination of the British mandate in that territory. The 'Palestinians' were used in training the Special Constables, thereby relieving the intense pressure on planters and miners who had hitherto been struggling with organising both production and security for their establishments.[6] In addition, to replace H.B. Langworthy, who was retiring as Commissioner of Police on grounds of ill health, W.N. Gray, formerly Inspector-General of the Palestine Police, who was said to have 'special experience in combating terrorism', was appointed in August 1948.[7] Meanwhile, the Army, 10 battalions strong in June 1948, was set upon the terrorists.[8] General Officer Commanding (GOC) Malaya District, Maj-General Boucher, reassured one and all that facing the MCP threat was the 'easiest problem' he had ever tackled,[9] while

Commander-in-chief, Far East Land Forces (FARELF), General Neil Ritchie declared that the arrival of the 1st Inniskillings from Hong Kong, combined with RAF support, would be sufficient to 'maintain the economic life of the country, and restore morale'.[10]

Two months after Gray's appointment, moreover, on 6 October, Sir Henry Gurney, formerly Chief Secretary in Palestine, arrived in Malaya as High Commissioner. The Malay Rulers initially opposed Gurney's appointment, worrying that his background as Chief Secretary in Palestine would prejudice him against their special position in Malaya and compel him to insist that like Arabs and Jews, Malays and Chinese ought to have equal rights. The Rulers wanted someone else with prior experience of Malaya who would be sympathetic to their interests. However, possible alternative candidates like Lord Milverton, Alec Newboult and John Macpherson, were unavailable.[11] Nevertheless, Gurney seemed equipped to cope with the peculiar challenge of Malaya. He possessed broad administrative experience – the fruit of having served, apart from Palestine, in the Gold Coast, Jamaica and East Africa as well.[12] Gurney's sheer intellectual power in fact prompted Hugh Carleton Greene, the man who was to re-organise Government spoken, printed and broadcast propaganda in September 1950, to opine that Gurney was 'one of the greatest men I've ever met in my life'.[13] To his MCS officers, Gurney was an excellent bureaucrat, 'shrewd in the ways of men and institutions', and was able to be firm and decisive without giving offence, arousing resentment and stoking jealousies. He thus quickly won a reputation as a man of high intelligence and imagination, yet modest, decent and fair-minded.[14] Templer himself later expressed 'the greatest admiration for all that the records showed Gurney had done'.[15]

However, for all his intellectual acuity, years spent 'working with files rather than human beings' had conditioned Gurney into seeing 'abstractions first and mundanity second'.[16] Thus, while Gurney certainly grasped that winning and holding Chinese confidence concerning their future role in Malaya was a key problem,[17] his rather 'theoretical'[18] approach to the Chinese question compelled him to seek an essentially political solution to the Insurrection. Thus although Gurney recognised the immediate need for creating 'confidence in Government's ability to exterminate the bandits',[19] his basic analysis was that the solution to the Insurrection involved securing a 'fair deal' and 'political rights' for the 'local Chinese'.[20] It was in this context that in December 1948 Gurney prodded the leading Chinese members of the Legislative Council, planting and mining communities, to help create a 'focus for loyal Chinese aspirations' so as to provide the mass of the Chinese with an 'alternate standard' to Communism.[21] The Malayan Chinese Association (MCA) was thus inaugurated on 27 February 1949 in Kuala Lumpur.[22] However, Gurney erred in assuming that by securing political concessions for all Chinese he would at one fell stroke also resolve the problem of the *military insurgency*. Although he himself recognised that the Malayan Chinese were by no means a monolithic community, he assumed that the differing interests of the various Chinese were mediated by a common quest for a political stake in Malaya.[23] But he was wrong, because the Chinese most affected by MCP terror, the exposed, unsophisticated *rural Chinese* – the squatters, tappers, timber workers – felt that 'politics and government were not the concern and responsibility of the people, but the concern of those who had acquired a special mandate to govern'. They just wished 'to be left alone to earn their living'.[24] Unfortunately, Gurney's pre-occupation with the political dimension meant that he 'put too much reliance on the aim of constitutional rights for the Chinese', and not enough urgency into seeking methods of improving their physical and socio-economic well-being, as through resettlement.[25] Consequently, because Gurney refused to sanction full-scale resettlement, some Government officials had to attempt local resettlement with inadequate funds and found it 'frustrating'.[26] More damagingly, it is possible to detect in Gurney's attitude a tendency to view the rural Chinese in largely operational terms – as a commodity to be denied the MCP. Hence he had 'no qualms whatever' in resorting to deportation to break up the squatter supply networks, something which as we shall see, caused the Chinese 'a great deal of distress'.[27] Compounding Gurney's political focus and essential lack of sensitivity to the fears and concerns of the rural Chinese was his temperament. He was not regarded as 'charismatic', or 'spectacular', but rather 'shy' and reserved. In fact some even perceived him as a 'bit too soft' to cope with the 'very serious situation in the country'. He was certainly not the type of leader who could by sheer force of personality alone dominate and impress upon the rural Chinese that Government could protect their interests.[28]

In fact, the high official who had a far more colourful persona and moreover seemed to grasp the need for visible, expressive leadership was the Commissioner-General, Malcolm MacDonald, who had arrived in April 1946.[29] MacDonald's awareness of the salience of public confidence was evinced as early as June 1948, when he insisted that the available Security Forces should not be sent off in speculative jungle-bashing operations in pursuit of the terrorists, but rather be concentrated in visible defence of installations vital to the 'life, economy and employment of the country'. The early appearance of the Special Constables at isolated estates certainly helped soothe 'the minds of the people'.[30] Moreover, MacDonald made it a point to project the image of the 'approachable proconsul'.[31] Old colonialists were often appalled at his informality and friendships with Asians, but it was precisely this quality which was badly needed in these first years of the Emergency when MCP terror had gripped the country.[32] In particular, MacDonald, like Gurney, understood the importance of securing Chinese confidence, and this was one reason that he encouraged the formation of the Communities Liaison Committee (CLC) in April 1949.[33] The CLC provided an informal mechanism which allowed leading Chinese like Dato Tan Cheng Lock to seek some concessions from their Malay counterparts in the 'matter of qualification for taking part in the public life of the community'.[34] MacDonald's efforts to project a more human face of Government to the Chinese were limited, however, for two reasons: as Commissioner-General he 'lacked political clout' and remained 'a broker without executive responsibility'.[35] More fundamentally, MacDonald chose to focus his energies on the attainment of the long-term goal of providing political security for the Chinese through constitutional safeguards. Like Gurney, MacDonald reckoned that the ultimate solution to the Insurrection was to be found in the political sphere; he thus assiduously cultivated the vocal, English-educated business classes, whom he felt to be the 'most important' Chinese as they were active in the Executive, Legislative and Advisory Councils and *ipso facto* the natural leaders of the Malayan Chinese.[36] Hence while he enjoyed very close ties with rich, influential Chinese like the formidable Dr Ong Chong Keng of Penang, he did not have a great deal of contact with the rural classes.[37] It was only with hindsight that MacDonald later conceded that the upper class English-educated Chinese were never able to match the MCP in articulating the aspirations of the Chinese squatters.[38]

To reiterate, although Government had pushed through tough Emergency Regulations and strengthened the Police and the armed forces, the basic concept for dealing with the MCP challenge was wrong: because Gurney and MacDonald adopted a political approach to the Emergency, they placed excessive stock by constitutional methods as a panacea for the Insurrection. This meant two things: first, it was assumed that all Malayan Chinese – including the strategic rural Chinese – would be won over to Government by the provision of political rights above all else. Second, it was held that all Government had to do was to co-opt the educated Chinese into the political process and they would serve as the channel for all classes of Chinese to articulate their interests. The basic disjunction between the urban wealthy Chinese and their strategically vital poorer rural cousins was not fully appreciated. The basically elitist, political thrust of Gurney and MacDonald and their overall focus on the MCA and the work of the Communities Liaison Committee meant that in the first three years of the Emergency, Government gave the rural Chinese relatively short shrift.

THE CONSEQUENCES OF THE LOSS OF THE CHINESE PROTECTORATE

The marginalisation of the rural Chinese in Government's basic appreciation of the Malayan *problematique* was reflected in and compounded by the virtual absence of a physical official presence amongst them, owing to the loss of the old Chinese Protectorate. Prior to 1877 immigrant Chinese coolies had been governed by headmen or 'capitan china' through the secret societies, and the Straits Settlement Government had had little contact with the community. With increased immigration however, there arose a need to monitor conditions on vessels from China and working conditions on tin mines, as well as to clamp down on secret society clashes. The first 'Protector' of Chinese was thus appointed in 1877 in Singapore, followed by one in Penang (1881) and Malacca (1911). Protectors were also appointed in Perak (1883), Selangor and Pahang (1890), Negri Sembilan (1914), Kedah (1923) and Johore (1927). With the emergence of the Chinese Protectorate, the old capitan chinas lost influence gradually as ordinary Chinese went directly to Chinese-speaking European officers for 'redress of grievances and settlement of troubles'. At first, there was one Secretary for Chinese Affairs (SCA) appointed to run the Protectorate in the Federated Malay States and one to do the same in the Straits Settlements, but in 1932 these two positions were fused, and the SCA was made a member of the Executive and Legislative Councils. The Federal SCA supervised the Protectors in the States and Settlements, who were charged with administering various laws relating to the Chinese community, for example the Banishment Ordinance, Pawnbroker's Ordinance, Societies Ordinance and the Women and Girls Protection Ordinance. Protectors also acted as detectives and informers keeping tabs on secret societies and brothels.[39] The Protectorate was 'an institution unrivalled' in British colonial history, 'touching the Chinese community at every point, with officers trained to observe and interpret every reaction throughout the body social and body politic of the Chinese in Malaya'. Hence Blythe argued that the Protectorate was 'in truth, the finger on the pulse' of the Chinese.[40] So close was the relationship between the Protectorate officer and the common Chinese that the former was treated as a 'village elder' or 'headman' and accorded the kind of respect reserved in China for the *Taijin* (Hokkien for 'great man'). Richard Broome was himself a pre-war Assistant Protector of Chinese, and recalled that much of the work of the 'Taijin' consisted 'of sitting in full divan and hearing the complaints and disputes of all and sundry Chinese. At these sessions, which took place virtually every day, everybody had direct access to the "Taijin" without the intervention of any interpreter, clerk, or other functionary'.[41] Naturally, the psychological hold of the *Taijin* on the ordinary Chinese was considerable. Frank Brewer, a senior Chinese Affairs officer during the Emergency, recounted that as a prisoner of war (POW) in Palembang he had been keen to conceal from his Japanese captors that he could speak Chinese. One day, because the school in which he and other POWs had been detained was overcrowded, he was ordered to investigate the Chinese Chamber of Commerce building to see if it was suitable for conversion into a detention centre. On entering the Chamber, Brewer found a few Chinese already there and carefully exchanged a 'few cheery words' in

Hokkien with them. To his chagrin, however, a party of them – with a Japanese officer in tow – later accosted him shouting 'Tai Jin [sic], help us to get a few days longer in here to pack our bags'.[42]

Until the Second World War, although the Protectorate had gradually been devolving powers to appointed Chinese Advisory Boards and was becoming more advisory in function, it was still very much the 'main force' for controlling the common Chinese.[43] However, Colonial Office opinion held that in the interests of a united post-war Malaya, the continued existence of a special department catering exclusively to the needs of the Chinese community was anachronistic. Hence, in September 1945, the Protectorate was abolished and its staff and functions were redistributed amongst other departments like Labour and Welfare, with no overall co-ordination.[44] In its place was a solitary SCA Malayan Union supported by one clerk and three translators. Because he had no 'field officers', the SCA 'sat on a cloud with no terrestrial contacts' with the mass of the common Chinese, and could only produce monthly confidential reports which were a 'pale version' of the 'very detailed and very informative' reports that had been produced in pre-war days. Furthermore, the SCA was not even on the Executive Council, while the Chinese Advisory Boards were abolished.[45] Thus, in the very period that the MCP was beginning to dominate the immediate environment of young, disaffected urban and rural Chinese workers, Government was *withdrawing* the very direct, personal contact needed to counterbalance the Communists' influence. Hence Blythe argued that the 'saddest' consequence of the abolition of the Protectorate was that 'the common man and woman who formerly brought their troubles to the Protectorate now [turned] to the Chinese Consul for help'. Brewer added that following the end of the Protectorate, Chinese Consuls stepped in to lead the Malayan Chinese middle classes while the MCP gained hold of the workers.[46] When the Emergency broke out, therefore, relations between Government and the ordinary Chinese were dangerously distant. One Chinese SEP later told Pye that Government 'had nothing to with me and I had nothing to do with them'.[47]

To close the gap between Government and the Chinese, Gurney as noted supported the setting up of the MCA, which grew in size to 15,000 members by June 1949.[48] While it has been suggested that the MCA was an 'ideal "power broker"' between Government and the Chinese squatters, there is evidence to suggest that the actual ability of the MCA to *replace* the Chinese Protectorate was dubious. The fundamental problem with the MCA was that it was a creature of the Chinese business classes, and its leaders, Dato Tan Cheng Lock, Tan Siew Sin, Khoo Teik Ee and Ong Yoke Lin among others, were English-speaking Chinese.[49] These men shared little in common with the rural Chinese, who basically regarded the MCA as a 'rich man's party', which was 'not attuned to the needs of the working man'.[50] Blythe thus observed in September 1948 that it was 'quite absurd' to expect that the Chinese members of the Legislative and Executive Councils could act as the conduit between Government and the rural Chinese. The elitist leading Chinese could never compete with the old Protectorate, which had dealt with 'persons, with people', and thus 'provided an unequalled reservoir of knowledge of Chinese affairs and reactions at the disposal of Government'.[51] In December, instead of resurrecting the old Protectorate -an idea apparently vetoed by Malcolm MacDonald – Gurney instructed Chinese-speaking Deputy Commissioners for Labour to spend more time advising State Governments on Chinese matters and advising District Officers (DOs) on contacting all strata of Chinese. Their secondary appointments as Secretaries for Chinese Affairs (SCAs) thus became more important, and by October 1949 they constituted, under the Federal SCA, the new Chinese Affairs Service, which, like the MCS, was a Federal *Service* rather than a discrete Department like the old Protectorate. Moreover, Gurney simultaneously resurrected the old Advisory Boards in six States/Settlements, which soon evolved into mechanisms for State Government-Chinese discourse on a range of domestic issues touching the lives of the ordinary Chinese, like sanitation, cheap housing, gambling and welfare, for instance.[52] To be sure, there was bureaucratic resistance to attempts to increase the number of Chinese specialists throughout Government. One of the objections to the old Protectorate had been that it was a 'snooping' Department. Blythe countered that in the current Emergency Government 'could do with more of such snooping', and insisted that it was a pressing need 'greatly' to increase the number of Chinese-speaking MCS officers throughout the administration.[53] In sum, the contraction of formal contact with the Chinese by the Insurrection meant that Government's ability to win and hold the confidence of the rural Chinese was greatly hampered. That developing visible, tangible, personal contact with the rural Chinese was of incalculable propaganda value was underscored by C.C. Too, who declared that 'putting down some sort of effective administration' of the 'masses of people at the grassroots level' was the 'overriding consideration'.[54]

THE PROPAGANDA IMPLICATIONS OF GOVERNMENT AND SECURITY FORCE BEHAVIOUR

Too also observed that traditionally, the ordinary Chinese villager had never had a positive concept of authority, given centuries of gross abuse and neglect by government officials, soldiers and 'persons dressed in uniform'. In fact, in China the soldier and the bandit had been perceived as equally representative of oppressive authority.[55] It was in this context that the loss of the sympathetic officers of the Chinese Protectorate was especially unfortunate: it meant that initially the only real contact the common Chinese had with Government was largely with the Police and Army, and in terms of both initial competence and disposition, they did nothing to secure rural Chinese confidence. On the one hand, the core of the post-war Malayan Police, under the supervision of Lieutenant-Colonel H.B. Langworthy, Officer-in-Charge Police Planning, Civil Affairs Malayan Planning Unit, had been trained on military lines by the North-west Army in India between August 1944 and September 1945; hence by the eve of the Emergency it was observed to possess only a 'rudimentary' knowledge of Police duties, and essentially co-operated with the Army in mounting surprise road blocks and mobile motor patrols. Civil, people-oriented policing was not its strong suit.[56] The Maxwell Police Mission which visited Malaya between November 1949 and February 1950 expressed reservations over this paramilitary bias of the Police, observing that 'training for jungle operations can do little or nothing to develop the habits of thought and action required for ordinary police work'.[57] In addition, the standard of hastily recruited Emergency Police recruits was poor, as evidenced by the standard of musketry: in a recent exercise, 131 out of 230 men had failed their shooting test.[58] In addition, the Special Constables – or 'Specials' – were 'easily intimidated' by the terrorists and in Negri Sembilan actually *supplied* the MCP with grenades and ammunition.[59] Incompetence coupled with the Malay character of the Police failed to impress the rural Chinese. The Chinese squatter thus regarded with disdain a Government that not only 'ran a Malay police force' but had the temerity to order him 'not to help the terrorists, yet failed to protect him'.[60]

On the other hand, initial Army operations were hampered by the lack of training and fitness of the troops, which were largely National Servicemen, and a serious consequence of this was, as in the case with the Police, poor marksmanship.[61] The record of the Army in Malaya was so worrying that the Secretary of State for War was forced to rebut the suggestion in the Commons that National Servicemen in Malaya should be replaced by a 'special volunteer force' of properly trained troops.[62] In addition, each of the six regular Gurkha battalions that made up the core of the British Army in Malaya were under-strength, inexperienced and untrained in jungle warfare.[63] These drawbacks were compounded by the clumsy introduction of the RAF air control doctrine to Malaya. From 10 air strikes a month during the first three months of the Emergency, the RAF was averaging 56 a month by March 1950.[64] Certainly, some terrorists were eliminated: for instance, in early 1949 an air strike in Kuala Langat District in Selangor killed eight terrorists and wounded one.[65] However, there were also instances when RAF bombs hit the wrong target, as on 7 February 1950, when the RAF accidentally bombed a Chinese school in Johore, killing five children.[66] The action was unintended, but it certainly did not help the ordinary Chinese trust Government any further.

However, a more serious problem than technical incompetence was the lack of communication with the rural Chinese, arising out of the acute shortage of Chinese Police. This meant that it was difficult for the rural Chinese to pass information to the Police even if they had been so inclined.[67] The lack of Chinese-speaking European Police was also a pity, as one SEP opined that those few Europeans who actually took the trouble to speak to the rural Chinese in their own dialects were 'liked and respected'.[68] This communication vacuum between the Security Forces and the rural Chinese was exacerbated by the fact that most terrorists were Chinese, and soon stereotyping had taken hold. Not only were MRLA terrorists labelled 'gooks', 'nignogs' and 'jiggerboos' which ought to be hunted like wild game,[69] the prevailing orthodoxy with respect to the wider Chinese community – articulated by no less than Gray and Boucher, Government's top Policeman and top soldier – held that the Chinese collectively possessed a 'streak of hysteria'.[70] They were also said to be subject to the so-called 'secret society complex', which meant that they were traditionally afraid of intimidation organisations – be they secret societies, trade unions and the MCP – and consequently the only way they could be compelled to comply with Government was if they were convinced that the latter represented an 'even stronger force'.[71] Thus it was felt that there was a need for a 'strong line with the Chinese'.[72] Such stereotypes and assumptions certainly made a contribution to the notorious Batang Kali incident of 12 December 1948. On that day, Scots Guardsmen descended upon the village at about four in the afternoon, sent the women and children to town and machine-gunned 24 men who had not even tried to escape. In addition, a soldier placed his rifle on the shoulder of one Chinese man, Chung, and fired two shots past his ears. He was later forced to carry ammunition for the troops and detained for interrogation purposes. Meanwhile the women and children were left in town without food or accommodation and only returned a week later to find the village razed to the ground and dotted with swollen, rotted bodies.[73] That Security Force misbehaviour – both Army and Police – was not at all isolated was hinted at when the Administrative Commandant of Ferret Force[74] and later Chief Instructor of Jungle Warfare at the Far East Land Forces Training Centre, Major A.G. Hayter, complained as late as May 1950 that the 'general attitude of the Government officials, the Army and the police is to regard the squatter as the enemy rather than as a civilian'. This meant that he was beaten and on occasion tortured into providing information, his possessions destroyed and house burnt.[75] Moreover, Hayter alleged that the Army leadership pointedly ignored reports about such methods which were 'turning the squatters against us and doing our cause more harm than any action of the bandits'.[76] In response to Security Force harshness, the rural Chinese engaged in passive resistance – which only engendered more of the same treatment.[77]

Worsening matters was the large number of hastily recruited and untrained Specials. A MCP Masses Executive, adopting the pseudonym

'Tan Chin Siong' wrote scathingly to MCA president Tan Cheng Lock that the Specials 'did all their best to line their own pockets, taking the opportunity of the promulgation of the Emergency Regulations by Government'. 'Tan' also claimed that the Specials also 'accused this person of financing the Malayan Communists, and that person of subscribing to the Malayan Communists'. The only way to avoid arrest was through bribery, and those who defied the 'Specials' risked being shot.[78] In sum, insensitive Security Force behaviour on this scale was incalculably detrimental to Government-Chinese relations. 'Tan' put it succinctly when he addressed the issue of whether the authorities had been informed of these incidents:[79]

> But no one reported to the Government. They considered [sic] to be of no avail in reporting to Government. Government is this sort of people and this sort of people are Government. Thus confidence in Government went on the rocks.

What was worse, such deplorable Security Force behaviour, when exploited by MCP propagandists, even compelled some Chinese to throw in their lot with the scarcely better-liked Communists. 'Tan' therefore observed sarcastically that 'Government helped the Malayan Communists to recruit'.[80] That there was a direct connection between such Security Force behaviour and MCP recruitment was attested to more rigorously in a 1954 study on reasons SEPs gave for joining the MCP. It found that fear of arrest by the Police was in many cases the 'final stimulus' to entry into the jungle to join the Party. Significantly, it was also found that fear of Police was a *greater* motivator of entry behaviour than fear of terrorists in almost every State. Moreover, fear of arrest was prevalent even among those who had done nothing illegal and regardless of whether the MCP had tried to influence them to join.[81] In short, the agents of Government, through the propaganda of ill-conceived acts, were inadvertently projecting the message that Government was not Provider but Tormentor of the rural Chinese.

DETENTION, DEPORTATION AND REHABILITATION

Not only did the rural Chinese experience the heavy hand of the Security Forces, the brunt of tough Government policies to deal with the Insurrection fell on them as well.[82] Stubbs[83] and Hack[84] have characterised Government's overall policy response to the MCP threat in the years June 1948 to June 1950 as the period of coercion or of the law-and-order approach. Certainly, Under-Secretary of State David Rees-Williams, commenting on the Emergency Regulations during a Commons debate on Malaya on 8 July 1948, confirmed that 'all necessary powers' had been given to the Government in Malaya and that there would be 'no sheathing of the sword' until the Communists had been wiped out.[85] However, merely possessing all 'necessary powers' was only part of the solution. There was a greater need to ensure that *discrimination* was applied in the enforcement of tough measures so that innocent Chinese would not suffer along with MCP supporters. This was not the case however. The same assumption of the need for a 'strong line with the Chinese' which contributed to Batang Kali also produced policies which fell most heavily on the rural Chinese.

Such policies included the provisions of the Emergency Regulations for individual and collective detention. Emergency Regulations (ER) 17 (1) provided for the issuance of detention orders for individual persons, though the latter possessed the right of appeal to a Committee of Review.[86] In addition, ER 17C authorised the High Commissioner in Council to deport any person – who was neither a Federal citizen nor a British subject born in Malaya – whose appeal against detention was unsuccessful, or who had not appealed.[87] Moreover, on 22 January 1949, ER 17C was amended to require the deportee's dependants to leave too.[88] The problem was that ER 17 (1) and 17C could be used against both the innocent and the guilty. This arose from the very real difficulty, when dealing with the squatters, for instance, of telling who was silent because he backed the Communists and who was silent until he could be sure of Government protection against reprisals. In this connection Gurney complained to the Colonial Secretary in December 1948:[89]

> Government of the Federation is most anxious to discern the black sheep but cannot in most cases be certain of doing so unless the others render themselves discernible by positive measures of co-operation with the authorities.

By demanding 'positive measures', however, Gurney – again evincing insensitivity to the practical dilemmas of the rural Chinese – was expecting too much courage than was fair in the circumstances of minimal protection against rapid and savage MCP reprisals for siding with Government. In the absence of voluntary indications of Chinese allegiance, therefore, Government had to discover other ways of separating the innocent from the guilty. This was where precise information was needed, but was in short supply, as the Police lacked trained staff and experienced investigators to examine all detention cases in detail.[90] In view of the difficulties of separating the sheep from the goats, then, much improvisation was the order of the day. For instance, in Johore, a 'Callus Index' arose as a rough basis for deciding whom to arrest. Thus squatters whose hands on examination were not found to be as callused as they were expected to be if they really were innocent manual labourers, could be detained for Police interrogation if they could not furnish a satisfactory explanation.[91] The virtual absence of precise information, compelling the resort to unorthodox methods for discerning the culpability of individuals, naturally meant that detentions were not always justified. Thus in September 1948, Frank Brewer and two officers, after reviewing the cases of detainees – mostly squatters on the jungle fringe – concluded that if more time had been spent on intelligence gathering, the number of detention orders could have been 'significantly reduced'.[92] Dubious grounds for detention were not the only problem. The Committees of Review had too few Chinese on them and had to concede the final decision on each case to the Police, who were too often disposed to act as 'Prosecutor, Judge and Jury combined'.[93] In addition, because of bottlenecks in the appeal review machinery, a good number of innocent persons had to languish in detention camps for a long time before finally being released.[94] What was worse, the period under which persons could be detained without trial under ER 17 (1) was increased on 17 May 1950 from two to three years, because it was held that those detained in 1948 could not be released in 1950 'without detriment to the public interest'.[95]

In addition, an Emergency Regulation that constituted far worse propaganda was that which provided for *collective* detention and deportation. As early as the first week of the Emergency, it was realised that the Communists were relying on the squatters for food, intelligence, recruits and other supplies.[96] There was thus an urgent need to separate the Communist 'fishes' from the 'sea' of squatters. Because the Committee to study the resettlement of squatters, appointed in December 1948, needed time to come out with concrete proposals, and there was an urgent need to take 'drastic action' to clear 'black areas' seen to be actively supporting the terrorists, Government decided to detain and deport rather than resettle. Hence the controversial ER 17D was inaugurated on 10 January 1949. This empowered the High Commissioner in Council to order the detention and deportation of all or any of the inhabitants of a particular area, who had been judged to have aided the terrorists or suppressed information to the authorities concerning the terrorists.[97] In addition, there was no right of appeal.[98] A 1953 Government study admitted that underlying ER 17D was the old imperial principle of 'collective responsibility'.[99] Thus ER 17D was imperial collective punishment in a new guise. The first operation under 17D was carried out on 11 January 1949 at Sungei Jeloh, near Kajang, Selangor. 564 persons, 'mainly women and children and some old men' were 'medically examined and detained'.[100] In all, ER 17D was used 16 times between January and October 1949.[101] This sweep resulted in 6,343 detainees.[102] In addition, in February 1949, the first 1,074 persons to be deported set off in two ships bound for China. Of these, 159 were being deported under ER 17C along with 84 dependants while 748 were squatters detained and deported under ER 17D.[103]

The extreme bluntness of ER 17D especially prompted the English and Chinese press to warn that ER 17D would punish the innocent as well as the guilty.[104] Certainly, even in Government, some officials were unhappy with it. Hence Edgeworth David, Deputy Chief Secretary to the Secretary of Defence, minuted after the seventh ER 17D operation:[105]

> Operations have been planned entirely by the Police and Military who are only concerned with the objective of denying the particular area to the bandits and not with the fate of wretched people who are being transplanted from their homes and forcibly removed for ultimate despatch to China where the majority arrive in a state of destitution.

David added that 'however strong the conception of collective guilt put forward in justification there is no question that these operations involve a degree of very severe hardship and inhumanity which is very difficult to defend'.[106] Actually Gullick points out that Government did recognise that poorly executed detention and repatriation constituted 'bad propaganda'. Hence a Chinese-speaking MCS officer was present at the port of disembarkation to ensure that each party of repatriates was despatched to the Chinese interior with some pocket money to help them on their way.[107] Nevertheless, it was an incontestable fact that many innocent rural Chinese had been unfairly targeted. Thus one SEP argued that moving squatters 'en masse' only proved the MCP line that Government was 'heartless',[108] while 'Tan Chin Siong' complained bitterly that some farmers who had been caught in the sweeps were not Communists at all but still lost houses, farm land and agricultural products 'which they [had] built and produced after 7 to 8 years' toil and sweat'.[109]

The situation was exacerbated when bottlenecks developed in the deportation process. With the success of Mao's forces on the mainland in October and November 1949, the receiving ports for Malayan deportees like Swatow and Amoy were closed, and this had the effect of seriously congesting the existing detention camps in Malaya, at Pulau Jerejak in Penang, Tanjong Bruas in Malacca, Majeedi, Muar and Kluang in Johore, Port Swettenham in Selangor, Ipoh in Perak, and Seremban in Negri Sembilan.[110] While Government immediately began studying the feasibility of building a large detention centre on Balambangan Island, off north Borneo, progress was very slow.[111] The congestion of the camps only played into the hands of the MCP which intensified propaganda activity amongst angry, disgruntled detainees.[112] In order not to worsen congestion, Government therefore eased off on further 17D operations.[113] But the damage to rural Chinese confidence had already been done.

The one policy Government implemented which actually constituted good propaganda was the Taiping Rehabilitation Centre, set up in November 1949. The idea for rehabilitation instead of detention and deportation of detainees was first broached by Federal SCA Fleming, who urged that an experiment along the lines of the Greek Mecronissos project be tried in Malaya. Mecronissos was an island off Greece where 21,800 Communists had been sent for rehabilitation.[114] Chinese Affairs staff proceeded to adapt the Mecronissos project to Malaya: David Gray and O.W. Wolters were responsible for initial planning and K.J. Henderson became the first Commandant of the camp. Detainees were selected by boards chaired by local advisers on Chinese Affairs. Members included an MCA representative, superintendents of detention camps, and members of Committees of Review. Generally, Taiping inmates were between 19 and 39 years old, were not MCP members or suspected criminals and terrorists. They were usually food suppliers, subscription collectors, couriers, propagandists and supporters. They could be illiterate tappers to skilled, educated tradesmen. Taiping aimed at inculcating in detainees self respect, discipline and leadership, based on a curriculum written by an MCS officer, J.M. Patrick.[115] Considering that many of the detainees had been innocent and wrongly incarcerated, the Taiping course gave them a sense of freedom and hope though many still felt hatred for Government. The idea was that the course would gradually help detainees to establish good relations with Taiping staff and by implication, Government.[116] Taiping alone, however, could never compensate for the 'strong line with the Chinese' manifested on numerous occasions through Security Force harshness and draconian policies like ER 17D. Overall, then, Government deeds communicated not concern but indifference bordering on malevolence; consequently the chasm between Government and the mass of the Chinese widened.

GOVERNMENT 'DEEDS' AND TERRORIST CONFIDENCE

While Government's lack of visible leadership and contact with the rural Chinese, compounded by Security Force misbehaviour and draconian detention and deportation policies were unwittingly eroding Chinese confidence, there was simultaneously little Government activity that actually exerted pressure on terrorist morale. This was essentially because a faulty concept for dealing with the MRLA was extant. Just as Gurney and MacDonald incorrectly emphasised constitutional methods as a panacea for coping with the Insurrection at a macro level, at the micro level of anti-terrorist operations, large-scale jungle-bashing was seen as the appropriate elixir. There were two reasons as to why this was the case. First, the lack of intelligence on terrorist movements. As intelligence did not 'merely arrive, [but] must be sought, obtained and put to the best use possible,'[117] the onus was on the Police to perform this crucial function. However, as noted the combination of a shortage of Chinese and Chinese-speaking personnel, negative attitudes toward the rural Chinese and lack of training prevented them from developing much useful information.[118] Even MacDonald complained in April 1949 that the Security Forces had little information on the MCP high command, order of battle, organisation and location.[119] Moreover, even if the Police were doing their job, there was as yet no effective co-ordinating mechanism for converting Police intelligence into forms the Army could use. Perry Robinson in this connection noted that many rows broke out between soldiers and Policemen because both had different conceptions of what intelligence was: while the Policeman was satisfied with clues as to where a suspect might be at a certain time, the soldier wanted more precise and detailed information.[120]

Differing conceptions of 'intelligence' aside, Gurney's decision to make the GOC operationally subservient to the Commissioner of Police was also not welcomed by the former.[121] Police-Army tensions, arising from the notion that Policemen should not give orders to soldiers thus developed, and permeated to the State and District levels, at which by July 1949, impromptu 'defence committees' were springing up.[122] These problems meant that the Security Forces simply lacked the information needed to plan more precise surgical operations. Intelligence paucity aside, however, imperial experience also suggested the value of large-scale sweeps. Commanders in Malaya recalled the use on the North West Frontier and Middle East of 'sweeps, drives or large mobile columns', and resorted to these.[123] Hence senior Army commanders emphasised that 'however meagre is the information available, [we need] to adopt an offensive military policy. Never leave the enemy alone, continually harry him and keep him on the move'.[124] The predilection for the big operation was illustrated by Operation Leo. This was mounted in October 1949 and involved 24 platoons setting out to seek and destroy terrorist elements 'thought' to be operating in 74,000,000 square yards of jungle. The troops were instructed to surround all four sides of this area, then 'sweep' inwards in lines of small columns toward the centre, all the time converging on ever-smaller boxes, entry into each box of jungle being preceded by bombing and strafing. It was held that in the last phase, the terrorists would have been hemmed in a very small area, and could be ferreted out by a single company in 24 hours. The outcome of the operation was zero kills – the commander of the operation later thought that the area was too big to sweep effectively, and the terrorists could easily slip out between the thinly spread lines of troops. Besides, the bombing would have given the Security Forces away anyway.[125] Bombing was in fact an integral aspect of the sweep, and in this respect the RAF's Middle Eastern experiences were perceived as instructive. For instance, a May 1949 RAF report suggested that – as in Palestine in 1938/39 – bombing of areas where terrorist activity was reported would not only 'flush' them like 'birds out of cover' into the waiting rifle sights of the Security Forces, it would also exert a 'great effect on enemy morale'.[126] In fact, it was generally accepted that the 'morale effect of air attack' was 'most marked'.[127]

Significantly, the terrorists did not share such sanguine assessments of bombing. For instance, Lam Swee – later C.C. Too's colleague in Emergency Information Services – and who had been Vice-President of the PMFTU and then the Political Commissar of the Headquarters 4th Corps,

MRLA prior to defection, argued that RAF strikes had little effect. He claimed that he himself had experienced seven days of continuous bombing for eight hours a day in the jungle at Mentakab in May 1950. While he conceded that during the bombing the Communists were in a panic, afterwards, 'everything seemed to be quite normal' – people went about cooking their food and so on. Lam added that bombing did not force the terrorists to evacuate, and moreover, most bombs exploded in the tops of trees. As for artillery fire, moreover, Lam pointed out that most shots 'invariably' went over the terrorists or fell short.[128] Lam's remarks were corroborated rigorously by a 1953 study investigating the impact of early Security Force activity on terrorist confidence. After interrogating 14 SEPs who had experienced air strikes, it found that not only were such strikes 'negligible' in terms of inflicting casualties on the terrorists, the 'psychological effect' of such attacks in the absence of casualties was 'very small indeed', and hence the contribution of air attacks in the early years to surrenders 'must be assessed as zero'. Moreover, the study suggested that instead of undermining terrorist confidence, air attacks actually *boosted* it. As evidence mounted that very few comrades were actually hurt by these attacks, terrorists felt that Government 'was wasting money by this kind of blind bombing', which was killing lots of 'leeches' rather than terrorists.[129] The study also found that artillery fire had little effect on the Communists, and if it did cause them to withdraw from an area, it was more a strategic withdrawal to avoid Security Forces rather than a panicked retreat.[130] The study was forced to conclude *inter alia*, that despite the assumptions of the effectiveness of air control as suggested by experiences in Iraq and the North-West Frontier, bombing in Malaya was not eroding terrorist confidence, and in fact was serving as 'battle inoculation' for them. The study also suggested that in order for air strikes to have greater effect, they simply had to be more 'lethal' – suggesting better target intelligence – and closely followed up by ground force attacks. The same year this study was carried out, the Scientific Advisers to the Admiralty, War Office and Air Ministry reported that they remained unconvinced that early air strikes had indeed eroded 'bandit morale'.[131]

As the Army in Malaya mounted successive fruitless sweeps and drives, some officers began to question if the right precedents were being applied. In this connection, Lieutenant-Colonel Walter Walker, a veteran of the war in Burma, was instrumental in calling attention to the experiences of small-unit jungle fighting during that campaign – lessons that had been crystallised in the famous Military Training Pamphlets 51 and 52.[132] Walker was subsequently involved, in July 1948, in retraining former Chinese Protectorate and ex-Force 136 officers who had operated against the Japanese in the war, forming them into the so-called 'Ferret Force'. The idea apparently originated in a June 1948 memorandum by R.N. Broome to GOC Malaya Boucher. The Force, divided into six groups of 80 men, including British troops, Chinese liaison officers and *Dyak* trackers, trained at the Malay Regiment Depot at Port Dickson and then set out for six weeks of jungle bashing and patrolling of Chinese squatter areas.[133] Ferret Force was disbanded by November 1948,[134] but despite its short existence it proved useful. First, by merely patrolling the squatter areas, the Force had encouraged the Chinese by suggesting that 'Government writ' still operated.[135] Second, in contrast to regular Police and Army units that 'did not stay in the jungle for long periods', the Ferrets had probed 'too deep' and stayed 'too long', thereby producing 'a most salutary effect on the terrorists'.[136] The morale effect of Ferret Force-like small-scale operations was further attested to by SEPs who admitted that what they really feared were not large scale Security Force extravaganzas but rather simpler 'ambushes laid in squatter areas'.[137]

Although Ferret Force was disbanded, steps were taken to ensure that the lessons learned were not lost. This was done in two ways: first, ex-Ferret men returned to parent units so as to 'pass on the "gospel" and raise the whole standard of operational efficiency throughout the units in Malaya'.[138] Second, in October 1948 Walker set up a jungle warfare school within the Far East Land Forces (FARELF) Training Centre (FTC) in Johor Bahru to 'train expected reinforcements'. The school henceforth ran courses for both officers and men with a view to 'perfecting methods of jungle fighting'.[139] Nevertheless, conservative military minds in HQ Malaya District were slow in making the transition to small unit patrolling. Thus, new commanders in Malaya ignored the FTC's instructions as well as the extremely useful MTPs 51 and 52 that were being circulated amongst units.[140] Furthermore, Boucher's replacement, Major-General Robert Urquhart[141] was against small-unit operations and criticised the FTC's instruction on it. This meant that in the spring and summer of 1950, the Security Forces continued with large-scale sweeps and drives.[142] Until the Ferret Force ideal of protracted small unit patrolling in the jungle had been more widely ingrained in Security Force culture, therefore, terrorist confidence was not about to be severely impacted.

Curiously enough, rather than Government's vigorous but ineffective military activities, it was in the realm of its less spectacular administrative work that a significant propaganda attack on terrorist confidence was inadvertently mounted: the national registration of the population, following the Palestine precedent. Registration was started in July 1948 and finished in only eight months.[143] Because terrorists and their supporters did not want to have their photographs and fingerprints taken and personal details noted by the authorities, they eluded registration, thereby rendering the exercise effective in 'separating the goats from the sheep'. It also enabled Government to note the physical distribution of the squatters in particular.[144] Without identity cards, moreover, Communist movement in villages and towns was made much more difficult. That registration greatly worried Central was unequivocally evinced by the MCP's vigorous response to the exercise – identity cards were stolen and burned,[145] photographers involved in the exercise were targeted, and considerable anti-registration propaganda was produced. These included the virulent 'Running-dogs who register will be killed' and 'Photographers will be killed. Authenticators will suffer'.[146] Other leaflets declared that 'ICs are really trouble-causing things', and 'should be torn up and treated as joss paper'.[147] That a relatively innocuous administrative exercise could precipitate more anxiety in Communist ranks than the more spectacular sweeps and bombing represented nothing less than a severe indictment of the Security Forces' ability to cope with the MCP revolt. It certainly was not turning out, as Boucher had boasted, to be the 'easiest problem' the Army had ever tackled.

THE DISORGANISATION OF GOVERNMENT WORD-PROPAGANDA

While Government was unwittingly attacking Chinese confidence while boosting that of the terrorists through its clumsy, ill-conceived deeds, it was also facing serious problems with respect to its propaganda of words. On the one hand, the organisation and co-ordination of spoken, printed and broadcast propaganda proved cumbersome; while on the other, the content and timing of propaganda to the rural Chinese public as well as the terrorists were deeply flawed. The relative newness of the Malayan propaganda machinery by the time the Emergency broke out clearly contributed to this initial disarray. The first-ever propaganda organisation in Malaya had been set up only in 1940 when the Far Eastern Bureau (FEB) of the Ministry of Information, under Robert Scott, shifted to Singapore from Hong Kong and assumed control of all white or overt propaganda. The FEB was joined by the Oriental Mission of the Ministry of Economic Warfare, led by George Sansom, in charge of black (non-attributable) propaganda and later sabotage. The Oriental Mission was later to become a part of the Special Operations Executive (SOE).[148] In Singapore Scott appointed Victor Purcell, a Chinese Protectorate officer, Director-General of Information and Publicity for Malaya. Labouring with inadequate facilities, Purcell was made responsible for all vernacular broadcasting in Singapore and Malaya, the installation of loudspeakers with amplifiers in towns and remote villages as well as a Chinese daily newspaper.[149] Following the fall of Singapore in early 1942, Sansom's deputy, John Galvin, assumed control of all white and black propaganda as well as paramilitary operations against Japan and set up operations in New Delhi under the FEB banner, controlled by the Political Warfare Executive in London. Then in November 1943, following a decision at the First Quebec Conference in August, Headquarters Supreme Allied Commander Southeast Asia (HQ SACSEA) was set up in New Delhi under Mountbatten. This body shifted to Kandy in Ceylon in April 1944, and in September the Psychological Warfare Division (PWD/SACSEA) was created by the transfer of Malay and Chinese broadcasting staff and equipment from FEB. Two months later the Malaya Section of PWD/SACSEA was formed under the supervision of J.N. McHugh, who transferred over from the Political Warfare Division of the FEB in New Delhi.[150]

The Malaya Section went on to produce 16,500,000 leaflets and newssheets for Malaya, and co-operated closely with both the Civil Affairs Malaya Section in Kandy and the Malaya Country Section of Force 136 in Colombo. McHugh was eventually ordered to shut down operations in August 1945.[151] The following month, the British Military Administration was set up in Malaya and created a military Department of Publicity and Printing in Singapore. This was disbanded the following April. However the Malayan Union Government recognised that it still needed a department to inform the public of 'the essentials relating to the new administration' in Malaya and so an attempt was made to maintain such a organisation. Moreover, a directive from the British Government required that such a body be created.[152] Accordingly, in April 1946 the BMA Department of Publicity and Printing became the Department of Public Relations (DPR), with its premises now located in Java Street, Kuala Lumpur. The DPR coalesced around a nucleus of 285 trained European and Asian staff that had become available after the Malaya Section of PWD/SACSEA shut down. The first Director of Public Relations was Mervyn Sheppard, an MCS officer who had been interned by the Japanese. McHugh became his deputy.[153]

By February 1947, DPR had more than 300 staff, employed a Public Relations Officer in almost every Malayan State, had set up 28 Information Centres in the urban centres and employed 11 mobile public address cum cinema units for the rural areas.[154] When the Emergency was declared, the DPR went into mass leaflet production. For instance, in 1948 30 million, in 1949 51 million and in 1950 35 million leaflets were produced and distributed to the isolated villages, estates, mines, riverine kampongs and squatter areas by aircraft, Police patrols and mobile units. These leaflets explained the Emergency Regulations to the rural population, and kept them abreast of Emergency news and what action Government was taking to deal with the MCP.[155] To target the rural Chinese in particular, the fortnightly *Farmers' News* was prepared by DPR in consultation with the Federal SCA.[156] Nevertheless, until late 1950, 'in spite of the millions' of leaflets which were printed, 'Communist leaflets and posters were a more common sight in the country-side than Government leaflets and posters'. This situation arose because DPR tended to despatch large numbers of leaflets to a small number of recipients in each State and Settlement, overloading them; the recipients could not cope with the volume of leaflets and 'too often used them as scrap paper'.[157] At any rate, even if the leaflet distribution system had been better, because the level of literacy in the post-war years was low – only 40 percent and as low as 15 percent in some States – leaflets and newspapers had to be supplemented by additional means of reaching the rural Chinese in Hokkien, Hakka, Mandarin and Cantonese.[158] Particularly important in this respect, was word-of-mouth propaganda by Chinese Field Officers manning the mobile units which had first appeared on a small scale in Malaya before the Japanese invasion.[159] There were 12 mobile unit teams at the outbreak of the Insurrection, and they reached 1.25 million people in the first six months of the Emergency alone.[160] However, there were not enough Chinese Field Officers.[161] So important did surrendered Communists regard spoken propaganda to the rural Chinese that as early as October 1949, some were urging Government to make greater use of Chinese SEPs in the role.[162]

Leaflet and spoken propaganda aside, the mobile unit teams also engaged in *visual propaganda* through 16 mm documentary films and newsreels on the Emergency produced by the Malayan Film Unit (MFU).[163] The MFU had been set up some months after the DPR. In April 1946, at the prompting of Director of Public Relations Sheppard, the equipment of the disbanding Crown Film Unit, which had served as part of PWD/SACSEA in Burma, was purchased by the Malayan Union Government, and by late November a small group of Malayan technicians who had served in Burma were producing documentaries and newsreels at Jalan Bangsar in Kuala Lumpur.[164] The output of the MFU following the outbreak of the Insurrection was unremarkable until August 1949, when MacDonald advised Creech Jones that he and Gurney had begun to believe that the Chinese were 'highly susceptible to visual propaganda'.[165] The MFU's output thus increased: between 1947 and 1949, while only 19 films were delivered for distribution, this jumped to 52 in 1950.[166] By early 1950, moreover, mobile unit Field Officers reported that MFU's fortnightly newsreels in Malay, *Berita Melayu*, were 'exceedingly popular with rural audiences',[167] and in March Stanley Hawes of the Australian National Film Board arrived to study how the MFU may be put on a firmer footing. Apart from noting that a locally-produced version of the Tarzan films chronicling the exploits of an anti-terrorist hero might be effective visual propaganda, Hawes recommended in particular that the MFU should be based permanently in Kuala Lumpur and housed in permanent buildings.[168] The sum of $295,350 was subsequently secured from Colonial Development and Welfare (CDW) funds for the necessary buildings.[169] Despite this progress, however, until the latter part of 1950, the value of film as a propaganda weapon to influence the 'largely illiterate rural population' was only very gradually appreciated.[170]

Spoken, printed and visual propaganda aside, the fourth way in which Government could get across to the rural Chinese was by broadcasting. In 1936 the British Malayan Broadcasting Corporation had been set up in

Singapore; four years later the Singapore Government organised the Malaya Broadcasting Corporation and in 1946 both corporations were merged to form the Pan-Malayan Department of Broadcasting, better known as Radio Malaya.[171] The headquarters of Radio Malaya was in Singapore, because the main studios and shortwave transmitters were there; Singapore was also the centre of international communications, cultural and educational life and had easy access to news agencies, while the technical opinion at the time held that the best radio coverage of the Federation could be provided from a point to the south of the territory, from whence shortwave paths could be followed on either side of the central mountain spine of Malaya. Singapore aside, another important station was in Kuala Lumpur, and relay stations were based in Penang, Malacca and Seremban.[172] Radio Malaya, however, had to deal with basic technical problems from the outset. The first was the state of its transmitters. Under long-term plans for the development of broadcasting in Malaya, worked out in the War Office in 1944, the Federation and Singapore were to have received two 10 kilowatt medium-wave transmitters and a single five kilowatt short-wave transmitter. These were actually supplied to Mountbatten's Southeast Asia Command and it was decided in early 1945 that they would be handed over to the civil administration in Malaya after the Japanese had been driven out. In the event, because the Allies did not have to re-invade Malaya, the transmitters were handed instead to the Foreign Office and the BBC. This meant that Radio Malaya had to rely on old transmitters left behind in 1942 and some worn-out Japanese transmitters. To rectify this situation, in March 1946, Colonel J.S. Dumeresque, who was to become the Director of Radio Malaya at the end of the BMA period, flew to London to recover the lost transmitters. He could only secure transmitters similar to those originally ordered – but which had been worn out by salt water and wartime exposure.[173] By December 1948, therefore, Gurney wanted very much to sell the old transmitters to secure hard currency to buy badly-needed new ones. This proved to be difficult.[174] So desperate was the situation that the *Straits Times* emphasised the urgent need for effective medium-wave and short-wave transmitters to carry out the task of 'information and enlightenment of colonial peoples' in Malaya.[175] Fortunately, funds were found to build a new 5 kilowatt short wave transmitter in Kuala Lumpur in January 1950 and plans were made to build further transmitters at Kajang in Selangor and Malacca by 1951.[176]

Transmitters aside, Radio Malaya also faced a potentially worse dilemma: the desperate shortage of receivers. When licensing began in 1947, there were by December only 11,043 licences.[177] Although the number of private radio receivers increased following the recovery of 1947, rising to 46,522 by the end of 1950,[178] there was little increase in the number of *community radio receivers*. While a normal radio receiver could be listened to by about 6 people at a time, with community radio receivers, about 50 could listen at a time.[179] Community radio was thus important for reaching very large numbers of the rural audience. Unfortunately, as late as December 1947, there was no provision for rural Community Listening.[180] Nevertheless, funds for securing such a scheme were soon forthcoming: on 26 May 1948, a paper on broadcasting in the colonies was circulated in the British Cabinet by the parliamentarian Ralph Glyn, who called for a major improvement in colonial broadcasting facilities so as to counter Communist propaganda.[181] Two months later, Cabinet overrode Colonial Office misgivings about the cost of such an endeavour and decided that sufficient funds did exist under the CDW vote to finance such an enterprise.[182] Subsequently, in January 1949, a paper on the experience of the community listening service of All India Radio was circulated by Creech Jones to Gurney and the Governor of Singapore Gimson. The Colonial Secretary also requested Gurney and Gimson to prepare a detailed scheme for the development of broadcasting in the two territories, showing in detail how the money should be spent. The latter issue precipitated disagreement on the relative importance of transmitters and receivers. While the Director of Colonial Information Services, Kenneth Blackburne, and Radio Malaya Director Dumeresque suggested that most of the CDW funds should be spent on receivers, Dumeresque's Deputy Director, W.H. Jackson, insisted that the money should be spent on new transmitters.[183] It was only in October 1949 that the Pan-Malayan Advisory Committee on Broadcasting decided that there was a primary need for community receivers.[184] This enabled the Colonial Secretary to release £41,639 from the CDW vote,[185] which financed the installation of 700 community receivers in 1950.[186] Unfortunately, because the State Governments influenced how these receivers were distributed throughout the Federation,[187] the community sets were installed almost exclusively in Malay kampongs, although the more urgent need for them, in light of the Emergency, was in the emerging Chinese Resettlement Areas.[188] In sum, basic infrastructural problems not only meant that there was virtually no Emergency broadcasting until September 1950,[189] more specifically it also implied that Radio Malaya was technically unable adequately to reach the rural Chinese throughout the first three years.

Not only were there problems afflicting each of the forms of propaganda of words: printed, spoken and broadcast, the task of co-ordinating them so that they projected one message also proved cumbersome. The Emergency Publicity Committee had actually been formed under the chairmanship of the Director of DPR for this purpose, but it soon ran into difficulties.[190] In October 1948 – significantly while Dumeresque was on leave in the United Kingdom – Blackburne wrote G.G. Thomson, Public Relations Secretary Singapore (PRS),[191] observing that 'a proper relationship' ought to be established between Radio Malaya and DPR/PRS. Blackburne averred that while Radio Malaya certainly ought to accept DPR/PRS guidance on topics to be given prominence in line with Government policy, DPR/PRS should defer to the station's views on the best way to 'present these matters to listeners' and the 'amount of entertainment programmes' necessary to attract an audience.[192] Thomson rather testily reiterated that Dumeresque had agreed to accept DPR/PRS advice before going on leave, and hinted that rather than going direct to the Colonial Office with his grievances, Dumeresque should air them at the Saturday morning meetings of the Emergency Publicity Committee.[193] The Committee was thus hamstrung by strained relations between Dumeresque, keen to safeguard Radio Malaya's autonomy, and McHugh and Thomson, eager to ensure that Radio Malaya adhered closely to Government propaganda policy. Moreover, because this was a Committee of more or less equals, Director Public Relations as Chair simply could not order other members to adopt a particular slant and take action on specific matters. Hence, throughout 1948 and 1949, Government propaganda of words was poorly co-ordinated.

In early 1950, however, things changed. The Governors' Conference on 30 January 1950 called for the setting up of a high-powered committee to overhaul spoken, printed and broadcast propaganda, and on 10 February 1950, the inaugural meeting of the Joint Information and Propaganda Committee (JIPC) was held on DPR premises in Kuala Lumpur. The JIPC was chaired by the Secretary of Defence, David Watherston, and provided a forum for the co-ordination of all Government propaganda resources. The dual terms of reference for the JIPC were: first, 'to co-ordinate all the information and propaganda services in Malaya so as to ensure that they speak with one voice; and second, to organise effective counter-propaganda to Communist-inspired propaganda, particularly that from Peking'.[194] JIPC forums were certainly an improvement over the previous arrangement. At the fortnightly meetings, propaganda chiefs were able to ensure that their output was co-ordinated according to a common line, through the issuing of regular 'Publicity and Propaganda Lines'. For instance the 'Publicity and Propaganda Lines' issued on 14 April 1950 stipulated maximum publicity 'through all channels' for Prime Minister Attlee's statement that Britain would remain in Malaya and defeat the Communist threat; that publicity should exert 'fullest pressure' on the population to assist Security Forces; and that a publicity drive should be directed at encouraging more volunteers to sign up as Auxiliary Police.[195] The JIPC mechanism also facilitated closer working relationships among Government bodies. Thus in March 1950 it was agreed that DPR would see all MFU productions, and the Defence Branch all MFU Emergency films, before final production.[196] Moreover, JIPC forums also provided opportunities for thrashing out various ideas: for instance, that Chinese leaflets should take the form of long strips that could be affixed to telegraph poles and trees; and that rewards for information leading to the capture of terrorists were a good idea and might take the form of money, passports or Federal citizenship certificates.[197]

While JIPC meetings did enhance the co-ordination of Government word-propaganda agencies from the beginning of 1950 onwards, better co-ordination however did not always ensure better implementation. While the JIPC had greater influence than the old Emergency Publicity Committee, it remained basically an advisory body,[198] never enjoying executive authority over all propaganda agencies per se. The JIPC thus acted like a clearing-house for propaganda ideas which when agreed upon, were implemented by individual officials in their respective executive capacities. In addition, the Secretary of Defence had too much else on his plate to undertake the task of cajoling the respective agencies to show more urgency in the propaganda effort. In sum, someone else had to be appointed with the sole mandate of marshalling Government's spoken, printed and broadcast propaganda resources in an efficient and rigorous way. Unfortunately, until the second half of 1950, no such person existed.

PROBLEMS WITH GOVERNMENT PROPAGANDA TO THE RURAL CHINESE PUBLIC

Not only was Government propaganda of words afflicted by problems of organisation and co-ordination, the content and timing of spoken, printed and broadcast propaganda to the public and the terrorists was far from ideal. On the issue of content, one issue related to the terminology used in characterising the terrorists. While London wanted to project to world opinion that the war in Malaya represented a battle between the West and Soviet Communism, it did not want to give the same impression to the Malayan public, thereby alarming it by suggesting that the MCP enjoyed external backing. The decision was thus taken in December 1949 to call the terrorists 'bandits' to project the impression that far from being supported by international Communism, the MCP was merely an isolated gang of thugs. Unfortunately, however, because 'bandits' was the precise term used by the Japanese and the KMT to characterise the Communists, it only encouraged the idea amongst the rural Chinese that as both had failed in wiping out Communism, the British would fail as well.[199] Terminology, however, was only one problem. DPR propaganda output intended for public consumption was also characterised by 'too much dwelling on bandit acts of terror (which was only calculated to help the other side)'.[200] The rural Chinese were hence exposed not only to Communist but even DPR leaflets inadvertently exploiting the impact of MCP terror. This unfortunate tendency for Government leaflets to do unsolicited propagandising for the MCP was evinced in a series of Mandarin leaflets called 'What Communism Means in Malaya', produced in May and June 1950. For instance, Leaflet No. 361, produced in May 1950 and entitled 'Destruction of the People's Water Supply', proclaimed:

bandits wantonly damaged the water supply to the town of Kajang (Selangor) thus interfering with the health and livelihood of the people… Communism means wrecking public utilities and causing hardship to the people.

Another example of Government doing the propaganda work on behalf of the terrorists was Leaflet No. 376, called 'No Respect for the Dead or Living':

23 mourners including women and children were wounded and four later died when a grenade was exploded by brutal Communists during a Chinese funeral ceremony in Ipoh. Communism means TERROR and MURDER. The bandits kill indiscriminately.

Other DPR leaflets which unwittingly advertised the deeds of the MCP included 'Killing of Worker's Children' (No. 351); 'Attack on Workers' Homes' (No. 348); 'Extortion from Farmers' (No. 349), and 'Damage to Worker's Transport' (No. 362). The impact of this extensive DPR coverage of the MCP's misdeeds only persuaded the ordinary Chinese that quite obviously Government was unable to contain the MCP rampage. Thus other Government leaflets that promised protection if the rural Chinese sent in 'information about the bandits and their helpers' were greeted with great scepticism.[201] Furthermore, Government pleas for information and co-operation in fighting the MCP – in the eyes of the rural Chinese – suggested, as C.C. Too observed, impotence rather than power. And the ordinary squatter was not impressed by weakness:[202]

For the government to ask defenceless squatters to help [it] fight against the communist terrorists is to tell them: "Look, chaps! The government is going to collapse and the communists are going to win!" The squatters will say: "Fine! Thanks for the information! We will go to the winning side!" It is as simple as that.

The utter bankruptcy of Government expertise in the area of spoken, printed and broadcast propaganda to the public reached its nadir during the pointless endeavour called Anti-Bandit Month, which ran from 26 February to 5 April 1950.[203] The idea for the Month had suggested itself to Gurney when it became apparent that the flow of information to Security Forces on terrorist movements, which had begun after the first steps at resettlement had been taken, all but ceased after the Chinese Communist success on the mainland in late 1949. He thus informed the Legislative Council in December 1949 of Government's intention 'to mobilise on a voluntary basis over a period of about a month all the civilian resources that can be made available to assist the security forces in an intensified combined operation'.[204] The whole idea was to make a massive propaganda statement that while public support for Government was spontaneous, its support for the terrorists was due to intimidation.[205] The three propaganda agencies did their bit for Anti-Bandit Month: DPR publicity material alone amounted to 170,000 posters, 4,100,000 leaflets and 40,000 booklets and other materials.[206] Radio Malaya put out no less than 96 talks, interviews, eye-witness accounts, features and broadcasts by SEPs and leading Asian community leaders.[207] At the same time, the MFU produced 17 trailers of varying length at the rate of one every four days, generally highlighting what the public could do in support of the Month.[208] The *Straits Times* opined that such intensive publicity represented 'an amazing demonstration of the effectiveness of a mass propaganda system never before employed in Malaya'.[209] Enrolment for Anti-Bandit Month commenced on 23 January 1950[210] and by 6 March the number of volunteers had reached 422,000.[211] Anti-Bandit Month activities were varied. Some members of the public volunteered for screenings at road blocks and checks on the movement of food. These were not without effect. For instance, in Bayan Lepas in Penang, volunteer screening produced the capture of a few wanted men, while at Pasir Puteh in Ipoh, the deputy leader of the Kepayang gang was captured and killed. DPR personnel also seized the opportunity at screenings to address the public on points relating to the Emergency. Other volunteers meanwhile helped expedite the process of resettlement, for instance in Pahang. Yet another surprising form of volunteerism was the formation of armed squads which in one case resulted in the capture of a female Communist and some sympathisers at Lahat, near Ipoh.[212]

However, it has to be said that Anti-Bandit Month made no fundamental contribution to the progress of the counterinsurgent campaign. It was conceived as a simplistic test of Chinese loyalty and its many diffuse and uncoordinated activities failed to impress the terrorists.[213] More importantly, the Month 'had little effect in Chinese rural areas surrounded by the jungle in which Communist armed forces lurked'.[214] In particular, like the infamous V Campaign of World War Two, the *timing* of Anti-Bandit Month was utterly inappropriate, as the psychological moment – the widely expected imminent collapse of the MCP – was simply not at hand. Hence there was no incentive for the terrorised rural Chinese in particular to rally behind Government – quite unlike the situation in the future when the Good Citizens' Committees were being formed.[215] The only positive result of the Month was paradoxically a negative one: it proved that Government 'word-of-mouth' or 'face-to-face' propaganda to the rural Chinese was in need of immediate augmentation.[216]

GOVERNMENT PROPAGANDA AND THE TERRORISTS

The difficulties attending propaganda to the population also affected that aimed at the terrorists. In the first place it was a major problem actually reaching them. Apart from the problem of distribution mentioned earlier, air-dropped leaflets frequently got stuck at the tops of trees, and rotted by the time they reached the ground. Hence as late as the summer and autumn of 1950, 'very few' terrorists 'had ever seen any Government propaganda material'.[217] Not that the terrorists would have been attracted by the content of DPR leaflets; the quality of the latter was severely diminished by a propaganda intelligence vacuum attributable to several factors. In the first place, McHugh noted that after the war 'propaganda' was not 'a word of appeal to the expatriate British official',[218] while Greene observed that until the second half of 1950 there was within Government circles 'a certain distrust of propaganda and propagandists'. Thus DPR faced difficulties securing access to Police intelligence.[219] In addition, Too recalled that in the first three years, whenever Security Forces discovered Communist documents in jungle camps the practice was to burn cyclostyled documents and keep only the hand-written ones. This deprived DPR of much vital raw material with which to construct an appreciation of the terrorist state of mind. This is not to say, however, that those MCP documents which did find their way to Kuala Lumpur unmolested were always properly handled. Because 95 percent of Communist documents were written in a quaint type of Chinese with obscure meanings and a peculiar construction which even an educated Chinese would have found difficult to work out, they really needed deciphering by specially trained translators. Unfortunately, Chinese Middle School students were employed to translate documents they did not understand. Consequently British officers reading the translations never discerned the 'real picture'.[220]

While a paucity of solid intelligence robbed DPR leaflets of much authenticity, little attempt was also made to take the line that the terrorists had been 'honourable' soldiers who had done what they did out of conviction and had fought bravely, and if they surrendered there could be no question of losing 'face'. Instead, Government leaflets generally employed a bullying, uncompromising tone. For instance, Leaflet No. 367 issued in Selangor in May 1950 warned ominously:

> If you want to save yourselves, the only thing to do is leave the jungle.
> If you do not do so, Government will use more troops and bombs against you. Your doom will be certain. COME OUT QUICKLY AND SAVE YOUR LIVES.[221]

The threatening approach was also a feature of Leaflet No. 341, produced in March 1950, which showed photographs of two dead terrorists, Chee Kiong and Ah Fong alias Eng Seng. It asked rhetorically: 'Why suffer the horrible fate of these two foolish men? Why not take the opportunity to surrender given to you by Government before it is too late?'[222] While such threats were easily dismissed by the hard core terrorists who were fully aware of how inept the Security Forces were at this stage, Government also frightened those within the terrorist ranks who were thinking of leaving the jungle. As C.C. Too observed, leaflets containing photographs of dead terrorists only convinced waverers that Government utterly hated them. They were thus too terrified to surrender.[223] In fact, the kind of leaflet that did attract potential SEPs was that which provided information on what they could expect after the all-important step of surrender had been taken. Such information was actually found in the second part of Leaflet 341:[224]

> Why endure unnecessary hardships and starvation and face death in the jungle, when food and medical attention await you when you surrender? ... Those who have voluntarily surrendered have all been well-treated. None of them have been sentenced to death for carrying arms.

The approach of actually telling terrorists what to expect after surrender, instead of threatening them with what would happen if they did not do so, represented the germ of a very good idea, but would only be developed into a major line of attack with the arrival of Hugh Greene. While Anti-Bandit Month revealed the weaknesses of Government propaganda to the public, all the shortcomings of Government propaganda to the terrorists were exposed by the Gurney Amnesty, arrangements for which were made in August 1949 and which was formally announced on 6 September 1949. This was intended to attract the 'lukewarm adherents' who had decamped into the jungle, corrode the trust between Central and the rank and file and enable the Security forces to build up an intelligence picture of the Communist organisation. The surrender terms provided that terrorists who gave up voluntarily would not be prosecuted on charges carrying a mandatory death penalty provided that they had 'still managed to avoid becoming assassins or committing the other more dastardly crimes against defenceless persons planned by the Communist leaders'. The rank and file was also exhorted to make up their minds quickly as the offer would 'not be open indefinitely'.[225] Certainly, the MCP did show concern at the Amnesty announcement. In Sungei Patani, terrorists tore down Amnesty posters, while Party propagandists began disseminating the line that Government's action indicated that it was losing the war, that mainland Chinese assistance would be forthcoming after the fall of Canton, and more to the point, traitors who surrendered would be shot once Malaya became a Communist State.[226] In fact, during the last three months of 1949, 155 terrorists surrendered after the Amnesty was announced, bringing the year's total to 251. However in 1950, the number of surrenders declined sharply – there were only 18 in January, 10 in February, and although it rose in March to 28, it dropped again to 17 in May, 14 in June, and then fell below 10 for the last six months of the year.[227]

The poor harvest of the Amnesty was due to a number of factors. In terms of content, the Amnesty was not a full-fledged one – it only promised to let terrorists who had not committed violent crimes off the hook – and in the *15 months* since the start of the Insurrection, many of the terrorist rank and file had had enough time to become guilty of some involvement in capital crimes. By September 1949, therefore, most potential SEPs had sullied hands to some extent, and worried over the 'degree of contribution or participation' in capital crimes 'taken into consideration by Government when reviewing each case'.[228] Little wonder then that 26 terrorists from Pulai who had been involved in an attack on Gua Musang in 1948 did not accept the Amnesty terms because they were 'in doubt as to whether the Government will regard them as "having blood on their hands"'.[229] Such uncertainty was precisely why Greene argued that 'surrender terms hedged in by reservations' would 'repel rather than attract'.[230] In addition, the actual Amnesty leaflet did not spell out precisely what would happen to SEPs after they gave up. The leaflet merely stated: 'Do not be afraid of harsh treatment when you come in. Your circumstances will be fully understood by the Government'. However, given the innate distrust of Government by the terrorists – many of whom had after all escaped into the jungle to get away from the Police – there was precious little confidence that Government would genuinely understand the circumstances of the terrorists. Hence, even in the unlikely situation that some terrorists actually qualified for clemency under the restrictive 1949 terms, they were still worried about their fate on surrender. They needed explicit information on what to expect at the hands of Government before they would even consider leaving the jungle. This became more critical once news of the 'gross ill-treatment' of captured terrorists by the Police filtered out, further nullifying the appeal of the Amnesty.[231] Clearly Government had to *win the confidence of the terrorists* by being more explicit in assuring them of fair treatment if they came over. Gurney himself fully recognised that the prosecution of SEPs might 'dry up the flow of surrenders', but felt that in view of the crimes they had committed – and general public opinion – it was quite impossible simply to 'let these people off without punishment'. Hence he felt unable to publicise widely that SEPs would be well treated. He complained to the Colonial Office that the problem was a 'difficult' one.[232] In sum, two reasons why the 1949 Amnesty failed were the fact that it was shot through with qualifications that created much uncertainty in the minds of wavering terrorists, and this unease was not helped by the dearth of much-needed information on what would happen to SEPs after surrender. This information lacuna only encouraged many wavering terrorists to conclude that 'death' was indeed 'everywhere': if the MCP caught them trying to defect to Government, they would be exterminated; if they did escape, Government would either force them to work against their old comrades, thereby exposing them to MCP retribution, or deport them to China, where they would fall into the hands of the Chinese Communists. The best bet, many reckoned therefore, was to remain in the jungle.[233]

In fact, F.H. Lakin, a Government officer closely involved in propaganda during the Insurrection, argued later that if Government as early as June 1948 had declared a full Amnesty proclaiming a clear policy on the legal status of surrendered terrorists, this could have 'led to a big reduction' in terrorist numbers, apart from the hard core.[234] However Lakin ignores the third reason why the Gurney Amnesty failed: the matter of timing. Between 1948 and 1951, Government was demonstrably not winning the war. Thus not only would the hard core terrorists have been unimpressed by a full Amnesty, the bulk of the terrorists who had joined the Party to secure material goals would not have had any incentive whatsoever for leaving the jungle while the MCP was on the ascendant and appeared fully capable of delivering on its promises. Hence even a full Amnesty with a clear policy on the legal status and fate of SEPs would not necessarily have led to the big reductions Lakin claims. In other words, the timing or psychological moment for a full Amnesty was simply not at hand. As Greene was to argue in September 1951, only when Government was clearly 'on top' and could dispense mercy from a position of strength, would a full Amnesty precipitate the mass surrenders of even the hard core. This was to prove very prophetic indeed.[235]

CONCLUSION

As we have seen, Government actions and policies in the first three years of the Emergency constituted propaganda which, rather than improving rural Chinese confidence, undermined it instead. Because of an erroneous preoccupation with seeking political advance for the Malayan Chinese as a panacea for the operational problem of the Insurrection, Gurney's administration paid less attention to how other features of Government would affect the rural Chinese. Hence, Government under Gurney, through the lack of visible, forceful leadership; the deplorable behaviour of some Army and Police units; as well as the indiscriminate application of very tough Emergency Regulations, utterly failed to project to the rural Chinese the idea that it was their Provider. At the same time, Security Force incompetence gave the bulk of the terrorists little reason to doubt that they were backing the right horse. Moreover, Government's propaganda agencies – DPR, MFU and Radio Malaya – were simultaneously racked with problems of organisation and co-ordination, while in terms of content and in particular timing, spoken, printed and broadcast propaganda were all found wanting – as the respective fiascos of Anti-Bandit Month and the 1949 Amnesty illustrated. At any rate, even if the machinery had been in order, propaganda of words aimed at raising Chinese while undermining terrorist confidence would not have been credible at this stage. It would only have been if the message of Government power, competence and concern projected in leaflets were congruent with the message being suggested by actual Government policy, Security Force behaviour and performance. Because this was not the case, Government failed to influence rural Chinese and terrorist confidence.

In addition, international developments complicated matters. On 6 January 1950, the British Government officially recognised the Communist Government of the People's Republic of China, which had had effective control since 1 October 1949.[236] In fact, since late 1949, fears had been expressed in both Kuala Lumpur and London that the act would lead Malayan Chinese to think that Britain approved of Communism in China and by implication in Malaya, and would thus adopt a more lenient attitude toward the MCP, even accepting Communist Chinese Consuls in Malaya despite the threat of subversion they posed.[237] MacDonald thus broadcast on 6 January that recognition of China only meant that Britain recognised the Communist Government's effective control over that territory – there was to be no change in Government's commitment to stamp out the MCP.[238] Prime Minister Attlee's Commons statement reaffirming Britain's commitment to Malaya was also publicised by the DPR.[239] These steps, however, did not seem to have much impact on the confidence of the Malayan Chinese. The educated, wealthy urban Chinese classes worried about Britain's political will to stay in Malaya, see the Emergency through, and set up a political framework that would accommodate their interests.[240] But for the mass of the rural Chinese, the fear had already endured for one and a half years and was largely visceral: that the once-invincible 'white man' who 'had been sent to rule over' them might at any moment fail again – as they had done so almost a decade earlier when the Japanese had come south.[241]

As for the terrorists, international Communist successes were of the utmost interest. Pye observes that the rank and file were encouraged by Central to see the MCP as 'the channel to the wisdom, the power, and the sheer successfulness of their Russian comrades'.[242] Thus, Mao's victory in October 1949 confirmed that the Party were surely riding the crest of a great Communist wave about to sweep across Asia. A Perak terrorist for instance, wrote excitedly:[243]

> If the reactionary KMT in China have failed although they enjoy the aid of the American Imperialists who supplied them with a great amount of material and ammunition, how then can the British Imperialists be victorious?

If cadres expected practical help from Communist Chinese troops soon, however, Central was more cautious. It published a paper called 'The Relation between Complete Victory of the Chinese Revolutionary War and the Overseas Chinese in Malaya', in order to discourage comrades from expecting practical aid from China.[244] Nevertheless, Central still felt it necessary to wave the China card in the faces of the comrades to bolster internal morale, especially after the September 1949 Amnesty.[245] In fact, Central was increasingly aware of the frailty of the morale of the bulk of its rank and file, which, as we noted in the previous chapter, was increasingly alarmed at the Party's failure to back its rhetoric with concrete deeds. Thus in January 1949, a mere seven months since the start of the Insurrection, rumblings were *already* being heard within the Party about the 'difficulties' associated with the Revolution. Some were saying that the time had not been 'opportune' for an armed revolt, and the understanding of the people had not been reached the 'required standard'.[246] Throughout 1949 and 1950, therefore, Central had to shore up terrorist confidence through circulating internal pamphlets with titles like 'Clarification of Doubts Arising out of Shaken Confidence' and 'Strengthening Confidence in the Communist Undertaking'.[247] Central had every cause to worry about the commitment of the rank and file, for once Government managed to improve, augment and synchronise its propaganda of word and deed, the impact on terrorist confidence would be catastrophic.

CHAPTER FOUR

Propaganda on the Mend

The Impact of Briggs and Greene, May 1950–February 1952

INTRODUCTION

The one and a half years between the inauguration of the Briggs Plan[1] and the arrival of Templer was a crucial, transitional period. On the one hand, the intensification of resettlement coupled with the appointment of more Chinese Affairs Officers at State and District levels, began to suggest to the Chinese that Government was perhaps beginning to show some interest in their plight. These developments arose because Lieutenant-General Briggs, the newly-appointed Director of Emergency Operations, correctly appreciated that if Government was to defeat the Communists, much more energy should be put into bringing the rural Chinese under Government's administrative fiat. Unfortunately, the impact on rural Chinese confidence of these positive measures was somewhat overshadowed by the persistence and even accretion of harsh Emergency Regulations, as well as the continuing hostile attitude and behaviour of the Security Forces toward the common Chinese. More positively, however, Briggs' insistence on protracted small-unit operations coupled with resettlement and the formal introduction of food control represented the right concept for undermining terrorist morale to the point of surrenders. In addition, very concrete progress was made in the area of Government spoken, printed and broadcast propaganda. Hugh Carleton Greene, appointed Head Emergency Information Services in September 1950, like Briggs appreciated that Government had to secure the confidence of the rural Chinese as a prelude to undermining terrorist morale. He thus sought to increase the capacity of Government propaganda of words to penetrate the rural Chinese community. As we shall see, however, the Briggs and Greene reforms, while steps in the right direction, were thwarted by administrative confusion, bureaucratic sloth and politicking. Thus, while Briggs and Greene laid the groundwork for eventual Government effectiveness in the propaganda of deeds and words, it would be left to others to build upon these foundations and reap the rewards.

BRIGGS, HIS PLAN AND THE RURAL CHINESE

In March 1950, the Labour Government in London, concerned about the progress of the counterinsurgency campaign in Malaya, appointed a high-powered Cabinet Malaya Committee to monitor the situation more closely. Chaired by the Minister of Defence, Shinwell, the Committee was charged with the task of studying the situation and recommending the measures necessary to 'preserve law and order in the Colony'.[2] In Kuala Lumpur, meanwhile, Gurney was pondering the possibility of 'appointing one officer to plan, co-ordinate and generally direct the anti-bandit operations of the police and the fighting services'.[3] He believed that Commissioner of Police Gray could not undertake the task of co-ordinating the overall campaign without jeopardising his main role of bringing the Police up to scratch.[4] Gurney therefore advised the Colonial Office that 'immediate steps' be taken to second to the Federation Government an 'experienced officer' who would be responsible for the 'preparation of the general plan for offensive action and the allocation of tasks to the various components of the security forces'. The High Commissioner added that the new man would 'exercise control through the heads of police and fighting services and aim at achieving co-ordination and decentralisation through this means'.[5] London was very sympathetic, and by the time two Cabinet Malaya Committee members, the Secretaries of State for the Colonies and for War[6] went out to Malaya in late May 1950 to get a better grasp of the situation, they were briefed on the Emergency situation not by the Police Commissioner but by Lieutenant-General Harold Rawdon Briggs, the newly-appointed Director of Operations, who had arrived on 6 April.[7] Briggs had commanded the 7th Indian Infantry Brigade in Eritrea and the Western Desert between 1941 and 1942, then the 5th Indian Division in the Western Desert, Iraq and Burma between 1942 and 1944, and was GOC Burma after the Japanese surrender. He had retired in 1948, but given his experience in directing anti-terrorist operations in Burma between 1946 and 1948, was persuaded by his old 14th Army commander General Bill Slim, now Chief of the Imperial General Staff, to accept the call to return to active duty.[8]

On arriving Briggs immediately engaged in a thorough appreciation of the situation in Malaya, talking to members of the various communities and businessmen, as well as senior Government and Security Force officers. He then prepared a note for Gurney on 10 April 1950, which he subsequently expanded into a formal document which was presented to the British Defence Co-ordination Committee Far East on 24 May 1950, and the Cabinet Malaya Committee two months later. This document has now become known as the 'Briggs Plan'.[9] It was, as Short notes, a 'counter-guerrilla classic'.[10] As we saw, while Gurney was conscious of the squatter problem, his political focus prevented him from fully grasping the urgency of dealing with it. Briggs, on the other hand, immediately understood that the 'uncontrolled squatter areas, unsupervised Chinese estates and small holdings, estate labour lines and timber kongsis' were the key source of sustenance for the Communists. To defeat the MCP in the jungles meant neutralising these areas and this in turn meant resettlement of their inhabitants away from the jungle fringe.[11] However, while previous analysts argue that the thrust of the Briggs Plan was squatter resettlement,[12] it was actually about something more fundamental: Briggs' more basic insight that above all else it was the 'confidence' of the rural Chinese which was the real key. Thus the whole point of resettlement was not so much to separate the terrorists from their supporters as to create 'a feeling of complete security' amongst the exposed Chinese. That is why Briggs underscored that the physical act of resettlement was not enough to win over the rural Chinese. In addition, the 'normal social services that go with effective administration', such as 'schools, medical and other services', must be provided to the resettled population.[13] In other words, Briggs was arguing that in order for the rural Chinese to repose their trust in Government, the latter had to first meet their needs for physical and socio-economic security. Only then would rural Chinese 'confidence' be secured and 'information' on terrorist movements flow toward Government.[14] Briggs thus synthesised, from pre-existing unstructured ideas and impressions extant in Malaya, the conceptual framework for thinking about rural counterinsurgency in Malaya:[15] to win Government had to secure rural Chinese confidence, and the key indicator of progress in winning over the Chinese was the volume of information flow to the Security Forces.

THE LIMITATIONS OF BRIGGS AS LEADER-PROPAGANDIST AND THE CONSEQUENCES

While Briggs had developed the concept for eventual victory, he also had to actualise it. Nicknamed the 'Ike' of Malaya by the *Evening News*,[16] he was on *prima facie* evidence capable of dominating Government and generating the image of visible, forceful and reassuring leadership amongst the rural Chinese. He was considered 'a man of immense charm, the best kind of soldier and gentleman', who projected an aura reminiscent 'in some way of Stilwell or Lawrence of Arabia'.[17] Briggs certainly won the confidence of Government officials, who appreciated his willingness to listen and give them plenty of leeway in doing their jobs. However – and this was to prove fatal – Briggs was so much a gentleman that he came across as 'quiet' and 'too kind' to his subordinates.[18] Hence he found great difficulty in imposing his will on the intractable Commissioner of Police Gray. The roots of Briggs' problems with Gray actually lay in the limitations placed on his authority from the outset. The Director of Operations portfolio was a civil post, and was ranked below the Chief Secretary.[19] He was moreover *not* in direct command of troops or Police.[20] Briggs could hence give instructions to the Commissioner of Police and the GOC Malaya, but they could bypass him and appeal directly to the High Commissioner.[21] In other words, Briggs' effectiveness depended on the goodwill of the senior soldier and Policeman. While Urquhart, the GOC was generally sympathetic,[22] Briggs failed to hit it off with Gray. Although Briggs himself noted initially that the Police Commissioner's 'drive' was needed to keep the problem-racked Malayan Police functioning,[23] Gray, a 'cold, reserved man', did little to heal the rift between the ex-Palestinian and Malayan Police officers over the criteria for determining seniority for promotions. As a result, Police morale was low and Gray's orders were increasingly ignored.[24] In addition, Gray's insistence that armouring Police vehicles as protection against ambush would dilute their offensive spirit was greeted with abject dismay by many officers.[25] Moreover, Gray's feud with Director of Intelligence William Jenkin led the latter to quit in October 1951.[26] It was only the month Jenkin resigned – October – that Briggs finally secured full executive authority in all Emergency matters – for the first time superseding the Chief Secretary in the chain of command[27] – which meant he had direct control of the Police. Gray at first wanted to resign, but relented,[28] only to be sacked by Conservative Colonial Secretary Lyttelton in December.[29] Thus Briggs belatedly succeeded in extricating the thorn from his flesh that was Gray, but this was a Pyrrhic victory.

While Briggs had his hands full coping with Gray, he was simultaneously being frustrated by the numerous bureaucratic obstacles strangling his Plan. A key plank of the Plan had been the creation of joint Civil-Army-Police headquarters at Federal, State and District levels to facilitate closer integration of administrative measures and military operations. Briggs himself chaired a new Federal War Council (FWC), which met for the first time on 14 April 1950 and included the Secretary of Defence, the Commissioner of Police and the service chiefs. The FWC, supported by a small Director of Operations combined staff, was responsible to the High Commissioner for 'policy concerning the Emergency and the allotment of resources thereto'.[30] In addition, to implement Federal plans at all levels, the existing unofficial local defence committees were formalised into State War Executive Committees (SWECs) and District War Executive Committees (DWECs). The basic SWEC structure consisted of the *Mentri Besar*, the British Adviser, the Chief Police Officer and the senior Army commander in the area; while the DWEC comprised the District Officer (DO), the Officer Commanding Police District (or Officer Superintending Police Circle) and the local Army commander.[31]

Briggs certainly clarified the DO's 'Emergency responsibilities', and this helped improve co-ordination between civil, Army and Police officials at the

District level.[32] However, the administrative efficiency of Briggs' 'war committee' system was generally hampered by the Federal political structure, which some observers as late as January 1952 still considered a 'political compromise' rather than an efficient instrument of administration.[33] The sacrosanct principle of State autonomy created a buffer between Kuala Lumpur and the Districts which meant that while 'KL, lacking the constant advice or experience of people in the field', tended 'to become academic, perfectionist and impractical', State Governments, 'by complaint, obstruction and jealousy of local privilege', tended to 'distort and delay the execution of Federal policy'.[34] Consequently, the Federal Government was not 'sufficiently in touch with conditions in the Districts' and found it difficult to push the States in increasing the tempo of Emergency work. While some officials argued that *Mentri Besars* and British Advisers simply needed time to adapt to their new roles in the State administrations following the constitutional re-organisation accompanying the inauguration of the Federation,[35] some responsible officials certainly took their time adapting. Thus, by November 1950, more than two years after the inauguration of the Federation, and five months after the adoption of the Briggs Plan, Gurney and Briggs were forced to admit to Prime Minister Attlee that the Plan was proceeding 'far too slowly', and that there was still 'a lack of urgency and the will to seek and solve difficult problems'.[36] Before the Attlee meeting therefore Briggs had asked Gurney himself to chair the FWC and foster a 'sense of urgency' throughout the machine. At the same time, at State/Settlement level, responsibility for Emergency matters was placed entirely into the hands of the SWECs, and State Legislative Councils were discouraged from meeting more often than was necessary. Provision was also made for a block financial vote to the FWC and SWECs to expedite speedy disbursement of funds for Emergency purposes.[37]

Nevertheless, by March 1951, Attlee summoned MacDonald and Commander-in-Chief FARELF Harding to complain once more that progress in clearing Malaya of the terrorists was still too slow. Consequently Gurney offered to resign but was dissuaded from doing so in April.[38] Significantly, Briggs had for some time been unhappy that Gurney was 'somewhat divorced from the operational side of the emergency', focusing instead on 'economic and social questions and on political reform'. Briggs even considered resignation himself at one point.[39] At any rate, in November, a month after Gurney's assassination, in yet another attempt to improve Government efficiency, the FWC was further expanded to include members of the Federal Executive Council, as well as the leaders of the communities and the larger Associations. At this point, Briggs, together with the original armed services and Government members of the FWC, formed a Director of Operation's Committee to handle the 'more detailed planning', supported by a substantial combined planning staff. This was the organisational set-up when Briggs left Malaya at the end of November 1951.[40] Unfortunately, even after Briggs' departure the political system in Malaya remained stubbornly 'ill-adapted to the needs of a small country at any time, least of all at a time of political convulsion and emergency'.[41] Thus the war committee system persisted in being cumbersome: one observer complained the month Briggs left that SWECs tended to issue 'long-winded explanations' to DWECs and in one case, a directive from the SWEC took *five months* to reach the DWEC.[42] He also observed that District officials on the ground were of 'pre-war vintage' when Malaya was a 'different country', and were either too busy or too frightened to visit Districts to see the situation on the ground. He lamented that 'the whole thing is being run as though it were a discussion group' instead of a 'WAR with innumerable people being killed'. Hence, he felt that people could not 'have confidence in Government.'[43] So bad was the situation that J.G.H. Brett, Chief Police Officer Pahang, told T.C. Jerrom of the Colonial Office that an 'Inspector of Emergency Measures' must be appointed to ensure on behalf of the Director of Operations that his directives were implemented at State and District levels.[44]

In sum, Briggs' war committee system, and by implication his Plan, was never efficiently implemented because of internal bickering, political complexity and administrative laxness. Consequently, Government's performance suffered and its capacity to win and hold the confidence of the rural Chinese was seriously hampered. Moreover, for all his unquestioned ability and achievements, Briggs utterly failed in exercising the propaganda function of leadership. Despite travelling extensively throughout his 20 months in Malaya, he was utterly unable to purge the dross of bureaucratic obstructionism and inertia and in Clausewitz's phrase, 'rekindle the flame of purpose' amongst officials at all levels.[45] While he was never 'completely satisfied with his powers', the real problem was that he remained the quintessential gentleman: he was 'patient, courteous and understanding' and was 'quiet of speech and of manner'. He was in short the avuncular 'General in the trilby' – when what he desperately needed to be was a ruthless, feared taskmaster.[46] Consequently, instead of dominating the war committee system, the war committee system dominated him. Briggs' exhausting administrative travails thus prevented him from infusing his 'Ike of Malaya' image with greater substance, thereby projecting to the rural Chinese the idea that Government was their Provider. He was a frustrated and sick man when he left Malaya, and died 11 months later.[47]

THE PROPAGANDA IMPACT OF FLAWED RESETTLEMENT

While the Briggs Plan underscored the importance of resettlement, Government had been grappling with it as early as August 1948 and by January 1950, resettlement schemes were in place 'all over the western

States'.[48] Moreover, the Federal Committee to study the squatter problem had reported at the end of January 1949.[49] Its chief recommendations were: first, wherever possible, squatters ought to be settled in areas already occupied by them and second, if this was not possible, then they should be resettled in suitable alternative areas. Third, Emergency measures to deal with the security problem of certain areas should be supported by administrative measures to re-establish the permanent authority of Government. It was only in the event of the Chinese refusing settlement or resettlement, that they should be liable for compulsory detention and repatriation.[50] Gurney ensured that the Committee's report was forwarded to the States and he urged them to take action without delay. Moreover, the Federal Legislative Council endorsed the report on 17 February 1949, and a new Emergency Regulation was passed in May: ER 17E. This empowered Rulers in Council in the Malay States to issue eviction orders to all illegal squatters in specified areas, and to give them one month's notice to leave those areas and proceed to certain prepared areas. In addition, a corollary amendment, ER 17F, was passed in August to empower *Mentri Besars* of States and Resident Commissioners of Settlements to order individual squatter families to be moved into an established area or to be regrouped into a 'compact community under effective administration'.[51] Colonial Office officials were certainly aware that resettlement constituted superior propaganda to mass detention. As one official put it:[52]

> It is one thing to keep persons in a resettlement area where they have the means of livelihood and reasonable conditions of existence. It is quite another to keep them in enforced idleness in detention camps.

Increased sensitivity to the propaganda benefits of resettlement was however less important than the ability to carry out such good intentions. In this respect, Gurney's basic neglect of operational Emergency matters such as resettlement was compounded by the States' disinclination to resettle on Malay land what were perceived as disloyal aliens. For instance, at a Rulers' Conference held on 24 May 1950, the Sultan of Kedah, unhappy that 'privileges' should be given to squatters who 'stole' Malay land, argued that they should all be 'sent away'.[53] Moreover Malay State officials did not like going out to the unpleasant squatter areas, while the Malay perception that resettlement provided Chinese squatters with amenities which were not even enjoyed in Malay kampongs proved so controversial that Government decided to downplay publicity on what the Resettlement Areas were like.[54] The net result was that very little resettlement was actually carried out until June 1950. In fact, Short suggests that more squatters were deported under ER 17D than were resettled by the end of 1949: about 6,000 to 5,000.[55] The momentum of resettlement did pick up in the new year, though. By 10 March 1950, 4,600 families of 18,500 people had been resettled in the Federation.[56] But it was still too little and too slow given the critical importance of the task to split the MCP from the mass of the squatters. As Gurney lamented in February 1950, 'speed of action had not been commensurate with the urgency of the case'.[57]

Because Briggs quickly recognised the importance of resettlement in securing Chinese confidence, he moved to speed it up from June onwards. In the four months following the implementation of the Briggs Plan on 1 June, about 26,000 people were resettled,[58] and by October, the figure had reached 69,872 persons, settled, resettled or regrouped.[59] By January 1951, there were 117,000 people in 82 Resettlement Areas and by the time Briggs left, there were 429 Areas with 385,000 people.[60] The rural Chinese were resettled into three types of Resettlement Areas: entirely new ones; those established as appendages to existing villages and towns but retaining a distinct identity; and those built next to and absorbed by existing towns and villages. The actual process of relocation differed from place to place. Sometimes a dawn raid was mounted to prevent squatters from slipping away. Usually, however, there was advance notice of perhaps 10 days, and each family given was an upheaval allowance ($70) and sold building materials well below cost price to help set up their new home. The early Resettlement Areas were all fenced in and were made up of small houses cramped together or large communal dwellings made of wood. These were sheltered by atap thatch, lalang or zinc roofs and served by bare laterite roads and unfinished drains. Gradually, space was created for the addition of a dispensary, Police station, well, school, and pig-sty.[61] In addition, to allay Chinese fears that they were in concentration camps guarded by Malay Police, an unpaid volunteer Chinese Home Guard was set up to assist in local security.[62]

The increased tempo of resettlement after June 1950 compelled the terrorists to seek new sources of supplies and cash, and they turned to the scattered workers on estates and mines. The smaller Chinese-owned estates and mines drew their labour force from the surrounding squatter areas, and these were resettled into Resettlement Areas as described above. However, larger estates with their own organic labour forces had to be dealt with differently.[63] Hence, a new regulation, ER 17 FA, was passed in August 1950 which empowered Government to declare any estate a 'controlled area'. That is, the inhabitants were required to reside within a specified residential part of the estate at all times, except at certain specified hours when they were allowed to proceed to work.[64] This process was called regrouping, which was intended to be completed in three months.[65] It was estimated that ultimately about 510,000 workers were regrouped on estates and another 80,000 on mines.[66] Regrouping posed some problems: sometimes regrouped areas were poorly selected and indefensible, and workers had to be moved a few times. Furthermore, although some estate accommodation included small semi-detached houses, rather 'uninspired labour lines' were the rule generally.[67] Still, while resettlement frequently relocated workers further away from the estates, regrouping merely meant closer settlement within the estates, and was thus less of an inconvenience. Moreover, in order to attract labour, some estates spared no expense in enhancing the quality of life in the controlled areas. Thus in addition to good accommodation, proper fencing and better-trained Special Constables, estates installed community radios, and organised basic medical and educational facilities.[68]

Resettlement of the half a million squatters scattered around Malaya, on the other hand, posed far greater potential for generating resentment at Government. In order for the scheme to succeed, there had to be careful co-ordination by all involved, so that eviction orders could be coupled with simultaneous arrangements for immediate resettlement in areas under effective administration.[69] A smooth transition from squatter to Resettlement Area was however, not easy to achieve. It was not feasible to build 'standard camps' for all squatters, because they were involved in different occupations. For instance, squatters engaged in market gardening needed land near markets where they could sell their produce, while others employed in rubber, tin or timber-cutting industries needed to be near their places of work. In addition, State planners had to organise and provide for, *inter alia*, social surveys, assessments of land availability, security arrangements, anti-malarial drainage as well as water supplies. Gurney thus conceded that while it was important to proceed with resettlement at some speed to snap the link between the squatters and the Communists, at the same time it was necessary to avoid *too fast* a pace as to compel harassed State authorities to select unsuitable resettlement areas and 'window-dress' them to meet resettlement 'quotas'. The rural Chinese would not be impressed.[70]

However, because the 'primary goal' of resettlement in this early period was 'quite simply, the rapid separation of the guerrillas from their principal source of supply, the squatter',[71] speed emerged by default as the overriding consideration, and this situation 'produced adverse effects on the morale of the people moved'.[72] This meant that the security and the suitability of the Resettlement Area were often neglected – with disastrous consequences, as in the highly publicised case of Mawai. Mawai, in Johore, was the site of a Resettlement Area into which 1,200 squatters had been moved in 1948. It was clear from the outset that Mawai was a bad choice: it was unsuitable for growing crops and too close to the jungle fringe – and by implication the terrorists. Moreover, Mawai was not wired in,[73] and only 12 Specials were detailed to guard 1,200 people in houses strung out for 2½ miles along a road next to the jungle fringe. It was 'abundantly apparent' that 'at no time' could the Mawai residents 'have felt any sense of protection by Government or security from the bandits'.[74] Since May 1951, moreover, the Police had known that Min Yuen Cells had been active in the Resettlement Area, and on 16 October 1951, information was received that the terrorists were going to attack Mawai the next day. The only official response, however, was to increase the number of Specials to 16 – hardly a decisive countermeasure. Sure enough, the very next day, terrorists attacked Mawai, killed four informers and abducted 36 young men. As the *Daily Telegraph* observed, Government's failure to provide protection was 'disheartening' because protection was 'the underlying reason in the concept of resettlement'.[75] But worse was to come: on 19 October, Government suddenly decided to close Mawai. This prompted an angry letter from Tan Cheng Lock to the Johore *Mentri Besar*. Tan pointed out that the Chinese had been brought to Mawai by Government in the first place and had been cultivating crops there for three years. Suddenly, without any assistance or compensation, they had been told to move elsewhere to restart their lives. While Tan admitted that Government probably wanted to close Mawai because it was unsafe for its inhabitants, he emphasised that the *way it was doing it was all wrong*:[76]

> It can never be a matter of pleasure for anyone to be told initially that they must leave what they have regarded as their homes and move into a Resettlement Area started by the Government; but once they have settled down in their new abode and have grown their crops, nothing but enmity can be expected when they are again told to move and in a manner which would appear to be without any consideration for their future livelihood or their recent losses.

Tan described succinctly the 'disastrous' propaganda implications of the Mawai closure:[77]

> These persons would ... have left the Resettlement Area with ... the feeling ... that they are being treated like cattle and ordered to move their homes and their crops upon a whim of Government which they must think results from Government's decision to harry them as much as possible because of Government's ill-will towards them.

Mawai crystallised a few hard facts: the rural Chinese were always going to be uncomfortable with resettlement because it meant having to leave behind their 'animals, fish ponds and their homes'.[78] Hence it was the height of folly to assume that 'the mere fact of herding squatters behind barbed wire' was enough.[79] Much more care had to go into 'the way the people are handled afterwards'.[80] Unfortunately, throughout 1951, Government was accused of 'gross negligence' in its 'administration of the resettlement areas' like Mawai, Changang, Jenderam and Tras.[81] Badly conceived and executed resettlement only constituted highly destructive propaganda which Government could ill afford.[82]

Nevertheless, the resettlement exercise resulted in a very significant by-product: the increase in the number of Chinese and Chinese-speaking officers roped in to help Government build contacts with the rural Chinese.

The Briggs Plan itself had identified the need for increasing the number of executive officers 'in the field' to 'maintain personal contact' with the resettled Chinese.[83] Accordingly, in mid-May 1950, Briggs expanded the Chinese Affairs Service, formally appointing additional Secretaries for Chinese Affairs in States where the size of the Chinese community justified it, local Chinese Affairs Officers (CAOs) to assist the State SCAs, and Chinese Junior CAOs to help District Officers in dealing with the rural Chinese. Furthermore, Chinese-speaking Europeans were recruited to serve as Resettlement Officers (ROs) while local Chinese came in as Assistant Resettlement Officers (AROs). By the end of 1951, therefore, there were 53 full-time ROs, 302 AROs and 51 additional officers from other Departments helping the rural Chinese settle into the Resettlement Areas.[84] Supervising the Chinese Affairs men was the Federal SCA who was appointed to both the Federal Executive and Legislative Councils in 1950.[85]

State Governments still viewed the 'pro-Chinese' State SCAs as 'interlopers' in the 'new world of the Federal Agreement', though, and disliking their links with that 'odd pre-war and therefore outmoded official', the Federal SCA, subjected them to 'close control', an exercise which was greatly facilitated as the State SCAs were paid from State, not Federal funds.[86] At any rate, R.P. Bingham, the Federal SCA, argued in November 1951 that as aftercare in the new Resettlement Areas was 'primarily a Chinese matter', more CAOs with greater executive powers were needed to attend to this task.[87] This was especially important given the MCA's continuing inability to act as the conduit between the rural Chinese and Government. Hence SCA Kedah Watts observed that rather than the 'ramshackle' and 'ill-disciplined' local MCA, it was the Government 'Taijin' who was regarded as able to 'do battle on behalf of the Chinese'.[88] Furthermore, S.R. Dawson, who spent 16 months in Malaya as an RO in Segamat District in Johore, noted that when ROs, AROs, and Public Relations teams all worked hard to 'sell' the idea of resettlement before the people had actually to move, the people came in willingly and often cheerfully'.[89] Importantly, it was also recognised that as many rural Chinese were illiterate, CAOs could engage them in word-of-mouth propaganda and 'gain the confidence of the people'.[90]

DETENTION, DEPORTATION AND COLLECTIVE PUNISHMENT

In addition to botched resettlement, the persistence of certain other Emergency Regulations also generated the powerful impression that Government was no friend of the Chinese. In June 1950, there were 10,000 detainees in Malaya, and Whitehall, eager to strengthen the Federal Government's detention powers even further, suggested that the suspension of the ER 17 (1) Review Committees might be advisable.[91] Gurney replied that the real problem was actually the serious congestion of detention centres and the resulting possibility of mass escapes. Hence the real need was to deport 'as many detainees as possible'.[92] Deportation to China thus continued throughout the year, stopping momentarily in September but resuming in November, so that 2,800 persons had been deported by February 1951.[93] Mass deportation may have appeared a seductively simple response to the Communist challenge, but its success operationally was premised on the notion that the detainees being deported were indeed Communists or Communist bedfellows. Government could not guarantee this however. As early as June 1950, Gurney himself admitted that many detained Chinese 'might well be innocent'. But he shrugged it off, opining that the 'most' that Government 'should do therefore was to keep them safely out of the way for the duration of the emergency'.[94] Given Gurney's incredibly callous attitude, it was unsurprising that the Chinese continued to bear the brunt of Government's sweeps. Accordingly, at the beginning of 1951, a deputation of leading Malayan interests warned Gurney and Briggs that 'by the detention of the wrong persons the Europeans were building up a heavy load of hatred which one day would react upon them'.[95] By December, however, of the 25,641 held under ER 17 (1) for more than 28 days since the start of the Emergency, a massive 22,667 were Chinese.[96] So strong was the sense of rural Chinese revulsion at Government that the same month Tan Cheng Lock offered the Police MCA assistance in screening detainees at regular intervals, to restore 'public confidence and trust in the Government'.[97] In addition, Chinese Affairs officers like John Litton, on visiting 'sullen' and 'apathetic' detainees at Tanjong Bruas in Malacca in 1951, felt conscious of their 'mute condemnation of our failure as administrators'. He felt that Taiping internees who had undergone rehabilitation had far better attitudes to Government than the detainees.[98] Litton lamented the fact that 'too many officers in the army, police and administration' were of the opinion that if 'the Emergency is to be ended the Secretary of Chinese Affairs' must reject 'the notion that bandits are capable of reformation'.[99]

Such a stern line was reflected in the continued application of the indiscriminate ER 17D at Jenderam in Selangor and Tras in Pahang. The inhabitants of Jenderam, evacuated in February 1951, were assumed to be 'mostly Communists on their own initiative and not through intimidation', but a number were released when screening after evacuation showed that they were not sympathisers at all.[100] Tras was evacuated on 7 November 1951, following Gurney's assassination, for failing to provide information as to the whereabouts of the terrorist ambush party. Again, the 'vast majority' of the inhabitants of Tras were released after initial detention. Although officials later tried to make the point that these operations were not meant to punish innocent people but rather to clear bad areas and separate the 'sheep' from the 'goats',[101] it was undeniable that the very process of evacuation itself had unfairly traumatised the innocent folk. The *Manchester Guardian* was moved to ask: 'Does such indiscriminate action really impress?'[102]

In fact, a further hardening of Government's 'bashing the Chinese' mentality had occurred around December 1950, accompanying official disappointment that intensified resettlement had yet to bear the fruit of increased Chinese co-operation.[103] Government attitudes were further exacerbated by a perceived continuing lack of Chinese civic consciousness: for instance following a terrorist grenade attack in Kuala Pilah, Negri Sembilan in late October 1950 which resulted in the deaths and injuries of several children and a woman, no passer-by either attempted to apprehend the terrorist who rode away on a bicycle, nor assist the injured. When British troops moreover asked a Chinese to drive an injured woman and child to hospital, he refused.[104] The resulting anti-Chinese mindset contributed to the passage of yet another Emergency Regulation: 17 DA, better known as 'collective punishment'. This empowered Government to impose sanctions on 'well-defined and comparatively small areas' where the inhabitants had clearly failed to do their duty in preventing the commission of crimes when they could, or in assisting the Police in discovering the culprits. These sanctions, taking another imperial precedent, took the form of a collective fine of a fixed amount imposed on all the male inhabitants of the area over 18 years old, and the closing of all shops within the area completely or part of the time. The amount of the fine and the length of time shops were to remain closed were decided by the competent authority on the spot, and reported to the *Mentri Besar* or Resident Commissioner. In addition, the inhabitants had to bear the cost of any additional Security Forces sent to reinforce the area.[105] Gurney opined that collective punishment was justifiable as long as it was 'balanced by constructive and progressive measures to assist the people who [showed] any signs of willingness to co-operate' with Government.[106] He identified such 'constructive and progressive measures' as the building of more Resettlement Areas with roads, water supplies, schools, medical services, transport and assistance in housing.[107]

However, the assumption of collective responsibility inherent in the collective punishment concept was simply unfair. In the case of the Kuala Pilah incident, for instance, the MCP, in the face of Police impotence, had simply intimidated the public through brazenly brutal slayings. People had thus been too terrified to help.[108] Moreover, even in 'well-defined and comparatively small areas', there were bound to be innocent people along with MCP supporters. Hence the *Singapore Standard* warned that the policy was bound to create enemies where none had existed before.[109] Colonial Secretary Griffiths even declared that he was doubtful of 'either the wisdom or the effectiveness' of this type of punishment, and expressed surprise that Gurney, who had had experience with it in Palestine, would want to try it in Malaya.[110] Most damagingly, moreover, collective punishment only reminded the rural Chinese of similar Japanese methods.[111] That collective punishment was of dubious value was illustrated in the case of Pusing. In February 1951, a European Resettlement Officer was shot dead within the barbed wire barricade of this tin mining town in Perak. When efforts to secure information from the miners came to nought, Government applied ER 17 DA: the town was fined $40,000, and all shops except for food shops were ordered to close except for two hours daily.[112] In response, terrorist supporters fled the town with the result that the innocent townspeople had 'to bear not only their own share of the fine but also two further levies in order to make up the total fine ordered for the area'.[113]

The propaganda perils of collective punishment were further illustrated in the case of Senai, in Johore. After terrorists had shot at a Police patrol in the main street in broad daylight, shopkeepers refused to give information because they believed that the 'timid, corrupt and ineffective' Police would be unable to protect them from Communist reprisals. In response, Government, 'like a prim governess who is afraid her charges are getting out of hand', promptly ordered all the shops to close except for two hours in the morning. The objections of the Senai Chinese were overruled by the official admonition that the added inconvenience would teach them to be more co-operative. Chinese Affairs staff complained that it was 'incredible that anyone in their senses should expect the Chinese to be the least impressed with half measures'.[114] In sum, the general impression created amongst the disgruntled rural Chinese by the combined impact of poorly executed resettlement, indiscriminate detentions and collective punishment was that Government was simply engaged in 'mass bullying'.[115] Still, Chinese frustrations were sometimes sublimated via the vehicle of black humour. When Penang Police were unable to arrest the terrorist who injured five people in a grenade attack on Carnarvon Street, *next* to Central Police Station, some wags whispered that perhaps a collective fine ought to be levied on the Police.[116]

THE PROPAGANDA CONSEQUENCES OF SECURITY FORCE BEHAVIOUR

While the harsh Emergency Regulations projected to the rural Chinese the image of an uncaring Government, the attitudes and behaviour of the Security Forces only confirmed the impression. This was certainly the case with the Police, who were in closest contact with the rural Chinese. The Malay regular Police and the Specials lacked the training to make greater use of the Criminal Procedure Code so as to build up sufficient evidence to identify and arrest individual terrorist suspects, preferring instead to invoke the sweeping Emergency Regulations in detaining persons, which often meant innocent Chinese.[117] Litton commented icily that reports of the Specials in particular being 'ill-trained, ill-disciplined, sometimes unreliable and occasionally corrupt', represented a 'masterpiece of understatement'.[118] There also persisted a shortage of Chinese Police. In mid-1950 Gurney had to ask the Governor of Hong Kong and the Australian Government for help in recruiting 50 Chinese or Chinese-speaking Police officers for Special Branch and CID work, able to 'establish friendly relations with the people'.[119] Government also introduced direction of manpower in December 1950 to get more Chinese recruits,[120] but sheer distrust of Government impelled thousands of eligible Chinese to evade the call up.[121] Thus, by December 1951, although there were more Chinese Inspectors and regular rank and file Police, there was still a shortage of gazetted Chinese officers, detectives and Special Constables.[122]

If Government could not get more Chinese Police, it tried to increase the number of Chinese-speaking Police. In July 1951, a Government Officers' Language School was set up in Cameron Highlands.[123] It was run by R.H. Oakeley of Chinese Affairs and he was assisted by Dr Nicholas Bodman, an American Associate Professor of Linguistics. Other Chinese staff were also recruited. From July 1951, the School ran six-month spoken Cantonese and Hokkien courses for Police and MCS officers, who were examined by Chinese Affairs staff at the end of each course. The courses were considered a success.[124] 20 Police and four MCS officers attended the first two courses.[125] Nevertheless, despite these efforts in putting out more Chinese and Chinese-speaking Police, by the end of 1951 there were still not enough to go around.[126] Hence the persisting communication vacuum between the Police and the rural Chinese facilitated stereotyping, and Police and Army officers continued to regard 'all Chinese as hostile'[127] and that it was 'no use being soft with them'.[128] In the face of such hostility, the average Chinese tapper, squatter, shop employee on a tin mine, artisan or shop assistant in a town naturally dared not go to Police Stations to give information.[129]

Chinese feelings toward the Army were just as negative. Litton recalled that the Head of the Criminal Investigation Department in Malacca admitted that he was under pressure from the Army to detain Chinese, even if they were innocent. Apparently, once troops had suffered casualties in terrorist ambushes and been unable to avenge their losses, they tended to arrest everyone in a wide area around the scene of the ambush on 'suspicion of complicity'. Litton complained bitterly that the 'detention of innocent people to satisfy the common soldier's lust for revenge is one of the best ways of ensuring that the Communists would get the full support of the people'.[130] Litton also pilloried the penchant of some senior Army commanders for large scale operations involving RAF air strikes instead of small unit patrolling in co-operation with the Police, and decried their 'strong dislike' for such an 'unmilitary' use of troops.[131] The Army's predilection for heavy weapons continued to create propaganda disasters on occasion: in late October 1951, accidental artillery fire killed two persons and injured four others in Sungei Perangin Resettlement Camp near Tanjong Malim, while during the same period a Royal West Kents mortar crew accidentally shelled a Chinese Resettlement Area in north Selangor, killing or wounding five Chinese.[132] The RAF's persistent faith in the 'insidious moral effect' of air bombardment was also costly propaganda-wise. In November 1950, a Lincoln bomber accidentally dropped its load on a rubber estate, killing 12 workers. RAF errors in fact were the subject of Commons debates.[133] In short, as long as the Security Forces clung to a simplistic mindset which preferred 'its campaigns neat and tidy with us (British and Malays) here and the enemy (the Chinese) there,'[134] Government relations with the rural Chinese would be imperilled. Little wonder that in December 1951 Tan Cheng Lock emphasised that there simply had to be a 'reduction to a minimum of the number of offences committed by the Security Forces against the general public especially in the rural areas so as to inspire more public confidence in them'.[135] Tan added that in general Government had to 'build up an attitude of love, confidence and trust of the people as a whole toward itself and avoid doing anything to antagonise them or alienate their sympathies in any way'.[136] Tan's impassioned pleas hint at the extent to which Emergency policies and Security Force actions were still unwittingly impressing upon the rural Chinese that Government was anything but their Provider.

GOVERNMENT MEASURES AND TERRORIST CONFIDENCE

The Briggs Plan had adduced that once an increasing 'flow of information' had enabled the Security Forces to break up the Min Yuen within the rural Chinese body politic, the terrorists would be isolated and would be forced 'to attack' the Security Forces on their 'own ground'.[137] This brings us to the other aspect of Briggs' strategy which has been virtually ignored: his awareness of terrorist physical/psychological vulnerabilities. As early as April 1950 he had noted that the 'morale' of the terrorists was an important consideration.[138] In February 1951, moreover, he declared that it was 'daily more clear that our object must be to break down Communist morale',[139] and by the time he left Malaya he was reiterating with conviction that the Insurrection would be won through 'maintaining the morale of the people' while 'at the same time destroying Communist morale'.[140] Significantly, Briggs held that destroying terrorist confidence could be achieved not only through the 'propaganda' of leaflets, but also through the psychological effects of 'methods' such as for instance, 'killing bandits' and 'breaking up Communist cells'.[141] One 'method' whose psychological effects and hence propaganda potential was becoming apparent was resettlement. One SEP in Negri Sembilan admitted that the 'most serious blow' the MCP had received was the 'removal and resettlement of squatters', because it was on these that units relied for 'foodstuffs and money'. Terrorists were thus afraid of Government's 'blockade of food-supply'.[142]

In June 1951, therefore, with resettlement fairly advanced, Briggs decided to further curtail the terrorist food supply by introducing controls on the movement of food. Food control was not a Briggs innovation. As early as 1948/49 such schemes had already been discussed for implementation in the Pusing/Menglembu area of Kinta, Perak.[143] Nevertheless it was Briggs who formalised food control:[144] briefly, every village, estate/mine controlled area and Resettlement Area were ordered to have their perimeters clearly demarcated and entrances and exits restricted to two each. Furthermore, all stocks of padi, rice, sugar, tapioca, cooking oil, dried fish, tinned foods and medicines, were purchased by local authorities in controlled quantities, placed in secure silos and closely monitored. Sales of these items were permitted from specific shops selected by DWECs, and only to identity card holders. In particular, sales of rice were strictly controlled and made only to holders of ration cards. In addition, shops were closed daily from 1900 to 0600 hours and no sales permitted during this period, while shopkeepers were required to keep a record of all stocks and order only the minimum stocks necessary for replenishment.[145] These in turn were allowed to arrive at the village, controlled area or Resettlement Area only at certain hours during the day – hence there was a general stoppage of movement by road of all foodstuffs by night, when they would be more prone to ambush.[146] Moreover, lorries travelling by day were not permitted to stop between stipulated halts nor deviate from the most direct route to the next destination. Finally, people leaving for work were allowed to take only liquids along and were searched at gates to ensure this.[147] In short, the general supply of food and necessities in the rural areas was sharply reduced by these food control measures.

The impact of food control on the terrorists was profound. Resettlement had ensured that some squatters could no longer grow crops in their old illegal holdings, while the Korean War boom had persuaded others to eschew food production for employment in estates, mines, smallholdings and nearby towns.[148] Now, as a result of food control, the already curtailed food supply was reduced even more, with serious consequences for terrorist confidence. Thus, in August 1951, for instance, just two months after food control began, four terrorists in northern Selangor surrendered, complaining that their gang had been reduced to eating fruit seeds in lieu of rice, and many were suffering from swollen and ulcerated legs.[149] Hence, if resettlement had compelled the terrorists to break into smaller groups, and Central to issue a warning to the comrades not to 'lose confidence',[150] food control provoked anxious terrorists to even greater levels of violence.[151] Consequently, the terror rate in 1951 was said to be appalling.[152]

If Briggs was spot on in his assessment of the efficacy of food control in attacking terrorist confidence, his North-West Frontier background perhaps misled him into feeling that RAF attacks on the terrorists lowered their morale.[153] The continuing evidence, however, was that the terrorists were not afraid of bombing as these raids were 'always inaccurate'.[154] However, Briggs was more progressive on the question of whether large-scale operations or small unit patrolling was the better Security Force strategy. In view of his own Burma experience, and those of officers like Lieutenant-Colonel Mike Calvert, who was to form the Malayan Scouts, the precursor of 22 Special Air Service (22 SAS) in August 1950,[155] Briggs moved decisively away from large-scale operations. The Briggs Plan had called for 'framework patrolling' by Security Forces in each State, whose task was to 'dominate the jungle up to about five hours journey from potential bandit supply areas', placing emphasis on dominating the 'tracks on which the bandits rely to make contact with their information and supply organisation'.[156] On finding in September 1950 that small-unit patrolling was being abandoned for long periods to allow 'large scale operations', he issued a Directive in mid-November insisting on 'six-week-long area patrolling' by 'small controlled units' with a view to 'interception' on 'the jungle fringes'.[157] By 1951, although sweeps were still used, 'some two-thirds of the army was engaged' in protracted small unit patrolling.[158] The gospel of Ferret Force was finally taking hold.

In addition, Security Force patrols in 1951 were no longer going out on 'prophylactic and will o' the wisp' operations, but were relying on better intelligence emanating from grateful squatters who were appreciative of the 'protection' afforded by Resettlement Areas.[159] Importantly, this information was also being better utilised because of the work of Director of Intelligence Jenkin.[160] By the time Jenkin resigned in October 1951, the re-organisation of Special Branch and the C.I.D. was 'well advanced', and a 'satisfactory Interrogation Branch' was in being.[161] Consequently, early in 1951, the contact rate was double the figure for the middle of 1950.[162] By this time, therefore, the terrorists were becoming increasingly rattled not so much by RAF attacks, artillery fire, nor large scale 'fire brigade'[163] operations, but rather 'a large number of small harassing patrols in the jungle over a period of days or weeks'.[164] In sum, Briggs' emphasis on protracted small unit patrolling on the jungle fringe with 'first class information' was a trump card, and once it was closely co-ordinated with food control, was to prove a major weapon in not merely physical, but psychological, warfare against the MRLA rank and file.

BRIGGS, GREENE AND GOVERNMENT PROPAGANDA OF WORDS

The Briggs Plan had recognised that 'good propaganda' was necessary in 'exploiting' the effects of increased Government administrative coverage of the rural areas.[165] However, because his immediate appreciation of

Government propaganda of words was that it was seriously deficient,[166] Briggs tried to rectify this by appointing Alex Josey as Staff Officer Emergency Information in early May 1950. Josey, as SO (EI) was directly responsible to the Director of Operations.[167] Described as a 'character of bohemian appearance and considerable wit',[168] Josey had been Controller of Programmes in the Palestine Broadcasting Service between 1946 and 1948, and had joined Radio Malaya in February 1949; prior to being appointed SO (EI) he had been doing 'a good job in the News Division'.[169] His new role was to 'intensify' both propaganda against the terrorists as well as that to the public in order to raise morale and increase the flow of information.[170] In the ensuing weeks, Josey did his best to help get Government across to the general public, for instance, through his *Malayan Affairs* broadcasts, which dealt with Emergency issues.[171] However, his efficiency was hampered by the fact that he was a 'one man band' and did not even have a secretary to attend to minor paperwork.[172] Moreover, as Josey's mandate overlapped with that of the Department of Public Relations – renamed the Department of Information in June – there quickly arose in early June a dispute as to the proper relationship between Josey and the DPR staff.[173] Worse was to come. Because Josey remarked in one broadcast that some of his friends had suggested that the Malayan rubber industry be nationalised, he prompted a furious response from some European planters, and this row contributed to his dismissal in September 1950. John Litton of Chinese Affairs argued that the chance remark had not constituted the main thrust of Josey's talk, and criticised 'the sheer emotional prejudice, the vulgar abuse and the lack of coherent thought' displayed in the spate of attacks on Josey.[174]

At any rate, during the 15th Commissioner-General's meeting at Bukit Serene in June 1950, Colonial Secretary Griffiths had conveyed London's concern at the poor state of word-propaganda in Malaya and offered to supply a specialist from the BBC to come out to Malaya. Gurney welcomed this offer.[175] On his return to London Griffiths promptly reported the need for 'an anti-Communist expert',[176] and by August, it was announced that Hugh Carleton Greene of the BBC was coming out for a year to Malaya.[177] Greene, brother of the novelist Graham Greene, and an Oxford graduate in English and Literature, had been the *Daily Telegraph's* correspondent in Nazi Germany from 1934 to 1939. He returned to England in June 1940 and worked for RAF Intelligence for a few months before being recruited by the BBC to head its German Service for the duration of the war. He then assumed responsibilities as Controller of Broadcasting in the British Zone of Occupied Germany till 1949 when he returned to Bush House to head the BBC East European Service. He left for Malaya the following year.[178] Greene later recalled that his had been 'a typically English sort of appointment': he had known the Secretary of State for Commonwealth Relations, Patrick Gordon Walker, since their BBC days in World War Two, and Walker had duly suggested him to Griffiths.[179] Greene belonged to that generation of British propagandists who had cut their teeth during the war, and in fact as BBC German Services Editor he had worked closely with the legendary Richard Crossman of the PWE German Section. It had been evident that both men had been like-minded on propaganda fundamentals.[180] In person, Greene came across as 'intellectual', 'a cold fish, unflappable and fair, maybe, but somewhat bleak'. He nevertheless managed to 'look dominating,' and carried an 'air of distinction'.[181]

He arrived on 19 September to take up the appointment of Staff Officer (Emergency Operations) on Briggs' staff.[182] Then, after a whirlwind tour of the Federation with armed escort, during which he talked to SWEC and DWEC staff, he returned to Kuala Lumpur to consolidate his findings.[183] This process resulted in the inauguration of the Emergency Information Services (EIS) in September 1950, created to fulfil three objectives: first, to raise public confidence in Government and increase the flow of information from the public to the Police; second, to 'attack the morale of the members of the MRLA, Min Yuen and their supporters' and 'drive a wedge between the leaders and the rank and file' so as to encourage 'defection'; and third, to 'create an awareness of the democratic way of life' being threatened by Communism.[184] At the same time Greene restyled himself as Head EIS, in order to make clear to all interested parties that he alone was empowered to 'direct and co-ordinate' all spoken, printed and broadcast propaganda on behalf of the Director of Operations. The fact that McHugh of the Department of Information went on long leave from July 1950 to January 1951, facilitated Greene's domination of the JIPC from October, which witnessed the shift of the locus of propaganda policy-making to EIS. JIPC henceforth existed a forum for co-ordination and exchange of ideas between the Federation and Singapore.[185] With Briggs' backing, Greene built up the EIS over the next few months. He reinstated Josey as Controller, Emergency Broadcasting in November and brought out Eliot Watrous from the BBC's Eastern European Department as Deputy Head of the EIS.[186]

Furthermore, in line with the wartime precept that special expertise was needed for devising propaganda directed at a specific audience, Greene, who could speak no Chinese, made it a priority to seek out suitable locals who could do the job. In particular, on 26 February 1951 Greene recruited a 'short, balding, bespectacled'[187] Chinese called Too Chee Chew, better known as C.C. Too, as Chinese Assistant. Too is so important that he deserves closer scrutiny. 31 when he was recruited, Too, a Cantonese, was from a family that had been staunchly Nationalist: his grandfather, Too Nam, had been a close associate of the Chinese Republican leader Sun Yat Sen. Too was educated in Chinese at the Confucian School (1926–34) and in English for his Cambridge certificate at the Methodist Boys' School (1934–38), both in Kuala Lumpur. He then spent a year at the Victoria

Institution, Kuala Lumpur, before proceeding to Raffles College, Singapore to read Pure Science. Because of the Occupation, Too graduated only in 1947 with a War Diploma in Science, equivalent to a degree.[188] What prepared Too for his later battle of wits with the MCP was his extensive fraternising with the Party during the BMA period. As the Communists lacked English-speaking members, they tried hard to recruit Too, inviting him to both public as well as private meetings, even granting him free access to Party headquarters in Kuala Lumpur. In the spring of 1946, they even asked him to accompany the MPAJA contingent to the post-war Victory Parade in London as interpreter, an 'honour' which Too respectfully declined. On the return of the contingent from London, moreover, a reception was held at the MPAJA Ex-Comrades' Association premises in Peel Road, Kuala Lumpur, and it was there that Too met Chin Peng, who was on hand to welcome back the contingent. Despite the attention, however, Too never joined the Communists. He noted that despite their 'pleasant manners and apparent sincerity', he could detect their 'naïve, syllogistic and contradictory theories and doctrines', and more importantly, their 'cynical' manipulation and coercion of their subordinates and the public 'in furtherance of their personal ambition for political power and wealth'.[189]

Instead Too worked in a voluntary liaison capacity for Field Security and RAF Counterintelligence until April 1946, and was then hired as Secretary to the Nationalist Chinese Consul-General in Kuala Lumpur until January 1950, when the Consulate was closed following the British recognition of Communist China.[190] After several months of unemployment, in November Too applied for the post of State Assistant, State Emergency Information Officer, after reading in the newspaper advertisement that Robert G.K. Thompson was on the Director of Operations Staff. Too had been impressed by Thompson's sincerity in 1947 when both men – Too representing the Chinese Consul-General and Thompson the British – had tried to persuade some KMT guerrillas in Betong, southern Thailand, to lay down arms.[191] When Too called up after two weeks without a reply to his application, Greene answered, informing him that Thompson had been posted to Johore and the original post had been filled. Still, Greene asked Too to turn up anyway. Too was immediately taken by Greene: although the Englishman dressed like a 'loafer', he had no 'colonial airs'.[192] Too thus joined EIS, and a month later Greene also secured Lam Swee, the high ranking SEP whom Tom Driberg had interviewed. Lam, 34 on joining EIS, had been a barber and rubber tapper, and during the Occupation was a member of the South Johore State Committee. After the war he had been Vice-President of the PMFTU and then the Political Commissar of the Headquarters 4th Corps, MRLA prior to defection. Lam was a useful acquisition. Due to his 'exemplary behaviour and sincere leadership', he had been popular and well known in Chinese labour circles prior to the

Emergency, and his voice had an echo throughout Malaya. Lam did such good work that his detention order was suspended six months after he had joined EIS.[193]

Greene set Too and Lam the task of 'consumer research' into Communist propaganda and state of mind. Too, ignoring the error-strewn translations of the Chinese Middle School students, went to work on the originals.[194] Too and Greene also insisted that 'every little bit of paper recovered in [sic] a live or dead body or recovered in any communist dump or camp' must be brought back to Kuala Lumpur even if local intelligence officers were not convinced of their value. Too personally examined them.[195] Greene also tried to improve EIS access to solid intelligence in another way: in March 1951 EIS was moved into new premises in Bluff Road, near Federal Police Headquarters, and Greene proceeded to build cordial relations with the Commissioner of Police and Director of Intelligence. From early 1951, moreover, Greene and Director Jenkin had regular weekly meetings and a member of the Federal Police Intelligence Bureau sat in at EIS meetings.[196] Furthermore, as individual Allied Army Headquarters had had organic Psychological Warfare Divisions to facilitate the drafting of propaganda appeals tailored to local tactical situations,[197] Greene ensured that each State and Settlement made provision for an Emergency Information Officer (SEIO), with a full-time Chinese Assistant. In August 1951, moreover, the Standing Committee on Finance approved the provision of SEPs as Special Assistants. The whole idea was for Government leaflets to move away from 'general exhortation' and provide more 'local detail'.[198] Greene also tried to ensure effective contacts 'down the line' between SEIOs and Chief Police Officers, Contingent Intelligence Officers and Officer Commanding, Troops, with the result that SEIOs by 1951 were attending SWEC meetings regularly. He also visited the DWECs to impress upon them the value of propaganda, and was rewarded with 'continual requests' to SEIOs from District Officers, Resettlement Officers, Police and Army officers for propaganda directed at the public and terrorists.[199]

Greene had his difficulties. Due to the very same shortages of Chinese-speaking officers afflicting the rest of Government, by the time he left in September 1951,[200] SEIO posts had yet to be filled with full-time men. Instead, Chinese Affairs officers had to be drafted to do the work part-time, and Greene opined that there seemed to be 'some mysterious connection between skill in Chinese Affairs and skill in propaganda, even when it is not directed to a Chinese audience'. In this respect Greene singled out Robert G.K. Thompson, SEIO Johore as having a 'real understanding of the principles of propaganda', while other Chinese Affairs men Greene praised for their SEIO work included A.W.D. James in Negri Sembilan, H.R. Howse in Selangor, John Litton in Malacca, W.J. Watts in Kedah and R.N. Jackson in Negri Sembilan.[201] Similarly, at District level, due to the lack of full-time District Emergency Information Officers (DEIOs), anyone who was deemed suitable was asked to do EIS work.[202] For instance, S.R. Dawson, Chinese-speaking Resettlement Supervisor in Segamat District, also took charge of SEP lecture tours in the area on behalf of the EIS.[203]

While he was expending considerable energy setting up a rational propaganda machine for raising Chinese and lowering terrorist confidence, Greene was also busy sharpening the various instruments of propaganda. In August 1951, the first 50,000 copies of a monthly newsletter called *New Path News* was inaugurated for the consumption of the rural Chinese. It was edited by Too and Lam Swee, and reactions to it were 'very favourable'.[204] More important to Greene was the availability of SEPs in lieu of the shortage of full-time Chinese-speaking SEIOs capable of undertaking word-of-mouth propaganda to the public. SEPs had for some time opined that Government propaganda was not sufficiently effective in reaching people, 'particularly by word-of-mouth'.[205] That the Communists placed great stock by word-of-mouth propaganda was evidenced by the comments of another SEP in early February 1950:[206]

> There appears to be no Government propaganda whereas Communist propaganda ... is constantly put out to the people. The most effective is verbal propaganda by talks to the people. Collect them together and talk to them... Leaflets are also important, but speech propaganda comes first.

Why was word-of-mouth propaganda so important to the Communists? Lucien Pye's valuable study found that the ordinary Chinese generally tended to evaluate 'communications media' on the basis of 'strength of personal relationship' with the source of the information. In other words, the more impersonal the source, the less trust was reposed in it. That was why SEPs later admitted that they did not feel fully comfortable with printed media as they were somewhat impersonal. One Chinese expressed it this way:[207]

> When people talk with you, you can tell whether their information is reliable or not. You can't do this with a newspaper. You can read the newspapers and you can find all kinds of ideas, but how do you know which ones are true and which ones are false? You don't know who wrote it, or why he wrote it, and therefore he might be cheating you.

The implication was clear: there was no substitute for friendly personal contact in any drive to win the confidence of the rural Chinese. Only when the deeds of Government agents communicated care and concern would the rural Chinese believe Government leaflets projecting the same message. In fact, six months before Greene arrived, in March 1950, Government was slowly beginning to grasp this fact, deciding that even after Anti-Bandit Month, volunteers would still be sought for dissemination of Government propaganda by word-of-mouth.[208] Greene took this further. Taking advantage of a major political decision by Gurney in August 1950 not to prosecute immediately SEPs 'with blood on their hands',[209] Greene secured SEPs for the purpose of word-of-mouth propaganda.[210] He believed that 'being of the same race and having the same background as the people they address', SEPs could understand the mentality of the people better than anyone else.[211] SEP teams were thus, from around November 1950, sent throughout the country on lecture tours.[212] In this way, Johore, Malacca, Negri Sembilan, Selangor, Pahang and Perak were covered in the first eight months of 1951.[213] Particularly noteworthy was the six-week tour of Johore, Negri Sembilan and Malacca by Lam Swee and other SEPs, between 1 June and 11 July 1951. They addressed 55,000 people and had a 'good' effect on public morale.[214] That SEP lecture tours were indeed effective propaganda was confirmed by complaints from the other side of the fence. For example, an editorial in the MCP's *People's Awakening News* warned the public:[215]

> The British Imperialists are using traitors and running dogs to go around every resettlement camp to spread rumours... Sometimes some people may think it is worth while to go and listen to them, but on the other hand you do not realise that you are influenced by their sweet flattering words or by those surrendered double-faced rogues.

Given the importance of the SEP lecture tour, Greene also ensured that it was well supported technically. A tour usually consisted of a convoy made up of a scout car, the SEIO car, an armoured wagon containing the SEPs, an armoured troop carrier with half a dozen Police and the all-important mobile unit.[216] Until November 1950, there were only 23 mobile units available. Greene secured approval from the Standing Committee on Finance to increase the number of mobile units to 53. This provided a mobile unit in every District in the States and Settlements most affected by the Emergency, and a unit for every two Districts in the other States. These new units became operational in July and August 1951, although Greene faced difficulty in securing enough Chinese Field Officers to man them, despite an advertised increase in emoluments from August 1951. This shortfall compelled Greene at one point to contemplate manpower direction.[217]

The expansion of the mobile unit fleet was followed by an increase in the output of visual propaganda. At the 15th Commissioner-General's Conference in June 1950, it was observed that film was a very useful form of propaganda.[218] Greene agreed, noting that despite the illiteracy of the Malayan rural population, film propaganda in Malaya had been 'comparatively neglected'.[219] In tandem with the expansion of the mobile units, therefore, Greene secured approval from the Standing Committee on Finance for a 'big expansion' in the equipment and European and Asian staff of the MFU, in order to facilitate a 'big increase both in its own production and the dubbing of specially chosen films'.[220] Greene envisaged a large number of mobile units plying not only the remote Malay villages and kampongs but also the Chinese Resettlement Areas, propagandising them with SEP talks and MFU films. Delays, however, meant that equipment for the MFU ordered in November 1950 did not arrive till April 1951. In addition, the continued lack of suitable buildings meant that the MFU had to move its equipment to new sites twice in 1951, causing disruptions in the production and delivery of films. Nevertheless, in 1951, the MFU delivered for distribution 111 films of which 24 were on the Emergency. This was more than twice the 1950 figure.[221]

Quantity aside, Greene paid close attention to the content of these MFU products. In order to keep the public informed, between January and September 1951, the MFU produced 13 issues of *News of Malaya* in Malay and a Chinese issue of *Malayan News*.[222] Other purely informational films produced until September 1951 included *The New Life: Resettlement in Johore*; *A Family Resettled*; *Rewards for Information*; *The Shame of Pusing, Communist Extortion Methods,* several shorts on the working of Police, and 10 Chinese anti-Communist slogan trailers.[223] Moreover, recognising that 'too much propaganda or information cannot be absorbed at one time', Greene urged MFU producers to put out 'entertainment' as a 'jam' to 'coat the pill' of propaganda. This was just as well, since Malayans were at the time considered as among the most avid filmgoers in the world.[224] MFU entertainment thus included *Love in the Jungle*, based on SEP statements and captured Communist documents and *The Adventures of Yaacob*, a 10-reel serial film about the eponymous hero's exploits against the terrorists. 'Yaacob' in fact bore a striking resemblance to Tarzan – a deliberate ploy, as it was realised that the national audience as a whole were at the 'Tarzan and Wild West stage'.[225] In addition, the rights for a period of three years, to exhibit 53 Tarzan, Wild West and Knockabout Comedy films produced by Metro-Goldwyn Mayer (MGM), were purchased. Coloured cartoon films were also brought in from the United Kingdom.[226]

The augmentation of spoken and visual propaganda was accompanied by the first important strides in broadcasting. In August 1950, it was announced that Radio Malaya would be receiving one medium-wave and one short-wave transmitter, which would enable it to add an additional three hours to its daily Chinese programming.[227] A month later, the Pan Malayan Advisory Council on Broadcasting advised that available CDW funds be used for the purchase of a separate transmitter to ensure the desired level of reception in the Kinta Valley area of Perak.[228] In October, the 17th JIPC meeting, which Greene attended, approved the provision for a 10 kilowatt medium-wave transmitter to replace the Japanese transmitter still in use.[229] There was progress on the receiver side of the equation as well. The Korean War boom enabled many rural folk to buy private radios.[230] Hence approximately 60,000 private radio licences were distributed throughout the Federation in 1951, compared to 46,522 in 1950 and 34,711 for 1949.[231] In addition, thanks to another CDW grant, by December 1951, the General Electric Company (GEC) had installed 645 powerful community receivers with loudspeakers of considerable range in kampongs, Resettlement Areas and villages. Meanwhile Government also installed 700 cheap small battery receivers chiefly in Resettlement Areas where they were set up in coffee shops and community centres. In addition, 274 estates installed receivers for their labour forces.[232] In sum, by the end of 1951, Radio Malaya for the first time 'reached right into the rural areas', and became an important 'medium of information, education and entertainment for the more isolated population who hitherto had largely been outside its range'.[233]

Meanwhile, efforts were also being made to upgrade the content of programmes being beamed to the population. As early as February 1950, Radio Malaya Director Dumeresque had warned the very first meeting of the JIPC that the station would find it difficult to provide suitable programmes for every race and class in Malaya. Six months later, he reiterated that Radio Malaya was currently producing material mainly for the 'educated classes', as the latter could afford private radio receivers, and was therefore unable to spare sufficient staff for the production of separate specialised programmes for other strata of the population. He thus asked the JIPC for guidance as to which of the following groups had priority: Malays in kampongs, urban Chinese working classes, Chinese squatters or Tamil rubber workers.[234] The 14th JIPC meeting in September replied that equal priority should be given to the rural Chinese and Malays. To facilitate increased Chinese and Malay rural programming, therefore, Radio Malaya recruited more staff for bringing programmes up to standard.[235] Greene was meanwhile seeking to influence Radio Malaya policy, and by 28 November he was made solely responsible for 'all broadcast programmes concerned with the Emergency'.[236]

In fact, at the 19th JIPC meeting 11 days earlier Greene had argued that the proposed Community Listening Scheme should be tailored to direct operational requirements: namely to keep the public abreast of Government progress in the Emergency with a view to raising morale and increasing the flow of information. This was accepted and Josey was appointed Controller of Emergency Broadcasting, starting work immediately on a detailed plan for Community Listening.[237] Subsequently, in January 1951, the Standing Committee on Finance approved funds for acquiring the staff and equipment for a separate Community Listening Organisation, and the first programmes, in Malay, Tamil and four Chinese dialects, went on the air in early February 1951.[238] By December, the Community Listening Programme for the Chinese in the Resettlement Areas and the mines comprised broadcasts in Hakka between 1700 and 1745, in Cantonese between 1745 and 1830 and in Mandarin between 1830 and 1900 hours.[239] Rural

Chinese could listen to SEPs talking or being interviewed in Hakka with translations into Cantonese, discussing how they had been duped into joining the MCP, life in the jungle and why they had surrendered. Moreover, regular programmes included the weekly *Spotlight on the Emergency*, which covered progress of the campaign; *This is Communism*, a simply-written weekly broadcast on Communism in practice, with examples drawn from China, Russia and the Eastern bloc; and the popular *Can I Help You?* in which every week listeners sent in questions pertaining to mundane issues such as identity cards, food control regulations, the manpower call-up, resettlement disturbance grants, and even marriage problems. There were also weekly talks and skits on farming by 'Uncle Ngee', health talks by the 'Radio Doctor', Dr. Low Nan Hong of the Kuala Lumpur General Hospital, and youth talks and plays with anti-Communist morals. In addition, apart from popular dance music, a major pulling factor of the Community Listening Programme was Lee Dai Soh, a Cantonese storyteller who was so popular that rural listeners without access to a community receiver were known to have walked long distances to coffee shops just to listen to him! Lee's stories were interspersed with talks and news, clearly conforming to the Crossman dictum that entertainment was the narcotic which made propaganda more palatable.[240]

GOVERNMENT PSYCHOLOGICAL WARFARE
AND THE TERRORISTS

Greene not only augmented Government spoken, printed and broadcast propaganda to the public, he strove to ensure that Government's message got across to the terrorists as well. In this respect he pronounced that leaflets, 'owing to local conditions, always must remain the main psychological warfare weapon against the bandits in the jungle'.[241] In order to ensure that terrorists came into physical contact with Government leaflets, Greene did two things. First, he secured waterproof material for leaflets so that they would not rot in the humid, wet jungle environment. Second, he changed the distribution system of the Department of Information. To recapitulate, what had transpired up to the end of 1950 was that large numbers of leaflets had been despatched to a small number of recipients in each State and Settlement, with the result that there had been wastage. Greene now asked Department of Information staff to deliver leaflet stacks to a *larger* number of recipients in each State, so that each recipient would only need to cope with a smaller and more manageable load, thereby ensuring that leaflets found their way to their intended targets in the jungle.[242]

The problem of distribution aside, there was the critical issue of content. On the one hand, Greene could do nothing about the issue of terminology. Terrorists were still called 'bandits', although from July 1950 onwards, the

Foreign Office view was that it was permissible for Government propaganda to dwell more on the Communism of the 'bandits', but highlighting the links with Russia rather than China.[243] Very importantly, Greene brought his wartime propaganda philosophy to bear. C.C. Too, a future Head of Government Psychological Warfare, revealed in 1981 that he 'learned the basic principles of psychological warfare' from Greene.[244] Too observed that the fundamental principle, as Crossman always maintained, was to establish credibility with the audience by telling the truth. In particular, the terrorists must always be able to verify what Government was promising in leaflets, so that they would gradually build up confidence in Government's good faith.[245]

This principle of establishing credibility lay at the heart of Government's continuing Amnesty deliberations. The JIPC meeting of 9 June 1950 had agreed to continue the 1949 Gurney Amnesty terms,[246] a position favoured by the departing Secretaries of State for War and the Colonies, who had held that a full Amnesty would only have suggested to the MCP that Government was weak, and that there should be no offer of a full pardon until 'Johore, Negri Sembilan and Pahang had been effectively cleared of bandits'.[247] They missed the point, however. In the anti-Chinese climate engendered by Government policy and Security Force misbehaviour, Government was simply *not trusted* by wavering terrorists, who felt that they would simply be used and then disposed.[248] To persuade them to come out was to ask them to put their faith in Government, and this meant that Government had to be more explicit about what SEPs could expect after surrender. The need for more publicity on how SEPs were actually treated by Government was made at the next JIPC meeting on 23 June by Acting Director of Public Relations A.J.W. Hockenhull. The JIPC thus considered a more explicit re-wording of the Gurney Amnesty: the main gist of the Amnesty remained – pardon was offered only to those terrorists who had were 'not found to have been guilty of murder of crimes of violence'. Now however, it was clearly stipulated that these SEPs would be after examination, either sent to Taiping for rehabilitation or repatriated.[249] Two weeks later, however, JIPC decided that the more explicit terms should not be put out at all, for fear of antagonising the European planters who were insistent that all terrorists be prosecuted. SEIO Johore, R.N. Broome thus suggested the more indirect approach of general publicity of life in Taiping.[250] This was hardly enough, however, to help close Government's credibility gap with suspicious potential SEPs.

Then, in August 1950 Gurney made a momentous decision. He quietly decided that Government would not immediately prosecute SEPs who were implicated in capital crimes.[251] In other words, even if a terrorist had 'blood on his hands' and did not qualify for pardon under the 1949 terms, he would not be prosecuted *at once* if he came out. This relaxation of the policy enabled Greene to get his hands on SEPs and send them out to be seen in public in the estates and Resettlement Areas. This spectacle of SEPs moving freely in public with the Security Forces and EIS was meant to project the impression in the rural areas that SEPs were being well-treated by Government.[252] The Gurney decision also influenced the content of leaflets. Greene could now assure terrorists of fair treatment on surrender, but *not* that they would never face prosecution. The emphasis was on what treatment terrorists could expect if they gave up.[253] Moreover, it was reckoned that if Government treated SEPs better than they had expected, the idea that Government was 'very humane and very reasonable' would make its rounds, raising Government's stock with the terrorists.[254]

Credibility aside, Greene also drilled into Too the maxim that threats should never be resorted to. This was important since as late as July 1950, the Department of Information was still producing leaflets like No. 365: 'Death to Min Yuen Workers'.[255] Greene urged that SEIOs use leaflets with photographs of dead terrorists 'with discretion' and not in areas where terrorist morale was still high, in case the leaflets stiffened their resistance.[256] Moreover it was then decided that such leaflets were bad propaganda because they deterred potential SEPs from giving up, for fear that they would be killed by Government. Rather, the new line taken was that they had made a genuine if 'awful mistake' in joining the MCP, and Government really wanted to help them rectify it. Another idea Greene imported was the value of straight news. Because terrorists were 'isolated' in their jungle lairs, they were starved for information, and to get their attention Government just had to provide this commodity. Leaflets were thus dropped on Sundays containing simple news of terrorists killed, wounded or who had given up. Moreover, SEPs were photographed and asked to write messages to their former comrades, giving them news of their fate under Government.[257] Particularly effective were leaflets showing groups of SEPs who had surrendered at different times during the Emergency together with freshly surrendered terrorists. This quashed Central's claims that SEPs were executed once Government had no longer any use for them.[258]

Apart from 'market research' into the Communist state of mind, Greene also capitalised on the empathy Lam Swee and Too enjoyed with the terrorist psyche by putting them to work devising Government propaganda to the terrorists. In this respect Lam Swee's *My Accusation*, put out in 1951, struck such a chord with the rank and file terrorists that considerable MCP internal propaganda was produced in an attempt to counter its effects.[259] Furthermore, Greene not only tried to persuade terrorists to give up, in line with a JIPC observation in July 1950 that terrorists faced difficulties in the physical act of surrendering, he also took pains to tell them *how* to surrender.[260] Every leaflet dropped on the jungle thus had a safe conduct pass on the reverse for the instruction of those keen to defect. It was signed by the High Commissioner and promised 'good treatment', food, cigarettes and medical attention for SEPs.[261] In addition, other leaflets like 'Hints and Advice on How to Surrender' were produced. Thus SEP Ah Tiew, who surrendered in Johore in October 1951 had a safe conduct in his pocket, while a Pahang SEP came out after reading the leaflet on 'Hints and Advice'.[262] Too also noted that leaflets were produced in a mixture of bright colours like red, yellow and orange and dull colours like grey, blue and green. This was because terrorists thinking of surrendering would not dare pick up bright leaflets for fear of being caught by their leaders, and would only risk picking up the less obvious leaflets.[263]

Another reform of considerable significance was Greene's introduction of the concept of the 'psychological moment' into Malaya. To recapitulate, this referred to the right timing for releasing leaflets to an audience. From the outset, Greene, like Crossman, was clear that the propaganda of words could achieve no miracles on its own:[264]

> It is not claimed that propaganda alone is responsible for surrender. The task of propaganda is to persuade a man that he can safely do what he already secretly wants to do because of disillusionment, grievances or hatred of life in the jungle and to play on those feelings.

In order to achieve maximum effect, therefore, propaganda of words had to be timed so as to exploit the psychological effects of any downturn in terrorist circumstances. As noted earlier, in Greene's mind, at the strategic level, the psychological moment for a full Amnesty was when the terrorists perceived that Government was clearly winning. In another more instantaneous, tactical sense, the psychological moment for targeting the terrorists was *immediately* after they had suffered serious reverses, such as the surrender of key leaders, or casualties at the hands of the Security Forces. In order to exploit *at once* the message of Government power and the concomitant terrorist anxiety generated by these setbacks, SEIOs had to rush out 'tactical' leaflets. Thus SEIOs, in response to a specific terrorist setback, would design an appropriate leaflet and submit it to Greene for approval. This would then be rushed to the Department of Information for mass production, and distribution in the terrorist locality would take place by patrols or airdrops.[265] Thus, when Tan Guat, second in command of the 4th Company, 3rd Regiment, MRLA, defected on 22 April 1951 after reading Lam Swee's leaflets, a mere 48 hours later, 250,000 leaflets bearing his photograph and instructions to his men to surrender were air-dropped in the area where the 4th Company was known to be operating.[266] In order to exploit the psychological moment created by a terrorist setback, speed was of the essence.

Another weapon emphasised by Greene was rewards for information on terrorists. Greene did not introduce this idea; Government had been offering rewards in a piecemeal fashion before he arrived. Thus during the first five months of 1950, $350,590 had been paid out for information.[267]

Greene believed in the concept because he felt that given the climate in Malaya at the time, 'the only human emotion' which could 'be expected to be stronger than fear among a terrorised population with very little civic consciousness' was 'greed.' In December 1950, therefore, Greene secured 'big increases' in the 'scale of rewards for information leading to the capture or killing of terrorists'.[268] These ranged from $60,000 for the Secretary-General of the MCP, $50,000 for a Politburo member, to $2,000 for the lowest rank and file.[269] Six months later, the bounty on the head of Chin Peng was increased to $80,000 if brought in alive; while the figures for 'live' Politburo members and members of the rank and file were raised to $65,000 and $2,500 respectively. If they were brought in dead, then the rates of December 1950 would be paid out.[270] While Greene hoped that the lure of large rewards would induce the public to provide information leading to the capture of terrorists, he also expected that the scheme might detach the rank and file from Central as well. Thus half the rates of rewards aimed at the public were offered to *terrorists* who could bring in the Secretary General or other members of the Party.[271] As a further inducement to give up, terrorists were offered payment for bringing in weapons – other than their own – and could again expect half what the public was offered. The public rate was as follows: Brens and stens fetched $500, rifles, pistols and revolvers $300, smooth bore guns $150, hand-grenades $20 and ammunition 25 cents per round.[272] Government paid out $500,000 in the first six months of 1951.[273]

By the end of 1951, Psychological Warfare had been worked in 'as an integral part at the planning stage' of major operations, and was increasingly appreciated by both the Police and the military.[274] It was also appreciated albeit for different reasons by the MCP. The MCP Johore/Malacca Border Committee for instance in the summer of 1951 had expressed concern at the new 'stiffening of the Government verbal and written propaganda' expressed in the form of 'leaflets written by surrendered bandits, the writings of Lam Swee, propaganda on the Siew Lau incident, rewards announcements, verbal propaganda by SEPs and film shows'.[275] Consequently, instead of the former attitude of scorn, terrorists by November were being ordered not to read Government leaflets but to 'take them immediately to the nearest platoon commander'.[276] Furthermore, Government leaflets proving that SEPs were well treated encouraged more terrorists to defect, and there was an increase in surrenders throughout 1951. While there had been only 74 surrenders between May and December 1950, there were 136 between January and August 1951.[277] Central was also forced to accept that surrender was 'inevitable' and wavering comrades should be given 'close indoctrination' to maintain 'right thinking' in the face of Government's propaganda onslaught.[278]

Nevertheless, there were limits to this remarkable progress in Government spoken, printed and broadcast propaganda to both the public and the terrorists. Greene as Head EIS may have driven Government propaganda policy, but he was never given the authority to match his drive. Hence he was never was able to attain his goal of centralising in his person full control of all propaganda agencies.[279] Thus no 'logical division of functions' between EIS and McHugh's Department of Information '[existed] or can be drawn', and much-needed co-ordination was only affected by means of a weekly meeting. This unwieldy arrangement resulted in untidy administration at State level, especially in the case of the mobile units. Although all mobile units were administered by the Department of Information, in some States, operational control of the units was shared between the SEIO and his counterpart from the Department of Information, while in others DWECs controlled the units. In addition, while EIS was responsible to the Director of Operations Staff, the Department of Information and the MFU were separately accountable to the Member for Home Affairs.[280] In addition, Radio Malaya was accountable to both the Singapore Government and the Home Member.[281] Greene may thus have worked a veritable miracle in the one year he was in Malaya, but even he could not overcome the impact on Government propaganda efficiency of this administrative tangle. He, like Briggs, had got the basics right, but again as in the case of the Director of Operations, somebody else would have to cut the Gordian knot.

CONCLUSION

By the end of 1951, despite the relatively short tenures of Briggs and Greene, Government propaganda of word and deed was on the mend. While the continued lack of clear, decisive leadership at the top, the persistence of draconian Emergency policies like detention and collective punishment, botched resettlement as in the case of Mawai and the insensitive behaviour of some Security Force units continued to preserve the image of Government as Tormentor, there were signs that Government was gradually recognising the harm it was doing to its own interests. Hence, the month Briggs left it was admitted in official circles that 'toughness' in itself was 'not sufficient and if injudiciously used is liable to turn the people against the interests of the country'.[282] On the other hand, while intensified resettlement helped to improve rural Chinese security to some extent, the increase in the number of Chinese-speaking and Chinese officers contributed materially to improving Government's image with the rural Chinese. At the same time, the impact of smaller Security Force patrols and resettlement-cum-food control began to have a serious impact on terrorist confidence. Thus, despite the still-numerous setbacks, a discernible start had been made to ensure that Government deeds projected the message that it was indeed Provider of rural Chinese needs. Meanwhile, on the propaganda front, Greene's setting up of the EIS; the raising of part-time

SEIOs; the advent of SEP lecture tours supported by more mobile units; the expansion of the MFU and the launch of the Community Listening Service, meant that by December 1951 the message of Government as Provider was reaching the rural Chinese as never before. Moreover, in the field of Psychological Warfare, Greene's recruitment of C.C. Too and Lam Swee, the importation of tried and tested propaganda precepts and greatly enhanced rewards for information, all began to play on terrorist anxieties.

Hence in 1951 it was felt that Government was progressing in the war against the MCP.[283] This optimism however was completely extinguished in the black period September to December. The major blow was the assassination of High Commissioner Gurney at Fraser's Hill in October 1951, and this, coupled with the departures of Briggs, Gray, Jenkin and Greene in the same three-month period, meant that Government was and was seen to be, bereft of any form of leadership at the top. Predictably, *The People's Comments* boasted that the MRLA had reduced the Briggs Plan to such impotence that its originator had to resign, and had also eliminated the 'highest official in the land'.[284] In this context, the new Colonial Secretary Oliver Lyttelton, on visiting Malaya at the end of 1951, found that the memory of the Japanese invasion was 'strong and recent', and the Chinese generally feared that a new British collapse before a Communist Chinese invasion was not impossible.[285] In addition, rural Chinese fears that Government would 'take revenge' for the Gurney assassination appeared justified by the collective punishment of Tras, noted earlier. Furthermore, the continuing 'incidents of ill-treatment and unsympathetic handling' of the Chinese compelled one observer to complain that the Emergency seemed to be conducted on a 'racial basis'.[286] As for Government, the events of late 1951 meant that morale hit 'rock bottom'.[287] Thus, although the machinery for building Chinese while attacking terrorist confidence was in place, it was moribund. It was a *matter of confidence* more than anything else – it was not so much that Government did not have the wherewithal to do the job, but that its officers and the public despaired that it could be done. What was therefore needed was not so much a material but moral infusion in the form of a leader of resolve, who would, in Montgomery's apt phrase, 'electrify' the formidable Emergency machine assembled by Briggs and Greene, and win over the strategic rural Chinese.[288] Fortunately, such a man was on the horizon.

CHAPTER FIVE

Propaganda Turning Point

Templer, February 1952–May 1954

INTRODUCTION

The period February 1952 to May 1954 was, as many commentators have noted, the turning point in the Insurrection. Lieutenant-General Sir Gerald Templer dominated the scene during this time and when he left the situation had been transformed. Apart from 'electrifying' the administration at all levels, Templer also ensured that Government finally projected unequivocally the image of Provider of rural Chinese needs and wants. This was done through the 'deeds' of improved Police professionalism; the Government-wide propaganda exercise Operation Service; the New Villages and the *Taijins* therein; the eventual abolition of the more draconian Emergency Regulations and the promulgation of White Areas. At the same time, building upon and refining Briggs' concept of food control and small unit operations, Templer began to make a sustained attack on terrorist confidence. Against this backdrop of improving Government effectiveness, moreover, Templer brought in A.D.C. Peterson to re-organise and centralise the Information Services. By arguing for a broad definition of 'propaganda', moreover, Peterson helped Government officials at all levels recognise that every agency, not just Information Services, had a role to play in winning and holding rural Chinese confidence. Meanwhile new innovations like Civics Courses and Voice Aircraft helped Government reach into the New Villages as well as the jungle with greater efficiency. Unfortunately, Peterson's centralising tendency was to create problems with his staff, and one damaging consequence was the split with C.C. Too, a development which was to hamper the Psychological Warfare effort.

THE MAN, THE PLAN AND THE RURAL CHINESE

That Gurney's assassination in October 1951 had been a deep shock to Government was attested to by former Director of Public Relations Mervyn

Sheppard, who as British Adviser Negri Sembilan recalled the gloom that permeated a meeting of responsible opinion soon after:[1]

> There was a general feeling of hopelessness at that time ... most people felt that the Briggs Plan had been tried ... the Army was doing its best, the police were doing their best; and nobody seemed able to win. There was a general feeling of depression.

MacDonald also recalled that amongst MCS officers there was a feeling that 'something's going wrong, providence is not on our side'.[2] The basic problem facing the country in January 1952 therefore was very much a question of morale: the eradication of the deep malaise afflicting not only the public but even Government. In this respect Montgomery informed Churchill the same month that determining 'the measures necessary to begin to put things right' were 'only half the answer, and the easiest half'. Fully persuaded as a result of his wartime experience that morale had tangible operational consequences,[3] he emphasised that in 'all this welter of trouble "the man" is what counts'.[4] Churchill, apparently convinced, decided after a brief search that the right 'man' for the job was General Sir Gerald Templer, whom he met in Ottawa on 12 January.[5] On that occasion, Templer, alleging that he was not used to getting up on his 'hind legs' in such company, made a very short and by his own admission, unremarkable speech. He recalled later that Churchill had grumbled:

> I have heard longer speeches, better speeches – much better speeches. In fact it is about the worst speech I have ever heard. I only hope he is a man of action.[6]

Templer was not to disappoint the Prime Minister. Commissioned in 1916 in the Royal Irish Fusiliers, he saw action against the Red Army in Persia and Mesopotamia between 1919 to 1921. He went on to serve in Palestine, experiencing guerrilla warfare firsthand, and rose so quickly that by 1942, he was a Lieutenant-General, the youngest in the British Army. After the Second World War, he was Director of Civil Affairs and Military Government in Montgomery's 21st Army Group over an area which included western Germany. He later held the posts of Director of Intelligence at the War Office and then Vice-Chief of the Imperial General Staff. Templer credited his times as Director of Civil Affairs, Director of Intelligence and VCIGS, as having prepared him for his task in Malaya. While the first post exposed him to the myriad responsibilities of Government in the social, economic and political spheres, the latter two conditioned him to the 'alleyways of Whitehall' and gave him confidence to meet the 'politico-military' challenge in Malaya.[7]

Templer arrived in February 1952 armed with a directive declaring that Malaya should in due course become a united self-governing nation with a common citizenship for all who considered Malaya their home, and that to achieve this end Communist terrorism was first to be stamped out.[8] Templer's ability to effect this directive was greatly assisted by the findings of Lyttelton's fact-finding mission at the end of 1951. The Colonial Secretary had recommended that one official should be Director of Operations as well as High Commissioner and hence responsible for both civil and military operations. This idea was endorsed on 22 January by the Cabinet. Hence Templer, in combining in himself the posts of High Commissioner and Director of Operations, achieved what Briggs never had: full powers.[9] Templer's appearance heralded further changes at the top: Chief Secretary Vincent Del Tufo, to the chagrin of the MCS, was passed over for the new post of Deputy High Commissioner in February 1952 in favour of Donald MacGillivray, who had been Chief Secretary in Jamaica, while the same month Colonel A.E. Young of the London Metropolitan Police arrived to replace Gray as Commissioner of Police. In addition, GOC Malaya Major-General Urquhart was eventually replaced by Major-General Hugh Stockwell, while Deputy Director of Operations General Rob Lockhart left in March 1953, to be replaced by General Bill Oliver as Chief of Staff rather than Deputy Director of Operations.[10]

Templer's mentor Montgomery always emphasised the need for the top commander to keep a firm grip on his military machine so that his 'master plan' would be implemented properly. This was to be done by delegating to aides the routine details of his daily duties so that he would be freed to make personal visits to the field to ensure that subordinate commanders were implementing the plan effectively.[11] Similarly, soon after arriving Templer set about 'electrifying' the machinery of Government in order to ensure that Briggs' 'master plan' was implemented adequately. To oversee this personally, Templer delegated the fine details of Government administration to Deputy High Commissioner MacGillivray.[12] He then went out three days a week on tour of the States, seeing personally every *Mentri Besar*, British Adviser, Chief Police Officer and military commander to 'quiz those responsible, encourage the fainthearted [and] congratulate the successful'.[13] These tours were mounted on short notice so as to enable Templer to see things as they were, and hence nobody could 'pull the wool' over his eyes.[14] Templer also set up a Combined Emergency Planning Staff (CEPS) under Lieutenant-Colonel Napier Crookenden, to visit SWECs and DWECs to monitor progress. They were regarded as Templer's 'spies' and were regarded with some apprehension, but all WECs were warned to give them their fullest co-operation.[15]

Templer also insisted on closer integration between the members of the SWECs and the DWECs. It was established that the DWEC was 'the sharp end of the stick' for it had to implement SWEC directives through 'detailed planning and strategy'. Hence it was 'absolutely vital' that the three members of the DWEC, the Policeman, District Officer and soldier, should 'hit it off'. To hammer this truth home, four three-day courses were held for all DWEC staff, between 28 August and 11 September 1952, at the Police Depot in Gurney Road, Kuala Lumpur.[16] It soon became obvious that if Briggs had been 'kind', Templer was the complete opposite. J.L.M. Gorrie recalled that Templer visited every State and 'read the riot act' to all Government servants, reminding them forcefully that they were civil servants with the accent on 'servants'.[17] His method, for instance, of resolving a row between the members of the WECs was threatening a mass sacking if they persisted with their grouses. This threat usually made 'all of them mind their P's and Q's and they did get on together'.[18] To further enhance the optimal functioning of Government at the ground level, Templer instituted a system of 'red minutes', which replaced the old system of filing. These were delivered by despatch rider to SWECs and DWECs when Templer wanted action on some especially urgent matter. The contents of these minutes were in red transcript, were numbered and at the bottom of each sheet the words 'An answer is required by ... days' were printed.[19] If a reply did not come, a reminder was sent, which usually settled the matter. Although the contents of the red minutes were known only to the recipient, Templer and three or four of his staff, the contents usually leaked out and acted as a 'deterrent' to 'sloth'. Templer later felt that the system 'worked a charm' and helped rectify an 'immense number of things which were wrong on the ground level'.[20]

But Templer's 'electrifying' of Government and the Security Forces did not represent simply a severe cracking of the whip. As Chinese Affairs officer J.D.H. Neill noted, Templer was always 'more than just a soldier with full powers from Churchill'.[21] Taking a leaf from his mentor Montgomery, Templer felt that the entire machine, from senior civil servants to the lowest Special Constable, must experience the impact of his personality.[22] Templer thus set about to dominate Government *morally*. Certainly, his physical mannerisms created an immediate impression. Templer projected an air of nervous energy, spoke with 'a rasping, acid voice' and had the habit of jabbing people in the stomach with his cane when he spoke to them.[23] Many were 'awfully frightened' of him.[24] However, it soon became clear that Templer also had an infectious enthusiasm and sense of fun: after having served two and a half years as Singapore Governor Gimson's Private Secretary, Gorrie was quite keen to get out to the rural areas and work with ordinary Malayans. However Templer wanted him to work at King's House in Kuala Lumpur as his Private Secretary. Because nobody dared tell Templer that Gorrie was not keen on working for him, he had to tell the man himself. When the nervous Gorrie met Templer in the Selangor Secretariat in early 1952, he started off by saying how honoured he was to be asked to work for the High Commissioner, to which Templer replied: 'Balls!' – but with a twinkle in his eye. Templer then accepted Gorrie's explanation and asked him to recommend someone else instead![25] For his part, Sheppard recalled being overwhelmed by Templer's 'electric personality', 'tremendous drive' and his 'great charm'.[26] After his first meeting with the High Commissioner, he returned to Seremban 'feeling like an electric torch' which had just been 'filled with new batteries'.[27] Significantly, Templer was also man enough to apologise to subordinates if he thought that he had treated them unfairly or if he had been mistaken on some matter. People remembered this.[28]

Completing the complex admixture that was Templer's magnetic personal aura was his obviously clear and quick mind. W.C.S Corry, the respected British Adviser to Pahang from 1949 to 1953, recalled that Templer grasped the complex situation in Malaya, its constitution and politics with 'incredible speed', and his speeches to the Legislative Council 'revealed a clarity of thought and a knowledge of detail which were outstanding'.[29] Indeed, after 'one such exposition to the heads of all Government Departments', a colleague told Commissioner of Police Arthur Young that he had 'no idea a General could talk so lucidly – somehow one expects a soldier to be dumb'.[30] Yet another MCS officer, John Loch, recalled that Templer's immense confidence was derived from an obviously 'constant and infallible intellectual process'.[31] Templer thus knew – and quickly projected that he knew – what he was about, and this quickly created confidence in Government circles. No surprise then that O.W. Wolters, a Chinese Affairs man who was to direct Government Psychological Warfare between 1955 and 1956, declared that he had 'never met a more effective and admirable leader than Templer'.[32] Hence, as early as June 1952, it was clear that Templer had somehow succeeded in 'electrifying a highly insulated and inert mass',[33] while the *Economist* reported a month later that there was a new air of resolution in Kuala Lumpur and that plans being considered for months had taken shape 'almost overnight'.[34] Lloyd Owen felt that on the whole, Government at all levels had been infused by Templer's 'infectious and confident determination to win' and his 'facility for making large difficulties seem mere stumbling blocks'.[35] Government, in other words, had been 'electrified'.

Templer also set about dominating the public. Peter Lucy, a European planter, felt that he 'was a man who gave confidence at once'.[36] The educated public aside, Templer 'very quickly appreciated that the only thing to do is to try and get the ordinary people on the side of Government'.[37] That is why he very early on campaigned against racist attitudes. He thus launched a tirade against the Lake Club in Kuala Lumpur for failing to invite the Sultan of Selangor to a St George's Day party, because he was Asian. Templer was especially livid since the Sultan was *Patron* of the Society as well as the Club's landlord. Following his threat to close the Club, the Committee resigned en masse and a new one introduced multi-racial membership from August.[38] Moreover, Templer, like Briggs, recognised that it was the rural Chinese especially whose confidence Government had to secure. Thus he declared in a speech to the Chinese Chambers of Commerce that 'by enlisting the support of the Chinese villagers we would solve not one-sixth of the Chinese problem in this country, we would solve at least half of it'.[39] In saying this Templer underscored that while efforts were made to forge a united Malayan nation in preparation for *Merdeka*, attention should also be paid to delivering the rural Chinese from the more immediate threats of Communist terror and poverty. Templer understood completely that without rural Chinese confidence in particular there would be no information flow on terrorist movements which the Security Forces needed. As he told a gathering of Government servants:[40]

> You cannot win this battle ... without information. The people who can give you that information are the ordinary simple people. They refuse to give you that information in more cases than not because they do not see that you are winning... It is this confidence that is needed.

To secure rural Chinese confidence, Templer embarked on a series of whirlwind tours of the rural areas which were intended to show that[41]

> Government extended right down the line into the lives of the simple people, and that Government – which on those occasions were represented by me – always kept its word when it made a promise.

One promise which Templer was keen to keep was Government's assurance of physical security for the Chinese. Apart from strengthening the security of the New Villages (see below), Templer – 'very conscious of his propaganda impact' and seeking to be 'feared and respected'[42] – deliberately projected the image of power. His numerous personal visits[43] to the rural areas were thus a propaganda exercise of the first order. Although his was a civilian appointment, he wore his uniform and travelled in a Humber armoured car or Churchill bullet-proof car, followed by a strong Army escort. When he travelled by train the convoy consisted of the pilot train, the main armoured train and then two armoured cars on rails. Armed troops were ubiquitous. When he visited Broga, Selangor, in July 1952, for instance, he rode into the village escorted by a strong force of armoured cars, stopped in the centre of the market place, put his hands on his hips and summoned the Village Committee, which 'came running' with 'hundreds of villagers looking on'. Templer's party included the Mentri Besar, British Adviser, Chief Police Officer, State SCA and the Commander 18 Brigade. Templer's cavalcades thus 'made an impressive sight which was long remembered with awe by the people in the communities he visited'.[44] At the same time, however, Templer wanted to impress upon the common Chinese that Government was not a Tormentor but a Provider, a Friend. This was the critical difference between Templer and Gurney. On a visit to a rubber estate, for instance, the latter would 'always pay particular attention to the Special Constables and wire fences', while 'Sir Gerald on the other hand, always made a bee-line for the estate labour lines to chat with the labourers and pick up some bouncing baby in his arms'.[45] Templer was in effect *campaigning* amongst the rural Chinese to win their confidence, and his sheer personal impact went some way in bridging the Government-rural Chinese gap. As Perry Robinson recalls:[46]

> [Templer] would stride rapidly from place to place, looking into their shops, their houses, their gardens... Then he would talk to the villagers – his cap on the back of his head, his hands on his hips – in that clipped harsh voice that could be so frightening (or so exhilarating). As they listened to him, there would come a suggestion on their impassive faces that here was a man to whom it might be well to accord respect, even at some future date a measure of trust.

Templer's sheer personal presence thus represented powerful propaganda which helped improve rural Chinese attitudes toward that Government. Hence as early as September 1952, Leslie Hoffman of the *Straits Times* noted that Templer had 'engendered a new spirit' amongst not only planters, Government servants and urban people but also in the New Villages, old kampongs and regrouped labour lines. Hence it was 'no longer unusual to see the people in the little towns and villages line the roadside and wave at the familiar convoy'. He added that 'more than just respect for higher authority', this signified 'that the unnamed fear of Communist reprisals [was] beginning to be replaced with a new confidence'.[47] Templer's personal impact as the ubiquitous '*Tuan* Governor',[48] however, had to be consolidated up by more 'materialistic' propaganda.

THE PROPAGANDA IMPACT OF THE NEW VILLAGES

One of Templer's first acts as High Commissioner evinced his sensitivity to the propaganda implications of official Government terminology. He thus decreed that the Resettlement Areas be renamed 'New Villages'.[49] By the time he arrived, resettlement had progressed some distance. Up to the end of March 1952, 423,000 rural folk had been resettled into 410 New Villages at a cost of $41 million. 85 percent of these people were Chinese.[50] This is not the place to go into great detail on the development of the New Villages, a subject which has been extensively studied.[51] From a propaganda perspective, however, the main issues confronting Templer were the security and quality of life in the New Villages. These values had not always been upheld. Some of the Villages were not sited near enough to cultivable ground, or they were too distant from lines of communication and thus exposed to terrorist intimidation. In addition, the houses in the early Villages were packed so close together as to create a 'concentration camp' feeling.[52] Furthermore, they lacked proper perimeter wire and the standard of protection provided by the Special Constables was generally poor: in Bukit Pisang New Village, for instance, the Special Constable post was situated at the top of a hill, while down below, the 200 huts where the villagers lived were too close to the fence, which was made up of wire hung on rotting poles.[53] Moreover, Government made repeated errors in siting of Resettlement Areas, and the people of Pulai, for instance, were resettled three times.[54]

Templer, like Briggs recognising that resettlement was critical to rural Chinese confidence, took a great personal interest in the New Villages. While he tried to ensure that the physical security of the New Villages was brought up to scratch through the provision of proper perimeter fences,[55] lighting[56] and even electrification of fences,[57] he was especially interested in 'aftercare' activities – that is, the administration of the New Villages.[58] Certainly, by late 1951, it had been recognised in Kuala Lumpur that the Resettlement Areas were 'getting in a mess' and there was a pressing need for cleansing, removal of night soil and other services.[59] Hence a committee had been formed in October 1951 under the chairmanship of the Chief Secretary to oversee the long-term development of the New Villages. Six months later Templer appointed a New Village Liaison Officer who, while responsible to the Deputy Director of Operations for security of the Villages, was also responsible to the Chief Secretary for their administration.[60] Templer knew instinctively that mere reliance on 'bullets and bombs and bayonets' was insufficient to win the confidence of the rural Chinese. Their physical and social needs had to be met as well.[61] The new life simply *had* to be better than the old, and Templer remarked that once the New Villagers set up beauty parlours, he would know that they were settled.[62]

The first way to give the former squatters physical security was to root them in their new surroundings. By 1953, therefore, it was policy that families of wage-earners on estates and mines be given a half-acre plot of land for cultivation, while families in purely agricultural villages be provided at least three acres and if possible five acres.[63] In addition, the villagers were now made aware of their opportunities to own land. By November 1952, Templer was able to report that State Governments had formulated land policies and enacted legislation to make land alienation a simpler process. Thus Penang offered 33-year leases, while Selangor, Perlis and Kedah offered 30-year titles.[64] By January 1953, therefore, 6,324 applications for land had been received from the New Villagers and 3,208 had been approved.[65] However, villagers were initially slow to take up the land titles because of the traditional suspicion of Government as well as Communist pressure.[66] Still, a start had been made.

Templer also formulated a checklist of criteria to measure the quality of life within the New Villages. These criteria included a reasonably adequate water supply; a school to accommodate most children in the Village, as well as adequate teachers' quarters; a Village community centre equipped with a Community Listening set, pictorial literature supplied by the Department of Information, a table tennis table, basketball court, and canteen selling items at controlled prices;[67] places of worship; good roads with side drains; trees along main streets and round the *padang* (field) and school; and reasonable conditions of sanitation and public health.[68] Of particular interest was the provision of schools and public health facilities. By the end of 1953, about 430 schools were built in the New Villages and extensions to about 70 schools completed, while 60 St John's Ambulance Brigade, British and Australian Red Cross relief teams as well as 100 Christian missionary workers were providing medical services.[69] In short, the New Village aftercare programme was nothing less than a mass exercise in propaganda of the deed. This was not lost on contemporary observers like Yong Shook Lin of the MCA. As he told his colleague Leong Yew Koh, 'welfare work amongst the masses' was 'realistic or materialistic propaganda', which he considered the 'best form of propaganda' and superior to 'talks', 'speeches' and 'pamphlets'.[70]

But just how effective was this exercise in 'materialistic propaganda'? Despite the improvements Templer wrought, there were still problems. There were grumbles that alienated land was poor, and 30 years was too short a lease, for example. Some villagers in Kedah even refused to pay the fees for the titles.[71] The biggest complaint of all, however, was life under the irksome Emergency Regulations. The average Chinese tapper left for work at dawn, after queuing up to be body-searched by the suspicious Malay Special Constables at the gates to ensure that the only nourishment he brought out was unsweetened tea – which meant he was hungry at work. Moreover, if he joined the queue late, he reached his smallholding late, which meant he tapped less rubber and earned less money. Also, because of the Emergency curfews, he had to leave the rubber plantation by 1615 hours, be within the New Village perimeter by 1900 hours and indoors from 2300 till 0500 hours the following morning. Moreover, in tandem with local Security Force operations rice rationing was implemented as well: three katis per week for adult males, 2.5 for women and 1.5 for children. In short, life was utterly regimented. Nevertheless, as John Davis observed, security *had* improved: although there was still the danger of being accosted by the terrorists when one was at work during the day, within the New Villages 'at least you could sleep well at night, and you leave your children at home comfortably'.[72] Physical security aside, the rural Chinese could also see other benefits: schools for their children, shops, meeting halls, temples, and most of all, land. It was not perfect, but it was better than anything they had ever had before.[73] In short, the New Villages, at least by late 1952, were beginning to offer physical security and welfare. By April 1953, moreover, while $26,248,000 had been spent on resettlement and regrouping, some $3,917,000 had gone into the provision of 'aftercare' services like education, medical facilities and agricultural development.[74]

Templer also rationalised the Home Guard scheme: he appointed an Inspector-General to be in charge of organisation and training but not operations. This officer supervised State Home Guard Officers and Home Guard inspectors who were responsible for training. The DO was given command of the Home Guard in his jurisdiction. By the end of 1953, the Chinese Home Guard was fully responsible for the defence of 72 New Villages. In Perak's Kinta Valley, in particular, Templer substituted a fully Chinese Home Guard for the Malay Special Constables in the defence of the tin mines, which were largely Chinese-owned. This was intended to make propaganda capital.[75] Another addition to life in the New Villages were local elections. When the New Villages were first set up, local village committees were nominated by the ROs and DOs to act as representatives of the villagers and serve as a channel between them and Government. In May 1952, Templer pushed through the Local Councils Ordinance which called for elected Village Councils. DOs and CAOs prepared the villagers for elections and assisted thereafter in Council meetings, which included the local ARO and a Police representative. By July 1952, there were 200 Village Councils in existence. The Village Councils did not have a great deal of power, however. They could collect taxes on residences only and mainly dealt with household registration, social welfare and sanitary works. Licence fees and taxes on established shopkeepers continued to go to the District Office.[76]

It is argued here that rather than the Home Guard and local elections, the true propaganda benefit of the New Villages was that it brought the rural Chinese into closer contact with Government and its representatives than before. In other words, the Chinese were able to build ties with new *Taijins*. Thus, although the Chinese had complaints, as Davis noted, 'all administration is built on complaints' anyway,[77] and what was really important was that – although there were still Communist Cells in the New Villages – the villagers were gradually *bringing their problems not to the Communists but to the agents of Government*. As Datin Jean Marshall, a Red Cross administrator in 1953 and 1954, observed, the New Villagers 'were glad to have people around who brought their needs to the notice of the authorities'.[78] These 'people' in 1952 included 55 ROs – 15 locals and 40 overseas Chinese-speaking personnel. In addition, in March 1952 all States were informed that Government must have 'more personal and constant contact with the people' through 'the employment of adequate Chinese field staff'.[79] Hence, by January 1953, 330 AROs were distributed throughout the Villages – which by April 1953 had risen in number to 509, and housed 461,822 people. A training school was also established at Taiping to train AROs to administer the New Villages. Interestingly, Gorrie feels that the AROs, who actually lived in the New Villages, were very important and never received the recognition they deserved.[80] Loh also suggests that AROs were the most important officials linking the rural Chinese and Government.[81] On the other hand, some State SCAs – who by early 1952 were members of SWECs and State Executive Councils – were positively 'adored' by the rural Chinese. Noel Alexander, for instance, was able to reduce them frequently to 'fits of laughter'. Other State SCAs liked and respected by the Chinese included Adrian Alabaster and Gerald Jolleye. In fact so popular was the latter that when he was accidentally murdered by the terrorists, the MCP was 'horrified'.[82] In like vein, Gorrie himself was a popular DO Kajang, Selangor, partly because he adopted a Chinese boy as his son. Thus MCP terrorists dared not harm him for fear of alienating the Kajang Chinese.[83] State SCAs continued to be assisted by Chinese CAOs and ACAOs at District level. By April 1953, 42 CAOs and 31 ACAOs were employed.[84] CAOs and ACAOs, although increasingly accepted as 'part and parcel' of District administration by the States, were however hampered by insufficient status and uncertainty as to their relationship to DOs and AROs.[85]

Because of the sheer size of the task of reaching out to the Chinese New Villagers, moreover, Government appealed to other organisations to come in and help. The MCA between 1950 and 1953 raised $4 million for New Village projects, which was used, *inter alia*, to finance the construction of school buildings, community halls, and playing fields. However, it failed to establish deep personal contact with the villagers.[86] More 'prominent' non-Government *Taijins* were the Red Cross, St John's Ambulance and Christian missionaries. These workers provided services such as clinics, adult literacy classes and vocational training.[87] So 'popular' and 'appreciated' were the Red Cross 'Misses' amongst the New Villagers, that the terrorists never ever 'shot up' any familiar white Red Cross vehicle for fear of incurring the opprobrium of the rural Chinese.[88] In sum, the work of the pre-war Chinese Protectorate was being resurrected in the New Villages by a host of new Government and non-Government *Taijins*. These discernibly raised Government's stock with the rural Chinese.

OPERATION SERVICE AND THE AGENTS OF GOVERNMENT

C.C. Too observed that:

> Without a fairly effective police system and without a fairly effective civil service, you cannot ... gain public confidence that the government is a good one which is working for the benefit of the people, and not as the communists say, oppressors and so on and so forth.

Too reiterated that people needed to regard the Police and administrators with respect as 'the properly accredited representatives of law and order. That is pretty basic'.[89] By 1952, however, it was increasingly obvious that the prevailing attitudes of the Malayan Police were a real obstacle to closer Government-Chinese relations. A major problem was that the entire force was geared toward 'anti-bandit operations' and not civil policing.[90] Hence a multitude of paramilitary Police formations abounded: by the third quarter of 1953 there operated 7 Police Field Forces of 69 platoons for framework operations on the Thai border, while Special Constables were re-organised into 876 Area Security Units to 'dominate' the populated areas. In addition, in May 1954 selected volunteers from the regular Police and the Specials were organised into Police Special Squads for operations against terrorists on the jungle fringes.[91] Overlaying the Policeman's military mindset, moreover, was continuing stereotyping of the rural Chinese. Because all Chinese were regarded as potential Communists, the Malay Police and European Lieutenants 'adopted a hostile attitude' toward them.[92] Moreover, the heavily guarded Police Stations overwhelmed most ordinary Chinese, while Special Constables appeared to be 'wired into New Village police posts', quite cut off from the Chinese they were supposed to be protecting.[93] Fear of the Police was supplemented by disgust. In Muar, Johore for instance, the ordinary Chinese were angry that local Police seemed to prefer penalising the Chinese for minor offences instead of defending them against the terrorists. It was thus suspected that the Police were either afraid of, or had come to terms with, the terrorists.[94] Templer recognised that to many people the Malayan Policeman was a 'bogey-man'.[95]

An attempt to rectify this state of affairs was made by new Police Commissioner Colonel Arthur Edwin Young of the City of London Police, who arrived in Kuala Lumpur on 21 February 1952. Young was a highly regarded officer who had served with distinction in the Gold Coast until December 1951.[96] Like Templer, Young travelled all over Malaya, meeting the highest to lowest ranks of the Police, and like the High Commissioner, greatly impressed his subordinates. A senior Malayan Policeman recalled that Young exuded confidence, restored morale and cemented the components of the fractured Federation Police together.[97] More significantly, apart from improving Police administration at all levels,[98] Young also brought with him a philosophy of policing which was to enable the Malayan Police to transform its relations with the public.

Declaring that essentially 'the police must be part of the people and the people part of the police', Young felt that the tasks of every Policeman were two-fold: to prevent crime and prosecute actual offenders. What is more, the Police must never carry out these tasks by resorting to too much force, otherwise it would become a quasi military body acting in units rather than individuals exercising judgement.[99] This then was the key difference between the Policeman and the soldier – while the former sought to root out the individual offender from amongst the larger community, the latter tended to impact the community as a whole through curfews and other communal restrictions that fell on 'friend and foe alike'. The latter approach thus jeopardised the 'public regard and public confidence upon which the Police essentially depend for their effectiveness'.[100] In the face of a terrorist threat, therefore, Young felt that the way to apply discriminate force so as to eliminate terrorists without harming the public, was to build sound relations with the community. This would start an information flow which would answer the following basic questions of Police intelligence, as put forth by the Police jurist:[101]

What was the crime, who did it, when was it done and where? How done and with what motive, who in deed did share?

It is clear that Young was sensitive to the propaganda implications of sound Police procedure as opposed to the quasi-military approach. As he argued, while the soldier was taught to make up his mind fast, and a wrong decision was better than none at all, the Policeman on the other hand had to take his time to make up his mind, 'because the important thing wherever the law is involved is to be right from the start'.[102] The Policeman had to be right from the start if he was to apply the full force of the law only against the criminal and not the innocent wider community. And in order to be right from the start meant that he had to possess expertise. Hence Young felt that 'instead of getting bigger the Malayan police must get better' and an enormous retraining programme was undertaken with the aim of ensuring that by June 1953 every Policeman in Malaya was trained.[103]

The retraining programme was inaugurated in June 1952.[104] By July 1953, the Special Constable training system was in place, including a two-month recruit training course at Tanjong Kling and a two-week refresher course for Specials at new Federal Area Training Schools. Moreover, the Police Depot and Setapak Sub-Depot were conducting eight-month regular Police recruit courses, while regular Police refresher courses started the following month. Altogether 60,000 regular Police and Special Constables were retrained under the watchful eye of former Chief Police Officer Perak, J.N.D. Harrison.[105] A Federal Police College with a capacity of 140 was also established the same year at Kuala Kubu Bahru to provide 'comprehensive basic training' and promote *esprit de corps* amongst gazetted officers.[106] In addition, Templer and Young tried to increase the proportion of Chinese Police recruits in order to improve relations with the rural Chinese. Templer secured MCA support in increasing Chinese recruitment, but this was not very successful. The problem continued to be deep-rooted Chinese attitudes towards men in uniform. In Selangor, for instance, a New Village headman proclaimed that 'We Hokkiens were never policemen in China'.[107] Thus while in November 1952, there were 602 Chinese out of 2,339 recruits at the Police Depot (about 26 percent), in April 1953 there were only 331 Chinese out of 2,235 recruits (about 15 percent).[108] At any rate, many of the 1,410 Chinese who did join the Police rank and file in November 1953 were consciously put in uniform to be seen by the Chinese public.[109] If Government could not get enough Chinese Police, Chinese-speaking European Police were the next best option. In May 1952, there were 42 European Police officers who could speak Chinese, but more were needed.[110] In this context the Chinese language course at Cameron Highlands continued to be useful. The second course started in the month Templer arrived and involved 16 officers learning Cantonese and Hokkien.[111] At the end of this course, the school was moved to Kuala Lumpur and housed in a Chinese temple, with Robert Bruce of the British Council taking charge. The third course involving 30 officers started in August 1952, and in April 1953 Bruce added Hakka and Kuo Yu to the curriculum.[112]

Although a crash retraining programme did increase Police profession-alism, Young felt that in the circumstances of the Emergency, this alone was insufficient to close the Police-Chinese gap. Extraordinary measures were instead required to help the Malayan Police achieve in months what the London Police took 100 years to secure with its public.[113] In this context he recalled watching the *Wizard of Oz* in which a dejected lion was transformed into a brave one by being awarded a medal for courage. He felt that this 'symbolisation' offered 'the prospect of a successful public campaign'. Hence, without consulting his senior officers, he committed them and the entire Malayan Police to a six-month campaign of seeking every opportunity, big or small, to demonstrate that they were in fact friends of the people. Young thus sent a letter to every member of the Force informing them that their promotion prospects would henceforth depend not merely on the performance of routine tasks but also their 'relationship with and attitude to the public'.[114] Operation Service was thereby launched on 15 December 1952 via press and radio.[115] Like the lion in the *Wizard of Oz*, every Policeman was issued a small oval badge showing clasped hands. The idea behind the 'psychological label' of the badge was that the

> policeman looked down at his arm and said, "That's me, I'm the friend of the public". And the public speaking to the policeman – the first thing they saw was his badge on his arm and said, "He is my friend".[116]

Young did not stop there. He looked around for other symbols to capture the public's imagination. He was attracted by the Scout motto 'Be Prepared' and the Rotary Club slogan 'Service above Self' and decided that the Operation Service equivalent should be 'Ready to Serve' or *Bersedia Berkhidmat* in Malay. Moreover, a new 'stirring Police March' was composed.[117] The Police seemed enthusiastic enough: in the first month about 10,000 'deeds of service' were recorded and subsequently the rate was 20,000 per month. These deeds included summoning a doctor for a member of the public and giving information on the functions of Government. Moreover, local Police visited schools to tell children that they were their friends, while Young hoped that the public would regard Police Stations as places not to 'get into but to get out of trouble'.[118] Templer even broadcast in January 1953 that henceforth Police Stations would no longer be called *rumah pasong* (house of incarceration) but rather *balai polis* (house of the Police). The same month Operation Service was extended from Federal level to the States as well.[119]

To what extent was Operation Service successful in transforming Police-public and in particular Police-Chinese relations? A Malayan whose views Templer valued declared that it was the 'best and most important thing' Government had attempted in the last few years.[120] On the other hand, John Gullick still considers it a public relations gimmick.[121] Lyttelton, however, although initially thinking that it was a 'gimmick', later came to realise that it was rather important, particularly in the context of Malay-Chinese relations:[122]

> There was a policeman who had mended a Chinese woman's tyres, or delivered the baby when there was no midwife – and it became a sort of game amongst the police, it looked a bit gimmicky but it wasn't.

Nevertheless, while there probably were scattered instances as described by Lyttelton, in general it cannot be claimed that Operation Service swung rural Chinese opinion solidly behind the Police. As late as June 1954 a Government study cautioned that it was too early to expect marked changes in the levels of Chinese confidence in the Police, as the scars of arrests and banishments in 1948 and 1949 had yet to heal fully.[123] Nevertheless, Operation Service was a positive step, because it coincided with and gave formal expression to a year-long soul-searching within Government over the need to recondition general attitudes toward the rural Chinese. In July 1952 for instance one observer noted that not only the Police but all Government servants needed to engage in the 'personal approach' toward 'the people in the New Villages and the kampongs', so as to win their 'confidence'.[124] The following month, moreover, the incoming Director-General Information Services Alec Peterson, recommended that *all* Government Departments had to become more 'propaganda-minded' in order to 'win the confidence' of the public.[125] In October Templer told a gathering of Division III officers:[126]

> You people in this room represent ... the sharp end [of Government] who meet the public... Be civil to them, be thoughtful to them, be helpful to them, when you meet them out in the field or when they come and see you in your office.

After Operation Service was launched by the Police in December 1952, Templer extended it to other branches of Government in January.[127] The next month, moreover, Templer urged a group of European civil servants to do their best to 'spread the spirit of Operation Service', and ensure that relations between Government and the public were much more 'friendly and trustful than they have been in the past'.[128] The Post Office thus launched Operation Courtesy and the Medical Department made preparations for its own campaign as well.[129]

While Templer was getting Government psychologically attuned to the idea of making Operation Service a way of life, the armed services also appeared to respond to it. Thus, Army units adopted New Villages on a company basis and helped organise sporting and social events, while Templer himself saw a National Serviceman giving advice to a New Village Council on local drainage problems. Moreover, RAF and Royal Navy helicopters where possible airlifted sick villagers to hospital.[130] Nevertheless, although a report on the Army in Malaya claimed that soldiers enjoyed exercising 'moral leadership'[131] amongst the ordinary folk of Malaya, there were hints that this was not always the case. Hence as late as June 1953 women tappers on an estate in north Johore laid themselves off because of the 'amorous advances' of Fijian troops.[132] Furthermore, the semi-fictional book *Jungle Green*, written by Major Arthur Campbell and based on his experiences as a company commander in Malaya, described the rural Chinese as a 'bastard Chink' and asserted that the way to end the Emergency was by sending 'these Chinks back to where they came from'. Templer carelessly described the book as 'authentic', and was promptly savaged by Victor Purcell.[133] Templer's view was that the British soldier 'does use expressions like this about pretty well everyone'.[134] Nevertheless, it must be said that in this case he may have allowed his intense dislike of Victor Purcell – 'that disgusting creature'[135] – to colour his better judgement.[136] Purcell may have taken wild swipes at Templer,[137] but at least on this issue – the racist baggage of some British soldiers – he appeared to be spot on. While it was the view of Vernon Bartlett, a Templer supporter, that after all, the MCP was Chinese and the British soldier was not unusual in using 'uncomplimentary adjectives about his enemies',[138] Purcell's point was that the book revealed that the Army did not seem to *differentiate* between the terrorists and the mass of the Chinese in Malaya.[139] Templer perhaps should have taken Purcell more seriously and clamped down on any such attitudes throughout the Army. Because he dismissed Purcell out of hand, however, some units lagged behind the rest of Government in re-orientating attitudes toward the Chinese. Thus M. Harvey, recalling his experiences with the Malay Regiment as late as 1954, noted that the British Army, well-conditioned by its imperial experience, tended to ask for 'one-sided co-operation' and to resort to 'a formal distribution of medical supplies' at best and 'plain intimidation' at worst to get that co-operation. Harvey felt that more effort should be made to emulate the work of the Police in Operation Service, and that 'good faith shown in deeds' was what the Army needed to win the 'friendship and confidence' of the rural people.[140] At any rate, the Templer-Young era could be characterised as the period when the Malayan Police experienced a 'renaissance'[141] which restored morale and enhanced professionalism, while Operation Service inaugurated the process – on the part of Government officers generally – of internalising a new attitude toward the ordinary Chinese in particular. While it cannot be claimed that Operation Service succeeded in persuading the rural Chinese that Government was their Provider, it certainly began the slow and tortuous process of doing so.

FROM COLLECTIVE DETENTION TO WHITE AREAS

Reconditioning official attitudes to the rural Chinese aside, Government also took steps to ensure that policy communicated the message that Government cared for the rural Chinese. In a memorandum to Templer of 5 February 1953, Young argued that the Emergency Regulations should not be 'applied for a moment longer than they are justified'.[142] The problem was that the Regulations tended to fall hardest on the Chinese, who were subjected to the 'most scrutiny and suspicion'.[143] Particularly onerous were those laws pertaining to detention/deportation and collective punishment. As early as December 1951, Lyttelton had balked at the large numbers of Malayans, especially the Chinese, who were in detention.[144] For instance, in January 1952, there were 3,717 Chinese, 902 Malays and 222 Indians in detention camps under ER 17 (1), and 2 203 Chinese and 11 Indians detained under ER 17D.[145] Moreover, 133 more deportation orders were made the same month, bringing the total number of deportations since the Emergency began to 12,715.[146] The following month, the numbers in detention swelled to 6,483 Chinese, 912 Malays and 300 Indians, while by April, the total number of persons deported since 1948 rose to 13,317.[147]

Templer was worried about these numbers and in April 1952 accepted that there were some innocent people in detention.[148] However, with the winding down of resettlement, the progress of the New Villages and steadily increasing administrative and Police control of the rural areas, Government relied less on the tougher Regulations.[149] Accordingly, the number of Chinese in detention was slashed to 2,790 by September, 2,358 in December, 1,788 by September 1953 and 1 614 three months later.[150] Moreover, the number of all persons detained under the notoriously indiscriminate ER 17D fell drastically from a peak of 2,037 in January 1952 to nil by December 1953.[151] It is highly significant in this respect that only a month after Young's memorandum, Templer cabled Lyttelton with the news that he was abolishing ER 17D. This was done on 17 March.[152] Gann at the Colonial Office observed that the abolition of ER 17D was 'timely' and would have a 'good effect on public opinion while taking only a very small tooth out of the ERs'.[153] It was in the same spirit of seeking ways of winning confidence through easing where possible, the impact of the Emergency Regulations, that Templer approached the entire issue of ER 17DA – collective punishment. However this was *not* the case when he first arrived in the country. Because he appreciated that he needed to 'show to the people of Malaya on all levels that Government was prepared to do something', he considered Tanjong Malim as 'just such an opportunity' to do this.[154]

The Tanjong Malim affair is a notorious aspect of Templer folklore and the precise details need not detain us here. Suffice to say that following the ambush and murder of an Assistant District Officer and his party on 25 March 1952, and the unwillingness of the Selangor town of Tanjong Malim to provide information to the Police on the identities and whereabouts of the terrorists, Templer imposed a 22-hour curfew and reduced the rice ration from five katis per head per week to three katis for adults and two and a half for children.[155] Accounts of Templer at Tanjong Malim paint him as brutally tough.[156] But the episode was above all a 'publicity stunt', and it was later admitted that Templer's ruthlessness was generally 'intentionally exaggerated in reporting in order to achieve the maximum deterrence with the minimum force'.[157] In fact Templer was equally anxious to try out new ways of assuring ordinary people that there would not be reprisals for giving information to Government. Thus he ordered the Tanjong Malim townsfolk, in the privacy of their homes and away from prying eyes, to fill in confidential questionnaires on what they knew about the terrorists. These were then placed in secure boxes opened by Templer *personally*, a point he wanted emphasised so as to reassure the townsfolk that no one would know what they had written.[158] He later sought feedback as to the efficacy of the questionnaire method and was told that this method, while ensuring confidentiality, was quite useless with Chinese who were illiterate.[159] Templer nevertheless persisted with the questionnaire method, called Operation Question, in other rebellious, largely Chinese villages such as Broga and Jenjarom in Selangor, Dangi in Negri Sembilan and Yong Peng in Johore.[160]

Templer actually endeavoured to be firm yet fair with villages implicated in terrorist incidents. For instance, following the collective punishment of Permatang Tinggi village in Province Wellesley for the murder of a Chinese ARO in August, Malay Police were searched by their superiors before going off duty to check if they had been guilty of theft, while the villagers were asked if they had lost any property. Furthermore, when Templer realised that some Permatang Tinggi villagers had been blackmailed into aiding the MCP and consequently felt too implicated to speak up, he made it clear that henceforth such persons would not be prosecuted if they informed the Police about this.[161] Similarly, when Pekan Jabi New Village was attacked with the collusion of some villagers in October 1952, once more a 22-hour curfew was imposed and rice rations reduced, while Operation Question was conducted. When Police enquiries resulted in the apprehension of a Communist Cell leader, however, Templer lifted sanctions and sent in Department of Information mobile units and the Red Cross more frequently.[162]

Thus Templer was fully aware that collective punishment carried with it potential propaganda pitfalls, and did not need to be told this by horrified observers.[163] He even showed better understanding of the problem than some Colonial Office officials: T.C. Jerrom had earlier suggested that once the High Commissioner considered that a village could not be weaned away from the Communists, it should be punished. Templer's real problem was how to identify and extricate the Communists *from amongst* the villagers.[164] Templer himself later conceded that he had never liked to use collective punishment and found it 'very difficult to estimate' its effectiveness. He added that while on balance, he felt it had done more good than harm, he admitted that he may have well been wrong to have ever resorted to the measure.[165] In fact, it is arguable that he had been feeling this way ever since early 1953, and Young's memorandum may have edged him closer to a decision to do away with it altogether. This he did on 25 November. Although he defended the move publicly as a recognition of the growing 'identity' of interests between the public and Government, he had probably made up his mind privately that ER 17DA was simply bad propaganda. Characteristically, he made capital out of its abolition, declaring that Government was keen to relax Emergency Regulations wherever possible.[166]

In his February 1953 memo Young had also urged that 'white' or 'safe' areas be designated where the security situation was deemed by SWECs to be good enough to reduce or even fully withdraw the resources of Security Forces. This was probably the origin of the White Area concept.[167] In White Areas, all curfews, gate searches and food controls ceased and normal everyday life resumed. Like the abolition of ER 17D and 17DA, and the continuing rehabilitation at Taiping of detainees and by March 1953 even SEPs,[168] White Areas represented an attempt by Government to communicate the idea that it genuinely cared for the people. On 3 September 1953, therefore, following a recommendation by the Resident Commissioner of Malacca, and in view of the relatively improved security situation therein, Templer decided to declare one-third of the State 'White'.[169] This area included 70,000 Chinese as well a 76,000 Malays.[170] It must not be imagined that all Malaccans had mysteriously been transformed into staunch Government supporters. In fact there had been initial opposition within the Malacca SWEC and the DWEC in question to the White Area suggestion, as despite the relative lack of terrorist activity in the Settlement, 'the CTs were receiving support from the rural population in the central district'. However, Brian Stewart, SCA Malacca, argued that 'there might be significant dividends to be gained from pretending that the area's freedom had been earned by co-operation with the government thus encouraging other districts to show more positive co-operation'. Templer, a 'supporter of the "ideas" men in Chinese Affairs', agreed with Stewart's assumptions and 'ruled that the experiment should take place'.[171]

The High Commissioner subsequently ordered the Information Services and the rest of Government to pull out all the stops when it came to publicity for the Malacca White Area. Accordingly, as he was describing the

White Area idea to 400 Malacca leaders in the garden of the Residency as 'one of the greatest advances' since the start of the Emergency, overhead, Voice Aircraft flew over the Area broadcasting Templer's congratulations and exhorting the people to keep the terrorists out. At the same time, Radio Malaya broadcast the news, while Information Services staff issued leaflets with a map of the area as well as the texts of Templer's speech and the announcement by the Resident Commissioner G.E.C. Wisdom. Furthermore, in order to stimulate the covetousness of neighbouring Districts, signs were erected proclaiming boldly: 'You are now entering the Malacca White Area'.[172] In his address to the people of Malacca, moreover, Templer pointedly emphasised that those irksome restrictions they used to grumble about were no more:[173]

> Everyone in this "white area" will be able to take out a proper mid-day meal to their tapping, their padi field or their garden. They can take food in and out of the village without restriction or the need for a permit. No one will be searched for food at the village gates.

Templer also urged the ordinary people to assist the Information Services by spreading the news of the White Area by 'word of mouth' to illiterate folk in the 'kampongs, the old villages, the New Villages, the labour lines, on rubber estates'. While Templer emphasised 'this very genuine attempt on the part of Government to make their lives easier and happier', he simultaneously threatened obliquely to re-impose restrictions if the people failed to use their new freedoms wisely.[174] The impact of the Malacca White Area was 'terrific', according to one observer, recalling driving up from Singapore 'in the dark emptiness, with everyone confined to their houses, and suddenly coming into the liveliness of the White area, with the streets full of people and lights everywhere'.[175] It was acknowledged in official circles in October that the 'psychological effect on the population of severe restrictions followed by their complete removal should not be disregarded'.[176] Templer maintained the propaganda momentum when, the same day he abolished collective punishment, he announced that there was no reason why more White Areas could not be declared throughout Malaya.[177] Sensitive to the propaganda nuances of White Area declarations, he ensured that announcements were always accompanied by carefully orchestrated publicity. For instance, two weeks before he left Malaya, he ordered officials in Johore not to tell anyone of the inauguration of the Mersing White Area. He wanted to leave that to 'the machinery for making this new development known to the people in the way most likely to serve our course best,' and did not want anyone to 'spoil the effect' of the announcement. Similarly, the North Perak White Areas were a 'complete surprise' to the public and civic leaders.[178] The White Area drive thus became the 'wedge' strategy which was to persist even after Templer had left. As Guy Madoc explained:[179]

[As] long as we continued this business of cleaning up a district, granting it "white area freedom", thus stimulating [the] civil population in the next district – "it might be ours next" ... we were sure we were going to win.

Thus, by the time Templer left in May 1954, about 1,314,400 people, including ordinary Chinese, were living in White Areas.[180] In sum, through his sheer personal impact; the consolidation of the New Villages and the creation of new *Taijins* in the form of the ROs, AROs, State SCAs, CAOs and the Red Cross; the inauguration of Operation Service; the abolition of the more draconian Emergency measures and the inauguration of the White Area strategy, Templer unequivocally projected the message that Government was Provider of rural Chinese needs and wants. This more positive Government image, when coupled with conspicuous Security Force success, elicited 'smiles and co-operation'.[181] Winning public confidence however had to be complemented, as Briggs always maintained, by lowering that of the terrorists.

THE IMPROVING ATTACK ON TERRORIST CONFIDENCE

Templer was well aware that psychological methods were needed to undermine terrorist morale and induce surrenders. He gave his 'personal attention', for instance, to a scheme called Operation 'Letter Box', which, *inter alia*, 'was intended to have a psychological impact on the Communist Terrorists (CTs) and make them uncertain as to whether they had been betrayed'. 'Letter Box' involved the despatch of a Government team of Chinese-speaking officers to selected New Villages at dawn, before the night curfew was lifted, so as to interview the villagers on an individual basis and extract from them in a refinement of the method first used at Tanjong Malim – confidential written responses to specially prepared questionnaires. The villagers were asked to 'describe any suspicions they had about terrorist activity in the vicinity and what they had heard of CTs and their supporters and methods in and around the village'. While the villagers were assured that their identities would remain secret, thus preventing the terrorists from knowing who had divulged information about them, this was not the point. As Brian Stewart observed, 'Operation "Letter Box" was more of a *psywar* than an intelligence gathering operation', because the main objective was to 'sow fear and doubt in the minds of the CT sympathisers and to shake the confidence of the CTs themselves in the benevolence of the environment in which they operated'.[182]

Specialised schemes like 'Letter Box' aside, Templer also recognised that well conceived and executed Security Force operations would have a powerful psychological impact on terrorist minds. He thus moved quickly to create an efficient machinery for conducting the war against the MCP. Determined to rid Government of a 'split personality guided by two separate Councils', on 1 March 1952 he abolished the War Council and concentrated its policy responsibilities in the Executive Council.[183] Meanwhile he chaired a Director of Operations Committee to cope with purely operational matters. He also brought in Jack Morton[184] as his Director of Intelligence to co-ordinate all intelligence assets in the Federation through the Federal Intelligence Committee,[185] and very important, split Special Branch from CID. Henceforth, while CID dealt with ordinary crime, the Special Branch focused its energies on 'Emergency crime detection'.[186] Furthermore, it was recognised that Asian officers should spearhead the Special Branch effort,[187] and before the end of 1952 Chinese Special Branch officers were gleaning valuable information in the Districts.[188] To improve Army-Police intelligence processing, moreover, a Special Military Intelligence Staff was created and integrated with Special Branch.[189]

Thus re-organised, Government began to mount Security Force patrols closely co-ordinated with food control, a process called food denial. In contrast to earlier food control schemes which, having been spread too evenly over Malaya, had failed to deal a concentrated blow to local MCP organisations, a food denial operation was targeted at a specific MCP District, and found to be better at clearing the area permanently. Significantly, underlying the food denial concept was an innate appreciation of terrorist psychological vulnerabilities. Hence food denial was premised on creating 'cumulative pressures, both mental and physical, over a period produced by privation, fear and hopelessness.'[190] The first food denial operations were Operation Habitual, conducted between May and August 1952 in Kuantan, and Operation Hive, conducted between August and October 1952 in Seremban. By July 1953, routine food denial operations included Operation Sting in Kuala Kubu Bahru and Operation Hammer II in Kuala Langat.[191] Essentially, a food denial operation began with the gazetting of a Communist District as a food control area in which District officials announced the reduction of rice rations and the removal of all surplus rice. Police enforced the regime through stricter checks on persons moving in and out of New Villages as well as surprise checks on nearby roads. The Security Forces simultaneously mounted protracted patrolling and ambushing operations on the jungle fringe for several months. This activity was needed to isolate the terrorists from their Min Yuen Cells in the New Villages and compel the former to use up their food dumps. Once this stage had been reached, the terrorists simply had to approach the New Villages to restore contact with their supporters, or starve. At this point, Special Branch deliberately weakened controls in one area of the Security Force net – it might have been a small village, or even one section of the village perimeter – where the Communist supporter on his way out to his tapping or cultivation, noticed that the Security Force presence was weaker, or gate searches were less strict. This was the 'honeypot', and word leaked to the terrorists that here was their best chance of making contact and securing supplies. Ambushes were thus laid on in the vicinity of the 'honeypot', and kills resulted. In addition, intensive Security Force patrolling *alone* also kept supporters as well as terrorists hovering on the jungle fringe in 'a state of nerves'. At some point, someone cracked and surrendered. Special Branch then exploited the information provided by these SEPs and more ambushes were laid, more surrenders obtained and the process snowballed.[192]

Templer had to ensure that the Security Forces played their part in the food denial strategy. First he brought in General Hugh Stockwell as GOC to prevent the Army from getting 'stagnant'.[193] In addition, after helicopters proved their worth for increasing troop mobility in 1952, they were quickly integrated into operations.[194] 'Weekly Intelligence Summaries' were also circulated internally to increase the collective wisdom on dealing with the MRLA. For instance, one Summary advised troops that cigarette packets, butt ends, food wrappers, talking, coughing, the scent of shaving soap and hair dressing, would all give their presence away to the terrorists. If they had to smoke, they should use the *Rough Rider* brand which terrorists liked. Another Summary advised that when attacking, shouting in Malay to terrorists to surrender might have some effect, while continuous mortaring, shelling or sporadic rifle fire would make the terrorists 'restless and sleepless'.[195] Templer also commissioned Lieutenant-Colonel Walker, who had trained Ferret Force, to write up a 'bible' for all troops in Malaya, the *Anti-Terrorist Operations Manual* (*ATOM*) in which was reposed the accumulated experience of jungle warfare. An Operational Research Section was also set up to study operational effectiveness with scientific rigour.[196] Marksmanship, so critical in jungle warfare where terrorist targets appeared for fleeting seconds, was emphasised and encouraged through inter-unit competitions.[197]

Moreover, in May 1953, 180 SEPs were organised into 12 15-man platoons – the so-called Special Operations Volunteer Force (SOVF). This was regarded as one of the 'most potent propaganda weapons' capable of 'inducing further surrenders of terrorists'.[198] Controlled by Special Branch and led by British Police Lieutenants, the extremely fit SOVF units mirrored terrorist units in dress, traits, weapons and tactics, and were usually deployed around villages. The MCP was only too conscious of the SOVF's existence.[199] While some observers did not think highly of the unit as an offensive force, it did score some tactical successes: for instance in Malacca, a SOVF patrol in Jasin District, acting on information, contacted five terrorists and killed two.[200] In addition, the RAF began to operate far more effectively in the Templer era. This was due in the first place to better liaison at all levels through the posting of an RAF officer to the Combined Emergency Planning Staff (CEPS), Federal Police Headquarters, the

Combined Operations Room and every SWEC operational subcommittee.[201] Furthermore, by May 1953, the RAF ceased its mass jungle bombing operations, and its offensive support operations henceforth consisted instead of harassing attacks based on 'sure information' that terrorists were in the area,[202] air strikes against definite targets with ground force follow-up,[203] and Voice Aircraft operations.[204] Moreover, in December the RAF geared itself decisively toward increasing ground force efficiency, by stipulating that its chief roles henceforth would be supply dropping, troop lift, communication flying and casualty evacuation.[205] By late 1953, therefore, simplistic assumptions about the 'insidious moral effect' of bombing 'semi-civilised' rebels had been ejected.

The cumulative impact of these efforts was significant. A study in 1953 of the psychological impact of Security Force pressure on 23 SEPs found that 'successive ground force attacks' were mentioned as 'lowering morale and leading to thoughts of surrender and among immediate reasons for surrender'.[206] Interestingly, the terrorists feared the Bren gun, regarding it as the 'most effective or dangerous weapon' used by the Security Forces.[207] In addition, from late 1952, the food supply situation became untenable: for example in September Negri Sembilan SEPs reported that the MRLA 5th Independent Platoon had broken down to section strength and was operating closely with the Min Yuen. Because of 'rapidly diminishing food dumps', the diet of the terrorists included 'boiled rubber leaves'.[208] In fact, incessant Security Force pressure compelled the terrorists to 'cease dependence on the masses for food supplies' and to rely more on food cultivation with the help of the aborigines in the deep jungle.[209] Hence, by mid-1953 deep jungle cultivation, which was only supposed to supplement food gathering by the Min Yuen, became more important.[210] This emphasis on food collection meant that there was a marked decrease in terrorist activity into 1953 and beyond: in October 1953, on interrogation the largest percentage of 54 SEPs (29 percent) gave 'food shortage' as the reason for the relative terrorist inactivity.[211] Moreover, while many terrorists who had surrendered in the first five years of the Emergency explained that they had given up because of dislike of their leaders and disagreement with their policy, throughout 1953, food shortage and Security Force pressure became gradually more important reasons for surrender.[212] The MCP thus began to complain that 'unsteady and feeble-minded elements who cannot stand hardship' were surrendering 'in many places'.[213] Thus, by May 1954, thanks to the impetus supplied by Templer and his associates, co-ordinated food control and protracted Security Force patrolling were beginning to communicate futility to the terrorist rank and file. The Operational Research Section therefore recommended that Government continue efforts with tightening food control and maintaining Security Force pressure, while urging that propaganda of words be employed to 'exploit' the psychological effect of such deeds.[214]

A.D.C. PETERSON AND THE BIRTH OF 'INFORMATION SERVICES'

Templer was in no doubt as to the importance of propaganda of the visual, spoken and written word in exploiting and publicising widely Government's deeds. Arguing that 'everything the Government does is intended for the benefit of the people', he emphasised that 'unless they know we are doing it and can take advantage of it, the whole point of it is lost'.[215] He thus regarded the strengthening of Government Information as one of his top priorities.[216] Following Greene's departure in September 1951, Eliot Watrous acted as Head Emergency Information Services (HEIS) until December. The following month A.W.D. James, who had been State SCA as well as State Emergency Information Officer (SEIO) Negri Sembilan, became Head and held the fort until October 1952. Meanwhile, J.N. McHugh continued as Head of the Department of Information until October as well.[217] Under James, EIS continued along the lines Greene had laid down, especially the exploitation of SEPs for propaganda purposes. For instance, SEPs were allowed to enter eating and drinking houses unaccompanied to talk about their experiences and contrast Government's fairness with so-called MCP 'justice'. In this respect SEPs like Ho Kei proved 'very forceful and influential' speakers. SEIOs observed in early 1952 that even if SEPs were not articulate, because they were known to the public, their 'mere presence was of propaganda value'.[218]

SEPs were of 'propaganda value' in the war against the terrorists as well. In March in Bentong, Pahang, two terrorists gave up after watching an SEP show at Sungei Pertang estate. Meanwhile in south Perak, SEP tours were integrated with Security Force operations and SEPs performed nightly in Resettlement Areas before audiences ranging from 200 to 1,400 people. In May, moreover, SEIO Perak formed an SEP drama troupe which performed a sketch called *Bloody Revenge*, dramatising how terrorists were thwarted by the Security Forces acting on information provided by brave villagers. The troupe performed 11 times before a total audience of 15,000 people and was extremely popular.[219] At the same time mobile units exhibiting American entertainment fare like *The Darkest Africa* and stories involving Tarzan, Charlie Chaplin and Laurel and Hardy, were as popular as MFU films with Malay commentaries, although sometimes rural folk got fed up when mobile units repeated the same films.[220] EIS also continued putting out SEP appeals via leaflets and the Community Listening Service to their former comrades to surrender. Certainly, throughout the first months of 1952, Central's concern at the potency of Government propaganda prompted a series of executions to deter potential waverers from escaping.[221] Hence C.C. Too recalled that EIS under James was 'bearing fruit' and functioning efficiently. In particular, desirous of exploiting the psychological moment created by every surrender, EIS would rush out leaflets 'immediately and keep on rolling'.[222] Again, however, the effectiveness of Government leaflets and tours was contingent on the degree to which the message they proclaimed was consistent with that emanating from actual Government performance. Hence, when the clearly positive effect of an SEP tour in Penang in March 1952 was nullified when the terrorists murdered a member of the audience only 30 minutes later, it was conceded: 'This is the problem – we may talk but terrorists' actions are extremely lethal'.[223]

Furthermore, A.D.C. (Alec) Peterson, appointed Director-General Information Services on 8 October 1952,[224] was not as sanguine about the state of Government propaganda of words as Too was. Peterson's family had had long links with Asia, and he had been educated at Radley and Balliol prior to directing black propaganda for Force 136 during the war. He was later Deputy Head of the Far Eastern Publicity Division in Southeast Asia Command, and after the war he had become headmaster of Adams Grammar School in Newport, Shropshire.[225] Actually, Templer had not settled on Peterson immediately. As late as June 1952, he had told the Colonial Office that he was thinking of Lillie-Costello, who was in charge of information work in the Gold Coast. Apparently this fell through, and Templer eventually picked Peterson's name from a list of officers who had worked in Southeast Asia Command. Accordingly in July Peterson was asked to come out and study the state of Government propaganda in Malaya. A month later he concluded that things were amiss, and was persuaded by Templer to stay on and put things right.[226]

As noted, the fundamental problem which Greene had been unable to resolve was the lack of direction and co-ordination, duplication of effort and separate lines of authority afflicting the Emergency Information Services, Department of Information, Malayan Film Unit and Radio Malaya. Second, Peterson did not agree with Greene's approach of allowing considerable latitude to local SEIOs in designing propaganda for their respective States; he was in favour of greater centralised control. Third, he was critical that it had been apparently 'assumed that the duties of State E.I.O.s could be carried out by other European officers on a part-time basis' – a comment not particularly fair to Greene, who had wanted full-time men but could not get them. Fourth, Peterson opined that the existing system made no provision for training of European or Asian staff. Hence some mobile unit Field Officers were apparently merely reading out what they had been told to read. Peterson argued that it was a 'waste of money' to send out 'clerks' who 'do not know what they are supposed to be doing and do not believe what they are supposed to be saying'. Fifth, he noted that the MFU had 'hitherto enjoyed too great a degree of independence', and that neither the 'Department of Information nor E.I.S. has been in a position to influence effectively the Film Unit's production policy'. This meant that not enough MFU films were being shown by the mobile units, which tended to exhibit 'cartoon films and short comedy films from America'. There was a great need for the MFU to increase its output of 'films with a simple message and a Malayan village background'. Sixth, because EIS had also been given the task of press relations, it was being distracted from its primary task of propaganda to the terrorists. Finally, Peterson, somehow overlooking the documentary research work being done by Too, opined that there was no 'planning and intelligence section' at EIS headquarters.[227]

The first thing Peterson therefore recommended was a centralisation of all propaganda assets under a single Director General of Information Services (DGIS). He should oversee a new organisation, the Department of Information Services, formed by fusing the EIS and the Department of Information. The DGIS would be supported by a Deputy Director in charge of administration, finance and training; a Films Officer responsible for ensuring that MFU products reflected Government propaganda themes; a Propaganda Officer tasked with collection and analysis of Communist intelligence, liaison with Government intelligence bodies and the planning and execution of Federation-wide propaganda campaigns against the terrorists; and a Press Officer in charge of issuing Emergency press releases to news organisations.[228] Moreover, at State level, full-time, not part-time, State Information Officers (SIOs) should be appointed to analyse all local intelligence on Communist morale and recruiting, advise SWECs on local propaganda campaigns and liaise with Army, Police and other Government Departments during operations.[229] Peterson also recommended that a propaganda training school be set up to train Asian Field Officers in 'the principles of oral, visual and written propaganda', the 'technique of Field Units – organisation of plays, meetings, film shows' and 'educational courses', as well as propaganda intelligence – 'the gauging of enemy propaganda and public reaction'.[230] Templer accepted these proposals. Hence Peterson as noted became DGIS in October 1952, and McHugh Deputy DGIS, although he left for the private sector and was replaced by the Malay Yaacob bin Latiff in December.[231] A.W.D. James, Head EIS, was posted to the Malayan Establishment Office as Deputy Malayan Establishment Officer. James was 'disappointed' at the transfer.[232] Major R.J. Isaac became the Propaganda Officer or Head Operations Section. Isaac, who had worked for James, actually wanted to resign when Peterson's 'new broom', ignoring 'past experience', 'abolished overnight' all EIS plans. He was however persuaded to stay on.[233] While B.H. Hopkins continued as manager of the MFU, Tom Hodge of the Foreign Office became Head of Films Division. The Press Division – occupying the old EIS premises at (ironically) Bluff Road! – was headed by R. Lindsay, assisted by A.R. D'Astugues.[234] Information Services headquarters was also housed in new buildings in Brockman Road, Kuala Lumpur, completed in only six weeks at a cost of $340,000, and declared open by Templer on 21 Nov 1952.[235]

In addition, the Standing Committee on Finance in May 1952 had approved an establishment of 22 full-time State Information Officer (SIO) posts, and recruitment for these started immediately from the United Kingdom. Peterson also recruited Europeans from Malta, Palestine and Indochina.[236] It was clear that SIOs were to have far less freedom under Peterson than SEIOs had had under Greene. The typical SIO was to act as the DGIS representative in each State with the remit of advising SWECs 'on the best way of carrying out Headquarters propaganda campaigns' and the 'initiation and operation of local campaigns, subject to Headquarters directives'.[237] Meanwhile Asian Field Officers were sent to the Information Training Centre, based in the Old Istana at Sri Menanti in Malacca, for three-week training courses starting in January and ending in August 1953. These courses basically covered three areas: instruction in the use and maintenance of mobile unit equipment such as the cinema projector, radio, tape recorder, generator, microphone and amplifier; the inculcation of leadership via training Field Officers to organise and lead a disciplined field team under pressure; and the instilling of 'showmanship' via practice in organising live shows and being masters of ceremony. 48 Field Officers were trained in the first two courses, and Philip Egerton, Training Officer at Sri Menanti, informed Peterson that since the courses only provided basic training, SIOs should ensure that freshly trained Field Officers applied the lessons learnt afterward.[238] It was hoped that the training would produce Field Officers 'with the gift of the gab' and able to hold audiences in rapt attention through 'impromptu talks'.[239]

Peterson also moved to increase the number of mobile units. He opined that mobile unit propaganda to the public was more important than that to the terrorists, because it often found its way to the terrorists anyway.[240] The units thus rose in number from 63 in March 1953 to 87 in April, 88 in June and 90 by November. The largest number of mobile units were allocated to the big States of Perak, Johore and Pahang.[241] Because of fiscal economies in 1954, moreover, the three-man units became two-man affairs by integrating the posts of driver and mobile cinema operator. At any rate, SEPs continued to accompany the units, telling listeners about their hardships in the jungle, the mistrust between leaders and rank and file, and why they finally quit.[242] In this respect, Peterson observed that putting SEPs before New Villagers tended to dissipate whatever myth of MCP superiority some of the latter may have harboured.[243] A critical aspect of the mobile unit interface with the rural Chinese, and of particular interest to Peterson, was the film shows. In this regard Peterson and Hodge tried to centralise and streamline the procedure for mobile unit film show exhibitions: they insisted that SIOs should tell mobile unit teams the exact programme of films to be shown at each New Village visited; that each State should only have sufficient films to feed their mobile unit programmes and unused films should be returned to the Federal Film Library; that the entire programme of films should be joined together on two 1,600 foot spools so that the mobile cinema operator need only change spools once during exhibitions so as to minimise interruptions; and the Federation flag must be shown at the start or end of every film show.[244] In addition, they ensured that the MFU, which had 121 staff by January 1954,[245] increased output of 'simple films relating to the constructive policies of the Government and designed to make contact with the rural public in a language they [could] understand'. Simultaneously, Peterson instructed that cartoons, if thought necessary, should only be shown after the completion of the MFU programme.[246] While 55 new MFU films consisting of 145 reels in all languages were produced in 1953, 59 new films were made in 1954 totalling 214 reels in all languages.[247] These included the following films shown by Mobile Unit No. 108 in Perak in April 1953: *Infant Care and Feeding* (Mandarin), *New Malayan Gazette* (Mandarin), *Loose Nut* (Cantonese), *Extortion* (Hakka) and *Use of Shotgun* (Mandarin).[248]

While Peterson tried hard to create a rational mobile unit instrument that would, through the expertise of Field Officers and MFU film exhibitions, close the Government-public gap, he did relatively little in relation to Radio Malaya. He acknowledged in August 1952 that the station should maintain its independence from Information Services lest it be perceived by the public as a mouthpiece of Government.[249] While he also remarked that it was unfortunate that Radio Malaya headquarters was in Singapore, which was rather isolated from the Emergency in the Federation, nevertheless, as the cost of erecting studios and moving equipment from Singapore to Malaya would be prohibitive, he advised against attempts to shift headquarters to Kuala Lumpur as yet. However, as DGIS Peterson ensured that firm policy control of Radio Malaya programming was safeguarded.[250] Meanwhile Radio Malaya continued to improve its transmitting infrastructure: in 1954 a Very High Frequency (VHF) link was established between Singapore, Malacca and Kuala Lumpur, which enabled regional stations to add local flavours to the General Programme. In addition, new transmitting stations were opened at Kuala Lumpur and Penang, which provided better coverage of northern and central Malaya.[251] Moreover, in line with Peterson's recommendation that Radio Malaya appoint staff reporters in the Federation to improve 'the local colour of news' and reduce the reliance on Government handouts,[252] teams of reporters equipped with portable recording equipment fanned out throughout the Federation from 'Ulu Kelantan to the Johore Straits'.[253] This mobility ensured that rural broadcasts on health, civics and agriculture had an authentic flavour to them and were popular in not only the rural but the urban areas as well. In 1953 Radio Malaya's General Programme carried Mandarin fare like *Radio Doctor*, *Talk on Information Department* and *Summary of 1952 Annual Report of Singapore Department of Fisheries*, as well as summaries of speeches by the Governor and other Singapore Government officials.[254]

Far more crucial operationally was the Community Listening Scheme. While by late 1954 the number of private radio receivers numbered 125,286,[255] by the end of 1953 946 Community Listening sets had been installed on New Villages, kampongs and estates and on completion of installation by the end of 1954 the final number of sets was 1,047.[256] The purchase of additional sets was made possible by a grant of £58,639 from CDW funds.[257] As in India, there evolved dual control of the Community Listening scheme. While State Governments were responsible for the selection of sites and general supervision of sets and operators, Information Services liaised with the General Electric Company for set installation, documentation and administration of funds.[258] Community Listening programmes, which were broadcast by Radio Malaya between 1700 and 1930 hours every evening, continued to be popular with the rural Chinese, and personalities like Lee Dai Soh, the Cantonese story teller, continued to enthral the ordinary Chinese in 'the mines, the New Villages, [and] the coffee shops'.[259] The Chinese also listened to talks by SEPs, news of Security Force operations, and talks on gardening, pork, fish and rubber prices, bringing up children, and health and hygiene matters. In general, Community Listening programmes were more straightforward than Chinese broadcasts on the General Programme, and included *A Visit to Cheras New Village* and *Six Golden Rules for the Home Guard*, as well as regulars like *Youth Talk*, *Health Talk*, *Civic Talk*, *Spotlight on the Emergency* and *Can I Help You?* There were also *Local Flashes* to keep the rural Chinese updated with current Emergency developments. To target rural audiences more closely, these programmes were not only in Mandarin but also in Hakka, Cantonese and Amoy.[260] In 1954, Community Listening staff, who had been on one-year contracts on the Emergency Establishment, were integrated permanently into the Radio Malaya establishment, and the Director of Emergency and Community Broadcasting became the Programme Director, Federation.[261]

In fact, the most important innovation in propaganda to the public during the Peterson era was the inauguration of Civics Courses. The idea, very much like Operation Service, gradually grew out of official musings throughout 1952 that Government simply had to come down to the level of the people, particularly the rural Chinese. In July 1952 for instance Lieutenant-Colonel Walker, author of *ATOM*, had criticised Government propaganda as 'puerile' as it generally lacked the 'personal approach'. Eight months later, SCA Kedah W.J. Watts told Peterson that the Government officer had to make a 'greater effort' to 'meet and get to know' the people, so that as a 'friend' who had 'eaten with them', who knew their names and the 'latest village gossip' he could 'spice his lectures with local examples'. A conscientious, people-oriented officer, Watts believed, was 'more likely to be listened to and believed than a semi-stranger who just appears with a cinema van occasionally'. To cement the 'personal touch' between

Government and the rural Chinese in an atmosphere of 'friendship and goodwill', Watts emphasised that the Government officer must 'get out from behind his desk and 'laugh, joke and play with the pupils', and that 'a wisecrack crude for preference will drive a point home much better than a formal ½ hour lecture and once one has got the confidence of the people they will accept anything one says'.[262]

In fact, in Malacca in May 1952 ROs and AROs were seeking ways and means of helping Government build closer contacts with the Chinese in New Villages, and were faced with the problem that there were simply too many new communities for Government officers, especially part-time SEIOs, to visit. Then State SCA K.J. Henderson suggested that instead of Government going to the New Villages, perhaps New Villages should come to Government. Thus the idea of the Civics Course was born. It was proposed that 30 New Villagers would be brought to Government offices for a week each time, and be exposed to a series of talks and demonstrations by Government staff, taken on conducted tours of Government installations and institutions, meet with other sections of the Malayan community and enjoy entertainment and sketches put on by Government.[263] The Civics Courses were a success in Malacca. While New Villagers were visibly moved by the experience, Government servants were able to 'see their work in terms of human values and to appreciate the broader aims of policy, rather than carrying on their work in isolation'.[264] The Civics Courses thus dovetailed very nicely with Templer's aim of bringing Government to the people, Young's emphasis on Operation Service and Peterson's insistence that all Government officials should be propaganda-minded. The Civics Courses were extended to all States by 1953.[265]

In 1953, moreover, State Information Officers (SIOs) took over co-ordination of Civics Courses, and with the help of State SCAs and other officials, arranged these events for the local public. For instance, the State SCA organised the Courses for Chinese New Villages, while the Superintendent of Chinese Schools did the same for Chinese teachers and schoolboys.[266] Throughout 1953, 116 Civics Courses were organised, 93 at State and 23 at District level. This involved about 3,600 people in batches of 30, each of which attended a Course strung out over three to six days. 1,400 Chinese were included in this number.[267] It was found that the most popular features of the Courses were the 'spectacular' or 'practical items', such as Army firing displays, Radio Malaya operations and entertainment by Commonwealth units like the King's African Rifles.[268] In particular, Civics Courses helped reduce the distance between the Chinese and the Police. For instance, it was found in Malacca that Police sketches were far more useful than mere conducted tours of Police Stations, while SIO Johore reported that members of a District Course 'shed' their suspicions after a visit to a Police Station. Moreover, in Pahang, talks by Special Branch officers given at Police Contingent Headquarters appeared to have 'convinced' students on the need for surrenders and information. In sum, Civics Courses, which from 1954 onward began to occupy a great deal of the time of Information Services, were an effective propaganda tool in reaching out to the Malay and Chinese villagers in particular.[269]

Overall, then, Peterson's re-organisation of the Information Services enabled Government to speak with one voice and brought that voice closer than ever before to the people of Malaya, especially the rural Chinese. Peterson's effectiveness even prompted Lucien Pye, in Malaya to study the motivations of the SEP's, to comment in January 1953 that 'Mr. Peterson is doing a very good job in organising the new department and rationalizing its administration'.[270] Certainly Peterson's emphasis on training bore fruit. In an attempt to copy MCP recruitment propaganda which catered for audience participation at meetings to demonstrate the power of the Communist cause,[271] trained Field Officers were soon employing a similar tactic of identifying the audience with Government through inviting their participation in anti-Communist sketches. Hence by 1953 there were two types of stage plays or live shows organised by mobile unit teams. The first type was the SEP play which was prepared in advance by the SIO. The second 'impromptu' type involved Field Officers inviting the New Villagers on stage with them. Impromptu shows were seen by SIOs as important,[272] and Perry Robinson has offered a glimpse of what they were like:[273]

> An astonishing amount of talent does present itself – several highly expert mouth-organ virtuosi, a complete family band, two jugglers, comic singers and sentimental singers, a large number of juvenile dancers (including one, a boy, who is studying classical ballet!) and the ever-popular lion dancers.

Peterson later claimed that this 'theory' of audience identification was innovated in Malaya.[274] Rationalising the propaganda machine aside, Peterson's perhaps greater achievement was to impress upon Government that 'propaganda, in its widest interpretation', will have to play a 'large part' in Government's drive to 'win and hold the confidence of the Malayan people'. To Peterson, 'propaganda' consisted not merely of the words put out by Information Services but also the deeds of all Government Departments; hence the messages transmitted by both word and deed had to be co-ordinated:[275]

> What is required is an extremely vigorous propaganda effort, carried out in accordance with a coherent plan, by all Departments and levels of Government... The additional function of the Department of Information in such an effort would be to stimulate and co-ordinate this campaign, keeping the master plan in mind.

To Peterson therefore goes the credit for ensuring that henceforth Government at all levels became aware of the propaganda implications of their actions. Apart from increasing the efficiency of Government propaganda to the public and publicising in Government circles the importance of being 'propaganda-minded', however, he did not change the philosophy of propaganda imported by Greene. He admitted that his work was 'of course a development of Greene's and James' general plan'.[276] Moreover, Peterson created an authoritarian organisational climate which stifled initiative. For instance, when SIO Pahang, G.N.H. Morris suggested to Head Films Division that film shows were not always more important than live shows and flexibility was needed, he was rebuffed. Furthermore, when SIO Penang, C.G. Mortlock, suggested that Field Officers also had to get Talking Points across to the rural people, Hodge replied scathingly that MFU films were quite capable of putting across Government's point of view, and were not at all intended merely to attract an audience so that Field Officers could put across Talking Points.[277]

Much more seriously, Peterson operated under the assumption that European propagandists were necessary to 'provide personnel of the requisite experience and authority', at headquarters, in the field and to conduct the training of propagandists, while 'Asian propagandists' should support the work of the Europeans in general.[278] When coupled with his insistence on tight control of the propaganda effort, Peterson's attitude was bound to irk the irascible C.C. Too. Too's original one-year contract had expired on 25 February 1952, but at James' insistence, on 12 June 1952 he was confirmed as Chinese Assistant to Head EIS for another three years. Once Peterson took over in October, Too became Assistant Head of the Operations Section of Information Services, under Isaac. Too's heavy workload throughout 1952 had included analysis of captured MCP documents; advice on general propaganda lines to the Chinese and specific lines to counter MCP propaganda; vetting of leaflets prepared by SEIOs; translation of important MCP documents and production of *New Path News*, which by January 1952 had attained a circulation of 90,000. Too had to draft not only the text of the *News* but also the cartoons. To keep up, he had to work late most days, weekends and holidays. Too was especially irritated that he also had to take Lam Swee and other SEPs on tour and deal with all the logistical arrangements that this entailed. He was getting a 'gastric ulcer' and wanted help.[279] Thus when Peterson arrived and seemed more intent on controlling Too than arranging for more assistance, the latter was very upset.[280] Peterson's ethnocentric attitude and authoritarian inflexibility ran counter to Too's fierce individualism and when no compromise was forthcoming, Too quit on 1 March 1953 because of Peterson's 'senile policy'. Years later Too was still bitter, charging that Peterson 'knew nothing about psywar' and was a 'bad choice' of Templer's.[281] The immediate consequence of Too's resignation was that propaganda intelligence fell into the hands of an 'old English Professor' who knew some Chinese but nothing about the MCP. Hence documentary research went into virtual limbo, which meant that Government Psychological Warfare was to be quite unprepared for the MCP 'peace offensive' of mid-1955.[282] Peterson, despite his sterling achievements, has to bear the blame for this.

GOVERNMENT PSYCHOLOGICAL WARFARE AND TERRORIST CONFIDENCE

In line with Peterson's recommendation that there should be more rigorous analysis of Communist morale and propaganda, and as part of the work of the Operational Research Section, on 18 March 1953 Templer set up a Psychological Warfare Interrogation Centre (PWIC) in the Police Depot in Kuala Lumpur. While Peterson as DGIS provided policy guidelines, F.H. Lakin was responsible for the technical direction of work, and P.B. Humphrey was appointed as OC, Interrogations. Information Services provided four Chinese interrogators. PWIC was tasked with investigating the reasons as to why people became terrorists, why they later surrendered, and a variety of issues about life in the jungle. It conducted its first study on 30 April 1953 with a sample of 28 Chinese SEPs who had surrendered since 24 October 1952.[283] Apart from putting the study of terrorist behaviour on a more scientific footing, Templer pressed on with propaganda appeals to the Communist rank and file, whose members were now called 'Communist Terrorists' or 'CTs'.[284] Leaflets remained the main medium of Psychological Warfare throughout the Templer era. Hence in 1953, about 54 million strategic leaflets and 23 million tactical leaflets were distributed.[285] That leaflets were now getting through to the terrorists was attested to by PWIC studies. For instance, in the April 1953 sample, out of 28 SEPs, only two had never seen a Government leaflet. In addition, 22 SEPs felt that leaflets had both reached them and provided sufficient information to have been a source of surrender. Meanwhile, of another sample of 50 SEPs from Malacca, Pahang and Selangor, 80 percent had seen Government leaflets.[286] In addition, while safe conduct passes continued to be the main means of assisting terrorists to surrender,[287] other methods of facilitating the latter were also tried. These included the provision of a 'pick up convoy' to patrol advertised roads to collect SEPs. Furthermore, leaflets stressed that the best time to slip away was while the terrorist party was near roads and that surrender would be very difficult once the party had retreated into deep cultivation areas. In addition, the importance of making the terrorist believe he was 'escaping', not 'surrendering' was also highlighted, as 'the difficulty believed to exist in surrendering makes the act one which calls for courage and determination'.[288]

As the physical obstacles to reaching the terrorists were disappearing, the bigger problem remained: that of convincing the terrorists of the *credibility* of Government's promise to treat them fairly if they gave up. On the one hand, some terrorists appeared to accept Templer's personal guarantee that they would be treated fairly and therefore surrendered. For instance, an SEP who had heard a Voice Aircraft broadcast in Mandarin by Templer assuring MCP men that it was 'safe to surrender', duly emerged claiming that 'all jungle men knew they could trust General Sir Gerald Templer'. A.S. Haynes remarked icily that this 'bandit has better judgement than Purcell'.[289] Nevertheless, many more terrorists remained afraid: over 40 percent of SEPs who surrendered between January 1953 and June 1954 had doubts as to how well they would be treated. They and other wavering terrorists were no doubt deterred from giving up by the sentencing to death in January 1952 of Goh Ah Khoon in Penang. Goh had been arrested in May 1951 and classified initially as an SEP, a fact that had been publicised. He was however reclassified as a Captured Enemy Personnel (CEP) and prosecuted,[290] *but EIS and thus the public were not informed.* Goh's prosecution was thus a propaganda disaster as another SEP immediately committed suicide in his cell, and the MCP gleefully propagated the line that Government milked SEPs and then executed them. It was admitted that Government's credibility amongst wavering terrorists would need 'many months' to recover.[291]

Nevertheless, a study in May 1953 found that terrorists were given hope by tappers' testimony that they had seen other SEPs moving about 'free and working' with Police and Information Services, thus confirming Government promises of fair treatment. Moreover, the policy of no longer dropping leaflets with photographs of dead terrorists – as this would only frighten potential SEPs – was supported. The study reckoned however that as SEPs basically feared for their long-term future, if possible Government should come out with a definite 'promise' that no SEPs would 'ever be hanged or imprisoned' for past crimes – in short, an Amnesty.[292] Otherwise, terrorists who wanted to surrender would be deterred from doing so because of they would simply not be sure of their fate at the hands of Government.[293]

Templer certainly had to think very hard about the Amnesty issue in 1952 and 1953. On the one hand, opponents of 'easy surrender' argued that such a policy was tactically flawed as it would enable the MCP to attract 'short-termers' who would be able to give up without fear of punishment after a certain period of time. It was also immoral as it would enable a man 'with several brutal murders to his discredit' to 'walk out of the jungle and get a job as washer-up in a police mess'. Police and administration officials on the other hand countered that liberal surrender terms would attract mass surrenders, and with the information from these SEPs, no terrorist hide-outs would be safe from the Security Forces. Besides, an easy surrender policy prompting an MCP recruiting drive on the 'short-termer' premise would also allow Government to insert its own operatives in the MCP organisation.[294] At any rate, as early as May 1952 Templer had decided against announcing an explicit promise of non-prosecution. On the one hand, he opined that given that some SEPs would have participated in 'particularly dastardly and notorious' crimes, Government simply could not, by promising non-prosecution, tie its hands and provoke public opprobrium. Also, taking a cue from Greene, whose report he had read,[295] he told Lyttelton that the 'psychological moment' for a general Amnesty leading to 'mass desertions' was not yet at hand anyway, and it was crucial not to declare an Amnesty 'hedged about with reservations' which would 'probably repel rather than encourage surrenders'. Until the psychological moment arrived, therefore, Government's surrender policy had to 'suffer from its self-imposed limitations'.[296] Thus the only potential SEPs whom Government could explicitly promise non-prosecution were those who had not been involved in capital crimes. These were of course the terms of the September 1949 Amnesty, which was still in force. Under these terms, 585 terrorists had surrendered by 31 March 1952, including 392 Chinese.[297]

Templer therefore continued the old Gurney/Briggs surrender policy: publicly, there was strict avoidance of explicit official promises that SEPs would not be prosecuted. Instead, all terrorists continued to be promised only fair treatment on surrender. Thus instead of saying: 'It is the generous policy of the Government to free men like me', SEPs could only say: 'I am now a free man'. The idea was to create only an 'impression of policy'.[298] In addition, in August 1952, Templer quietly reiterated to the Police that SEPs should not be prosecuted 'save in exceptional circumstances'. Instead SEPs were put to work for the Government for three months before being kept on, released or sent to Taiping Rehabilitation Centre. From 1 March 1954, moreover, SEPs could also be sent to Kemendore Agricultural Settlement to learn a trade.[299] The fact that no SEP was ever prosecuted was deliberately not publicised.[300] In sum, SEP word-of-mouth propaganda emphasised news on what to expect after surrender, not promises that Government would not prosecute. Disappointed PWIC officers lamented that it was a 'pity' that Government was 'at present unable to offer [formally] nearly as much as we are in fact giving'.[301]

That Templer was right that the psychological moment for an Amnesty had not yet arrived was proven by the experience of Operation Bison in October 1953. On 28 October, 18 million leaflets were dropped all over the Federation carrying an appeal for mass surrenders. This exercise was carried out because two months earlier, Kang Wei, an Armed Work Force commander, had surrendered with seven of his men, claiming that many lower-ranking terrorist leaders wanted to give up but were afraid to do so. One side of the Bison leaflet thus promised that any terrorist leader below the rank of SCM who brought out five other comrades would earn the right to an identity card and a 'an immediate new life'. Not only that, he would receive $500 for every person he brought out – which was the prevailing rate paid to the public for helping members of the MCP to surrender.[302] The other side of the Bison leaflet showed a photograph of SEPs, and readers were told that these former comrades had 'received a fair and sincere welcome' and had taken up civil employment, were learning a trade at the Taiping Rehabilitation Centre, or had joined Information Services or the SOVF. The leaflet concluded that all 'are happier, healthier, more contented, and have peace of mind now they have left behind them the injustice, misery, sickness and uselessness of the jungle'.[303]

The results of Bison, however, were disappointing. 11 SEPs who surrendered between 28 October 1953 and 31 January 1954 correctly identified Bison leaflets at PWIC, saying they had seen them whilst in the jungle. Six of these 11 admitted that the leaflet affected their decision to surrender, and 10 were affected by Government promises of good treatment and group photographs of SEPs. However, the aim of Bison – to secure mass surrenders of six or more terrorists, was not met. The largest number who surrendered at a time was three persons. Moreover, the offer of a reward to lower ranking leaders to facilitate mass surrenders did not seem to have worked. Post-Bison SEP interrogation also showed that discussions of surrender within the terrorist rank and file were actually *less* in the first six months of 1954 than in the last six months of 1953. The study concluded that unless there was a 'change in the circumstances initiating surrender', discussions about surrender, let alone actual group surrenders were unlikely in the immediate future.[304] Hence, terrorist confidence, though shaken by Security Force pressure and food control, had not yet reached the point of general collapse. According to SEPs, a major reason for the absence of a general collapse of terrorist morale in late 1953 was the MCP's internal propaganda that 95 percent of French Indochina was under Vietminh control, and once the country had been overrun, Communist armies would sweep south toward Malaya. Many terrorists were thus holding on to that hope. In addition, Central had tightened discipline, withdrawing the rank and file into the deep jungle as well as cutting back on all activity. This meant fewer opportunities for the contact and disruption of MRLA units by the Security Forces, which in turn meant fewer chances for terrorists to get disenchanted enough to defect.[305]

The disappointment of Bison aside, rewards for information leading to the kill or capture of terrorists still proved valuable. Up to 10 June 1952, $2 million had been paid out in rewards for such information.[306] Templer, in an attempt to target the higher leadership of the MCP, now increased the bounties on their heads markedly. For instance, the reward offered to the public for bringing in Chin Peng, which had been $80,000 under the June 1951 scale, was raised to $250,000 if he was taken alive and $125,000 if he was brought in dead. Politburo members like Lau Lee, Chen Tien and Wu Tien Wang could fetch $200,000 if taken alive and $100,000 if brought in dead, while State Committee Members could now fetch $75,000 if brought in alive and $35,000 if their bodies were produced.[307] By January 1953, however, there was a reassessment. It was felt that the reward policy in operation since December 1950 did not stipulate a 'proper relationship' between the amount paid and 'degree of risk' incurred by the informant or 'effort involved in elimination' of the wanted terrorist. Moreover, it was increasingly realised that such large public bounties on the heads of terrorist leaders, coupled with their continued immunity from Government, were turning them into objects of 'hero worship' among the rank and file. Government thus decided, from 13 August 1953, to stop publicising reward amounts. Furthermore, maximum rates paid out were quietly reduced. Hence the bounty on Chin Peng was reduced from $250,000 to $100,000 if brought in alive, and from $125,000 to $70,000 if brought in dead. In addition, amounts paid out were henceforth dependent on the 'motive, effort, risk and ingenuity' on the part of the informant. For instance, a member of the public providing information leading to the capture of Chin Peng could receive, depending on effort and risk, up to a maximum of $100,000. He would receive a maximum $70,000 if Chin Peng was killed.[308]

Government studies also found that Radio Malaya and the Government papers *New Path News* and *Farmers News* were ineffective in reaching the terrorists,[309] while tests between October 1952 and August 1953 on Landrover-mounted ground loudspeakers were also unsuccessful.[310] The big breakthrough, however, in Psychological Warfare media was air broadcasting. In September 1952 news filtered out that the Americans were having 'great success' with loudhailer aircraft in the Korean War.[311] Egged on by Brigadier Henniker, who had 'ideas on this subject', Templer asked for details of the American equipment, and the status of airborne loudhailing research in Malaya to date.[312] He then borrowed an American C-47 Dakota for trials conducted between 27 October and 21 November. The first trial was staged between 27 and 28 October at RAF station, Kuala Lumpur and compared the audibility of 'live voices' speaking into microphones as opposed to recording the same voices on tape. Over the next two days, trials were held over open country as well as primary jungle in Malacca and Negri Sembilan, to investigate the extent to which observers at ground level could hear C-47 messages in all languages by male and female speakers.[313] Thereafter on 3 and 4 November, the C-47 was put through operational trials over six selected target areas in southern and western Selangor. This time two Mandarin messages were broadcast by a female speaker. The first informed any terrorists listening that Liew Kon Kim[314] had been shot dead, while the second exhorted them to give themselves up to the nearest Police Station where they would be well treated. Results were soon forthcoming. District Committee Member Wei Keiong gave himself up and on 9 November, he broadcast to the same areas that he had surrendered and urged others to give up. Six days later, Ah Yoke and Ah Fong, both surrendered. Ah Yoke's voice in turn was broadcast between 16 to 18 November in the same areas, and on 22 November, two more terrorists, Ah Kong and Kong Swee, surrendered. The Voice Aircraft had proven its worth even during its trials! Wei Keiong expressed the opinion that this weapon constituted a 'fundamental advance' in Psychological Warfare especially since terrorists were forbidden to read Government leaflets. It was also noted that the Voice Aircraft could deliver a tactical message exploiting a terrorist surrender 'rapidly and personally' in the same areas where the SEPs had been known. Implicitly endorsing the principle that propaganda of words was only credible if actual deeds communicated the same message, it was concluded that the best use of the weapon appeared to be as a follow-up to a large ground and air operation, which in this case had been Hammer.[315]

Buoyed by this success, Templer had two Valetta aircraft fitted with broadcasting equipment and by April 1953, operational Voice flights had commenced.[316] Within months, Voice Aircraft sorties were being mounted as follow-up to Security Force operations.[317] But there were teething problems, given the newness of this weapon. For instance, a group of SEPs from Johore who surrendered in August 1953 were unable to hear what a Voice Valetta had been broadcasting.[318] Tests were thus continued from February to September 1953, but were not always conclusive. For instance, an experiment conducted in September 1953 found that both 'live' and recorded broadcasts could be effective in reaching listeners on the ground, while there was uncertainty over the relative merits of straight line flying versus circling.[319] By January 1954, however, a test conducted with a Dakota – which had replaced the noisier Valetta in December – confirmed that recorded broadcasts of 30 seconds' duration dubbed onto continuous recorded tape were effective. Moreover, it was found that a comparatively brief message broadcast several times in one run over the target area, was better than a longer message which could only be broadcast fewer times. Furthermore, parallel straight line flights in opposite directions at 3000 feet and 2000 yards apart, were found to give good coverage of an area.[320] Around the same time, moreover, a test on an Auster – deemed more suitable and economical for accurate broadcasts over small targets on the jungle fringe or adjacent to roads – [321] discovered that studio-recorded tapes and direct speech were both effective in certain conditions, and flying in a static circle of a radius of 400 to 800 feet, at a height of 1500 feet, allowed for continuous intelligible reception at the ground. In addition, two parallel straight line flights at 1500 feet and 500 yards apart allowed for good reception even up to 120 seconds.[322] Until February 1954 the RAF's Voice Flight of No. 267 Squadron was made of one Dakota, one Valetta and two Austers, but the Valetta crashed in Johore and was replaced by a second Dakota in March.[323] The Voice Aircraft, because of the speed and efficiency with which it could exploit the psychological moment created by any Security Force success, was to become an even more refined weapon over the next few years.

CONCLUSION

Templer's sojourn in Malaya undoubtedly turned the tide decisively in Government's favour: he dominated the administration and the public through a deliberate projection of personal power and breathed new life into the Briggs Plan, with consequences for rural Chinese and terrorist confidence. In particular, by paying close attention to New Village aftercare through appointing more Chinese-speaking and Chinese officers; extending Young's Operation Service from the Police throughout all Government Departments; abolishing draconian Emergency Regulations and inaugurating and extending the White Areas, Templer effectively projected to the rural Chinese that Government was their Provider. To ensure that the ordinary Chinese were kept appraised of Government's 'deeds', moreover, Alec Peterson set about centralising and rationalising Information Services. Thus, the ubiquitous mobile units, the MFU, Radio Malaya's Community Listening Service and Civics Courses were all co-ordinated so as to 'exploit' efficiently Government's achievements. While Peterson's injunction to all Government officials to be 'propaganda-minded' was a massively important step, his overall record, however, was marred by a personal inflexibility which led to the loss of C.C. Too, a development which weakened Government propaganda intelligence analysis considerably. Nevertheless, Templer's placing of Psychological Warfare on a more scientific basis produced rigorous studies of the terrorist psyche, while the advent of Voice Aircraft enabled a more rapid exploitation of the psychological moment created by terrorist reverses. In fact, soon after Templer left, as we shall see, terrorist confidence began to haemorrhage seriously. Thus although Central proclaimed that help would be coming from Indochina and backed propaganda with warnings that comrades keeping Government leaflets would be severely punished,[324] the decay persisted. Government's major challenge in the final phase was thus the selection of the correct psychological moment for an Amnesty to precipitate mass surrenders. The responsibility for this was to fall upon a new Man for the Plan: Tunku Abdul Rahman.

CHAPTER SIX

❦

Propaganda Most Optimal

Tunku Abdul Rahman and the Collapse of the Communist Terrorist Organisation, June 1954–December 1958

INTRODUCTION

On 27 July 1955, Tunku Abdul Rahman's Alliance Party won the first Federal elections in Malaya overwhelmingly. From that point on, Tunku, first as Chief Minister, and then after independence or *Merdeka* on 31 August 1957, as Prime Minister, dominated both the administration and the public. By maintaining the confidence of his expatriate officials despite the dislocation caused by Malayanisation, Tunku ensured that there was no serious slackening of Government and Security Force momentum. This enabled on one hand the continuation of official policies and behaviour which communicated to the rural Chinese that Government was their Provider, while simultaneously, through unrelenting Security Force pressure, projecting to the remaining terrorists that there was no hope of an MCP victory and it was best to switch sides. Meanwhile under Alec Peterson's successor, the able Yaacob Latiff, Information Services continued to reach into the bosom of the New Villages, estates and mines, and an immensely important innovation, the Good Citizens' Committees, was inaugurated which hastened the end of the insurgency. Finally, the returning C.C. Too was instrumental in girding Government Psychological Warfare for the climactic contest with Central for the confidence of the remaining hard core rank and file; a struggle which at its apex involved a clash of wills between Tunku and Chin Peng. We shall see that Tunku's steady refusal during and after the Baling Talks to recognise the MCP – despite pressure from some quarters to end the Emergency by cutting a deal with the Communists – contributed directly to the collapse of terrorist confidence. Hence the 1957/58 *Merdeka* Amnesty became a powerful weapon precipitating the devastating mass surrenders of 1958.

TUNKU ABDUL RAHMAN: THE LAST MAN FOR THE PLAN

Templer's departure from Malaya at the beginning of June 1954 coincided with a marked improvement in the security situation. For instance, terrorist-inspired incidents fell from a monthly average of 507 in 1951 to 89 in 1954, while the average number of civilians killed declined from 44 toeight in the same period.[1] However, this situation instilled a misguided sense of complacency on the part of the general public,[2] given the increase in subversion. For instance, in March 1954, the MCP South Malaya Bureau intensified the infiltration of junior Middle and Higher Primary Chinese schools, Old Boys' Associations, and basketball teams.[3] Moreover, Government could not as yet rest on its laurels. It was recognised that the rural Chinese had merely moved from total indifference to what Alec Peterson termed 'reasonably friendly apathy': many villagers were still too scared to stop helping the terrorists.[4] Hence, although the Emergency was being won, it was far from over. To maintain the drive of the administration therefore, a continuation of the dynamic leadership that Templer had provided was all the more essential. Who then was to be the new Man for the Plan? In this important interim period before the Tunku's emergence as Chief Minister in July 1955, two figures stepped into the breach.

One was Donald MacGillivray, who was promoted to High Commissioner in June 1954. In contrast to Templer, MacGillivray came across as 'very nice', 'suave' and 'different'.[5] He also possessed an 'acute and analytical mind with tremendous powers of concentration', an 'enormous' capacity for hard work, and got on 'extraordinarily well' with 'everyone',[6] including Tunku, despite a rocky start to their relationship.[7] Importantly, MacGillivray, appreciating Templer's concern to symbolise the friendly face of Government to the rural Chinese, also made it a point to visit the New Villages.[8] Nevertheless, it has to be said that MacGillivray had limitations as a leader-propagandist. Like Gurney, he was by temperament a 'shy and self-effacing' man,[9] and it is difficult to imagine that so soon after experiencing the boisterous and memorable Templer, the rural Chinese would have readily reposed their confidence in someone as relatively nondescript as the new High Commissioner. MacGillivray's strength lay instead in his administrative and political acumen: MCS observers later admired the way he handled the transition to independence with 'a sure touch'.[10] In sum, MacGillivray's instinct and ultimate contribution, was to maintain the drive and confidence of the administration and the general public, in particular the Europeans and educated Asians.[11]

In fact, it was the new Director of Operations rather than the new High Commissioner who probably did more to maintain Government's momentum in its quest to secure the confidence of the rural Chinese. He was Lieutenant-General Geoffrey Bourne, who assumed duty on 1 June 1954, combining in his person the posts of Director of Operations and

GOC Malaya.[12] Bourne, educated at Rugby and Woolwich, had had a distinguished army career, and had been GOC-in-Chief, Eastern Command just before coming to Malaya.[13] Described as 'decisive' and 'shrewd',[14] he plunged immediately into the task of keeping the sharp end of the Government machine – the DWECs, the Army and the Police – in fine mettle.[15] Moreover, taking a leaf from Templer's tactic of 'dominating' the public, Bourne deliberately maintained a high profile, regularly using Radio Malaya to review the Emergency situation and meeting Chinese community leaders.[16] In particular, he made a distinct impression on the rural Chinese. Like Templer and Briggs, Bourne recognised that the 'half-million Chinese on New Villages and estates' were the key to the military insurgency, and he was completely pragmatic about Government's task: it was, he felt, 'not so much a matter of winning their hearts as a question of convincing them which side is going to win the struggle'.[17] In order to do this, Bourne continued Templer's policy of bringing Government power as close to the ground as possible, which meant meeting the Chinese personally – as at Kerdau New Village in Pahang and Titi New Village in Negri Sembilan in July 1955 – an exercise in which his missing arm[18] must have left an indelible impression![19]

The Federal elections of 27 July 1955, however, shunted both MacGillivray and Bourne into the background. After his Alliance party had won about 80 percent of the vote, Tunku Abdul Rahman became Malaya's first Chief Minister.[20] The significance of Tunku's mandate was not lost on Colonial Office officials. Hence at the Lancaster House constitutional conference in London in early 1956, full responsibility for internal security was immediately vested in a Malayan Minister for Internal Defence and Security, while August 1957 was identified as the date by which Malaya would achieve 'full self-government'.[21] The assumption of responsibility for internal security by Tunku's Government represented a significant Malayanisation of the Emergency machine. Prior to this internal security had been the responsibility of the Director of Operations Committee – an exclusively British preserve until October 1954, when, in order to associate Asian leaders with the 'practical application of emergency measures', leading Malayans had been drafted in. Hence the Director of Operations Committee until March 1956 had consisted of Bourne as Chairman and Director of Operations, the Chief Secretary, the Principal Staff Officer, the Secretary of Defence, the Director of Intelligence, the Commissioner of Police, the Air Officer Commanding, the Naval Liaison Officer and the Chief of Staff HQ Malaya. The inducted Asians by this time had been Tunku, Dato Abdul Razak, Colonel H.S. Lee and V.T. Sambanthan.[22] On 1 March 1956, following the London talks, as Chief Minister and Minister for Internal Defence and Security, Tunku assumed the chairmanship of the new Emergency Operations Council (EOC). The EOC also included Bourne, Lee, Razak, Sambanthan, the

Principal Staff Officer, and A.H.P. Humphrey, the Secretary for Internal Defence and Security. In August 1956, the Air Officer Commanding, the Commissioner of Police and the GOC Federation Army were added.[23]

The EOC aside, from 1 January 1955, all SWECs and DWECs had also included Malayans.[24] Gradual Malayanisation from 1955 onwards did not however eradicate British participation in the direction of anti-terrorist operations. Despite MacGillivray's anxieties in mid-1956 that Tunku's 'nationalist emotions' might 'overpower his judgement' and he would insist at *Merdeka* (independence) that 'the Federation could deal with the Emergency unaided',[25] the Chief Minister proved reassuringly sensible. By March 1957, Tunku had accepted the principle that rather than Federation forces having 'first go' at the terrorists and Commonwealth assistance sought only if the Federation forces were ineffective, British and Commonwealth forces would have areas of operations assigned to them for which they would have 'prime responsibility' after *Merdeka*. Such was Tunku's pragmatism that he even accepted that if the Emergency situation in an area assigned to the local Federation Army deteriorated, then Commonwealth forces could be called in to assist. However, it was understood in both Whitehall and Kuala Lumpur that after *Merdeka* British troops should not be used for maintaining communal harmony.[26]

In sum, under Tunku, Malayanisation in the context of Emergency operations implied the twinning of the principles of Malayan responsibility and British operational control. Hence, although the Director of Operations from 1 March 1956 did not chair the EOC, he still enjoyed 'operational command' of all Security Forces.[27] Moreover, at *Merdeka*, although it was politically imperative that the Alliance Government be seen to have assumed complete and sole responsibility for anti-terrorist operations, a way was still found to retain British oversight: hence the post-*Merdeka* Director of Operations ceased to be concurrently GOC Malaya Command – emphasising his independence of British forces – and was seconded as the 'exclusive servant' of the Alliance Government, directing all Security Forces on their behalf. The first Director of Operations after *Merdeka* was Lieutenant-General James Cassells, who was appointed on 16 September 1957. He replaced Lieutenant-General Roger Bower, who had taken over from Bourne in May 1956.[28] With Cassells' appointment, Malaya Command was abolished and the indigenous Malayan units came under GOC Federation Army[29] while all non-Malayan Army units came under GOC 17 Gurkha Division/Overseas Commonwealth Land Forces. In a reversion to the Briggs arrangement, Cassells was a co-ordinator more than a supreme commander, acting through these two GOCs. Tunku continued to chair the post-*Merdeka* EOC, which now included Razak as Minister of Defence, and four other Malayan Ministers: Sambanthan, H.S. Lee, Ong Yoke Lin and Tan Siew Sin. The other members were Cassells, Secretary of Defence Frank Brewer (a former Federal SCA), the Commissioner of Police, the two GOCs, and the air and naval commanders.[30] In short, from July 1955 Tunku may have personified the new Malayan face of Government, but in the sphere of Emergency operations, he continued to lean fully on British prowess.

Tunku had not always enjoyed cordial relations with the British, however. The latter had been worried initially about his commitment to multiracialism, as they wanted to hand over power to a united multiracial political elite. Dato Onn bin Jaafar, Tunku's predecessor as UMNO president, had tried to transform UMNO into a non-communal party, but had failed. He had then left and in September 1951 created the Independence of Malaya Party (IMP) which espoused a multiracial political vision which was more to the British liking. Tunku, on the other hand, in seeking to purge UMNO of remaining pro-Onn elements and re-establish its credentials as the Party of the Malays, had succeeded in appearing unrelentingly communal.[31] However, Tunku soon acquiesced in the UMNO-MCA alliance which won the February 1952 Kuala Lumpur municipal elections, and institutionalised UMNO-MCA co-operation at the national level in March 1953[32] – an alliance which culminated in the Federal election victory in July 1955. He was then accepted as the best available local to lead a united Malaya to independence.[33] Nevertheless, the British still regarded Dato Onn as 'intellectually head and shoulders above most of his fellow-countrymen',[34] and they bemoaned the fact that through a series of misjudgements, he had lost his influence with the Malay elites.[35] Tunku thus came into office bearing the burden of unfavourable comparisons with Onn. W.C.S. Corry initially regarded the Chief Minister as a man 'whose personal enthusiasms are apt to outrun his discretion' and who was 'yet to prove himself as a leader'.[36] MacDonald felt that Tunku did not 'have the brains of Dato Onn'[37] while Lyttelton even averred that Tunku, though 'nice' was a 'second-rate', 'silly little man'.[38] Yet Tunku was to prove himself the last and most important Man for the Plan.

Tunku Abdul Rahman was a member of the Kedah royal family. He was never an outstanding intellectual, as evidenced by the fact that at Cambridge in December 1925 he had barely secured his degree in History, and had then taken 'twenty-five years to qualify as a barrister', partly because he had 'preferred horse-racing, dog-racing and dancing to the law'.[39] Tunku's strong suit, however, was not his brain but his personality. This gift was amply demonstrated when on being called to the Bar at the Inner Temple, he quipped: 'Tonight I not only celebrate my coming to the Bar, but also my silver jubilee as a student at this Inn'.[40] Tunku's sense of humour certainly was needed during his first weeks as Chief Minister. One observer reported that the Alliance Government was hampered by the fact that everyone had to start from scratch and 'the Ministers were as much as sea as everyone else'.[41] Tunku himself behaved at first like a sort of Chief

District Officer, unwilling to turn away anyone who came to see him with problems which their District Officers could well have handled.[42]

However, Tunku gradually settled into the job and began to deal with the most immediate problem: European officer morale in the face of Malayanisation of public services. In July 1953, a Committee on the Malayanisation of the Government Service had been constituted to investigate 'the extent to which higher posts in the Public Service are at present filled by Malayans and the prospects of increasing the number of Malayans in such posts'. In August 1954 the Committee reported that there were too few Malayans with the necessary qualifications and experience to be appointed to the higher posts, and therefore recommended that Malayanisation should be implemented slowly by filling natural wastage with Malayans and not expatriates.[43] However, deeming natural attrition too slow, the Alliance Party had issued an election pledge that once in power, full Malayanisation would be effected within four years – something which naturally worried many expatriates.[44] Once in power, however, Tunku recognised the need for continuing expatriate expertise and persuaded his Cabinet colleagues of this reality during stormy Malayanisation Committee meetings.[45] In pushing for the adoption of the Committee's final report,[46] which envisaged gradual, not precipitate, Malayanisation of public services over a period lasting till 1965, Tunku warned against a 'drastic and sudden change' in the administration which would seriously affect the efficient working of Government.[47] The Legislative Council adopted the Paper's recommendations.[48]

Tunku's success in securing better Malayanisation terms for his British staff by late 1956, coupled with his earlier success at the Baling talks[49] – perhaps marked the beginnings of his rehabilitation in their eyes. Instead of comparing him with Dato Onn, they began to value him on his own merits. His British staff now admitted that he possessed 'a seriousness of purpose' and a 'very shrewd judgement' which made him difficult to outwit.[50] Emulating Templer, moreover, Tunku tried to make his presence felt at all levels. For instance in March 1956 he visited the Sungei Patani and Alor Star DWECs in his home State of Kedah,[51] while the following month he accompanied Bourne on a visit to Pahang SWEC and Temerloh DWEC.[52] Tunku's visits to the field were quite unlike Templer's. While the latter gave the impression that he was on top of the situation, Tunku looked 'slightly dazed', probably because 'suddenly' he had the 'top job in the land' and had to 'do all sorts of things and go and see all sorts of activities which he probably had never experienced before'. Still, Tunku 'carried it off very well', and projected the impression that he liked to be there and meet people, though he was a 'bit at a loss'.[53]

Tunku's general air of mild befuddlement coupled with the ever increasing realisation by expatriate officials that there *was* substance to the man, gradually created affection and even loyalty. Ivan Lloyd Phillips,

Tunku's Secretary, noted that on the one hand Tunku exasperated him by having an 'almost pathological dislike of detail', preferring to talk about the file in question and giving verbal decisions which Phillips recorded on the papers. Moreover, Tunku was not above reading out wrong answers to parliamentary questions. On the other hand, Phillips could not help but find Tunku 'endearing': the latter used to talk about his Cambridge days, soccer and racing and always communicated his sense of fun to listeners. But importantly, Tunku trusted Phillips, telling him 'exactly what was going on with the conviction that his confidence would not be abused'.[54] Similarly, Gullick recalled that when he asked Tunku for his signature on a document, Tunku, instead of interrogating him, simply said: 'If you say it's alright, I'll sign it'. Gullick could not help but contrast Tunku's attitude with that of Dato Onn, who in 1946 had 'scandalised' a gathering including Gent and the Constitutional Working Party revising the Malayan Union scheme, by insisting that no legal draughtsman should alter a 'comma' on any draft document until Onn's own legal team had vetted it.[55] By *Merdeka*, therefore, although 413 expatriates had left public service under Malayanisation terms, it is probable that if had not been for Tunku, expatriate morale would have been worse off, and consequently Government efficiency harder hit.[56]

Tunku's great humanity affected not only Government officials but also ordinary Malayans as well. MacDonald observed that Tunku had:[57]

> a very great ability to deal with other people, not just Malays, but with non-Malays. He was a good mixer with everybody. He was gay, he was laughing, he was interested in all sorts of things.

Tunku's easygoing persona and openness to all races was effective propaganda. It has to be emphasised: Tunku was extremely proud to be a Malay, and as first president of the Malay Society of Great Britain he had urged his members to be proud of things Malay and to speak Malay when in one another's company.[58] Yet Tunku was at the same time a *Malayan* in every sense. Hence as District Officer in Kedah in the 1930s, he had distinguished himself as a friend of all races, and during the Japanese Occupation had risked his life on several occasions interceding for the Chinese.[59] As Chief Minister moreover Tunku even adopted several Chinese children, who were in the habit of running up and sitting on his knee as he entertained people in his home.[60] Gullick was thus told by a Chinese journalist that while other Malay leaders sought communal peace as a means of maintaining Malay political hegemony, Tunku 'aimed at communal harmony' because that was 'his instinct'.[61] Hence, as Tunku was 'remarkably acceptable' to the Chinese, he was well-placed to personify Government to that critically important community.[62]

While he was already well-known in the countryside, having campaigned on behalf of Alliance candidates for the Federal elections,[63] as Chief

Minister and later as Prime Minister, Tunku maintained his high profile. For instance, in March 1956, he visited Ladang Geddes rubber estate in Negri Sembilan to talk to the estate labourers and ask for their co-operation,[64] while in July, accompanied by Bower, he visited Kampong Pantai New Village to urge the inhabitants to provide information to the Security Forces.[65] Tunku also got his Chinese Alliance Ministers to speak at New Village Councils and public meetings, something which was effective in further closing the Government-Chinese gap.[66] Tunku's charismatic appeal to the rural Malays as well as the Chinese comes out in this account of his visits to the New Villages and kampongs.[67]

> His oratory is by no means of the highest order, but he speaks with a simplicity and directness that strikes a responsive chord in his audience. Wherever he goes ... whole villages turn up to meet him. ... When he rises to leave he is immediately surrounded by villagers who want to shake his hand or ask for his autograph.

In short, Tunku's charisma was an important propaganda asset, and between 1955 and 1958, he 'dominated' Government and the public with 'determination, humanity and great good humour'.[68] As we shall see later, moreover, Tunku's ability to win the trust of Chinese terrorists would prove even more crucial.

THE NEW VILLAGES UNDER TUNKU

By late 1954, 438 New Villages had been built,[69] and eventually 573,000 people, mainly Chinese, were residing in 480 New Villages.[70] How did these new centres of the rural Chinese community rate as 'materialistic propaganda' under Tunku? An October 1954 study by W.C.S. Corry observed that New Villagers became settled when apart from physical security and ownership of the titles to their house lots, they enjoyed good amenities like schools, water supplies, lighting, drainage and community halls.[71] In fact, 'the fluctuating but generally high international price of natural rubber' boosted Government revenues in the late 1950s and enabled the continued provision of facilities to New Villages. Hence by the end of 1958 every New Village had a school, 10 percent had static clinics, 67 percent were served by mobile clinics and a number of others had access to medical facilities in nearby towns. It was thus estimated that by *Merdeka*, 80–85 percent of all New Villages had become pretty much settled.[72] In fact some observers have noted that by 1960, the New Villages had become 'a permanent feature of the Malayan landscape', and a very small minority of their number actually closed down.[73] Amenities aside, a very important factor determining the efficacy of New Villages in securing rural Chinese confidence was the availability of sufficient economic opportunities. In this regard, the inhabitants of 222 New Villages living near big urban centres were able to find employment in secondary industries like sawmills, pineapple canneries, rubber shoe and biscuit factories.[74] Where economic security was lacking, however, the rural Chinese attitude to Government soured. Thus, C.H.F. Blake, DO Batang Padang District in Perak, contrasting why Temoh New Village had a better record of co-operation than Kampong Pahang New Village, noticed that although there was no agricultural land near Temoh, there were plenty of jobs on local Chinese tin mines. On the other hand, Kampong Pahang suffered from a dearth of jobs and had an uncertain outlook.[75] Generally, a small number of remote New Villages in Selangor, Perak, Johore, Kedah and Pahang suffered from economic insecurity arising from a lack of employment opportunities on mines, estates and factories, as well as sufficient good agricultural land to provide an alternative source of income. These Villages not only ultimately failed to survive, they represented the Communists' strongest bases of support until the end of the Emergency.[76]

There were other problems: if one of the aims of the New Village project had been to secure rural Chinese confidence through providing the opportunity to participate in local elections and local defence, then there were big question marks as well. On the one hand, the attitude of the New Villagers to their Local Councils varied. In some areas, villagers apparently supported them: in Sungei Dua New Village in Pahang, for example, 94 percent of eligible voters turned out for the elections.[77] But in the New Village studied by Judith Strauch, only 41 percent of eligible voters bothered to cast their vote in the 1956 Council election. Moreover, Loh argues that in general, few New Villagers participated in local elections.[78] Furthermore, Corry in October 1954 observed that while a good number of Local Councils in Johore and Perak had healthy bank balances and functioned well, Councils in Selangor, Negri Sembilan and Pahang were 'mediocre', and the people in those areas did not seem interested in self-government.[79]

In addition, while the Malay Home Guard was considered effective,[80] the Chinese Home Guard, which by September 1954 had assumed responsibility for the defence of 129 New Villages,[81] was generally seen as unreliable: some Chinese Home Guards were prone to losing arms to the terrorists and even after training, were liable to backslide into passivity.[82] For example, in March 1955 Inspector-General of the Home Guard E.B. de Fonblanque had personally to exhort the Chinese Home Guards at Pokok Sena New Village in Kedah to take their duties more seriously.[83] By the end of 1955 therefore, it was reluctantly recognised that if a New Village was 'bad' then its Home Guard would be 'bad' too.[84] There were thus calls for some Chinese Home Guard units to be disbanded. Government however demurred, arguing that disbanding would only encourage 'inefficiency' amongst other Chinese Home Guards, who, it was admitted, did not like to serve. Instead of disbanding them, therefore, Government exerted greater efforts in attempting to 'stiffen' their 'will to fight'.[85]

Thus in June 1956, the Chinese Home Guard was comprehensively re-organised. 400 Operational Sections were trained to carry out not the static defence of New Villages but rather a mobile, offensive defence within and without the village perimeter. The re-organisation was completed in three months, and the remainder of the Chinese Home Guard were stood down and given unarmed duties within the New Villages.[86] This new approach was put to the test in October when two patrols of Chinese Home Guard Operational Sections from Kulai and Scudai New Villages in Johore engaged the terrorists. That de Fonblanque promptly exclaimed that 'a turning point' had been reached[87] only reinforced the perception – albeit unwittingly – that the Johore action was an exception to the rule. In fact, even after the re-organisation it remained unclear to what extent the Chinese Home Guard would prove itself reliable.[88]

It is tempting at this point to conclude that despite the economic well-being of most of the New Villages by the end of 1958, the relative lack of rural Chinese enthusiasm for local politics and defence must suggest that on balance, the New Village project failed as propaganda. However, were elections and village defence really important in winning and holding rural Chinese confidence? Although Police Commissioner Young in mid-1953 had held that it was important to give the New Villagers 'the opportunity to elect their own village committees',[89] the reality was different. Frank Brewer of Chinese Affairs noted in February 1955 that the Chinese accepted that 'the Government officer stands in relation to the public as a parent to his children', and if the officer acts justly, his right to rule would be readily accepted.[90] Hence what the rural Chinese wanted, as another Chinese Affairs man, W.J. Watts, argued, was not 'political rights' but rather that Government should be 'intelligent, scrupulously just and efficient'.[91] Watts emphasised that the former squatter, 'fully wrapped up in his struggle for existence', tended to ask: 'What value is it to me if I became a Federal citizen'?[92] Similarly R.N. Broome complained that the rural Chinese, being 'first class backseat drivers', had to be 'ruthlessly booted into democracy'.[93] The point is, the rural Chinese did not want to administer himself, he wanted to be administered. The same logic applied to the area of local defence as well. Although in May 1952 de Fonblanque had opined that 'Action by the people to safeguard their own homes' spread 'a far greater confidence' than if they were 'being protected by strangers, be those strangers police or soldiers',[94] the Chinese view was actually the opposite: if Government was supposed to administer them, surely it was supposed to protect them as well. Hence the ordinary Chinese reluctance to serve in the Home Guard and the general view that the Emergency was Government's problem, not theirs.[95]

It is instead reiterated that the true propaganda value of the New Village environment was that it continued to offer a plethora of *Taijins* to whom the rural Chinese could bring their complaints, instead of seeking the assistance of the lurking MCP Masses Executives. Among the *Taijins* were 34 Red Cross teams which in 1955 ministered to 243,000 Chinese.[96] More importantly, by February 1956, the Chinese Affairs Service was at 'full strength', with a Federal SCA and a Deputy in Kuala Lumpur, supported by two senior State SCAs in Perak and Selangor, and other State SCAs in Penang, Johore, Kedah, Negri Sembilan, Pahang and Malacca. The Federal SCA was no longer on the Federal Executive and Legislative Councils, but remained as adviser to the High Commissioner on 'Things Chinese'.[97] At the District level, moreover, while the ARO scheme from mid 1955 was being run down, it was accepted that the CAO was generally the staff officer to the DO on Chinese matters, assisted by ACAOs. In fact some AROs sought to be re-appointed as ACAOs.[98] Unfortunately, in some Districts CAOs continued to be regarded as 'errand boys' with little status, causing resentment.[99] At any rate, by *Merdeka*, the Federal SCA and State SCA posts were abolished, and part of the functions of Chinese Affairs were absorbed by the Ministry of the Interior. Nevertheless, CAOs and ACAOs by this time 'were being accepted as an integral part of district administration', and the posts were placed on District estimates.[100] For instance in Johore by March 1957, there were seven CAOs and 14 ACAOs assisting the DOs in the Districts of Johor Bahru, Muar, Segamat, Batu Pahat, Kluang, Kota Tinggi, Mersing and Pontian.[101]

In sum, apart from meeting the physical and socio-economic needs of the bulk of the rural Chinese, the real propaganda success of the New Villages was to be found in the continued provision of *Taijins* to whom the rural Chinese could bring their problems. This had the critical effect of freezing the MCP out of the picture. Moreover, there was ultimately a larger benefit. The New Villages over time turned out to be a mass exercise in not merely materialistic, but *civic*, propaganda: sustained exposure to Government officials, together with of course regular contact with nearby urban centres, had the gradual effect of subjecting the former 'squatter and his family to an infinitely wider spectrum of beliefs, customs, attitudes and values than was even imaginable to him in his previous situation'. In other words, the New Villages helped to expand the frame of reference of their occupants beyond the traditional preoccupation with their immediate, proximate circumstances. Hence by the 1960s, observers like John Humphrey, who studied 85 New Villages in Perak, Selangor, Negri Sembilan, Johore, Pahang and Penang over a two and a half year period, detected a discernible increase amongst New Villagers in the levels of civic consciousness, awareness of national politics, as well as participation in village elections. Nevertheless, the deeply ingrained insularity of the Chinese New Villager proved resilient, as he continued to 'consider elections other than those concerned with local issues as exercises in futility and not worth worrying about'.[102]

THE SECURITY FORCES AND CHINESE CONFIDENCE

After a six-week visit to Malaya in early 1955 during which he toured several States and Districts, Inspector-General of the Colonial Police W.A. Muller reported that the Malayan Police Force was now working 'smoothly'.[103] As the Force was gradually Malayanised[104] it was also reduced in size. From a total established strength of 47,601 at the end of 1955[105] the Force shrunk to 44,950 at the end of 1957[106] and then to 36,260 by July 1958.[107] The Special Constables, in particular, continued to be demobilised steadily, their strength shrinking from 23,155 in December 1955[108] to 15,071 in July 1958.[109] The basic problem which Muller identified however was that the Police were still biased toward paramilitary operations rather than civil policing. For instance, the number of paramilitary Police Special Squads increased from 22 groups at the end of 1955 to 50 at the end of 1956.[110] His assessment was that the average regular Police constable, though smart in dress and drill, was still not well-versed in the skills of criminal investigation required to precisely identify suspects.[111] In addition, Muller emphasised that the OCPDs (Officer Commanding Police District) should be allowed to get to know their Districts and the people in them, and not be subjected to frequent transfers. However, the system in some Penang Districts of allocating constables to wards, thereby facilitating close ties with the people, was 'excellent' and should be extended throughout the country.[112] Government implemented Muller's suggestions.[113] Thus for instance, 41 Village Constable posts were started up in rural areas in 1956 and 12 more in 1957.[114] Associated with this attempt to bring the regular Police in even closer contact with the public was the continued emphasis on Operation Service.[115]

Another problem which Muller identified was the continuing dearth of capable Chinese Police to secure the trust of the rural Chinese.[116] Chinese recruitment remained patchy. At the end of 1957, only 15 percent of Gazetted Officers, 39 percent of Inspectors and 11 percent of Subordinate Police Officers were Chinese.[117] There were of course the rather small corps of Chinese-speaking European Police, trained by the Government Officers' Language School. Up to June 1954, 57 European Assistant Superintendents and 23 Police Lieutenants had been trained in either Cantonese, Hakka, Hokkien or Mandarin at the School. In addition, 17 Malay, nine Indian and four Eurasian Inspectors had also been trained.[118] That speaking in the native dialect was excellent propaganda and cemented the *Taijin* relationship with the Chinese comes out in the following report by Police Lieutenant John D. Slimming at Chemor in Perak:

> As I see it, I ought to do my best to get the confidence of the people rather than frighten them. Since they are slowly finding out that I can talk with them, they're starting to turn up (either in the Police station or at my door) with all sorts of problems.[119]

However, it was found that some Police officers, though trained in Chinese dialects, were too busy with paperwork to go out and converse with the Chinese.[120] Robert Bruce, the Director of the School, criticised this attitude, declaring that only officers who consciously made the effort to use the language could succeed in winning the 'sympathy, respect, understanding and even friendship' of the rural Chinese.[121]

Like the Police Force, the Army also sought to secure the confidence of the rural Chinese by building closer contacts with the community. Thus British units continued to engage in routine community relations exercises: for instance, at Christmas 1955 the Royal Lincolnshire Regiment's First Battalion in Pahang organised a Christmas party for 200 children, complete with Regimental band music, a film show, treasure hunt and a tea party.[122] These exercises were now supplemented by more conscientious attempts to win the confidence of the rural Chinese. Thus in May Johore Ops SWEC, in order to 'gain the confidence' of the local Chinese New Villages, had decided to station small parties of troops in them. The hope was that 'local inhabitants will gradually acquire a sense of security both in their villages and at their work', and provide information of 'immediate operational value'.[123] As Lieutenant-Colonel R.C.H. Miers of the South Wales Borderers remarked, the idea was to create an impression of Security Force omnipresence 'so that the next time our rubber tapper comes out working around his rubber trees and the bushes part, it is not terrorists who appear but it is British soldiers sharing the jungle ... like a policeman on his beat'.[124]

Unfortunately, the evidence suggests that despite this genuine effort on the part of the Army to win the confidence of the Chinese, some elements within its ranks continued to cling to damaging stereotypes of the community. One Chinese who enlisted in the Federation Army recalled the propensity of some British soldiers to regard all Chinese as potential Communists and thus to dehumanise them as '"slant-eyes", "chinks" and a hundred other names'.[125] The propaganda implications of clinging to dehumanising stereotypes comes out in the notorious case of Semenyih New Village in the Kajang District of Selangor. Semenyih was home to mostly Hakka Chinese, who made their living mainly from tapping on the nearby rubber estates. Every morning tappers passed through four gates in the perimeter fence to get to work, and one gate, Kachau Gate, was the busiest. It was estimated that 2,500 tappers, 60 percent of whom were women, had to pass through this gate each morning to get to work. The District had in fact been a bad area, and from mid-October 1955 to January 1956 there had been much terrorist activity along with 'ample' evidence that there were terrorist supporters amongst the Semenyih population.[126] In order to deal with the situation, a food denial operation was planned and as part of preparations, the 17th (Gurkha) Provost Company – with both Gurkha and British personnel – was sent to the New Village to enforce a stricter regime of gate checks from 5 January 1956.[127] The Semenyih villagers had never liked gate checks and found the daily process of actually getting out of the New Village extremely irksome. With the end of the house curfew at 0500 hours, the tappers – men and women in separate lines – usually filed past two decrepit booths just outside the Kachau Gate. While most were simply frisked by Police and moved along, some men and women were randomly picked and led into the booths to be searched by having their clothing loosened and their bodies felt under them, or even having their outer garments removed. The tappers then had to wait outside in a group till the perimeter curfew was lifted at 0600 hours.[128]

With the arrival of the Military Police, searching was intensified considerably, and the tappers at Kachau[129] Gate reacted negatively, shouting and bustling against the Police and refusing to be searched. Their resistance to such checks boiled over into a near riot on 12 January 1956 followed by another disturbance on 14 January.[130] An official investigation into the incidents unearthed several disturbing facts: 61 women tappers complained that their outer garments had been removed by force after they had refused to remove them on their own volition; the searching booths used for the full searches were not only decrepit, they were covered in hessian cloth which was practically transparent in the early morning darkness when illuminated by pressure lamps – creating an effect akin to watching a 'cinema show'; 10 women complained that their women searchers had flung their clothing out of the booths so that they had to fetch them in their undergarments; a Malay Special Constable had looked under the cloth of the women's booth and remarked in Malay that 'They are all the same'; and finally, one woman tapper on the way to another gate was stopped by a British soldier who forced her at the point of his rifle to the verandah of a nearby shop where he felt her body through her clothes.[131]

The official enquiry made the point, justifiably, that given the scope of the operation – between 5 and 14 January 1956 25,000 tappers had been searched at the Kachau Gate alone – it was far more surprising that more incidents of this nature had not occurred. It attributed this – correctly – to the general good humour and discipline of the troops on the whole. Nevertheless, the fact that such incidents had occurred at all was blunt testimony to the continuing proneness of some soldiers to take liberties with people who in their eyes were nothing more than 'slant-eyes'. Although there were clearly terrorist supporters amongst the Semenyih tappers, the official enquiry concluded significantly that the disturbances were not so much terrorist-engineered as the spontaneous outburst of a people who had tired of seven years of being subjected to draconian infringements on their individual liberties and dignity.[132] While Government later insisted that food control measures could not be helped in the war against the terrorists, it did announce 'full and detailed plans' for all future operations of this nature. In particular, it was decided that in future all body searches would no longer require removal of outer garments, except in very exceptional cases and in complete privacy by a person of the same sex. In addition, women searchers would be given better training and supervision. With respect to Semenyih, new corrugated iron booths were constructed immediately and the British soldier who had allegedly molested the female tapper was sought by Police.[133] Nevertheless, even after the improvements Semenyih women tappers remained 'scared' of searchers.[134] Semenyih reinforced the lesson that it only needed 'one demonstration of the contrary' to destroy Chinese 'confidence' in Government's 'good intentions'.[135]

GOVERNMENT'S INCREASINGLY 'PROPAGANDA-MINDED' POLICIES

Tunku and the British remained sensitive throughout to the possibility of lifting or modifying the Emergency Regulations so as to ease restrictions on the rural Chinese, while not jeopardising operational effectiveness. In this regard Tunku oversaw in particular a further thinning out of the detention camps; the innovation of more discriminate 'surgical swoops' to eliminate terrorist supporters lurking in the midst of the wider public; the tactic of offering White Areas to induce the public to co-operate actively with the Security Forces; and the introduction of central cooking. Detention figures, which had fallen precipitously between 1952 and 1954, fell again in this period. At the end of 1954 there had been 1,463 persons and dependants detained under ER 17 (1), falling to 754 by the end of 1955[136] and 337 by the end of 1956.[137] So dramatic was the fall in detention figures that some centres had to be closed down, and by the end of 1956 only three major camps were left: Ipoh Detention Centre, Ipoh Female Rehabilitation Centre and Taiping Rehabilitation Centre. By the end of 1956, 2,958 persons had passed through Taiping since its opening in 1949.[138] Facilitating the decrease in detention figures was the setting up in December 1955 of a Review Commission headed by a Supreme Court judge assisted by unofficials. This supplemented the existing Committees of Review which heard individuals when they were first detained under ER 17 (1). The Review Commission reviewed detention cases every six months and could modify detention orders, order the conditional release of detainees or even quash detention orders. Generally, the Commission tried to prevent detentions longer than six months, unless faced with very strong evidence.[139] As detention figures went down, so too did those for deportation. In 1955, 491 detainees and dependents were deported to China under ER 17C,[140] dropping sharply to 122 a year later,[141] and 76 in the first six months of 1957.[142]

While Templer had abolished collective punishment, the problem which that ill-conceived policy had been designed to deal with – the lack of information flow from a community which had witnessed or had to some extent participated in a terrorist outrage – still presented itself. As always Government's problem was how to identify the wolves amongst the sheep, so that countermeasures could be directed only at the wolves *without* injuring the sheep amongst which they hid. The key was information. However by the end of 1953, an increasingly professional Special Branch was penetrating MCP District and Branch Organisations.[143] Thus Banting, a small town in Selangor long saddled with the dubious reputation of being a source of terrorist support, was suddenly in January 1955 purged of its Communist elements when a Special Branch operation netted them.[144] By November the following year, moreover, the Special Branch tactic of the discriminating surgical swoop had been perfected, as exemplified by Operation Tartan Rock in Johore. A series of terrorist outrages had culminated in attacks on Kulai, Senai and Scudai New Villages – but the people had been too intimidated by the Min Yuen in their midst to give any information outright. While in the not too distant past the New Villagers – both the culpable and the completely innocent – could have expected a collective fine and 22-hour curfew, Government had by now refined its methods. Rejecting the old notion of collective responsibility, the aim of Tartan Rock was to 'remove the bad elements' who had been intimidating the 'considerable amount of loyal elements in these villages'.[145] Accordingly, on the night of 28 November, Police and Army holding and search teams, accompanied by Johore Information Services staff and guides, formed into groups at preselected points in Kulai, and on the stroke of midnight descended upon certain homes in the New Villages, estate regrouped areas and labour lines which had been identified – thanks to information received over a 'considerable period of time' – as Min Yuen centres. While the Police did the searching, the Army cordoned off the area, and by noon on 29 November, 158 arrests had been made. Meanwhile welfare teams looked after the dependants of those who had been arrested. In conception and execution a 'propaganda-minded' operation, the success of Tartan Rock – the biggest of its kind up to that point – prompted the Combined Emergency Planning Staff to call for its wider application.[146]

Another crucial manifestation of Government's increased propaganda-mindedness toward the general public was the continued growth of White Areas. In July 1954 there were 1,444,620 people living in White Areas in Malaya.[147] By April 1956 the 2,500,000 mark was reached,[148] and by the end of 1957, 3,471,500 people were living in White Areas.[149] Always, whenever one was declared, maximum propaganda capital was squeezed out of the occasion. For instance, when at dawn on 4 May 1957 180 square miles of north Perak was declared White by the Raja Muda, the announcement was made from five main centres, and publicised by mobile units in every village, kampong and estate in the area. Simultaneously Voice Aircraft flew overhead broadcasting the Sultan of Perak's congratulations while a RAF Auster dropped 130,000 leaflets emphasising what privileges the people now enjoyed. That evening free cinema shows and talks were also organised to inform the people how they could guard their new freedoms and status.[150] SWECs knew they had a powerful weapon in hand, and they routinely dangled the White Area carrot before rural folk in bad Districts in order to induce increased co-operation.[151] The White Area strategy was not without its risks, however. A June 1955 study by the Combined Intelligence Staff found that there had been a recrudescence of MCP activity in the White Areas in some States.[152] However, these had been small in scale and generally concerned with reconstructing discreet supply lines to the terrorists in adjoining black areas, rather then actual terrorism or subversion. The study had recommended that as the benefits of the White Area idea outweighed the disadvantages, it should be continued but with careful Special Branch oversight.[153] Moreover, in order to induce the public in borderline Districts to give more information to the Security Forces, an intermediate step to White Areas, Selected Areas, was introduced in 1956. In Selected Areas, some but not all restrictions were lifted. The public were told that they could earn full White Area freedom if they co-operated more with Government. Eight Selected Areas were declared in 1956, but were unpopular with SWECs, which preferred to wait till a District was completely cleared of terrorists before declaring it White.[154]

It was however the introduction of central cooking which probably went furthest in communicating to the rural Chinese that Government cared for their plight. Early experiments had been carried out in Bahau District in Negri Sembilan in May 1954, and the very first central kitchen had been set up on the Dunlop rubber estate. Altogether 21 rubber estates and one New Village, comprising 11,500 people altogether, had been affected. The exercise had been overseen by Mervyn Sheppard, the first Director of Public Relations, in his capacity as British Adviser, Negri Sembilan. With the abolition of all British Adviser posts as part of Malayanisation in 1956, moreover, Sheppard was made Head of the new Emergency Food Denial Organisation on 1 July, and proceeded to implement central cooking Federation-wide.[155] At the end of 1956, 24,000 people were drawing rice from central kitchens on 34 rubber estates, 2 tea estates, six sawmills, two tin mines, six New Villages and one town. Instead of cooking an austere Operational Rice Ration in their homes, the rural Chinese now received cooked rice from central kitchens. For instance, in Broga, Selangor, where central cooking was introduced on 15 October 1956, two rice kitchens were constructed and four rice cooks recruited locally with the help of the Village Council. The cost of the kitchens and cooks were paid from Government Food Denial Funds, and two Chinese AROs were employed to supervise the scheme. Rice, stored securely in the Police compound, was taken to the central kitchens and cooked in two large *kualis* under Police guard between 0200 and 0430 hours before being given to tappers at 0500 hours to consume at home with their own home-grown vegetables.[156]

Because cooked rice spoiled in 24 hours, and was too bulky to smuggle out anyway, there was little danger of a terrorist supporter saving and giving it to the terrorists. This meant that there was no reason why the mass of the Chinese could not eat as much rice as they wanted. They could thus do away with the Operational Rice Ration and did not have to go hungry at work. The psychological effect of this was considerable.[157]

Between June 1956 and July 1957, moreover, the Emergency Food Denial Organisation was deployed in Selangor, Negri Sembilan, Johore and Perak, at incorrigible villages like Broga, Semenyih, Sungei Siput and Yong Peng. Very significantly, even hard core villagers and terrorist supporters seized the opportunity to eat normally once more. So popular were the central kitchens, their cooks, and Emergency Food Denial staff, that the terrorists dared not touch them.[158] In sum, by thinning out the detention centres; refining countermeasures for rooting out terrorist supporters without harming the wider public; extending White Areas and introducing central cooking, Government tried to send the message that it was no enemy of the rural Chinese and wanted to lift restrictions completely, but needed their help. As we shall see shortly, by 1955 this message had begun to sink in.

GOVERNMENT DEEDS AND THE STEADY EROSION OF TERRORIST CONFIDENCE

By the end of 1956, there was real concern amongst senior British officials that the reduction – due to Malayanisation – of British personnel in the Police, Special Branch and the MCS, as well as the loss of the British Advisers who had been chairing SWECs, would hamper efforts to allot the 'First Eleven' team to areas where it was necessary to exert maximum pressure on the terrorists.[159] However, because Malayans as noted had been involved in SWECs and DWECs since January 1955, local politicians and businessmen had been exposed to the nitty-gritty of managing operations for some time before *Merdeka*. They had thus been 'brought to grips with difficult problems', and were able to use 'their influence to organise a greater war effort' by the public.[160] Furthermore, by this time, the SWEC/DWEC system was functioning at optimal capacity. Operational decisions were taken by 'Ops SWEC', while policy matters were discussed by 'Full SWEC'. In addition, the SWECs continued to monitor and co-ordinate the activity of the DWECs, which also had Malayan unofficials in addition to key officials like the DO and the OCPD.[161] Meanwhile, by the end of 1954, 30 Military Intelligence Officers had been integrated into Special Branch to assist with the production of tactical intelligence useful to the Army.[162]

Furthermore, from late 1954 a more offensive strategy was pursued. While in the past food denial operations within the Briggs-Templer framework had certainly disrupted local terrorist organisations, it was found that with experience terrorists were able to 'weather' these tactics, returning later to reconstruct their supply networks after Security Force pressure had eased off. At any rate, no matter how rigorous food denial had been, rice still trickled toward the terrorists, especially in heavily populated areas. It was estimated that only 0.1 percent of the total rice consumption in Malaya was needed to feed the entire Communist organisation. To deal with the situation Bourne thus inaugurated 'domination' tactics, in which the Army now descended upon certain areas of the jungle where MCP District Committees were known to be hiding and remained there for longer periods, dominating the area until the MCP organisation was disrupted permanently.[163] Domination tactics in conjunction with food denial measures succeeded spectacularly in Pahang, where the State terrorist organisation collapsed in 1955, enabling 80 percent of the State to be declared White.[164] Thereafter Government's strategy involved 'projecting success' outward from areas where Communist Districts had collapsed and Government had consolidated. Accordingly, in 1956 Government tried to project success from Pahang in Central Malaya to the west coast, creating a 'White belt' across the middle of the country. The intention following this was to thrust simultaneously northwards into Perak and southwards into Johore. By *Merdeka*, the White belt across Malaya had become a reality, although the proposed north-south White belt had not.[165]

To facilitate the creation of the criss-crossing White belts, in July 1956, the Federal Priority system was inaugurated in which the major Security Force effort was directed at so-called Priority areas where the Communist Terrorist Organisations were the strongest. Thus while Selangor, Pahang and Negri Sembilan received Federal Priority in 1956, in 1957 and 1958 Perak and Johore received attention. In addition, the experienced 17 Gurkha Division/Overseas Commonwealth Land Forces were deployed in the Federal Priority States of Perak and Johore after *Merdeka*, while the emerging Federation Army assumed responsibility for the remaining two-thirds of Malaya.[166] More focused and intense Security Force pressure aside, central cooking also subjected the remaining terrorist rank and file to increasing psychological stress. The point of central cooking was this: because all available rice in the New Villages and estates were guarded in the Police compound before being cooked in central kitchens, villagers did not need to keep any uncooked rice at home. This meant that bulky, rapidly-spoiling cooked rice aside, there was no longer even any uncooked rice for hard core supporters to smuggle out.[167] Central cooking thus virtually cut off even the small amounts of rice that had been trickling out despite food denial.

In sum, the ever-increasing effectiveness of co-ordinated food denial and intensified Security Force pressure constituted powerful propaganda to terrorists. SEPs testified readily that relentless and co-ordinated air and ground attacks, by compelling them to keep moving, prevented them from settling and finding food. Their morale was utterly shaken.[168] Meanwhile starvation produced not only physical but also severe psychological suffering, as illustrated by the cases of Selangor SEPs Kim Fook and Lim Kong. Emaciated and desperate to surrender for many weeks, they deserted their unit and 'trudged slowly and painfully' toward 'freedom', having to take frequent long rests because of weakness. Yet they knew they had to keep going because they were terrified that their 'comrades' would catch up with them. Finally they stumbled across some tappers, to whom they surrendered their weapons, visibly 'glad to be rid' of the 'burden'. Once in Police custody, moreover, they were so hungry they had to be physically stopped from gulping down handfuls of rice too quickly. Days later, suffering from 'extreme malnutrition' and despite medical attention, they were still prone to buckle at the knees when trying to walk.[169] Once central cooking had tightened up food denial in July 1956, moreover, within a year the number of such starving, anxious terrorists increased dramatically.[170] Chin Peng himself admits that central cooking proved a key 'turning point'.[171]

The cumulative effect of such sustained physical/psychological attrition began gradually to tell on the MCP. By mid-1954, it had been recognised that the relatively less committed terrorists had been excised from the rank and file, leaving behind a 'psychologically tougher' if paradoxically militarily weaker target.[172] But within months, it became apparent that even this hard core rank and file was being worn down psychologically.[173] It appears that the Pahang terrorist collapse was the turning point. Many of the SEPs generated by the disintegration were 'very high ranking CTs' who had brought out their subordinates as well.[174] These included Pahang State Committee Member Ah Tan, who gave up in February 1955 – the highest ranking MCP member to surrender since Lam Swee in June 1950. Two months later, another Pahang SEP, SCM Hon Leong, broadcast that Communism no longer had the support of the 'broad masses', that there was 'widespread suspicion and distrust within the ranks of the party' and 'morale' was at 'a very low ebb'.[175] In addition, a further sample of 54 hard core SEPs from the rest of Malaya interrogated at the same time as the Pahang SEPs, admitted that the main reason for surrender was 'loss of hope in final victory'.[176] Significantly, because of ignorance of Government's declared policy of fair treatment of SEPs, terrorists in both samples had worried that they would be imprisoned, hung, poisoned, tortured or simply 'never seen again'. But they had *still* given up, despite this lack of confidence in Government – such was the extent of their disillusionment.[177]

Government deeds aside, another factor that must have played on the minds of these hard core SEPs was the external environment: between mid-March and early May 1954 the Vietminh had laid siege to General de Castries' French forces at Dien Bien Phu, and following the Geneva Conference between May and July, a settlement was reached providing for the temporary division of Vietnam at the 17th parallel. At least nine out of

31 SEPs interrogated in late 1954 felt that news of the Indochina ceasefire had been a factor in their decisions to surrender. They reported that the MCP had been arguing that the Indochina conflict distracted the imperialists and in the long run help would come from the Vietminh. Now that that war was over, some SEPs reasoned that the imperialists could focus on Malaya.[178] In sum, between 1955 and 1956, it was clear that the devastating psychological effect of intense Security Force pressure/food denial, and to some extent the external environment, *were of themselves* persuading more of the hard core rank and file and even their leaders that there was 'no hope'. Because the circumstances of the terrorists increasingly suggested futility, the timing was right for 'Information Services and Psychological Warfare' to 'play a decisive part in finishing off the Emergency'.[179]

GOVERNMENT PROPAGANDA OF WORDS
IN THE FINAL PHASE

Information Services underwent a re-organisation at the end of June 1954 with the departure of Peterson. Yaacob Latiff, who had been Deputy DGIS,[180] was promoted to Director of Information Services (DIS) with effect from 1 July.[181] Of Bugis descent and a scion of a famous Selangor family – his grandfather had been the first Malay magistrate after British intervention in 1875, while his father had been the first Malay doctor in Government service[182]- Yaacob was 'a man of great ability and charisma', and 'a very good general administrator'. He had had considerable experience even before becoming DIS. A recruit to the Malayan Administrative Service in 1937, Yaacob had joined the old Department of Public Relations in 1948, where he soon rose to be Senior Information Officer. Following a five-month stint in Britain on a Special Information Officers' Training Course, moreover, Yaacob headed the now-renamed Department of Information when J.N. McHugh went on home leave from July 1950 to January 1951.[183] Yaacob proved to be an active and interventionist DIS, mixing not merely with both kampong Malays and young educated town Malays, but also the Chinese, as in March 1955 when he addressed 30 Chinese women from Kerling New Village in Kuala Lumpur, encouraging them to be good citizens and to guard their children against 'bad influences'. Yaacob also made frequent use of Radio Malaya to broadcast periodic assessments of the MCP's intentions and strategy, drawing particular attention to the threat of subversion of schools, trade unions, businessmen, youth and intellectuals.[184]

Assisting Yaacob was F.W. Bustin, the Deputy DIS, who supervised the work of three Senior Information Officers[185] who looked after the deployment and discipline of mobile unit Field Officers and their equipment, finance and service matters, and print materials. In addition,

A.R. D'Astugues ran the Press Division, David Lyttle maintained Radio Malaya's liaison with the Information Services, while Tom Hodge remained in charge of the MFU.[186] In fact, on 1 March 1954, the Operations Division of Information Services had been hived off to the Director of Operations Staff, and renamed Psychological Warfare Section (PWS). Head Operations Division, Major R.J. Isaac, was re-designated Head PWS or HPWS. HPWS acted as the Psychological Warfare Adviser to DIS.[187] It was also reckoned that while Information Services should speak for the High Commissioner to the public, Psychological Warfare should speak for the Director of Operations to the terrorists.[188] HPWS was charged with co-ordinating the Psychological Warfare element in all Federal-level Security Force operations; drafting all propaganda material aimed at the terrorists – whether Federally or locally produced – and representing the Principal Staff Officer on the Voice Aircraft Committee.[189] DIS in turn assisted HPWS by producing, storing and distributing all propaganda material aimed at the terrorists; providing State/Settlement level support and heeding HPWS advice on the production of publicity material directed at the public which had a Psychological Warfare implication. Co-ordination was effected through a daily morning meeting at Information Services headquarters at Brockman Road, Kuala Lumpur.[190] By the end of 1954 it was actually found that 'exact compartmentalisation' was not always easy as Psychological Warfare increasingly spilled over 'into the area of Information to the civil population'. Fortunately, the amiable relationship between HPWS and Information Services prevented friction from hamstringing efficiency.[191]

Thus re-constituted, Information Services proceeded to get Government across to the rural Chinese. In this respect, Civics Courses continued to be important because they afforded the opportunity to bring the rural Chinese and Government representatives into personal contact with one another.[192] The format of the Courses, organised at State level by SIOs,[193] was by 1956, somewhat diversified. On the one hand, the original format persisted: groups of New Villagers were collected at one centre in the District and over the next three to seven days, were exposed to lectures and demonstrations in the neighbourhood.[194] On the other hand, less expensive 'Civics Days' were increasingly popular: in July 1955 for instance 60 Chinese youth from Senai New Village were brought to Johor Bahru for a Civics Day, where they were given a talk on the forthcoming Federal elections, brought to a Police Operations Room, and introduced to the Tunku Mahkota at the Johore Istana.[195] In addition, from the beginning of 1955 Government, besides bringing the rural Chinese to the State/Settlement capital, also returned to the New Villages. This decentralised approach was useful because lecturers frequently discovered and dealt with problems 'personal to the listeners rather than with departmental policies above their heads'.[196]

At any rate, peripatetic Civics 'Tours' remained both important and popular: this usually involved transporting groups of Chinese to Kuala Lumpur itself or another large centre to see Government flex its muscles.[197] Thus, in Ulu Klang District in Selangor in April 1955, 200 Chinese were treated to a demonstration of Government's 'powerful' Psychological Warfare. They watched as an SEP playing a 'District Committee Member', complete with terrorist uniform and red star cap, emerged from the *belukar*[198] waving a Government surrender leaflet, and were 'thrilled' as an Auster swooped low over the jungle-clad hills to drop leaflets 'with pin point accuracy', while a Voice Dakota boomed out surrender appeals in Hokkien and Mandarin.[199] In 1957, 3,611 people attended 102 Civics Courses; 26,015 attended 237 Civics Lectures, 1998 attended 44 Civics Tours, and 6,220 attended group discussions. In addition, from 1954 Civics Course 'old boys' in the New Villages and kampongs increasingly assisted Information Services in distributing propaganda to their neighbours. These were known as Honorary Information Officers and were useful in the remoter areas.[200]

Civics Courses aside, mobile unit field teams continued to be active. From 90 units (83 vehicles and seven river boats) in 1954 and 1955, 102 (94 vehicles and eight river boats) became available by *Merdeka*.[201] The units continued their visits to the New Villages and estate lines exhibiting film shows interspersed with talks on the burning issues of the day.[202] The teams also organised live demonstrations such as voting at elections, while on occasion they were joined by troupes of SEPs performing 'live' anti-Communist sketches.[203] For example, on 4 October 1958 at 1500 hours, Chinese Field Officer (CFO) Ong Chih Hua brought Unit 61 and a Government party to Ayer Jerneh where SEP Fook Thien told 60 Chinese and Malays why he had surrendered. Following this, the Area Information Officer (AIO)[204] and Deputy Special Branch Officer appealed to the gathering for information so as to eliminate the remaining nine terrorists in the jungle. Two hours later another 'SEP conference' was held at Kampong Ibok where 70 villagers attended. That evening, the Unit exhibited a film show, and Ong talked to the people about the Fook Thien surrender as well as registration of electors.[205] Despite the clearly useful work done by the mobile unit field teams, there were shortcomings. As late as the end of 1958, Field Officers were still not happy about mobile unit administration: while there was over-centralisation of control of the units at State level in some State/Settlements, in others the DOs, not the SIOs, controlled the mobile units. Furthermore, there was generally a lack of co-ordination between SIOs, AIOs and FOs. In addition, some of the mobile unit equipment was ageing and needed replacing; there was a lack of standby film projectors, public address systems and of spare parts generally and apart from Johore and Perak, there were no technicians to repair damaged equipment.[206]

The FOs themselves were not above reproach, either. It was found that they tended to lack a sense of professionalism, not only neglecting to keep abreast of the latest Government policies, but allowing the standard of their film show presentations to dip as well. More damagingly, FOs were seen by some rural folk as arrogant and impolite – they failed to pay courtesy calls on village headmen on arrival; expected to receive hospitality from villagers; and were generally uninterested in the real problems facing the rural people.[207] To rectify this situation, Yaacob decided that six 12-day refresher courses for FOs would be held at the Home Guard Training Centre at Siginting, Negri Sembilan between November 1958 and March 1959. In all, 183 FOs and 16 AIOs attended the refreshers.[208] Following the courses it was decided that a full-time Training Officer would be appointed to conduct periodic retraining for FOs while SIOs would conduct spot checks on field teams to keep them on their toes and weed out 'deadwood'.[209]

By February 1955 the MFU, having in Hodge's words, 'laid a solid foundation of basic films', began to establish a reputation for itself on the international stage. Thus neighbouring Southeast Asian countries such as Burma and South Vietnam sent over technicians for training, while a Senior Film Editor was sent to Saigon to help start up that Government's film production programme.[210] Meanwhile *Buffaloes are Ploughing* was lauded by UNESCO as a model instructional film, while *Serve to Lead* – about the Federal Military College – was hailed by British experts as the 'best recruiting film' they had seen and was purchased for exhibition in Britain. Unsurprisingly, MFU revenue surged from $17,000 in 1952 to $500,000 in 1956.[211] International impact aside, the MFU continued to contribute to the propaganda war within Malaya, although general film output began to decline in this period: from 74 new films of 254 reels made in 1955, 35 films of 178 reels were made in 1956 and 28 films of 164 reels produced in 1957.[212] The drop in output occurred because of the shift to more ambitious types of subjects and colour films.[213] Nevertheless, MFU productions continued to be exhibited by mobile units in the New Villages and estate lines. For instance, Mobile Unit No. 68 in Trengganu showed MFU films to 16,800 people in the month of October 1955 alone.[214] Coverage aside, how effective were MFU films as propaganda? It may appear that on balance, Hugh Greene rather than Peterson was vindicated on this score. It will be recalled that Peterson had called for more MFU films with a 'social, not necessarily anti-Communist purpose', and acted by Malayan peasants in a Malayan setting.[215] But FOs attending the late 1958 refresher courses actually complained that these more serious MFU films were 'too fast' for rural audiences, and did not cater to their 'intelligence and mentality'. They recommended instead that more feature films along the lines of *Hassan's Homecoming* and *Rohani Steps Out* – as well as variety programmes based on Malayan songs and dance went down better.[216] These observations confirmed the Crossman/Greene thesis that entertainment always had a role to play in propaganda.

In June 1956, because of tensions emerging between Information Services headquarters and the MFU, Tunku appointed an official committee to study the relationship between both bodies, as well as other staff problems.[217] By the time Hodge left Malaya on 7 June 1957[218] and was replaced by Ow Kheng Law,[219] it was reaffirmed that although MFU would remain part of Information Services and operate within policy guidelines set by DIS, it would enjoy complete creative freedom in film production.[220] Nevertheless, one problem remained unsolved: the perennial headache of securing better premises. In September 1957 Yaacob complained that working drawings for MFU studios had still not been completed and construction could only take place in 1958. He wanted the Public Works Department to give the building of the studios priority.[221] Exactly a year later, moreover, Ow himself was compelled to write a memorandum explaining how bad the situation was: the existing MFU premises at Jalan Bangsar dated back to the Japanese Occupation and were a mixture of temporary and permanent buildings. Because the temporary structures were made of timber walls and attap roofs, they were a fire hazard of the first order, as there were no fire hydrants nearby. Moreover, there was hardly any space for MFU films to be stored, and the lack of proper ventilation only hastened the deterioration of films. Furthermore, staff working conditions were 'deplorable': Assistant Producers had to work within extremely cramped, sweltering rooms, while the four Film Directors were all packed into a single room with two tables. In addition, because ventilation in the film laboratory was poor, technicians at times suffered from fumes. In sum, it was 'an absolute disgrace' when foreign VIPs visited the MFU, and staff morale was not all good.[222] It was not until 1962 that new MFU buildings were finally ready, at Jalan Utara in Petaling Jaya.[223]

Up to December 1958 Radio Malaya still had its headquarters at Singapore, while a Kuala Lumpur sub-headquarters oversaw the Kuala Lumpur, Penang and Malacca studios and transmitters.[224] Meanwhile there was further growth in the number of private receivers: from 135,437 at the end of 1955 the figure grew to 154,875 in 1956 and 175,000 at the end of December 1957.[225] In particular, as increasing numbers of New Villagers began to purchase their own private radios, Community Listening sets were transferred to less well off Villages.[226] The event that dominated this phase of Radio Malaya's history was however the renewed moves to break up the pan-Malayan broadcasting organisation. The onset of *Merdeka* brought the issue into sharp focus: how could the headquarters of Radio Malaya, the national broadcasting station of independent Malaya, be based *outside* Malaya? Rumours of a split between Malaya and Singapore therefore gathered momentum as early as May 1957,[227] and was confirmed in December when Government announced its attention to withdraw from the pan-Malayan broadcasting system and set up its own separate service.[228] Obstacles appeared immediately, though. Radio Malaya staff based in Singapore flatly refused to transfer to the Federation because of fears of lower pay, uncertain promotion prospects and lower quality of life.[229] In February 1958, therefore, a Government working party reported that the idea of setting up a completely separate Radio Malaya with its Singapore staff relocated to Kuala Lumpur was not feasible.[230] Two months later, therefore, the Deputy Director of Broadcasting, A.T. Read, was asked to prepare a new establishment, which was approved in December, and on 4 January 1959 listeners in the Federation and Singapore woke up to find that there were now two stations on air: Radio Malaya and Radio Singapore.[231] The specialist staff who had refused to relocate to the Federation were now Radio Singapore staff, and Radio Malaya had to look for 160 staff to fill its own establishment.[232] Because of this manpower shortfall, therefore, Kuala Lumpur still had to rely heavily on Radio Singapore for all early morning broadcasts in the four languages until 0900 hours, most news broadcasts, all schools broadcasts and all entertainment programmes. However, 'rump' Radio Malaya intended to start Federal Regional Bulletins in July 1959 to follow after the main bulletins from Singapore. In addition, Read, new Director of the separate Radio Malaya organisation, indicated that henceforth Radio Malaya would rely on medium-wave transmitters to provide Federation-wide coverage, and four such transmitters were set up in Kajang in Selangor and on the east coast at Kuantan, Kuala Trengganu and Kota Bahru by 1960. These, as well as new studios at Penang and Malacca, were financed by a 100 million dollar loan from Brunei.[233] Furthermore, Radio Malaya planned to introduce three transmissions on medium-wave to serve Selangor initially and the other States later. One transmission would be exclusively Malay, another exclusively English, and the third, Mandarin and Tamil.[234] In particular, once sufficient new staff were trained, it was intended to increase programming for rural audiences.[235]

On the issue of rural audiences, the Community Listening Service still represented the sharp end of radio propaganda towards this group. Because of Emergency demands, the Service had been run from the Kuala Lumpur studios, so the break-up of the pan-Malayan broadcasting organisation did it no lasting harm as its staff were not based in Singapore.[236] In November 1954, because it was established that 'battery failure' was hampering the efficiency of the Community Listening Scheme, and as more New Villages were having access to power supply, it was decided to withdraw battery sets, convert them into mains sets, and reinstall them at their original sites. While the conversion process was free, State Governments bore the electricity bills for the operation of the converted sets.[237] Conversion proceeded slowly. In 1955 there were 102 mains sets out of a total of 1050 Community Listening sets; this figure had only risen to 127 by 1957.[238]

Nevertheless, by 1957, Radio Malaya was becoming more sophisticated in targeting the rural Chinese audience. At a policy meeting in January, for instance, it was agreed that since Chinese rural workers ate their evening meals between 1730 and 1830 hours daily, the best time for Community Listening broadcasts was between 1900 and 2130 hours. It was also accepted that rural Hokkiens could understand Teochew broadcasts, and Teochews Hokkien, while rural Hakkas could understand Cantonese and Cantonese Hakka. It was emphasised that it was better to use the listeners' own dialect if a direct approach over an important matter was needed.[239]

As for content of broadcasts, it was reiterated – as Greene would have done – that 'rural broadcasting' must 'entertain and assist', rather than 'get at' listeners. It was added that broadcasts must also help rural Chinese cement their relations with Government Taijins by instructing them how to seek assistance from officials.[240] Chinese programmes carried on the Community Listening Service at this time included *Village Gossip*, a weekly programme in Cantonese and Hakka, which dealt with issues like application for licences, business registration, radio licences and identity cards; *Farming Talk*, another weekly programme in Cantonese and Hakka, in which experts advised listeners on how to rear chickens and how to prevent crop diseases; and *Surveys of Market Prices for Local Produce*, a daily broadcast in Hokkien, Cantonese and Hakka, which was widely acclaimed by primary producers. In addition, Radio Malaya's General Programme continued to carry the popular *Radio Doctor* two times a week in Mandarin and Cantonese.[241] In sum, Radio Malaya, despite the massive distraction of a fundamental re-organisation, continued to bring Government and the rural Chinese closer.

The intensive barrage of Government propaganda – of words and deeds – described in the preceding paragraphs and directed at the rural Chinese in particular, eventually bore fruit by 1955. This assumed the form of perhaps the most critical propaganda device ever yet developed – the Good Citizens' Committee (GCC). As noted, by the end of 1954, Bourne had been forced to concede that although there had been an improvement in the level of public co-operation with the Security Forces, 'reasonably friendly apathy' prevented the rural Chinese from doing any more. If the insurrection was to be defeated, they *had* to do more: they had to provide more information, and they had to resist terrorist demands more actively. This was not a military problem. As Bourne observed, 'the political or psychological side of the struggle is three-quarters of the problem'.[242] In short, it was a matter of rural Chinese confidence. However, a local success at Banting in Selangor in early 1955 ushered in a process in which the mass of the rural Chinese came down decisively on Government's side. As indicated earlier, a Special Branch swoop on the town had eliminated the Min Yuen in the area. The Banting Chinese were so relieved at this that, with the help of SIO Selangor Jack Hackett, in March 1955 they formed a Good Citizens' Committee

(GCC) to rally public support behind Government. Sensing a propaganda opportunity, the same month Yaacob reiterated to 37 Banting Chinese including members of the GCC that if the rural Chinese could work with the Security Forces in freeing their Districts of the MCP, they could all enjoy White Areas. It was terrible, he added pointedly, that innocent people had to suffer because of 'a few bad sheep'.[243] The following month, 200 Banting residents gathered at nearby Sungei Manggis village to watch nine members of the Banting GCC, including 62-year old Tee Leong Sih, take turns to fire a 25-pounder of the 93 Field Battery at MCP positions eight miles away.[244] A week later, moreover, for the first time since the Emergency began, a tea party was organised in which Banting residents entertained District officials, military, Police and local planters.[245] Two months later, the first large scale processions appeared on Banting's streets. The GCC put 2,300 people on parade, shouting anti-Communist slogans and waving banners. In a deliberately orchestrated manner, they saluted the Selangor State Secretary who told them 19 terrorists had been eliminated in Selangor's South Swamp, and if the people continued to co-operate, a White Area would be declared soon.[246] Suddenly, the Banting 'bug' appeared to bite. The Village Committees of Triang and Kerayong New Villages in Pahang fired 25-pounders at terrorist positions and as a reminder of their having partaken of Government's power, were allowed to keep the expended shell casings as souvenirs.[247] Then Pulau Banting and Telok Bunut, two villages near Banting, formed an anti-Communist organisation.[248] By the end of the year the GCC movement was extended throughout Malaya,[249] Bourne proclaimed the GCC 'technique' a 'success',[250] and in March 1956 MacGillivray himself personally feted the founder members of the Banting GCC at King's House.[251] As we shall see, the growth of the GCCs in particular was to greatly assist Government Psychological Warfare in applying the final blow against the MCP.

THE RETURN OF C.C. TOO AND THE STATE OF GOVERNMENT PSYCHOLOGICAL WARFARE

Following his resignation in March 1953 over Peterson's interference in Psychological Warfare, and despite attempts to bring him back in the interim, C.C. Too had been 'too bitter' to budge. He thus spent the next two years 'wandering around', having a rest, and at one point even tried to join the National Museum.[252] It was only after Peterson had long left the scene – late March 1955 – that Too changed his mind. By this time O.W. Wolters, a Chinese Affairs man, had taken over as HPWS from Isaac.[253] Wolters had known Too since the late 1940s and despite having been discouraged by Peterson, did his best to get Too to come back. Too, irascible as ever, first informed Wolters to 'go to hell', then relented and agreed to return on his old pay for six months.[254] He added that if at the end of that time he had not set Wolters up as the authority on 'psywar' in Malaya he would 'walk out' as it would have been clear by then that he was 'no damn good'.[255] In the event, Too worked under Wolters on a monthly basis from 1 April 1955 to 1 June 1956 when he was offered a three-year contract.[256] True to form, Too promptly rejected the new contract and while he settled down to fight Chin Peng over the terms of the MCP's surrender, on the side he also engaged in internecine warfare with the Federal Establishment Office (FEO) and later the Public Services Commission (PSC) over the terms of his contract. Finally, Too was grudgingly appointed acting HPWS in November 1956 following Wolters' departure, and after Yaacob pointedly informed the Public Services Commission that 'none' of his staff wanted to be appointed to the post of HPWS, all resistance crumbled and Too was confirmed as HPWS with effect from 6 February 1958.[257]

Meanwhile the ability of Government propaganda physically to reach the terrorists continued to improve rapidly. Hence between July 1954 and February 1955 for instance 95.5 percent of a sample of SEPs had seen a Government leaflet, and on average each SEP had seen six leaflets.[258] In addition, despite earlier studies predicting that ground-hailing equipment had no future in Malaya, some breakthroughs were achieved from 1955. These included *Magnavox*, a powerful public address system mounted on an armoured Police vehicle, which could broadcast messages up to two and a half miles depending on type of terrain and time of day;[259] *Stentor*, a powerful amplification unit mounted on a truck with a range of two miles from the jungle edge;[260] and the *Thunderer* loudspeaker unit with a range of three miles from the jungle fringe.[261] Of particular interest was the Voice Aircraft, which was important because of the speed at which it could 'exploit' the psychological moment created by a specific terrorist setback. Between July 1954 and February 1955 79 percent of the earlier sample had heard at least one clear Voice Aircraft broadcast while complaints of lack of clarity had all but disappeared in 1955.[262] By 1954, moreover, a system of requesting Voice Aircraft support was in place. Demands for an event to be exploited usually originated from SIOs or SWECs and a signal was sent to Kuala Lumpur where it came before the Voice Aircraft Committee (VAC), consisting of two members of the PWS and a Police officer. The VAC met daily and was responsible for liaison with the RAF, composition of messages suitable for air broadcasting, preparation of tape recordings of such messages and the assignation of priorities for the various demands.[263]

By 1954, air broadcasting in Malaya had settled into two main types: 'tactical' broadcasts to individual terrorists or groups of terrorists either ad hoc or as part of an operation to secure surrenders and 'strategic' broadcasts concerning a general theme to both terrorists and the public. The chief problem that emerged by April 1955 was delays in exploiting the psychological moment created by terrorist setbacks. At the VAC end, delays occurred because of unavailability of aircraft (only three Dakotas and two

Austers for the whole country), poor weather over the target, unavailability of studios at Radio Malaya for recording of messages, or lack of announcers who could speak the right dialects. It was found, however, that the chief source of delay was at the State end. For instance in late 1954 Pahang took nine days and Negri Sembilan six days to provide the VAC with news for exploitation by Voice Aircraft. Sometimes this was because Special Branch, with an eye on operational considerations, would not clear the information for exploitation.[264] Richard Miers later put it this way:[265]

> If you've got a surrendered man who comes in and says there are four or five terrorists out there, well I as an infantryman will want to go and deal with them straight away. The psychological warfare people want me to project a message over to them. It's a bit difficult to work the thing out [sic] that is best to do. Once you project the message in and say "come out and surrender," obviously, I can't sit on the jungle edge and shoot them as they come out. It is a bit difficult to get a balance.

As a result of such delays, States like Pahang, Selangor and Johore did not exploit the surrender of as many SEPs as they could have. The PWS view was that a Voice broadcast up to two days after surrender would have had some impact on the remaining terrorists, but if the broadcast were made a week later, the 'news' value would have been less and the overall effect on terrorist morale nugatory. In other words, in order to exploit the psychological moment created by a terrorist setback, 'news' of the event had to be 'speedily utilised'.[266] Miers expressed it succinctly when he argued that 'tactical psychological warfare' was all about 'hitting the iron when its hot'.[267]

Another powerful weapon remained rewards. Throughout the last six months of 1954 and into January 1955, the policy of not making public the amounts of rewards offered or paid, so as to prevent high ranking terrorists making propaganda capital out of the high prices on their heads, was still in force. It was held that both the terrorists and the public knew informally that substantial sums were paid out anyway.[268] In February 1955, however, it emerged that one of Central's tactics to clamp down on the desertion rate was to suggest that Government paid out more money for information leading to *kills* rather than surrenders. To counter this, Bourne once more made public the reward scale to drive home the point that Government sought surrenders rather than kills. He also simplified the scheme to four basic tiers: members of the public who induced the surrender, captured, or provided information leading to the surrender or capture of leaders above District Committee rank would now receive $20,000. On the other hand, information or action resulting in the killing of the said rank of terrorist would earn $16,000. The corresponding figures for leaders of District Committee rank were $12,000 and $10,000; for leaders of Branch Committee rank, $4,000 and $3,000; and for persons below Branch Committee rank, $2,000 and $1,500 respectively. These were minimum sums which could be increased by the Commissioner of Police contingent on the degree of risk and effort put in by the informant. In addition, half these rates were payable to SEPs in the first three months after surrender. After this period, if an SEP joined the Security Forces voluntarily he was no longer eligible for rewards. On the other hand, if he was released for rehabilitation, following this he could claim full rewards as an ordinary member of the public.[269]

In addition, any member of the public and SEP who was able to recover from the terrorists the following grades of serviceable arms were eligible for the corresponding rewards: for each light machine gun and light automatic, $1,000; for each rifle, pistol, revolver and automatic, $300; for each smooth bore gun, $150; for each grenade, $50; and for each mortar bomb, shell, landmine or aerial bomb, $100. Moreover, unlike before, SEPs could now earn rewards for surrendering their own weapons. It was hoped that this would act as a further incentive to surrender. In addition, Government reiterated that any member of the public who physically assisted terrorists *in the act of surrender* (as distinct from inducing him to surrender) by guiding him to the nearest Police or Government officials would receive $500, and would be immune from the charge of consorting with the terrorists if they first informed Government officials of their intention. Finally SWECs took pains to persuade the terrorists in leaflets and other media that Government paid out higher rewards for 'inducing or causing surrenders than for action resulting in death'.[270] By the end of 1955, $822,082 had been paid out as rewards.[271]

In sum, 1955 was a key year for Government Psychological Warfare: C.C. Too returned in April, Tunku as noted earlier became Chief Minister in July, while Government had by then perfected or was about to perfect the various instruments of Psychological Warfare: the ubiquitous leaflets, powerful ground hailing equipment, the flexible Voice Aircraft and the reward policy. Moreover, the circumstances for utilising these media were looking propitious, judging by the rise of the Good Citizens' Committees, the favourable international situation and the increasing evidence – caused by successful Security Force/food denial operations – of a decay in the confidence of even hardened terrorists. The stage was thus set for the climactic battle between Tunku and Chin Peng for the confidence of the remaining terrorists.

PROPAGANDA ENDGAME: JANUARY 1955–DECEMBER 1958

On 6 January 1955, Tunku told the *Malay Mail* that if the Alliance won the July Federal elections, it would declare an Amnesty for the terrorists.[272] While the Colonial Office appeared open to the idea,[273] British officials in Malaya were none too keen. MacGillivray and Bourne feared that Tunku would commit the Alliance politically to an Amnesty at a time when there was no evidence at all that such an offer would precipitate the collapse of the MCP.[274] Accordingly, at a Director of Operations Committee meeting on 17 January, Tunku was persuaded to drop all public discussion of an Amnesty, as the prevailing surrender policy already embodied a 'measure' of Amnesty, and would be reviewed if the situation truly warranted it.[275] To recapitulate, under the prevailing Gurney Amnesty, only SEPs with no 'blood on their hands' – that is, who had not committed a capital offence – were not prosecuted. Culpable SEPs were only promised fair treatment. However, although Government had never explicitly promised it in propaganda to terrorists, generally, SEPs who *had* committed capital offences were not only fairly treated but had never been prosecuted either.[276] Now in March 1955, in a hugely significant step, and in an attempt to forestall further UMNO/MCA pressure for an Amnesty, Government finally revealed to the general public the fate of all SEPs who surrendered – with 'blood on their hands' or not: they were detained the first three months after surrender, and after this they were rehabilitated or joined the Security Forces voluntarily.[277] By this time it was routine that during the first three months after surrender SEPs worked with Special Branch, and following this period, were rehabilitated. They could then work for Special Branch permanently or find employment outside, at which point they had their Restricted Residence Orders cancelled and were issued identity cards. Rehabilitated SEPs could also join SOVF or live in Kemendore Agricultural Settlement. SEPs who could not find employment, serve in SOVF or work in Kemendore were released on a suspended order of detention with a Restricted Residence Order.[278]

Despite Government's uneasiness about public Amnesty discussions, these early debates *had* got Central worried, and from January, its internal propaganda decried this attempt to 'shake the thoughts of our comrades whose resolve is not sufficiently definite' and 'produce wavering confidence among them'.[279] Central was only too aware of the rot already setting into even its State Committee leaderships, as the Pahang surrenders were demonstrating. Furthermore, it was most likely disturbed by Government's March announcement which clarified the fate of all SEPs for the benefit of the general public, who could now see that there was substance in Government's claim that its current surrender policy was already pretty generous. Moreover, Chin Peng knew that in London in April 1954, the second Conference of Communist and Workers' Parties of the British Commonwealth had called for the resolution of the Malayan Emergency by 'the method of peace'.[280] The bottom line, however, was simple: Central had to act fast to prevent a collapse of terrorist morale given the 'very remote' prospect of a military victory. Thus it now decided to launch a 'political attack, which is more severe than our military offensive'. The aim was to split the Government camp and win over neutral elements for a 'peace movement'.[281] Hence the so-called Ng Heng letter, dated 1 May 1955, was posted in Haadyai, Thailand, on 7 June 1955 and sent to several Government and Malayan interests.[282] It was received by Government in late June. The Director of Operations Committee appreciated that the Party, exploiting the public's natural desire for the end of seven years of Emergency conditions, sought to build up public pressure on Government to recognise the MCP as a 'body' to be parleyed with. The offer was thus rejected and it was reiterated that the terrorists should instead take advantage of the prevailing 'generous surrender policy' which promised fair treatment.[283]

Government then counterattacked. Beginning in July, 71 million leaflets were dropped on the jungle, emphasising that the MCP peace offer was tacit admission of political failure and that it was useless to continue the struggle.[284] In fact, the rank and file heard about the Ng Heng letter from Government, not Central, and this precipitated 'repeated discussions and uncertainty and even controversy among units in the jungle'.[285] At the same time, however, it was recognised that the Emergency-weary public were wondering if Government had been unreasonable in rejecting the MCP offer. This sentiment was encouraged by MCP propaganda which insisted that although Government had rejected the Ng Heng offer, Central still wanted to talk. MacGillivray and Bourne feared that such rhetoric would stimulate public demands that the MCP be accorded legal recognition as the price for ending the Emergency. It was to forestall this that the Director of Operations Committee decided to mount a 'new and fresh approach' to seize the propaganda high ground: an Amnesty. The hope was to persuade the public to reject the MCP version of a peaceful resolution: the emergence of the Party from the jungle as a legal entity with full political rights, in favour of Government's interpretation of 'peace': the emergence of a surrendered enemy with its rights sharply curtailed.[286] Hence MacGillivray cabled London at the end of July, arguing that a fresh Amnesty would 'offset the propaganda value of the Communists' negotiation proposals' as well as 'convince neutral opinion that the government were not seeking to prolong the shooting war but were prepared to make a positive proposal to end it'.[287] The 1955 Amnesty was thus intended primarily to assure the public that Government shared its desire to end the shooting war. In addition, it was hoped that the Amnesty would spur the people to pressure the terrorists to come out of the jungle on *Government's* terms.[288] Furthermore, while the terrorists per se were in fact seen as a secondary target of the Amnesty,[289] MacGillivray nevertheless added that the 'psychological moment to make a fresh offer' had arrived, and Government should make a renewed attempt to 'drive a wedge between' the rank and file and 'their leaders'.[290]

Another factor affecting the proposed timing of the Amnesty was the July 1955 Federal elections. MacGillivray accepted Tunku's view that the

Amnesty would enjoy enhanced legitimacy and thus greater bite if it were made not by the British but rather the newly elected *Malayan* Government which would assume power after the elections.[291] Finally, the content of the Amnesty was critical. To be sure, given the tense strategic situation in Southeast Asia at the time, deciding on the surrender terms proved a tricky task. MacGillivray vehemently opposed the view of the Chiefs of Staff Committee that the Amnesty leaflet ought to announce how SEPs would be 'held in detention' once they came out. Warning that the term 'detention' would deter terrorists from leaving the jungle, he argued instead that the word 'investigation' ought to be used, as it represented the 'best possible compromise between the aim of making the amnesty successful and the need to leave the Federal Government with a free hand in dealing with hard core Communist terrorists'.[292] In addition, the phrase 'if any of them wish to go to China, their request will be given due consideration' apparently 'suffered many birth pangs before it was born'. It was eventually felt that it would be unwise to expand the sentence to include other countries in Southeast Asia, such as Thailand and Indonesia, as it might alarm them.[293] Ultimately, after 'much discussion' between Kuala Lumpur and London, by late August, the text of the Amnesty was hammered out,[294] and Tunku, now Chief Minister, immediately announced that he had secured the agreement of the Colonial Secretary Lennox-Boyd, MacGillivray and Bourne for a new surrender offer.[295]

The new Amnesty was declared at midnight on 9 September 1955, superseding and more generous than the 1949 Gurney Amnesty. Its terms were: all terrorists who had committed 'any offence, connected with the Emergency' under 'Communist direction', would 'not be prosecuted' if they would 'come in and surrender' immediately. Government would then 'conduct investigations on those who surrender'. Those 'AMSEPs' who 'show that they genuinely intend to be loyal to the Government of Malaya and to give up their communist activities, will be helped to regain their normal position in society and be reunited with their families'. Those who refused to recant Communism would have 'restrictions' imposed 'on their liberty'. Requests for repatriation to China would be 'given due consideration'.[296] It was decided not to impose a time limit for the surrender offer, though this fact was not made explicit in the leaflets.[297] In addition, to allay the fears of certain supporters that they would be implicated by terrorists whom they had previously assisted and consorted with – and now helped to surrender – Tunku announced that such people would not be prosecuted either. To facilitate the safe surrender of terrorists, moreover, 186 safe areas were declared throughout the country. In such safe areas, the Security Forces were withdrawn and surrender points designated within them. Meanwhile the existing rewards for bringing in terrorists alive were also emphasised and publicised.[298] A massive propaganda drive was mounted to publicise these Amnesty terms. Hence 2,000 people of all races from Tanjong Sepat New Village in Selangor and nearby kampongs and estates, divided themselves into six parties and marched into the jungle – some for up to *five miles* – and shouted messages to terrorists Ah Thian and Sze Kwan to come out and surrender, or else all 15,000 people in the area would unite to wipe them out. The people significantly complained that everyone was sick of the Emergency restrictions and wanted a White Area.[299] More pro-Amnesty rallies of 3,000 people each were mounted in Seremban and Gemas in Negri Sembilan, Tangkak in Johore and Bentong in Pahang. Tunku addressed the Gemas rally.[300]

Meanwhile, C.C. Too, who had been back at work since the beginning of April, was shaking his head: a senior British intelligence officer admitted to him that Government had been caught out by Ng Heng. Too promptly 'resuscitated and intensified' documentary research, examining Special Branch files for the previous two years, and found that captured MCP documents cyclostyled in Chinese had not been translated, sorted and studied. In particular, he discovered in a document 'gathering dust' that the 1954 Conference of Communist and Workers' Parties in the British Commonwealth had passed six resolutions which served as directives, the last of which had called for the war in Malaya to be ended by 'the method of peace'. This directive had been transmitted by Central to the rest of the Party.[301] Sensing that the public was open to MCP peace initiatives like Ng Heng, Too warned Wolters in June 1955 that Central was going to send another open letter stressing the positive public response to Ng Heng and proposing that Tunku and Chin Peng ought to meet without 'British interference'. To this end, Too predicted that Central would send propaganda head Chen Tien, who knew some English, to meet British representatives and discuss protocol for peace talks. Too recalled that PWS staff had 'laughed' at 'the Great Prophet, C. Too'.[302] Not for long, though. Three days after the Amnesty announcement, Chin Peng wrote to Tunku proposing exactly what Too had 'prophesied'. There followed three preparatory meetings at Klian Intan in northern Perak between Chen Tien of the MCP and Government representatives in 17 October, 18 November, and 13 December, and the dates for the Baling Peace Talks were finally fixed: 28 and 29 December 1955.[303]

The British were very anxious about Tunku meeting Chin Peng. At a meeting with MacGillivray on 18 October, while Tunku indicated that he was not prepared to recognise the MCP, he was willing to discuss with Chin Peng: the possibility of providing an assurance that terrorists surrendering under the Amnesty would not be deported; that they would be allowed to take part in politics and would not be detained for more than a very short period; the release of present detainees, and the repeal of the Emergency Regulations. MacGillivray disagreed, reiterating that Tunku should only clarify the Amnesty terms at Baling.[304] MacGillivray felt that any attempt to stop the meeting, however, would lead to a breach with the Alliance and play into the Communists' hands.[305] The possibility of Tunku being trapped into disastrous concessions at Baling was reinforced alarmingly during a Baling dress rehearsal staged following Chin Peng's September letter, in which Too, playing Chin Peng, had squared off against Maj-General Lindsay,[306] playing Tunku. Too/Chin Peng offered the following 'package deal': in return for laying down of arms, the 'only' thing the MCP wanted was legal recognition and the ability to walk out as free men. Lindsay/Tunku was unable to sensibly counter this, and was left in a 'cold sweat'.[307] It was thus felt that Singapore Chief Minister David Marshall would be needed to help stiffen Tunku at the talks.[308] However, the prognosis was greatly improved when following discussions with Whitehall, MacGillivray assured the Executive Council at the end of November that the continuation of the Emergency at its present level was no obstacle to Malaya's progress to independence. This eased the pressure on Tunku, because he did not now have to secure the end of the fighting at whatever cost in order to pave the way for *Merdeka*. In other words, whether Chin Peng surrendered or not, *Merdeka* was coming anyway. Coupled with news of the Too/Lindsay dress rehearsal, therefore, Tunku approached Baling with a stiffer, cautious but confident attitude, primed to merely 'clarify' the Amnesty terms and nothing more.[309]

However, Tunku's announcement in late September 1955 that he would meet Chin Peng enabled Central to inform the rank and file to hold out for the outcome of the Baling Talks, as it was possible that all might walk out as free men.[310] The Baling Talks thus nullified the Amnesty: up to the end of December 1955, only 62 AMSEPs were generated.[311] Moreover, some terrorists took advantage of the safe areas to perpetrate atrocities. This resulted in the revocation of all such areas from 21 November.[312] At Baling, moreover, Chin Peng rejected the September Amnesty and – as Too had predicted – instead offered to cease hostilities in return for 'recognition of the M.C.P., no detention, no investigation and no restriction of movement' of MCP members who came out of the jungle. While Tunku clarified that AMSEPs wishing to be repatriated would not be investigated, only those wishing to remain in Malaya would be, it was his position on what to Chin Peng was the 'primary question' which led to the breakdown of the Talks: Tunku insisted that he would never recognise the MCP, and added that it had to be dissolved. Nevertheless, Tunku did wring out of Chin Peng a significant declaration that if Tunku managed to gain control of internal security the MCP would cease hostilities – although Chin Peng clarified that this did not mean a surrender of weapons to Government.[313] At any rate, Tunku announced on 30 December that the Amnesty and all other surrender terms in force prior to the Amnesty would be withdrawn on 8 February 1956. He added that he had no intention of meeting the MCP again unless they wanted to discuss surrender.[314] Tunku emerged from Baling not merely with an enhanced reputation for toughness; because he got precisely full control of internal security and even a promise of independence by August 1957 at the London constitutional conference, he was to put Chin Peng on the propaganda defensive.[315]

Once the Amnesty was withdrawn on 8 February 1956, moreover, with the very disappointing final score of 74 AMSEPs,[316] it became imperative to replace it with a new surrender policy. It was not very simple. Government did not want to return to the generous pre-Amnesty terms of fair treatment of SEPs with 'blood on their hands' and appear weak. On the other hand it still had to offer *something* to convince the hard core left in the jungle to surrender.[317] In March, new surrender terms were approved which offered fair treatment and freedom (or repatriation to China), *only* to those terrorists who had 'genuinely foresworn [sic] Communist terrorism and [had] not been guilty of acts of atrocity or murder'.[318] This strict stipulation however meant that most of the remaining terrorists would be prosecuted if they surrendered. In July, however, the EOC agreed to a 'less stringent interpretation of the exclusion clause', which meant that except for a few thugs who were guilty of extremely brutal crimes, the rest could be offered terms which resembled the pre-Amnesty ones. By the end of 1956, therefore, terrorists intending to give up could be credibly assured by Government Psychological Warfare of fair treatment.[319]

In any case, the effectiveness of the March 1956 surrender terms was nullified by Central's quick response to the breakdown of the Baling Talks. It embarked on intensive internal propaganda which suggested to terrorists 'severely shaken' by the failure of Baling and the end of the Alliance Amnesty that the real failure at Baling was Government's: because Tunku had 'failed' to secure the surrender of the MCP at Baling, as *Merdeka* approached, the will of both Government and the public to continue fighting would weaken and they would seek accommodation with the MCP eventually. Hence the call to the comrades was to 'hang on' and conserve strength for that inevitable day. This internal campaign was effective, as the terrorists by mid-1956 were clearly adopting a 'wait-and-see' attitude. Hence the monthly surrender rate dropped from 20.66 in 1955 to only 11.25 in 1956.[320] To counter this 'wait-and-see' policy, PWS tried to attack terrorist morale by stiffening the public against helping the terrorists. Part of this involved a continuing attempt to 'sweeten' the bitter pill of food control and other restrictions so disliked by the rural Chinese.[321] Too in this respect recounted how the New Villagers were coached into turning the Emergency Regulations into an excuse for not assisting the MCP:

> I am 100 percent supporter of the National Liberation War. You are no end of a hero! Fine we like to support you but we cannot. The horrible imperialists-colonialists have put us in a concentration camp! ... They fence us up like pigs and they search us. You don't believe, comrade?

Why don't you come down and see for yourself? ... Why don't you and your comrades come down and shoot up the gate! Then you liberate us and we help you.

Too recalled that the New Villagers 'took great delight' in resisting the terrorists, and the latter, confronted with increasing numbers of tappers who actually answered back, were shaken.[322] By mid-1956, moreover, PWS intensified its already close co-operation with Information Services, producing material for mobile unit teams, and increasing emphasis on briefing the public on the progress of the Emergency in their Districts and why the end was in sight. It was held that letting the public into what were hitherto regarded as the 'secrets of professionals', 'made for confidence both in the superiority of the Government forces and the wisdom of those who [controlled] those forces'.[323]

Furthermore, by 1956 it was clear that the public and the rural Chinese especially 'desperately wanted the violence to end, and were generally very co-operative'.[324] This sentiment was expressed in the continued formation of GCCs. The GCCs were in fact used by PWS for passing on information to the public, while GCC-organised mass demonstrations were useful in 'giving the people a feeling of strength in number and unity'. These mass rallies also made it plain that it was safe to pass information to the authorities, while underscoring to both the public and the terrorists that Communism was a lost cause. Little wonder then that by the end of 1956 it became clear that in Districts where the people publicly turned against them, terrorist gangs rapidly collapsed.[325] Against this background of growing overt public – and rural Chinese – support, Tunku engaged in three main countermeasures against the MCP 'wait-and-see' policy. In April 1956 he rejected a second attempt by the MCP to negotiate peace terms, this time via a letter dated 5 March from Chen Tien, sent to a number of organisations and people but not himself. Dismissing Chen Tien's arguments that the MCP did not want terms which subjected it to 'political indignity or personal retaliation', Tunku reiterated that he would only talk about arrangements for the unconditional surrender of the MCP. He also reminded the public that at Baling Chin Peng had agreed to lay down arms once he had secured control of internal security, and that thus far the MCP had failed to do so.[326] On 27 September, moreover, following Chin Peng's letter to the Eighth Chinese Communist Party Congress, he rejected any notion whatsoever of international mediation of the conflict between the MCP and Government. Finally, in November, via the Operation Iceland mass leaflet drop, Tunku personally informed the terrorists that Yeong Kwo, Chin Peng's deputy who had planned the 'political offensive', had been eliminated by Security Forces; that it was pure folly believing Central's line that Chin Peng had almost succeeded at Baling and would succeed the next time; that the situation was getting worse for the MCP, not better; that there was no hope of external aid for the MCP; and with *Merdeka* in 1957 they would be bereft of a reason to fight. He concluded by promising that he and the Malayan people would be determined to stamp out Communism even after *Merdeka*.[327]

As *Merdeka* drew closer, Central once again tried to seek new negotiations. In March 1957 a cyclostyled letter from Central reached several Chinese Guilds and Associations. It was 'absolutely identical' to the Chen Tien letter of a year earlier. Tunku once more did not budge.[328] Then in July, he announced that he expected very soon to receive a letter from Chin Peng announcing the MCP's unconditional surrender, and that the Emergency would end in December 1958.[329] Tunku was meanwhile under heavy pressure to negotiate with the MCP so as to begin independence with a 'clean slate', and stop the shooting war, which had been such a 'colossal drain' on the country's finances. For instance, the same month he announced his projected end-date of the Emergency the Malayan Trade Union Congress called on him to seek an 'honourable settlement' with the MCP.[330] Nevertheless, in August, Tunku announced a 'secret plan': an 'intensified' Psychological Warfare campaign involving all Cabinet Ministers and Alliance Federal, State, town and village councillors going to all parts of the country to secure the help of the public in eliminating the terrorists.[331] Then three days before *Merdeka* he declared that Government would give the terrorists one last chance to surrender.[332]

The *Merdeka* Amnesty was therefore announced on 3 September. The latest surrender terms were the result of the Baling script being 'studied afresh' for several months beforehand. Intended to last until 31 December 1957, the Amnesty stipulated that terrorists 'who genuinely desire to give up the armed struggle may come out of the jungle', and that they would 'NOT be prosecuted for any offence connected with the Emergency' which had been 'committed under communist direction before this date'. In addition, terrorists 'who show that they genuinely intend to be loyal to the elected Government of Malaya and to give up their communist activities will be helped to regain their normal life and to be reunited with their families, if they so wish'. Those who refused to recant Communism would be 'repatriated to China (with their families if they so wish)'. As in the case of the 1955 Amnesty, moreover, the *Merdeka* offer assured terrorist supporters who induced terrorists to give up that they would not be prosecuted. However, what made this latest Amnesty the most liberal ever was that, given Chin Peng's opposition at Baling to any form of restrictions or investigation of terrorists, SEPs opting for repatriation were explicitly assured that they would 'not be made the subject of any investigation or interrogation but will be given fair treatment while waiting for repatriation'. Finally, Too drafted the Amnesty text in 'a most palatable language' to the hard core terrorists and their leaders. For instance, instead of 'surrender', Too substituted 'wishes to leave the jungle'; while in place of 'Communist terrorists', he inserted 'MCP personnel'. Government also timed the Amnesty announcement soon after *Merdeka* so as to force Central into reacting rather than the other way around.[333]

In truth, the *Merdeka* Amnesty represented the final throw of the dice. Government hoped to persuade the Emergency-weary public, especially of course the ordinary Chinese in New Villages, estates and mines, that since *Merdeka* had been achieved, eliminating the MCP's most critical ostensible rationale for their revolt, there really was no reason why the Communists should not accept the surrender terms. Equally significant, there was widespread agreement – even amongst Tunku's political opponents such as the Labour Party and the People's Progressive Party – that the terms themselves were unprecedentedly reasonable and even generous. While Government in this fashion exerted moral pressure on the terrorists, in the realm of the physical, pressure was applied too: unlike the 1955 Amnesty with its safe areas, this time there was to be no relaxation of Security Force operations while the Amnesty was in force. The Amnesty leaflet stipulated this.[334] The *Merdeka* terms were publicised via Operation Greenland, in which 12,412,500 leaflets were dropped between 6 and 9 September 1957.[335] Mass leaflet drops were followed up by intensive activity on the ground. Hence the month the Amnesty was inaugurated 100 Perak State and Federal Councillors, in conjunction with SIO Perak, launched a six-week campaign in 700 New Villages and kampongs in a drive to get the terrorists to quit.[336] Also in September Sauk New Village GCC in Perak organised a 2,000-strong rally in which the people pledged to help Government destroy the terrorists to the last man unless they accepted the Amnesty offer.[337] Significantly, the GCC movement by 1957 had penetrated even the 'bad' areas: Broga, Semenyih, Tanjong Malim and Pusing, for instance. The Tanjong Malim GCC for example in August had organised a mass plunge by 2,000 residents, flanked by Security Forces, into the jungle in order to get DCM Chi Lui to surrender. Tan Boon Jin, Chairman of the GCC, had declared that it was 'stupid' of the terrorists not to give up, and that the people had 'enjoyed' themselves.[338] In early October Tunku himself addressed the biggest ever anti-Communist rally of 5,000 people at Kuala Pilah and introduced the first SEP to give up under the new Amnesty: Ah Ying, wife of the DCM Li Hak Chi who had been killed the previous month.[339] The Amnesty also sparked a marked increase in the flow of public information especially from people living on the jungle fringes. This helped the Police round up 38 terrorist sympathisers.[340]

Also in October, newspapers in Malaya received a MCP manifesto dated 1 September that had been posted in Haadyai. It reiterated that the MCP would lay down arms in return for participation in the democratic process within 'constitutional limits'.[341] Tunku's response was that this was nothing new and if Chin Peng could make new and constructive proposals based on the MCP's complete surrender he could write to Tunku direct and a meeting could be arranged.[342] Meanwhile the Amnesty was beginning to bite – hard. On 23 October, a big fish – Regional Committee Member Yee Foong, whom Special Branch had believed would never give up – surrendered in Kluang District and was repatriated, 'no questions asked'.[343] The rot was setting into even the hardest of the hard core.[344] Meanwhile Chin Peng had written to Tunku on 12 October to ask for a second round of talks to obtain 'a just and fair agreement to end the war'. On 8 November Tunku announced that he would agree to a preparatory meeting and wanted Chin Peng to write for more details on the talks.[345] Later that month, Government identified Kroh, near the Thai border as the site for new talks.[346] By early December, however, Tunku had still not heard from Chin Peng. It became obvious that as he had done so two years earlier, Chin Peng had thrown up the hope of peace talks so as to persuade his battered rank and file to hold on and wait for a better deal.[347]

On 6 December Tunku therefore issued an ultimatum: if Chin Peng failed to send out an emissary to make arrangements for the meeting by 31 December, the talks would be off.[348] 10 days later, moreover, Tunku announced that 122 terrorists had surrendered under the Amnesty. This indicated a huge jump in the surrender rate. While the rate had been only eight a month in the first eight months of 1957, in October and November this had hit as many as 40 a month. In addition, for the first time in the Emergency, the number of SEPs actually exceeded the number of terrorists captured or killed. Moreover, 36 of the 122 SEPs were ranking terrorists.[349] Tunku had the propaganda upper hand and he knew it. Five days later, on 21 December, he finally received Chin Peng's reply, dated 9 December. Chin Peng indicated that he would send two lieutenants for preliminary talks, but added that the question of surrender did not arise. Tunku replied the same day that in that case there was no point meeting at all, dismissed the possibility of future talks, and extended the *Merdeka* Amnesty by another four months.[350] PWS thus mounted Operation Greenland II between 17 to 20 December 1957, dropping a further 13,735,000 leaflets.[351]

Significantly, one official assessment of the state of the Emergency at the end of 1957 noted that 'it becomes increasingly obvious that the end to the Emergency will not be brought about by shooting, but must be induced by psychological or other means'.[352] This was confirmed within 12 months, thanks to the *Merdeka* Amnesty. It is suggested that the exact psychological moment that the *Merdeka* Amnesty became irresistibly potent was 21 December 1957. This is because from that date onwards the terrorists knew they had no hope whatsoever of waiting for a 'better deal' – Tunku had ruled out future Balings. Only two clear choices were left, therefore: death from Security Force pressure and starvation, or survival on Government's liberal *Merdeka* terms. In short, the remaining hard core were forced to conclude – not so much that since *Merdeka* had been achieved, there was no point fighting – but rather that since even a political victory was to be denied them, it was best to make the most of the liberal surrender offer. Terrorist morale thus cracked. Captured documents illustrate the extent of the breakdown of discipline in January 1958: increased reading of Government leaflets; more group discussions of surrender within the terrorist ranks and lack of interest in carrying out Party tasks.[353] Little wonder that between March and May 1958 Regional Committee Secretary Ah Ann in south Johore had to execute five of his men, before he himself was eliminated by Security Forces in November.[354] It must be noted that from September 1957 loss of faith in the Party was complemented by increasing confidence that Government would honour its promises. In this connection Tunku's personal credibility was crucial: several terrorists reported that they came out because they trusted Tunku to keep his word regarding the Amnesty terms.[355] At any rate, 1958 was the year of the mass surrenders. While 130 terrorists surrendered under the *Merdeka* Amnesty by 31 December 1957,[356] by 27 March 1958, this figure had risen to 215, and compelled Tunku to extend the Amnesty a final time, till 31 July.[357] 8.5 million leaflets were therefore dropped under Operation Greenland III.[358] Particularly spectacular were the collapse of the Communist organisations in the last bastions of Perak and Johore, orchestrated by Special Branch. 118 terrorists, including a State Committee Member, four District Committee Secretaries, seven District Committee Members, and 10 Branch Committee Members, gave up in south Perak between 15 October 1957 and 10 July 1958, which meant that since the *Merdeka* Amnesty commenced in September 1957 a total of 304 had given up only in that area by July 1958.[359] South Perak was eventually declared White in January 1959.[360] In Johore, the surrender of Hor Lung – the first Central Committee Member to do so – ensured the collapse of the MCP Southern Malaya Bureau and 160 surrenders. Johore was declared White on 31 December 1958.[361] Such large losses were disastrous to the MCP because of its reduced overall numbers: by the end of 1957 there were only 1,681 terrorists left in Malaya, including 500 on the Thai/Malaya border. A year later, this had fallen to 868, including 485 on the Thai side of the border.[362] To all intents and purposes, therefore, as a meaningful contest, the Emergency was over by the end of 1958.[363]

CONCLUSION

We have seen that Tunku Abdul Rahman played a key role in maintaining the efficiency of Government despite the distractions of Malayanisation, thereby ensuring that it could continue to generate the deeds needed to influence the minds of the rural Chinese and the terrorists. In addition, Tunku's personal appeal to all races and classes, especially the rural Chinese, was not only unique but crucial. Rural Chinese confidence was also enhanced by the increasingly secure New Village environment where Government and associated *Taijins* were on hand to address problems. On the other hand, despite Police and Army recognition of the importance of rural Chinese confidence, residual caricaturing of the ordinary Chinese at times gave rise to propaganda disasters like Semenyih. Nevertheless, it was now Government practice to be 'propaganda-minded', and in the policy field the message that Government cared was communicated through, *inter alia*, increasing the number of White Areas, central cooking, easing off on the use of detention and deportation, and implementing more discriminate measures by which to extricate terrorist supporters from the larger community. At the same time Security Force pressure in conjunction with central cooking communicated 'no hope of victory' and precipitated sheer defeatism in terrorist ranks, while the Indochina ceasefire convinced them that notions of external assistance were illusory.

We also noted that Information Services under Yaacob Latiff, through Civics Courses and mobile unit visits, continued to bring the rural Chinese into the bosom of Government, while the MFU and Radio Malaya projected Government's presence into the New Villages and estate lines. Of particular importance was the growth of Good Citizens' Committees, which from 1955 to 1957 both promoted rural Chinese confidence in Government as well as expressed that commodity. Moreover, the transfer of PWS to the Director of Operations Staff, the improving reach of Government tactical propaganda and importantly the return of C.C. Too, also set the scene for Government Psychological Warfare to mount its final campaign against the terrorists. Finally, the period January 1955 to December 1958 represented the climax of the contest between Government and Central for the confidence of the terrorists. Against a background of Government words and especially deeds which were sending the message to both the rural Chinese and the terrorists that Government was winning, Tunku's contribution to the terrorist collapse was two-fold: his steadfast refusal during and after Baling to allow the MCP to emerge from the jungle with political recognition and freedom of movement in hand, and his personal aura and credibility that convinced surrendering hard core Chinese terrorists that he could be trusted.

Finally, although the official end of the Emergency was one and a half years away, as a serious contest it really ended in December 1958. Chin Peng recently admitted that following the mass surrenders of that year, the MRLA was 'hard up' and 'finished'. This compelled Central to 'discontinue the battle and lie low', and to introduce in December a demobilisation policy permitting MCP members to have their Party membership revoked as a prelude to leaving the jungle.[364] Certainly, this formal de-emphasis on military operations augured an intensification of the lower-cost strategy of subversion: at the end of June 1958 a secret MCP document was captured stipulating that as the shooting war could not be won, it was imperative that cadres penetrated progressive political parties to form a United Front Government as a prelude to a Communist regime.[365] Nevertheless, the MCP demobilisation implied that Government – although it did not know it then – had effectively won the shooting war.

Conclusion

While previous explanations of the outcome of the Emergency, such as Thompson's principles of counterinsurgency, Stubbs' 'hearts and minds' approach and Mockaitis' British counterinsurgency style have provided important and useful insights, they have not effectively teased apart the operational and political aspects of the conflict. Thus, while past analysts may have discussed discrete methods, strategies and tactics of counter-insurgency, they have had little argument with the assertion that fundamentally, constitutional advance toward self-government and in particular political rights for the Chinese community represented the ultimate formula for counterinsurgency success. As we have seen, however, while the progress of the rural insurgency certainly influenced the pace of advance toward *Merdeka*, the converse was not true: progress toward citizenship and self-government did not *ipso facto* imply that the public most affected by MCP terror – the rural Chinese – would throw their weight behind Government. Rather they instinctively sought physical and socio-economic security ahead of political rights and aspirations. These rural Chinese – the squatters, rubber tappers, tin miners, timber workers and the artisans of varying skills that populated the jungle fringe – represented the true centre of gravity of the military insurgency. It was they that provided both material sustenance to the Malayan Communist Party as well as its combat strength. As successive Directors of Operations from Briggs onward recognised, moreover, the key to defeating the rural insurgency was to secure that elusive psychological commodity of rural Chinese confidence, the well-spring of everything else. Without confidence, the Chinese would not pass intelligence to Security Forces on terrorists and their Min Yuen helpers; without confidence they would not march in the crucial anti-Communist processions organised by Good Citizens' Committees. Similarly, without confidence in Government's good faith, many terrorists – who themselves largely emerged from the rural Chinese community – would never have surrendered. The key *operational* question of the Malayan Emergency was therefore not so much how to win the 'hearts and minds' of the Malayan public, but more precisely, how to win and hold rural Chinese and terrorist confidence?

The recurring answer to this question throughout the study has been: propaganda. However, this subject has not been given sufficient attention in past works because of their focus on counterinsurgency technique to the virtual exclusion of any sustained examination of the psychological dimension – a mistake, since as Clausewitz observed, the physical and the moral can never be separated. We have seen that propaganda comprises not merely words and images, but also actions or deeds. In fact propaganda is more accurately conceived as those relevant mass communications – words and deeds – which influence the state of mind – or confidence – of a specific audience. We also noted that a basic precept of propaganda was that for propaganda of words to be credible, the messages conveyed by words and actual deeds must be consistent. If the propagandist's words communicated an impression which was contradicted by the message emanating from his actual deeds, then the audience would dismiss his words and lose faith in him. In this respect, despite its voluminous leaflets suggesting that it represented the oppressed masses in the fight against British Imperialism, the MCP's basic inclination to violence – even after the October 1951 policy – only destroyed its credibility in the eyes of most rural Chinese. Moreover, most of the terrorist rank and file were basically interested in the Party's ability and willingness to keep the promises of material benefits which had attracted them to join in the first place. Thus – quite apart from Security Force pressure and food denial – the jungle reality of uncaring and selfish leaders, broken promises and draconian discipline, similarly compelled them to lose faith in the Party. Furthermore, even the smaller group of hard core terrorists of the Tunku era lost confidence in the Party when they realised that Central after 21 December 1957 would not be able to secure political victory from the jaws of military defeat and thus provide them with the short-cut to power they had craved. In short, a main reason why the MCP contributed to its own demise was that Central, through its deeds, lost the confidence of both the rural Chinese and the bulk of its rank and file. In the words of the leading American counterinsurgent Edward Lansdale, the attitude of the rural Chinese and the rank and file was: 'I cannot hear what you say because I see what you do'.[1]

On the other hand, while British actions were able to secure the confidence of the mass of the rural Chinese and even the terrorists by late 1958, this was a tortuously slow process. The problem was that British administrators and soldiers took years to jettison certain habits of mind that had been forged during the long experience of imperial policing. One damaging trait carried over into Malaya was the post-Indian Mutiny propensity of soldiers and officials to stereotype a particular ethnic group as 'cunning' and in need of a firm hand to keep them in check. This found fresh incarnation in Malaya as the 'strong line with the Chinese', and was reinforced by the circumstantial realities that the rural Chinese were not very enthused about authority in the first place and it happened that most terrorists were Chinese. Moreover, the short-sighted abolition of the Chinese Protectorate and the severe shortage of Chinese-speaking Police contributed to the communication vacuum in which stereotyping flourished. Consequently British soldiers, British and Malay Police and Specials in the first four years subjected the rural Chinese to rough treatment when the real reason they were not talking was the lack of effective protection from MCP reprisals for co-operation with Government. A similar phenomenon obtained during the Second Indochina War when language difficulties were compounded by 'racist clichés' that 'Orientals [were] lazy, dirty, untrust-worthy, and ignorant of the value of human life'.[2] In an atmosphere where all Vietnamese were stereotyped as 'gooks' or 'dinks', atrocities like My Lai were a logical consequence.[3]

That the Security Forces did not perpetrate further Batang Kalis in Malaya was due to the fact that by the end of 1951 and into 1952 serious and sustained reflection on the propaganda implications of troop behaviour occurred in official circles. Of particular importance was DGIS Peterson's insistence in August 1952 that all Government departments had to be 'propaganda-minded' and the inauguration of Operation Service at the end of 1952. Operation Service represented nothing less than an official recognition that the attitudes and behaviour of the agents of Government constituted propaganda which had to be orchestrated so as to project the idea that Government rather than the MCP was the Provider of the rural Chinese in particular. This was not an idea peculiar to Malaya. In the Philippines at the same time every Battalion Combat Team (BCT) had a Civil Affairs Officer who ensured 'the creation and maintenance of the "image" of the troops as friends and benefactors of the people'.[4] While it cannot be claimed that Operation Service alone transformed rural Chinese attitudes toward Government, it certainly influenced the attitudes of all Police and Government servants toward the Chinese. In fact, 'throughout the Templer and MacGillivray period the government was fully aware that its policies and practices had to match its pronouncements'.[5] Operation Service was materially enhanced by the work of the Government Officers' Language School, which Briggs had opened in mid-1951 and which produced a small but useful coterie of Chinese-speaking European and non-Chinese Police and Government officers. On the other hand, Chinese Police recruitment was never very successful throughout. For its part, while the Army did engage in community relations programmes like organising picnics and adopting New Villages, evidence like Semenyih in January 1956, however, suggests that it might have lagged behind the rest of Government in terms of attitudinal re-orientation toward the rural Chinese.

While harsh troop behaviour was one manifestation of the 'strong line with the Chinese' in the first four years, Government policy represented the other. As in Ireland and in Palestine, mass detention was used heavily in the early years. Until the end of 1951, thousands of rural Chinese and their families were subjected to detention on mere suspicion under Emergency Regulation 17 (1) and if their appeal failed, to deportation under ER 17C. Far worse, ER 17D uprooted and deported entire communities, on suspicion of complicity, and without right of appeal. As if this was not enough, Gurney introduced yet another imperial practice. ER 17DA or collective punishment, at the end of 1950, which authorised the imposition of punitive curfews and collective fines on localities judged to have been less than co-operative with the authorities. The basic premise of these punitive policies – collective responsibility – meant that many innocent rural Chinese suffered along with the guilty – or even at the expense of the guilty, as the case of Pusing in early 1951 suggested. Again, however, Templer's arrival inaugurated a change. Like Operation Service, the abolition of both ER 17D and ER 17DA in a matter of months in 1953, was meant to convey the message that Government cared for the plight of the rural Chinese. Furthermore, the White Areas from September 1953 projected the same image of Government as Provider whilst acting as a powerful psychological inducement to public co-operation against the MCP. Once Chief Minister from August 1955, Tunku carried on Templer's approach, where the security situation permitted, of making sure that Government policies were 'propaganda-minded' in conception and execution. Hence detention and deportation figures continued to fall drastically, White Areas continued to emerge, central cooking did away with the unpopular Operational Rice Ration, and significantly Special Branch swoops exemplified by Operation Tartan Rock protected the innocent while eliminating the guilty. In sum, by the Tunku era, 'British deeds were certainly not alienating the public – even the Chinese people in the New Villages'.[6]

A very important policy which constituted 'materialistic propaganda' was of course the New Villages. Resettlement as noted had been an old imperial tactic, dating from the Boer War, and officials in Malaya had tried it locally as early as August 1948. Moreover Gurney appointed a Squatter Committee in December 1948 to examine the possibility of Federation-wide resettlement, but, despite ushering through enabling legislation, he oversaw very little physical resettlement. It was thus Briggs who implemented the programme with great energy between June 1950 and the end of 1951. Briggs recognised that resettlement had to be followed by the provision of not merely physical security to the rural Chinese, but also 'aftercare' in the form of economic opportunities, health and educational facilities and amenities. Unfortunately, the haste with which resettlement was executed meant that some Resettlement Areas were very unsuitable, and the inhabitants had to be re-resettled, much to their resentment, as the Mawai affair of October 1951 demonstrated. Nevertheless, under Templer and Tunku, the majority of the Resettlement Areas, now called New Villages, received more aftercare than before. We noted, moreover, that despite Government attempts to secure rural Chinese confidence through the creation of a Home Guard and elected Village Councils, these were not particularly successful, given the traditional Chinese lack of interest in politics and dislike of soldiering. In addition, while it is true that there were continuing rural Chinese complaints about the New Villages, as John Davis observed all administration was built on complaints anyway, and the real point was to whom were the rural Chinese complaining? We saw that by 1953 the MCP Masses Executives had been virtually frozen out of the New Village environment by a plethora of Government and non-Government *Taijins*: State SCAs, CAOs, ACAOs, AROs, the Red Cross, and church workers. These were generally so popular that the terrorists dared not molest them. By way of contrast, in South Vietnam, the Diem and succeeding administrations never sunk roots in the countryside, and haughty, corrupt officials alienated the peasants.[7]

A key argument throughout this study has also been that the personal styles of senior Government officials represented powerful propaganda in the war for rural Chinese and even terrorist confidence. Gurney, because of a preoccupation with seeking political concessions for the educated Malayan Chinese, was largely out of touch and did not have a significant impact on the operationally crucial rural Chinese community. Even if he did, his uninspiring and dour demeanour would not have gone down well anyway. MacDonald was more colourful, but like Gurney, focused his energies on the educated Chinese stratum, as evidenced by his work with the Communities' Liaison Committee. For his part, Briggs, while fully aware of the salience of the rural Chinese, unfortunately possessed the right attributes in the wrong place at the wrong time: given the resistance of stubborn, parochial subordinates and a war committee system rendered moribund by inertia, he could not afford to be 'the best kind of soldier and gentleman'; he needed to be ruthless, even feared. Moreover, his amiable image as the 'General in the trilby' did not impress rural Chinese who needed above all assurance that Government could protect them from MCP terror. Rather it was Templer, applying the lessons of his charismatic mentor Montgomery, who 'electrified' an administration demoralised by the Gurney assassination and consciously and very deliberately projected the image of Government strength and concern amongst New Villagers. The documents suggest that Templer did indeed have 'instant and transmogrifying effects' on the Emergency.[8] Similarly the amiable Tunku Abdul Rahman, who personified Government to the rural Chinese in the final years, though very different from Templer, in his own way maintained the moral momentum the General had bequeathed him. The very real if intangible propaganda of visible, demonstrative leadership was evident elsewhere: in the Philippines at the height of the Huk insurgency the popular Filipino Secretary of Defence and later President Magsaysay, won the confidence of the ordinary people by fully identifying with them. A big, rugged man, he wore the same dress as the villagers, ate with his hands, walked barefooted through the rice paddies, and jumped over fences and ditches.[9] Similarly, with 'his wispy figure, his shorts and sandals', Ho Chi Minh 'took pains to promote that family feeling which Vietnamese have often had for their leaders, and which he felt was the proper relationship between the people and their government'.[10]

Government deeds also constituted propaganda to the terrorist rank and file. Again British soldiers quarried the imperial experience for pointers on dealing with the insurgents, and again some lessons were good and some were not. A dubious assumption imported into Malaya was the supposed 'moral effect' of air bombardment. This belief had unfortunate consequences: RAF attacks on occasion injured, even killed civilians while the lack of reliable target intelligence meant that there was – as SEPs observed – a great deal of 'blind bombing' going on which utterly failed to demoralise and even acted as 'battle inoculation' for terrorists. Fortunately by late 1953 the RAF shifted gear, refocusing its resources on support of the ground forces through supply dropping, troop lift, communication flying and casualty evacuation. Its offensive role was strictly circumscribed, limited to attacks only on sure information, and mainly in conjunction with ground force follow-up. In contrast, throughout the war in South Vietnam, circumspection in the use of bombing was less pronounced: for instance, during Operation Masher/White Wing in the densely populated coastal region of Binh Dinh in 1967, 1,126 fighter bomber sorties dropped 1.5 million pounds of bombs, killing not only enemy troops but also hundreds of civilians.[11]

Bombing aside, other imperial precedents had far greater effects on terrorist confidence in Malaya. Until 1950, the Palestine precedent of national registration and the short-lived Ferret Force experiment caused more anxiety within terrorist ranks than large scale Security Force sweeps and drives. From the latter half of 1950, however, Briggs' insistence on protracted small-unit patrolling on the jungle fringe, coupled with the intensification of resettlement and the introduction of food control in mid-1951, began to make the first dents in terrorist morale. Food control and protracted small unit patrolling began to be closely co-ordinated in the food denial operations of the Templer era, which targeted MCP Districts, and the concept received further refinement during the MacGillivray/Tunku era when Bourne introduced domination tactics to ensure that disrupted MCP Districts did not resurrect later. Food denial was further strengthened by the introduction of Sheppard's central kitchens from mid-1956, especially in the bad areas. This British emphasis on targeting the MCP District infrastructure required less application of firepower and consequently posed less risk of collateral damage than the American tendency to target with full military resources the Vietcong units which that infrastructure supported.[12] As noted, the impact of Security Force pressure and food denial was by mid-1954 the major factors precipitating the surrender of the less committed terrorist rank and file, and by 1955 was bringing out even ranking SEPs, as the Pahang success suggested. By the time central cooking was producing emaciated and forlorn hard core SEPs by 1957, the stage had been set for the Information Services and Psychological Warfare in particular to bring about the collapse of the morale of the remaining hard core terrorists.

Actually, in June 1948, Government had relatively few propaganda instruments to target the public and the terrorists. Until 1950, about two dozen mobile units, as well as leaflets, were used by McHugh's Department of Public Relations as the main media of communication with the public. There was a lack of word-of-mouth propaganda due to the shortage of Chinese Field Officers, the output of the MFU was unremarkable, while Radio Malaya suffered from problems with both transmitters and receivers, and did not have a specialised service for rural areas. As far as the terrorists were concerned, moreover, they hardly ever saw Government leaflets. Once Hugh Greene arrived in September 1950, however, he increased the number of mobile units so that by the second half of 1951 the Districts were adequately served, while to compensate for the continuing shortage of Chinese Field Officers Greene sent out Chinese SEPs on lecture tours. Greene also arranged for community radio receivers to be distributed in Resettlement Areas and by early 1951 the Community Listening Service was serving them. Meanwhile he increased the Emergency-related output of the MFU. Furthermore, by improving the leaflet distribution system and using waterproof paper, Greene ensured that more leaflets found their way into the hands of terrorists, and in December 1950 he introduced the first large public rewards for information or action leading to the capture or killing of all grades of terrorists.

During Alec Peterson's tenure, moreover, between October 1952 and June 1954 Government was able to reach the public even more effectively via mobile unit teams that numbered 90 by November 1953, and which conducted SEP and 'live' shows as well as exhibited films produced by a revitalised MFU under Tom Hodge. In addition, the by now familiar Community Listening broadcasts included the very popular Lee Dai Soh while the important Civics Courses were bringing people to the bosom of Government. Peterson's tenure also saw the inauguration of the Voice Aircraft which was able to reach terrorists with news of important developments very quickly, and hence joined the leaflet as a key tactical propaganda instrument. In addition, although in May 1952 there were even bigger increases in the rewards for information or action leading to the capture or killing of terrorists, from August 1953 the reward amounts were no longer made public, while instead of fixed rewards, the amounts paid out were henceforth made dependent on the informant's ingenuity, risk and effort. With the emergence of Yaacob Latiff as DIS in July 1954, Government propaganda media were reaching their optimal potential: the various instruments of propaganda to the public were now joined by the Good Citizens' Committees from April 1955, which organised anti-Communist rallies and demonstrations that served as vehicles for expressing growing public and in particular rural Chinese confidence in Government and disdain for the terrorists. Meanwhile in the war against the terrorists, the Voice Aircraft and leaflets were now joined by powerful new ground hailing equipment like *Stentor, Thunderer and Magnavox*, while in March 1955 minimum reward amounts were once again made public so as to counter MCP whispers that Government paid out more money for information leading to kills than for surrenders.

The gradual growth of the scale and sophistication of Government propaganda instruments was matched by the equally slow evolution of propaganda organisation. The three main agencies for Government propaganda of words, the Department of Public Relations, the Malayan Film Unit and Radio Malaya, were all formed in 1946, but were quite independent of one another. After the Emergency broke out, attempts by first the Emergency Publicity Committee in 1948 and then from early 1950 the Joint Information and Propaganda Committee (JIPC), to improve co-ordination and increase output to the public and the terrorists, were generally ineffective. Although the arrival of Hugh Greene resulted in the locus of Emergency propaganda policy-making being situated in the Emergency Information Services, with the result that he was able to exert some influence over the MFU and Radio Malaya, the fact remained that Greene's EIS did not have a clear division of responsibility between itself and J.N. McHugh's now-renamed Department of Information. This was reflected in the untidy and haphazard control of mobile units in the States. Unfortunately, Greene, and his successors Eliot Watrous and A.W.D. James, never achieved full centralisation of all Government propaganda assets under EIS. The situation was analogous to that obtaining in South Vietnam as late as 1969: while the 4th PSYOP Group conducted tactical and national PSYOP campaigns, the body called Civil Operations and Revolutionary Development Support (CORDS) supervised all PSYOP campaigns in support of pacification. Meanwhile, the Joint United States Public Affairs Office (JUSPAO) was responsible for 'U.S. PSYOP policy, supervision, co-ordination, and evaluation of all U.S. PSYOP in Vietnam, and for PSYOP support' of indigenous Vietnamese programmes. There was much jurisdictional overlapping and duplication of effort.[13]

Fortunately in Malaya, Alec Peterson, on being appointed by Templer in October 1952 as Director-General Information Services (DGIS), unified EIS, the Department of Information and the MFU under the Department of

Information Services, while maintaining policy control over Radio Malaya's Emergency programming. Meanwhile Community Listening was also integrated permanently into Radio Malaya in 1954. To be sure, the efficiency and co-ordination of all Government propaganda assets were generally enhanced from Peterson's watch onwards, and persisted into Yaacob Latiff's tenure. Especially important, in March 1954, the Operations Section – a part of the old EIS which dealt with Psychological Warfare against the terrorists – was transferred to the Director of Operations Staff and renamed the Psychological Warfare Section, first under R.J. Isaacs until March 1955, followed by O.W. Wolters till November 1956, and from then on, C.C. Too. Moreover, by the end of 1958 Radio Malaya had split into two separate organisations, and rump Radio Malaya continued to rely heavily on the new Radio Singapore for certain broadcasts, although Community Listening, based in Kuala Lumpur, remained unscathed.

In terms of propaganda expertise, McHugh's Department of Public Relations until June 1950 was rather deficient. On the one hand propaganda to the public inadvertently advertised the Party's misdeeds and made Government appear weak by appealing to the bemused rural Chinese for 'help' against the terrorists. On the other hand, propaganda to the terrorists themselves lacked authenticity due to a dearth of propaganda intelligence, thanks to the general antipathy in Government and Police circles toward propagandists in the early years, as McHugh complained. Tactical propaganda thus came across as clumsy and blunt, as evidenced by the use of threats and leaflets with photographs of dead terrorists. While this approach only stiffened the morale of the hard core terrorists, it terrified the waverers and deterred them from surrendering. Moreover, Anti-Bandit Month was inaugurated by Gurney in circumstances where it was patently obvious to both public and terrorists that Government was not winning, and achieved little. Meanwhile the September 1949 Gurney Amnesty was also badly timed while its promise of clemency to only those terrorists with 'no blood on their hands' only stimulated doubts amongst the waverers as to how much participation in capital crimes constituted culpability. Given the background of Security Force persecution of the rural Chinese in the early years, such uncertainty did nothing to assuage wavering terrorists' basic lack of trust in Government. Consequently, the Gurney Amnesty was a failure.

Hugh Greene's arrival, however, ushered in a period of change. Importing and applying a philosophy of propaganda that he, together with others like Richard Crossman had helped forge during the Second World War, Greene immediately recruited local Chinese like C.C. Too and Lam Swee and employed SEPs to produce and engage in the propaganda which would be authentic to the rural Chinese public and the terrorists; he appointed part-time State Emergency Information Officers (SEIOs) to ensure that propaganda was tailored to local contexts; unlike McHugh, he succeeded in improving co-ordination with the Police and secured access to its intelligence on the MCP; he ensured that MFU and the new Community Listening Service produced straight news while working in entertainment to coat the 'pill' of propaganda; he introduced into operations the principle of the psychological moment and the need to exploit rapidly terrorist setbacks, and by the same token ruled out a general Amnesty as the strategic timing was not right. He also inaugurated the long-term surrender policy of officially promising only fair treatment, not non-prosecution, and most importantly, he taught C.C. Too the basic propaganda fundamentals, especially the dictum that in propaganda it was the credibility of the propagandist that mattered most. As a future HPWS, Too was to apply these ideas.

For his part, Alec Peterson was certainly responsible for creating a centralised propaganda machine; appointing full, not part-time State Information Officers; and setting up a training school for Field Officers to hone their skills. Moreover, it was Peterson who insisted in August 1952 that propaganda was not merely the job of Information Services, but every agent of Government in contact with the public. Thus every Government official had to be 'propaganda-minded' in order to 'win and hold the confidence' of the public. This injunction helped provide the intellectual justification within official circles for Operation Service, which was launched in December, as well as Government's attempts thereafter to be 'propaganda-minded' in policy and action. These contributions aside, however, it must be conceded that Peterson really did not add a great deal more to the stock of propaganda expertise which Hugh Greene had imported – Peterson himself later admitted that he had built on Greene's work. In fact, Greene's imprint remained evident throughout the Peterson era – and it is significant that Templer in May 1952 informed Lyttelton that he was against a full Amnesty because the 'psychological moment' leading to mass surrenders was not at hand. In addition, Templer basically continued Greene's surrender policy of officially promising all potential SEPs – with 'blood on their hands' or not – fair treatment.

In stark contrast to Greene, moreover, Peterson failed to show sufficient respect for the abilities of Asian propagandists, maintaining that they were simply needed to support Europeans. He thus attempted to exert too much control over, and refused to accommodate, prickly subordinates like the valuable C.C. Too, and was directly responsible for Too quitting. This hampered the documentary research work of the Operations Section of the Information Services, and led to the overlooking of the April 1954 resolution of the Conference of Communist and Workers' Parties of the British Commonwealth for a switch of Communist strategy to political methods. Thus Government failed to anticipate the June 1955 Ng Heng letter. Peterson's uncompromising proclivity for centralisation had other consequences: his insistence – with Tom Hodge – on the elevation of MFU film exhibitions as the centrepiece of every mobile unit visit to New Villages and estates, tended to smother the initiative of State Information Officers who felt that at times live shows were more effective. In addition, Peterson's decision to de-emphasise Hollywood entertainment fare and increase the number of simple films with a serious message against a Malayan background was also later criticised by Field Officers, who felt that these were 'too fast' for rural audiences. Greene, on the other hand, always recognised the need for both local initiative as well as entertainment in propaganda.

In the final analysis, therefore, it is hard to escape the observation that Peterson's replacement by Yaacob Latiff in July 1954 was perhaps necessary to the continuing vitality of Government propaganda. Yaacob was a competent administrator and his particular contribution was the encouragement, with SIO Selangor Jack Hackett, of the Good Citizens' Committees which began at Banting, Selangor, in April 1955. As we saw, from 1956 onwards, the highly visible anti-Communist rallies organised by the GCCs even in the bad areas were causing local hard core terrorist gangs to fold. Hence GCCs by no means 'had little effect on the guerrillas or on their hardcore supporters'.[14] Particularly critical, unlike Peterson, Yaacob accommodated the independent spirit of C.C. Too and fully backed Too's installation as acting HPWS in November 1956. Had Peterson remained in charge, Too would never have returned and hence would not have been able to play a role in drafting the wording of the climactic *Merdeka* Amnesty. In sum, while crucial roles were played in the final years of the Government propaganda effort by Too and Yaacob, the main contributions overall were as others have suggested, made by Peterson and Greene. But which of the latter two made the bigger impact? It is argued that while Peterson does deserve plaudits for his work in rationalising Information Services between 1952 and 1954 and for his broadening of Government's overall concept of propaganda, it must be said that the basic precepts of operational propaganda were identified by Hugh Greene, and as this philosophy was passed on to C.C. Too, Greene's influence long survived Peterson's.

This brings us to a key contribution of the study: the analysis of the psychological dynamics of the MCP's collapse by the end of December 1958. It has to be asked: why did the catastrophic collapse of terrorist morale compelling Central to inaugurate the demobilisation policy occur only in 1958 and not between September and December 1957, when the original *Merdeka* Amnesty was in effect? To recapitulate, by this time a harder core of terrorists remained in the jungle who would surrender only if it was demonstrated to them that there was 'no hope of victory'. To Central, 'victory' as early as January 1955 was no longer defined as military victory. Not only was the military situation discouraging, the Indochina ceasefire mitigated against any 'help' coming from outside Malaya.

'Victory' was therefore seen as the securing of political recognition and complete freedom from restrictions should the MCP decide to emerge from the jungle – a scenario which would have been anathema to Government. Thus the Government-Central propaganda endgame commenced, beginning with Tunku's January 1955 announcement of his intention to announce an Amnesty if in power, and proceeding through subsequent phases, including the Ng Heng letter of mid-1955, the Baling Talks at the end of that year, the *Merdeka* Amnesty of September 1957, and ultimately culminating in Tunku's far reaching repudiation on 21 December 1957 of further Baling-type talks. In the war for the confidence of the terrorists, it was at this point, 21 December 1957, that the psychological moment – that moment when the terrorists became most receptive to the liberal *Merdeka* Amnesty terms – was reached. This was because from that date on they were bereft of any hope whatsoever that the MCP would be able to secure favourable exit terms. Hence the confidence of the remaining terrorist rank and file evaporated. While the MCP demobilised in December 1958, subversion was to continue at a higher pitch, but the shooting war was effectively over. In sum, while extant circumstances, mainly the capture of the strategic initiative by the Security Forces and the growing anti-Communist, pro-Government mass movement embracing even the hard core MCP supporters, represented 'deeds' which communicated to the remaining hard core the futility of continued resistance, Government Psychological Warfare exploited this message optimally with telling effect. Hence the last effective phase of the rural Insurrection, from the *Merdeka* Amnesty of September 1957 to the MCP demobilisation policy of December 1958, represented a triumph for Government propaganda – of word *and* deed.

Notes

CHAPTER ONE

1 Richard Stubbs, *Hearts and Minds in Guerrilla Warfare: The Malayan Emergency 1948–1960* (Singapore: Oxford University Press, 1993), p. 250.

2 *Ibid.*; Karl Hack, 'Screwing Down the People: The Malayan Emergency, Decolonisation and Ethnicity', in *Imperial Policy and South East Asian Nationalism*, ed. by Hans Antlov and Stein Tonnesson (Surrey: Curzon Press, 1995), pp. 84–93. See also Hack, 'British Strategy and South East Asia, 1941–1957', Unpublished PhD Dissertation, Oxford University, 1995, p. 162.

3 Robert Thompson, *Defeating Communist Insurgency: Experiences from Malaya and Vietnam* (London: Chatto and Windus, 1966); Richard Clutterbuck, *The Long, Long War: The Emergency in Malaya and Vietnam* (London: Cassell, 1967); *idem, Riot and Revolution in Singapore and Malaya 1945–1963* (London: Faber and Faber, 1973); Ian F.W. Beckett, 'Robert Thompson and the British Advisory Mission to South Vietnam, 1961–1965', *Small Wars and Insurgencies*, Vol. 8, No. 3 (Oct 1997), pp. 43–44. For the so-called British school of counterinsurgency, see Thomas R. Mockaitis, 'The Origins of British Counter-insurgency', *Small Wars and Insurgencies*, Vol. 1, No. 3 (Dec 1990), pp. 209–225; *idem, British Counterinsurgency, 1919–1960* (London: Macmillan, 1990). See also Anthony Short, 'The Malayan Emergency', in *Regular Armies and Insurgency*, ed. by Ronald Haycock (London: Croom Helm, 1979), pp. 66–67; Stubbs, *Hearts and Minds in Guerrilla Warfare*, pp. 250–251.

4 Leon Comber, *13 May 1969: A Historical Survey of Sino-Malay Relations* (Singapore: Graham Brash, 1988), p. xvi; Beckett, 'Robert Thompson', p. 43; Short, 'The Malayan Emergency', in Haycock, ed., *Regular Armies and Insurgency*, p. 64; Stubbs, *Hearts and Minds in Guerrilla Warfare*, p. 250; Brian Lapping, *End of Empire* (London: Paladin, 1989), p. 226; Brian Crozier, *Southeast Asia in Turmoil* (Harmondsworth, Middlesex: Pelican, 1966), pp. 74–75.

5 Stubbs, *Hearts and Minds in Guerrilla Warfare*, pp. 1–2; Susan L. Carruthers, *Winning Hearts and Minds: British Governments, the Media and Colonial Counter-Insurgency 1944–1960* (London and New York: Leicester University Press, 1995), pp. 1–2; John Cloake, *Templer: Tiger of Malaya* (London: Harrap, 1985), p. 477, note.

6 Mockaitis, 'The Origins of British Counterinsurgency', pp. 211–215.

7 Hack, 'British Strategy and South East Asia', p. 144, n.1.

8 For a good anecdotal account of the impact of the Malayan jungle on the minds of British troops, see Charles Allen, *The Savage Wars of Peace: Soldiers' Voices 1945–1989* (London: Futura, 1991), pp. 19–35. Graham Greene well captures the sense of paranoia afflicting everyday life in Malaya in the early years of MCP terror. See his *Ways of Escape* (London: Penguin Books, 1981), p. 119. For some discussion on how the jungle had its psychological pitfalls even for Communist terrorists, see David Owen, *Battle of Wits: A History of Psychology and Deception in Modern Warfare* (London: Leo Cooper, 1978), pp. 158–159; Anthony Short, 'Communism and the Emergency', in *Malaysia: A Survey*, ed. by Wang Gung Wu (London and Dunmow. Pall Mall Press, 1964), p. 156.

9 Richard Clutterbuck, *Conflict and Violence in Singapore and Malaysia 1945–1983*, revised, updated and enlarged edn. (Singapore: Graham Brash, 1985), pp. 193–194; Brian Crozier, *The Rebels: A Study of Post-War Insurrections* (Boston: Beacon Press, 1964), p. 214; J.B. Perry Robinson, *Transformation in Malaya* (London: Secker and Warburg, 1956) pp. 154–155.

10 Those favouring Peterson include: Harry Miller, *Jungle War in Malaya: The Campaign against Communism 1948–60* (London: Arthur Barker, 1972), p. 85; Robert W. Komer, *The Malayan Emergency in Retrospect: Organisation of a Successful Counterinsurgency Effort* (Santa Monica: Rand, 1972), pp. 69–75; Riley Sunderland, *Winning the Hearts and Minds of the People: Malaya, 1948–1960* (Santa Monica: Rand, 1964), esp. pp. 50–57; John Coates, *Suppressing Insurgency: An Analysis of the Malayan Emergency* (Boulder: Westview Press, 1992), pp. 125–129.

11 Stubbs, *Hearts and Minds in Guerrilla Warfare*, pp. 120–121, 180–184; Anthony Short, *The Communist Insurrection in Malaya,1948–1960* (London: Frederick Muller, 1975), pp. 416–438; Clutterbuck, *Conflict and Violence in Singapore and Malaysia*, pp. 190–193.

12 Susan Carruthers in fact examines the contribution of both Greene and Peterson, but with emphasis on the former. Moreover, her analysis is very brief, as she is more interested in propaganda for consumption in the United Kingdom and the United States. See Carruthers, *Winning Hearts and Minds*, especially pp. 93–95. An even briefer treatment of the two is offered in Donald Mackay, *The Malayan Emergency 1948–60: The Domino that Stood* (London and Washington: Brassey's, 1997), pp. 130–131. On the other hand, Zarougui attempts to examine the work of both men in some detail, but his analysis is constrained by an over-reliance on Colonial Office sources. More fundamentally, his study is compromised by a narrow definition of propaganda which compels him to overlook the psychological consequences of Government and MCP 'deeds'. Thus he practically ignores, *inter alia*, the propaganda implications of the leadership style of senior Government leaders, troop behaviour, Operation Service, the Gurney assassination, and the Communist terrorist campaign. M. Zarougui, 'Propaganda and Psychological Warfare in Guerrilla and Counter-Guerrilla Warfare: The Malayan Emergency 1948–1960', Unpublished PhD Dissertation, Reading University, 1992.

13 Charles Townshend for instance contends that the insurgency was effectively neutralised by 1954. Townshend, *Britain's Civil Wars: Counterinsurgency in the Twentieth Century* (London: Faber and Faber, 1986), p. 164. Mackay agrees that by the time Templer left the 'military battle *was* all but won.' Mackay, *The Malayan Emergency*, pp. 140, 147–148. Short is probably more correct in asserting that 1953 was the 'breakthrough' year, which is not the same as asserting that the Insurrection was 'virtually over'. There was a lot more fighting to be done. Short, *Communist Insurrection in Malaya*, p. 387.

14 There is virtual silence on Yaacob Latiff's work, while C.C. Too receives cursory and unsystematic treatment as the so-called Malayan mastermind of Government

Psychological Warfare. Noel Barber, *War of the Running Dogs: Malaya 1948–1960* (London: Arrow, 1989), pp. 139–146; Miller, *Jungle War in Malaya*, pp. 105–106; Clutterbuck, *Conflict and Violence in Singapore and Malaysia*, p. 193.

15 C.D. Cowan, *Nineteenth-Century Malaya* (London: Clarendon Press, 1961); Emily Sadka, *The Protected Malay States, 1874–1895* (Kuala Lumpur: University of Malaya Press, 1970); Eunice Thio, *British Policy in the Malay Peninsula 1880–1910, Vol. 1: The Southern and Central States* (Kuala Lumpur and Singapore: University of Malaya Press, 1969); Nicholas Tarling, *British Policy in the Malay Peninsula and Archipelago 1824–1871* (London: Oxford University Press, 1969); C. Northcote Parkinson, *British Intervention in Malaya 1867–1877* (Singapore: University of Malaya Press, 1960).

16 S. Husin Ali, *Malay Peasant Society and Leadership* (London: Oxford University Press, 1975), pp. 15–22; Richard Winstedt, *The Malays: A Cultural History* (London: Routledge and Kegan Paul, 1961), pp. 120–121.

17 Kernial Singh Sandhu, *Indians in Malaya: Some Aspects of their Immigration and Settlement, 1786–1957* (London: Cambridge University Press, 1969); Sinnapah Arasaratnam, *Indians in Malaysia and Singapore* (Bombay and Kuala Lumpur: Oxford University Press, 1970); J.H. Drabble, *Rubber in Malaya 1876–1922: The Genesis of the Industry* (London: Oxford University Press, 1973).

18 Stubbs, *Hearts and Minds in Guerrilla Warfare*, p. 12; Wong Lin Ken, *The Malayan Tin Industry to 1914: with Special Reference to the States of Perak, Selangor, Negri Sembilan and Pahang* (Tucson, Arizona: University of Arizona Press, 1965), pp. 11–21; Victor Purcell, *The Chinese in Malaya* (London: Oxford University Press, 1967), pp. 37, 61; Wilfred Blythe, *The Impact of Chinese Secret Societies in Malaya: A Historical Study* (London: Oxford University Press, 1969); Francis Loh Kok Wah, *Beyond the Tin Mines: Coolies, Squatters and New Villagers in the Kinta Valley, Malaysia c. 1880–1980* (Singapore: Oxford University Press, 1988), pp. 27–32; 84; Robert Heussler, *British Rule in Malaya: The Malayan Civil Service and its Predecessors, 1867–1942* (Oxford: Clio Press, 1981), pp. 144–145; K.S. Sandhu, 'Chinese Colonization in Melaka', in *Melaka: The Transformation of a Malay Capital c. 1400–1980*, Vol. 2, ed. by Paul Wheatley and K.S. Sandhu (Singapore: Oxford University Press, 1983), pp. 119–120.

19 Blythe, *The Impact of Chinese Secret Societies in Malaya*, pp. 43–44; Loh, *Beyond the Tin Mines*, pp. 23–39, 84–85; Ray Nyce, *Chinese New Villages in Malaya: A Community Study* (Kuala Lumpur: Malaysian Sociological Research Institute, 1973), pp. xxx–xxxii.

20 See Heussler, *British Rule in Malaya*, pp. 166–167; *idem, Completing a Stewardship: The Malayan Civil Service, 1942–1957* (Westport: Greenwood Press, 1983), pp. 206–207; A.J. Stockwell, 'The White Man's Burden and Brown Humanity: Colonialism and Ethnicity in British Malaya', *Southeast Asian Journal of Social Science*, Vol. 10, No. 1 (1982), pp. 57–62.

21 Heussler, *Completing a Stewardship*, p. 60; Stubbs, *Hearts and Minds in Guerrilla Warfare*, pp. 44–45; Cheah Boon Kheng, ed., *From PKI to the Comintern, 1924–1941: The Apprenticeship of the Malayan Communist Party* (Ithaca: Cornell University Press, 1992); *idem, Red Star over Malaya: Resistance and Social Conflict During and After the Japanese Occupation 1941–1946* (Singapore: Singapore University Press, 1983); F. Spencer Chapman, *The Jungle is Neutral* (Singapore and Kuala Lumpur: Times Books International, 1997); Short, *Communist Insurrection in Malaya*, pp. 20–21; Paul H. Kratoska, *The Japanese Occupation of Malaya 1941–1945* (St Leonards, New South Wales: Allen and Unwin, 1998), pp. 95–103.

22 Albert Lau, *The Malayan Union Controversy 1942–1948* (Singapore: Oxford University Press, 1991); James de V. Allen, *The Malayan Union* (Connecticut: Yale

University Press, 1967); A.J. Stockwell, *British Policy and Malay Politics during the Malayan Union Experiment, 1942–1948* (Kuala Lumpur: Malayan Branch of the Royal Asiatic Society, 1979); *idem*, 'British Imperial Policy and Decolonisation in Malaya, 1942–52', *Journal of Imperial and Commonwealth History*, Vol. 13, No. 1 (Oct 1984), pp. 68–69.

23 Stubbs, *Hearts and Minds in Guerrilla Warfare*, pp. 16–22, 46–48; Cheah Boon Kheng, *The Masked Comrades: A Study of the Communist United Front in Malaya, 1945–48* (Singapore: Times Books International, 1979); M.R. Stenson, *Industrial Conflict in Malaya: Prelude to the Communist Revolt of 1948* (London: Oxford University Press, 1970), pp. 78–81, 100 109.

24 A.J. Stockwell, '"A Widespread and long-concocted plot to overthrow the government in Malaya"? The Origins of the Malayan Emergency', *Journal of Imperial and Commonwealth History*, Vol. 21, No. 3 (Sep 1993), pp. 66–88; Cheah, *Masked Comrades*, pp. 140–158; Short, 'Communism and the Emergency', in Wang, ed., *Malaysia*, pp. 152–153; *idem*, *Communist Insurrection in Malaya*, pp. 55–60; Stenson, *Industrial Conflict in Malaya*, passim; *idem*, *The 1948 Communist Revolt in Malaya: A Note on Historical Sources and Interpretation; A Reply by Gerald de Cruz* (Singapore: Institute of Southeast Asian Studies, 1971); Frank Furedi, *Colonial Wars and the Politics of Third World Nationalism* (London: I.B. Tauris, 1994), pp. 143–174.

25 Discussion between Chin Peng, Secretary-General of the Malayan Communist Party, and Dr. Anthony Short, Professor R.B. Smith, Professor A.J. Stockwell, Mr. Robert Lemkin and the author, held at 11 Bedford Square, London, on 18 June 1998. Hereafter Group Discussion with Chin Peng. The latest historiography seems to reflect this view. See T.N. Harper, *The End of Empire and the Making of Malaya* (Cambridge: Cambridge University Press, 1999), pp. 142–148.

26 Thomas K. Adams, 'LIC (Low-Intensity Clausewitz)', *Small Wars and Insurgencies*, Vol. 1, No. 3 (Dec 1990), pp. 266–268.

27 A leading student of Clausewitz, Michael Howard, suggests that the Trinity idea is so integral to an understanding of conflict in general that it would be 'a good place for any contemporary strategic thinker to begin'. Michael Howard, *Clausewitz* (Oxford and New York: Oxford University Press, 1983), pp. 72–73.

28 *Ibid.*, p. 39; Carl von Clausewitz, *On War*, ed. and trans. by Michael Howard and Peter Paret (Princeton: Princeton University Press, 1989), pp. 595–597.

29 Clausewitz, *On War*, ed. by Paret and Howard, p. 596.

30 Harold D. Lasswell, *Propaganda Technique in the World War* (London: Kegan Paul, Trench, Trubner and Co., 1938), pp. 8–10. Lasswell was a prolific academic who made significant contributions to mass communications theory. For more on Lasswell, see Christopher Simpson, *Science of Coercion: Communication Research and Psychological Warfare 1945–1960* (Oxford and New York: Oxford University Press, 1996), p. 130.

31 Short, 'The Malayan Emergency', in Haycock, ed., *Regular Armies and Insurgency*, pp. 62–63.

32 Peter Paret, 'Clausewitz', in *Makers of Modern Strategy: From Machiavelli to the Nuclear Age*, ed. by Peter Paret (Oxford: Clarendon Press, 1991), p. 206.

33 Cited in Daria Frezza, 'Psychological Warfare and the Building of National Morale during World War II: The Role of Non-Government Agencies', in *Aspects of War in American History*, ed. by David K. Adams and Cornelis A. Van Minnen (Keele: Keele University Press, 1997), p. 174.

34 *Ibid.*, p. 185.

35 Slim was said to have 'a force that came out of him, a strength of personality' that 'gave Fourteenth Army its overwhelming confidence'. See George MacDonald Fraser,

Quartered Safe Out Here: A Recollection of the War in Burma (London: HarperCollins, 1995), p. 36; Duncan Anderson, 'Slim', in *Churchill's Generals*, ed. by John Keegan (London: Warner, 1995), p. 314. Slim was obviously well qualified to talk about 'morale'.

36 Field Marshal Sir William Slim, *Defeat into Victory* (London: Cassell, 1956), pp. 182–183.

37 Joint Memorandum by Sir Henry Gurney and Lieutenant-General Harold Briggs, 'Federation of Malaya: Combined Appreciation of the Emergency Situation', 4 June 1951, CO 537/7263.

38 Charles Roetter, *Psychological Warfare* (London: B.T. Batsford, 1974), Preface.

39 Lasswell, *Propaganda Technique in the World War*, p. 9.

40 Philip M. Taylor, *Munitions of the Mind. War Propaganda from the Ancient World to the Nuclear Age* (Wellingborough, Northamptonshire: Patrick Stephens, 1990), p. 11.

41 Paul M.A. Linebarger, *Psychological Warfare*, 2nd edn. (New York: Duell, Sloan and Pearce, 1954), p. 39.

42 See Carl von Clausewitz, *On War*, ed. by Anatol Rapoport (London: Penguin, 1982), pp. 251–252; Clausewitz, *On War*, ed. by Paret and Howard, pp. 184–185.

43 See Alex P. Schmid and Janny de Graaf, *Violence as Communication: Insurgent Terrorism and the Western News Media* (London: Sage Publications, 1982), p. 12; Grant Wardlaw, *Political Terrorism: Theory, Tactics and Counter-Measures*, 2nd edn. (Cambridge: Cambridge University Press, 1989), pp. 20–21.

44 Lasswell, 'Political and Psychological Warfare', in *Psychological Warfare Casebook*, ed. by William E. Daugherty and Morris Janowitz (Baltimore, Maryland: Johns Hopkins Press, 1958), p. 22.

45 Kay Saunders, '"An Instrument of Strategy": Propaganda, Public Policy and the Media in Australia during the Second World War', *War and Society*, Vol. 15, No. 2 (Oct 1997), p. 80.

46 Francis M. Watson, Jr., 'PSYOP and Related Activities', in *The Art and Science of Psychological Operations: Case Studies of Military Application*, ed. by Ronald De McLaurin *et al.*, Vol. 1 (Washington, D.C.: American Institutes for Research, 1976), p. 53.

47 *Ibid.*, pp. 54–56; 58–59.

48 Alexander R. Askenasy, 'Role of Psychological Operations within the Military Mission', in De McLaurin *et al.*, eds., *The Art and Science of Psychological Operations*, Vol. 1, p. 70.

49 Edward N. Luttwak, 'The Impact of Vietnam on Strategic Thinking in the United States', in *Vietnam: Four American Perspectives*, ed. by Patrick J. Hearden (West Lafayette, Indiana: Purdue University Press, 1991), pp. 66–67.

50 Askenasy, 'Role of Psychological Operations within the Military Mission', in De McLaurin *et al.*, eds., *The Art and Science of Psychological Operations*, Vol. 1, pp. 73–74.

51 Cited in Thomas Perry Thornton, 'Terror as a Weapon of Political Agitation', in *Internal War*, ed. by Harry Eckstein (New York: Free Press, 1964), p. 83.

52 Johannes Most cited in Schmid and de Graaf, *Violence as Communication*, pp. 13–14.

53 Phillip P. Katz, 'PSYOP and Communication Theory', in De McLaurin *et al.*, eds., *The Art and Science of Psychological Operations*, Vol. 1, p. 39.

54 Clutterbuck, *Conflict and Violence in Singapore and Malaysia*, pp. 190–191; Thompson, *Defeating Communist Insurgency*, pp. 95–96.

55 See especially Chapter Six.

56 See Chapter Three.

57 Linebarger, *Psychological Warfare*, pp. 39–40; Taylor, *Munitions of the Mind*, pp. 11–14.

58 Askenasy, 'Role of Psychological Operations within the Military Mission', in De McLaurin *et al.*, eds., *The Art and Science of Psychological Operations*, Vol. 1, p. 70.

59 *Scotsman*, 2 Nov 1951.

60 Philip Towle, *Pilots and Rebels: The Use of Aircraft in Unconventional Warfare 1918–1988* (London: Brasseys, 1989), pp. 16–20, 40; Thomas Pakenham, *The Boer War* (London: Abacus, 1996), p. 535; John Pimlott, 'The British Army: The Dhofar Campaign, 1970–1975', in *Armed Forces and Modern Counterinsurgency*, ed. by Ian F.W. Beckett and John Pimlott (London and Sydney: Croom Helm, 1985), p. 17; Roetter, *Psychological Warfare*, pp. 83–84.

61 Rex Stevenson, 'Cinemas and Censorship in Colonial Malaya', *Journal of Southeast Asian Studies*, Vol. 5, No. 2 (Sep 1974), pp. 221–222.

62 Rosaleen Smyth, 'Britain's African Colonies and British Propaganda during the Second World War', *Journal of Imperial and Commonwealth History*, Vol. 14, No. 1 (Oct 1985), p. 75.

63 *Ibid.*, p. 77; Victor Purcell, *The Memoirs of a Malayan Official* (London: Cassell, 1956), pp. 314–315. Purcell, a pre-war Protector of Chinese, was made Director-General of Information and Publicity for Malaya and Singapore just before the Japanese invasion. He reported to Robert Scott, the Far East representative of the Ministry of Information, headquartered in Singapore.

64 Smyth, 'Britain's African Colonies', p. 78.

65 *Ibid.*, p. 77.

66 Purcell, *Memoirs of a Malayan Official*, pp. 314–315.

67 In the inter-war years Crossman was a young Oxford don who specialised in the works of Plato and Marx. After the Second World War he became a journalist for the *New Statesman and Nation* and was also the Labour Member of Parliament for Coventry. Crossman later became a Cabinet Minister during the Wilson Government, holding the portfolios of Minister for Housing and Local Government, Secretary of State for Social Services and head of the Department of Health. During the war, Crossman was head of the Political Warfare Executive (PWE) German Section, later serving as Chief of Operations and then Deputy Chief of the Psychological Warfare Division, Supreme Headquarters, Allied Expeditionary Force (PWD/SHAEF). Both British and American propagandists regarded him as a leading, if not the leading, Allied propagandist during the war. See William E. Daugherty, 'Richard H.S. Crossman', in Daugherty and Janowitz, eds., *Psychological Warfare Casebook*, pp. 246–248; Daniel Lerner, *Psychological Warfare against Nazi Germany: The Sykewar Campaign, D-Day to VE-Day* (Cambridge, Massachusetts: The MIT Press, 1971), pp. 59, 73, 78; Tam Dalyell, *Dick Crossman: A Portrait* (London: Weidenfeld and Nicolson, 1989); *Times*, 6 April 1974.

68 Richard H. S. Crossman, 'Psychological Warfare', *RUSI Journal*, Vol. XCVII, No. 587 (Aug 1952), hereafter 'Psychological Warfare I', pp. 324–326. In 1952 and 1953, Crossman delivered three talks on British propaganda philosophy at Royal United Services Institute (RUSI). These RUSI talks were so well received in British military circles that the great military historian and analyst Basil Liddell Hart wrote him to express his 'admiration' for his 'brilliant and masterly treatment' of the topic of Psychological Warfare. Liddell Hart to Crossman, 5 June 1953, Liddell Hart Papers, 1/205, Liddell Hart Centre for Military Archives, King's College, University of London (hereafter LHCMA).

69 Leslie Glass, *The Changing of Kings: Memories of Burma 1934–1949* (London: Peter Owen, 1985), pp. 166–168.

70 Crossman, 'Psychological Warfare', *RUSI Journal*, Vol. XCVIII, No. 591 (Aug 1953), hereafter 'Psychological Warfare II', p. 358; Charles Cruickshank, *The Fourth Arm: Psychological Warfare 1938–45* (London: Davis-Poynter, 1977), pp. 67, 184–185;

Daniel Lerner, 'Is International Persuasion Sociologically Feasible?', in De McLaurin
et al., eds., *The Art and Science of Psychological Operations*, Vol. 1, p. 49. Lerner, an
American, was another key student of propaganda, and had served during the war as
the editor of the PWD/SHAEF *Weekly Digest*, working closely with Crossman. He
later wrote at least 18 books on propaganda and collaborated with Lasswell on four.
See Lerner, *Psychological Warfare against Nazi Germany*, p. xvi; Simpson, *Science of
Coercion*, p. 130.

71 Crossman, 'Psychological Warfare I', p. 324; *idem*, 'Psychological Warfare II',
pp. 358–359.

72 Lerner cited in William E. Daugherty, 'Personnel Qualifications for Psychological
Warfare', in Daugherty and Janowitz, eds., *Psychological Warfare Casebook*, p. 160.

73 Crossman, 'Psychological Warfare I', p. 331, *idem*, 'Psychological Warfare II', p. 358.

74 Dalyell, *Dick Crossman*, p. 57; Richard H.S. Crossman, M.P., 'Supplementary Essay',
in Lerner, *Psychological Warfare against Nazi Germany*, p. 344

75 Glass, *The Changing of Kings*, p. 163.

76 Cited in Daugherty, 'Personnel Qualifications for Psychological Warfare', in
Daugherty and Janowitz, eds., *Psychological Warfare Casebook*, p. 158.

77 Delmer spoke German and French fluently, and had followed Hitler on his tours
around Germany in 1932 and 1933, getting to know his lieutenants intimately.
Crossman spent some time in Germany after his university training in 1929 and
developed 'a superior knowledge' of German and the Germans. Greene arrived in
Berlin in 1933 and by 1938 had become chief German correspondent for the *Daily
Telegraph*. He had, like Delmer, a close-hand view of the Nazis. See Michael Tracey,
A Variety of Lives: A Biography of Sir Hugh Greene (London: Bodley Head, 1983),
p. 32; For Delmer, see Roetter, *Psychological Warfare*, pp. 170–173; for Crossman,
see Daugherty, 'Crossman', in Daugherty and Janowitz, eds., *Psychological Warfare
Casebook*, pp. 246–248.

78 Crossman, 'Psychological Warfare I', pp. 323–324, 326.

79 Glass, *The Changing of Kings*, p. 189. In one instance, Allied leaflets directed at
Japanese officers in Burma in June 1945 appealed to their 'superior education and
wide knowledge of the world' to confirm that further sacrifice was useless.
Psychological Warfare Information Review, No. 17, 10 June 1945, WO 219/4757.

80 Crossman, 'Psychological Warfare I', p. 325.

81 Crossman, 'Supplementary Essay', in Lerner, *Psychological Warfare against Nazi
Germany*, p. 342; 'Reference Notes for Lecture 5: The Short-Range Leaflet', Feb
1944, FO 898/101.

82 Crossman, 'Psychological Warfare I', p. 326. This was an observation corroborated
by the interrogation of Japanese Prisoners of War in Burma in May 1945. They felt
that true and verifiable 'news is the best form of propaganda'. *Psychological Warfare
Information Review*, No. 16, 10 May 1945, WO 219/4757.

83 Crossman, 'Supplementary Essay', in Lerner, *Psychological Warfare against Nazi
Germany*, pp. 342–344.

84 A.D.C. Peterson to Riley Sunderland, in Sunderland, *Winning the Hearts and Minds
of the People*, pp. 51–52.

85 Sir Robert H. Bruce Lockhart, 'Political Warfare', *RUSI Journal*, Vol. XCV, No. 577
(1950), p. 195.

86 Crossman, 'Psychological Warfare I', p. 321.

87 Lockhart, 'Political Warfare', p. 198; Roetter, *Psychological Warfare*, pp. 110–113;
Michael Balfour, *Propaganda in War, 1939–1945: Organisations, Policies and
Publics in Britain and Germany* (London, Boston and Henley: Routledge and Kegan
Paul, 1979), p. 214.

88 Balfour, *Propaganda in War*, pp. 214–215.

89 Crossman, 'Psychological Warfare I', p. 320.

90 Roetter, *Psychological Warfare*, pp. 110–113; Crossman, 'Supplementary Essay', in Lerner, *Psychological Warfare against Nazi Germany*, p. 335.

91 Crossman, 'Supplementary Essay', in Lerner, *Psychological Warfare against Nazi Germany*, p. 339.

92 Thus in Burma it was recognised that 'timing and pinpointing of leaflets' were the key to effective propaganda. *Psychological Warfare Information Review*, No. 14, 10 March 1945, WO 219/4757.

93 Crossman, 'Supplementary Essay', in Lerner, *Psychological Warfare against Nazi Germany*, pp. 339–340.

94 Lerner, 'Is International Persuasion Sociologically Feasible?', in De McLaurin *et al.*, eds., *The Art and Science of Psychological Operations*, Vol. 1, p. 49.

95 Crossman, 'Supplementary Essay', in Lerner, *Psychological Warfare against Nazi Germany*, p. 339; *idem*, 'Psychological Warfare', *RUSI Journal*, Vol. XCVIII (Nov 1953), p. 529. Hereafter 'Psychological Warfare III'.

96 See Chapter Five.

97 Templer first worked under Alexander at Northern Command Headquarters in York in 1933, and ten years later as Commanding Officer, 56th Division, he again reported to 'Alex' who was Supreme Allied Commander, Italy. Montgomery was Templer's instructor at the Staff College at Camberley in 1928; 12 years later Templer was one of 'Monty's' brigade commanders in 5th Corps. In May 1945, moreover, Montgomery appointed Templer as Director of Civil Affairs and Military Government in Germany. Montgomery was then Commanding Officer 21st Army Group. Finally, from April 1946, Templer worked as Director of Military Intelligence under Montgomery who was now Chief of the Imperial General Staff. Parkinson's opinion is that Montgomery was the greater influence on Templer, while Cloake argues that Templer picked up vital pointers from both generals. See C. Northcote Parkinson, *Templer in Malaya* (Singapore: Donald Moore, 1954), p. 17; Cloake, *Templer: Tiger of Malaya*, pp. 47, 52, 87, 114–115, 144–146, 168, 454.

98 Michael Carver, 'Montgomery', in Keegan, ed., *Churchill's Generals*, p. 152.

99 Brian Holden Reid, 'Alexander', in Keegan, ed., *Churchill's Generals*, pp. 104–105, 116, 125.

100 Nigel Nicolson, *Alex: The Life of Field Marshal Earl Alexander of Tunis* (London: Weidenfeld and Nicolson, 1973), p. 126; Nigel Hamilton, *Monty: The Making of a General 1887–1942* (London: Hamish Hamilton, 1981), p. 565.

101 Christopher Hibbert, *The Great Mutiny, India 1857* (London: Penguin, 1988), pp. 389–391; Ronald Hyam, *Britain's Imperial Century, 1815–1914: A Study of Empire and Expansion*, 2nd edn. (London: Macmillan, 1993), pp. 140–141, 155.

102 Bernard Porter, *The Lion's Share: A Short History of British Imperialism, 1850–1995*, 3rd edn. (London and New York: Longman, 1996), p. 71.

103 *Ibid.*, p. 46.

104 Hyam, *Britain's Imperial Century*, p. 169.

105 *Ibid.*, p. 155.

106 Cited in Lawrence James, *Rise and Fall of the British Empire* (London: Abacus Books, 1997), p. 233. See also V.G. Kiernan, *The Lords of Human Kind: European Attitudes to the Outside World in the Imperial Age* (Middlesex: Pelican, 1972), p. 159.

107 Helen Fein, *Imperial Crime and Punishment: The Massacre at Jallianwala Bagh and British Judgement 1919–1920* (Honolulu: University of Hawaii Press, 1977), pp. 21, 45–46.

108 *Ibid.*, p. 20.

109 *Ibid.*, pp. 41–42.
110 Charles Townshend, *The British Campaign in Ireland 1919–1921: The Development of Political and Military Policies* (London: Oxford University Press, 1975), pp. 120, 149; *idem*, 'The Irish Insurgency 1918–21: The Military Problem', in Haycock, ed., *Regular Armies and Insurgency*, p. 46.
111 Tom Bowden, *The Breakdown of Public Security: The Case of Ireland 1919–1921 and Palestine 1936–1939* (London and Beverly Hills: SAGE Publications, 1977), p. 32; Bruce Hoffman, *The Failure of British Military Strategy within Palestine 1939–1947* (Jerusalem: Bar-Ilan University Press, 1983), p. 80.
112 Townshend, 'The Irish Insurgency', in Haycock, ed., *Regular Armies and Insurgency*, p. 43. H.J. Simson provides an account of detention during the Arab Revolt. Simson, *British Rule and Rebellion* (London and Edinburgh: William Blackwood and Sons, 1937), p. 214.
113 Hoffman, *The Failure of British Military Strategy within Palestine*, pp. 29–30.
114 *Ibid.*, pp. 33–34; Townshend, *The British Campaign in Ireland*, pp. 149–150.
115 Towle, *Pilots and Rebels*, pp. 12–15.
116 'Memorandum by the Air Staff on the Psychological Effects of Air Bombardment on Semi-Civilised Peoples', Air Staff Memorandum No. 19, 7 Feb 1924, AIR 9/12.
117 Towle, *Pilots and Rebels*, p. 53.
118 'Reasons why the Bombing of Villages Overseas is Essential', undated note, AIR 9/12; Arab villages had been bombed during the Arab Revolt as well. Hoffman, *The Failure of British Military Strategy within Palestine*, p. 19.
119 'Reasons why the Bombing of Villages Overseas is Essential', AIR 9/12; Towle, *Pilots and Rebels*, pp. 19–20.
120 David E. Omissi, *Air Power and Colonial Control: The Royal Air Force 1919–1939* (Manchester: Manchester University Press, 1990), pp. 44–45.
121 George Orwell, *The Collected Essays, Journalism and Letters of George Orwell, Vol. 1:An Age Like This, 1920–1940*, ed. by Sonia Orwell and Ian Angus (London: Secker and Warburg, 1969), p. 403.
122 George Orwell, *The Road to Wigan Pier* (London: Penguin, 1989), p. 138. See also John Newsinger, '"Pox Britannica": Orwell and the Empire', *Race and Class*, Vol. 38, No. 2 (1996), p. 36.
123 Townshend, *The British Campaign in Ireland*, p. 95.
124 Bowden, *The Breakdown of Public Security*, pp. 27–28.
125 Keith Jeffery, *The British Army and the Crisis of Empire* (Manchester: Manchester University Press, 1984), p. 73. See also A.J. Stockwell, 'Policing during the Malayan Emergency 1948–60: communism, communalism and decolonisation', in *Policing and Decolonisation: Nationalism, Politics and the Police 1917–65*, ed. by David M. Anderson and David Killingray (Manchester: Manchester University Press, 1992), p. 110.
126 Jeffery, *The British Army and the Crisis of Empire*, pp. 71–72.
127 Thomas R. Mockaitis, 'Low-Intensity Conflict: The British Experience', *Conflict Quarterly*, Vol. 13, No. 1 (Winter 1993), p. 12.
128 Cited in Trevor Royle, *Orde Wingate – Irregular Soldier* (London: Weidenfeld and Nicolson, 1995), p. 121.
129 *Ibid.*, p. 119.
130 Mockaitis, 'The Origins of British Counter-Insurgency', p. 219; John Masters, *Bugles and a Tiger* (London: Four Square, 1967), p. 9; Townshend, 'The Irish Insurgency', in Haycock, ed., *Regular Armies and Insurgency*, p. 46.
131 Eversley Belfield, *The Boer War* (London: Leo Cooper, 1993), p. 129.
132 Pimlott, 'The British Army: The Dhofar Campaign', in Beckett and Pimlott, eds., *Armed Forces and Modern Counterinsurgency*, p. 16; Ian F.W. Beckett, 'The Study

of Counterinsurgency: A British Perspective', *Small Wars and Insurgencies*, Vol. 1, No. 1 (1990), p. 48.

133 Tim Jones, 'The British Army, and Counter-Guerrilla Warfare in Transition, 1944–1952', *Small Wars and Insurgencies*, Vol. 7, No. 3 (Winter 1996), pp. 266, 275–276.

134 These ex-prisoners were grouped into the National Scouts, of which 1500 were based in Transvaal and 480 in the Orange Free State. See Philip J. Haythornthwaite, *Colonial Wars Sourcebook* (London: Arms and Armour Press, 1995), p. 205; Pimlott, 'The British Army: The Dhofar Campaign', in Pimlott and Beckett, eds., *Armed Forces and Modern Counterinsurgency*, p. 17.

135 Hoffman, *The Failure of British Military Strategy in Palestine*, pp. 23, 59.

CHAPTER TWO

1 According to C.C. Too, the terms 'CPM' and 'MCP' are interchangeable. The former term is the more formal one, used when issuing official statements, policy directives and pronouncements, while the latter is used in less formal propaganda. See C.C. Too, 'The Communist Party of Malaya and its Attempts to Capture Power', Nov 1989, C.C. Too Papers (PP), in author's possession.

2 Short, 'The Malayan Emergency', in Haycock, ed., *Regular Armies and Insurgency*, pp. 65–66; Stubbs, *Hearts and Minds in Guerrilla Warfare*, p. 254; Lucien W. Pye; *Guerrilla Communism in Malaya: Its Social and Political Meaning* (Princeton: Princeton University Press, 1956), pp. 95–102; Robert O. Tilman, 'The Non-Lessons of the Malayan Emergency', *Asian Survey*, Vol. 6, No. 8 (August 1966), pp. 413–415; Charles B. McLane, *Soviet Strategies in Southeast Asia: An Explanation of Eastern Policy under Lenin and Stalin* (Princeton: Princeton University Press, 1966), pp. 398–400; Leon Comber, '"The Weather has been Horrible": Malayan Communist Communications during "The Emergency" (1948–60)', *Asian Studies Review*, Vol. 19, No. 2 (Nov 1995), pp. 37–57.

3 Crozier, *The Rebels*, pp. 166–168; J.H. Brimmell, *Communism in South East Asia: A Political Analysis* (London: Oxford University Press, 1959), p. 323; Julian Paget, *Counter-Insurgency Campaigning* (London: Faber and Faber, 1967), p. 76.

4 W.L. Blythe, 'The Significance of Chinese Triad Societies in Malaya', 16 March 1949, W.L. Blythe Papers, MSS.Ind.Ocn.s.116; Frank Brewer, 'The Chinese Protectorate and the Chinese Affairs Department', Oct 1954, Frank Brewer Papers, Box 1, MSS.Ind.Ocn.s.306, RHO; B.W.F. Goodrich, 'Secret Societies', *Malaya: The Journal of the British Association of Malaya* (March 1959), pp. 32–34.

5 C.F. Yong, *The Origins of Malayan Communism* (Singapore: South Seas Society, 1997), pp. 216–235; Goodrich, 'Secret Societies', p. 33; Stenson, *Industrial Conflict in Malaya*, pp. 23–24; Cheah, *The Masked Comrades*, pp. 32–36; W.L. Blythe, 'The Interplay of Chinese Secret Societies and Political Societies in Malaya', 3 Aug 1949; *idem*, 'The Significance of Chinese Triad Societies in Malaya'; V. Purcell, 'Reports on Chinese Affairs', 18 Feb 1946 and 30 March 1946, Blythe Papers, RHO.

6 Granada Television Interview with C.C. Too, Aug 1981, 'End of Empire' Papers, MSS. Brit.Emp.s. 527 (EEP), RHO; P.B. Humphrey, 'A Preliminary Study of Entry Behaviour among Chinese Communist Terrorist Terrorists in Malaya', Operational Research Section (Psychological Warfare) Memorandum No. 2/53, June 1953, WO 291/1764; Pye, *Guerrilla Communism in Malaya*, pp. 216–217.

7 Humphrey, 'A Preliminary Study of Entry Behaviour', WO 291/1764; Pye, *Guerrilla Communism in Malaya*, pp. 240–242.

8 'The present day situation and duties of the Malayan Communist Party': note by Mr Strachey for the Cabinet Malaya Committee commenting on a captured MCP

document, PREM 8/1406/2, MAL C(50) 12, 12 May 1950, in *BDEEP Series B, Vol. 3: Malaya, the Communist Insurrection, 1948–1953, Part II*, ed. by A.J. Stockwell (London: HMSO, 1995), Doc. 215. See also Geoffrey Fairbairn, *Revolutionary Guerrilla Warfare: the Countryside Version* (Middlesex: Penguin, 1974), pp. 161–163.

9 David Gray, Acting Secretary of Chinese Affairs, Federation of Malaya to W.J. Watts, 17 Dec 1951, *idem*, 'The Chinese Problem in the Federation of Malaya', July 1952, W.J. Watts Papers, MSS.Ind.Ocn.s.320, RHO.

10 P.B. Humphrey, 'A Study of the Reasons for Entering the Jungle within a Group of Surrendered Chinese Terrorists', ORS (PW) Memorandum No. 8/54, 17 June 1954, WO 291/1781.

11 Humphrey, 'A Preliminary Study of Entry Behaviour', WO 291/1764; D.F. Bayly Pike, 'Interrogation of 112 Surrendered Communist Terrorists in 1955', Operational Research Unit Far East, Memorandum No. 4/56, May 1956, WO 291/1699.

12 'Tan Chin Siong' to Dato Tan Cheng Lock, 18 May 1950, TCL.11.5, Tan Cheng Lock Papers, Institute of Southeast Asian Studies, Singapore (hereafter TCLP-ISEAS); R.N. Broome, 'Communism in Malaya: Background to the Fighting', 1949, Blythe Papers, RHO.

13 Too interviews, Tapes 1 and 2, EEP, RHO.

14 'Tan Chin Siong' to Dato Tan Cheng Lock, 18 May 1950, TCL.11.5, TCLP-ISEAS; Broome, 'Communism in Malaya', 1949, Blythe Papers, RHO. See also F.H. Lakin, 'Psychological Warfare Research: Its Role in the Cold War', Army Operational Research Group Report No. 5/56, n.d., WO 291/1509.

15 W.L. Blythe, 'Commentary on Purcell, *The Chinese in Malaya* (Oxford University Press)', March 1949, Blythe Papers, RHO; Lakin, 'Psychological Warfare Research', WO 291/1509.

16 Humphrey, 'A Preliminary Study of Entry Behaviour among Chinese Communist Terrorist Terrorists in Malaya', WO 291/1764; *idem*, 'A Study of the Reasons for Entering the Jungle', WO 291/1781; Lakin, 'Psychological Warfare Research', WO 291/1509.

17 Bayly Pike, 'Interrogation of 112 Surrendered Communist Terrorists', WO 291/1699.

18 'Tan Chin Siong' to Dato Tan Cheng Lock, 18 May 1950, TCL.11.5, TCLP-ISEAS.

19 Frank Brewer, *The Chinese Problem in the Federation of Malaya* (Kuala Lumpur: Government Printer, 1955), p. 7; Gray, 'The Chinese Problem in the Federation of Malaya', Watts Papers, RHO.

20 Humphrey, 'A Preliminary Study of Entry Behaviour', WO 291/1764; Pye, *Guerrilla Communism in Malaya*, p. 190.

21 Humphrey, 'A Study of the Reasons for Entering the Jungle', WO 291/1781.

22 This was the abbreviated form of *Min Chong Yuen Thong*, or 'people's movement'. See Extract from 'Abstract of Intelligence', 16–31 Dec 1951, Appendix A, CO 1022/188. See also Edgar O'Ballance, *Malaya: The Communist Insurgent War, 1948–60* (Hamden, Connecticut: Archon Books, 1966), p. 92.

23 Group Discussion with Chin Peng; C.C. Too, 'Schematic Diagram of Typical Min Yuen Activities in Support of the Communist Terrorists in the Jungle', Sep 1990, PP; Extract from 'Abstract of Intelligence', 16–31 Dec 1951, CO 1022/188; Extract from 'Secret Abstract of Intelligence', 1–15 July 1951, Extract from 'Secret Abstract of Intelligence,' 16–31 Jan 1951 and Extract from 'PMR 5/1951', all in CO 537/7300; Federal Government Press Statement, 30 April 1952, CO 1022/152; *Scotsman*, 14 June 1952; O'Ballance, *Malaya*, pp. 89–92; Clutterbuck, *Conflict and Violence in Singapore and Malaysia*, pp. 170–172.

24 Short, 'Communism and the Emergency', in Wang ed., *Malaysia*, p. 150; *idem*, *The Communist Insurrection in Malaya*, p. 19.

25 Brimmell, *Communism in Southeast Asia*, p. 327.

26 Yong, *Origins of Malayan Communism*, pp. 56–57, 134–141; Cheah, *From PKI to the Comintern*, pp. 31–32; Too interview, Tape 2, EEP, RHO.

27 Yong, *Origins of Malayan Communism*, pp. 145, 168–169, 188–194, 276; Stubbs, *Hearts and Minds in Guerrilla Warfare*, pp. 54–58; Mackay, *The Malayan Emergency,*, pp. 18–25; Blythe, 'The Interplay of Chinese Secret Societies and Political Societies in Malaya', Blythe Papers, RHO; Group Discussion with Chin Peng, 18 June 1998.

28 Miller, *Jungle War in Malaya*, pp. 52–53. Chin Peng, born in 1924, had risen to be State Secretary Perak and commander of the 5th MPAJA Regiment during the Japanese Occupation. Yeong Kwo, born in 1914, had been Selangor State Secretary during the Occupation, and during the Emergency had been based in the vicinity of Kuala Lumpur. He was killed by the Security Forces in 1956. Lau Lee, born in 1916 and also known as Lee Aun Tong, had been a school teacher before the Emergency, and during the conflict he edited the main jungle newspaper *Humanity News*. He replaced Yeong Kwo as Deputy Secretary General in late 1955.

29 Broome of course was in a position to comment on the MCP's top leaders as he had known them intimately during the Occupation, along with John L. Davis and Spencer Chapman, among others. Chapman, *The Jungle is Neutral*, pp. 198–199, 274–288.

30 Broome, 'Communism in Malaya', Blythe Papers, RHO; Stenson, *Industrial Conflict in Malaya*, pp. 95–96.

31 Too interview, Tape 2, EEP, RHO. See also Cheah, *Masked Comrades*, pp. 58–60; Short, *Communist Insurrection in Malaya*, p. 54; Yong, *Origins of Malayan Communism*, pp. 140, 182.

32 Group Discussion with Chin Peng, 18 June 1998; Short, *Communist Insurrection in Malaya*, p. 53. The Canberra workshop with Chin Peng was organised under the auspices of the Australian National University, from 22–23 February 1999. It was convened by Prof. Anthony Reid, and leading scholars of the Emergency such as Anthony Short and Richard Stubbs were invited to interview Chin Peng. Information taken from Karl Hack, 'Corpses, Prisoners of War and Captured Documents: British and Communist Narratives of the Malayan Emergency, and the Dynamics of Intelligence Transformation', *Intelligence and National Security*, Vol. 14, No. 4 (Winter 1999), pp. 222–223, 233.

33 C.C. Too, 'Curriculum Vitae', n.d., PP.

34 The work of the English-educated recruits was confined to publishing the Communist-controlled English newspaper *The Democrat* (1946–1947) and working in united front organisations like the Malayan Democratic Union (1945–1948). De Cruz was a Eurasian who had been a journalist with the *Straits Times* before the Japanese Occupation, who joined the MCP in late 1945. He fled Singapore when the Emergency was declared in June 1948. Osman China was a Chinese who had been adopted by Malay parents and brought up as a Muslim. Going underground at the onset of the Emergency, he achieved the rank of District Committee Member in Pahang but surrendered at the end of 1954. Cheah, *Masked Comrades*, pp. 58–60, 90–91; Perry Robinson, *Transformation in Malaya*, pp. 155–156. See also Gerald de Cruz, *Rojak Rebel: Memoirs of a Singapore Maverick* (Singapore and Kuala Lumpur: Times Books International, 1993), pp. 65–67.

35 Too, 'Curriculum Vitae'.

36 Too, 'The Communist Party of Malaya', PP.

37 Too interview, Tape 2, EEP, RHO; Chin Kee Onn in Stubbs, *Hearts and Minds in Guerrilla Warfare*, p. 58; Crozier, *The Rebels*, pp. 44–45; Short, *Communist Insurrection in Malaya*, p. 54.

38 Brimmell, *Communism in Southeast Asia*, p. 323.

39 Stubbs, *Hearts and Minds in Guerrilla Warfare*, p. 253.

40 *Selected Readings from the Works of Mao Tse-Tung* (Peking: Foreign Languages Press, 1967), p. 236.

41 Mao Tse-Tung, *Selected Military Writings,* 2nd. edn. (Peking: Foreign Languages Press, 1966), pp. 58–61.

42 *Ibid.*, pp. 57–58.

43 *Ibid.*, p. 260.

44 *Ibid.*, p. 229.

45 McLane, *Soviet Strategies in Southeast Asia*, pp. 389–390; Brimmell, *Communism in Southeast Asia*, p. 322.

46 See the document 'Decisions of the Standing Committee, Central Committee, Malayan Communist Party', 13 June 1940. Reproduced in Gene Z. Hanrahan, *The Communist Struggle in Malaya* (Kuala Lumpur: University of Malaya Press, 1971), pp. 163–170.

47 *Ibid.*

48 Harry Miller, *Menace in Malaya* (London: George G. Harrap, 1954), pp. 101–102; J.N. McHugh, 'Psychological, or Political Warfare in Malaya', Part II, *Journal of the Historical Society University of Malaya*, Vol. 5 (1966/67), pp. 84–85.

49 J.N. McHugh, *Anatomy of Communist Propaganda* (Kuala Lumpur: Department of Public Relations, 1949), pp. 1–2.

50 Cited in Pye, *Guerrilla Communism in Malaya*, p. 302.

51 *Ibid.*, p. 304.

52 Gerald de Cruz, *Politics and Everyman Today* (Kuching, Sarawak: Government Printer, 1963), p. 21.

53 Cited in Pye, *Guerrilla Communism in Malaya*, pp. 264–265.

54 'Decisions of the Standing Committee, Central Committee, Malayan Communist Party', 13 June 1940.

55 De Cruz, *Politics and Everyman Today*, p. 20.

56 Mao, *Selected Military Writings* , p. 58.

57 See the testimony of Fong Sin, who surrendered on 26 July 1952, and was broadcast over Radio Malaya. Federal Government Press Statement, 26 July 1952, Sir Arthur Edwin Young Papers, Box 1, MSS.Brit.Emp.s.486, RHO. See also Pye, *Guerrilla Communism in Malaya*, p. 257.

58 'Decisions of the Standing Committee, Central Committee, Malayan Communist Party', 13 June 1940.

59 Miller, *Jungle War in Malaya*, p. 56.

60 *Selected Readings from the Works of Mao*, p. 120.

61 C.C. Too, 'Psychological Warfare and Some Aspects of the Psychology of the People in Southeast Asia in Areas Where Communist Insurrection is Likely to Arise', impromptu Speech to the Staff of the Faculty, US Army Command and General Staff College, Fort Leavenworth, Kansas, 15 Oct 1962, PP. Hereafter Too US Lecture.

62 Federal Government Press Statement, Kuala Lumpur, 3 June 1952, CO 1022/49.

63 *Times*, 30 May 1952.

64 See Extract from 'Malayan Weekly Intelligence Summary No. 35 for week ending 4 Jan 1951', CO 537/7291; Extract from the 'Security Forces' Weekly Intelligence Summary No. 24, week ending 19 Oct 1950', CO 537/6015.

65 Mrs. A.D.C. Peterson, 'Immediate Interrogation of Surrendered Enemy Personnel', ORS (PW) Technical Note No. 7/53, n.d., WO 291/1798.

66 F.H. Lakin and Mrs. G.J. Humphrey, 'A Study of Surrenders in Malaya during January 1949-June 1954', ORS(PW) Memorandum No. 11/54, July 1954, WO 291/1783.

67 Pye, *Guerrilla Communism in Malaya*, pp. 338–339.

68 See Mao Tse-Tung, *Selected Works*, Vol. 2 (Peking: Foreign Languages Press, 1965), pp. 136–137; Robert Taber, *The War of the Flea: A Study of Guerrilla Warfare Theory and Practice* (London: Paladin, 1970), pp. 52–56.

69 Mao Tse-Tung, *Selected Works*, Vol. 4 (Peking: Foreign Languages Press, 1969), pp. 155–156. See also Peter Paret and John W. Shy, *Guerrillas in the 1960's* (London and Dunmow: Pall Mall Press, 1962), pp. 26–27.

70 Frances Fitzgerald, *Fire in the Lake: The Vietnamese and the Americans in Vietnam* (New York: Vintage Books, 1973), pp. 215–216.

71 Cited in Pye, *Guerrilla Communism in Malaya*, p. 294.

72 Aloysius Chin, *The Communist Party of Malaya: The Inside Story* (Kuala Lumpur: Vinpress, 1995), p. 30; Group Discussion with Chin Peng, 18 June 1998. Aloysius Chin is a retired senior Malaysian Special Branch officer who spent 30 years combating MCP subversion.

73 McHugh, 'Psychological, or Political Warfare in Malaya', Part II, pp. 82–86.

74 Cited in *Ibid.*, p. 83.

75 Group Discussion with Chin Peng, 18 June 1998; 'Supplementary Views of the Central Political Bureau of the Malayan Communist Party on "Strategic Problems of the Malayan Revolutionary War"', 12 Nov 1949. Reproduced in Hanrahan, *The Communist Struggle in Malaya*, pp. 197–220.

76 While against a pre-war figure of 80 651 tons, only 8 432 tons of tin had been mined in 1946, by 1947, this had jumped to 36 079 tons, and three years later the pre-war figure had been surpassed. In addition, because the Japanese had only managed to damage 2½ percent of the total of 3 302 000 acres under cultivation, rubber production was able to recover faster. See D.G.E. Hall, *A History of Southeast Asia*, 4th edn. (London: Macmillan, 1988), pp. 872–873.

77 Stenson, *Industrial Conflict in Malaya*, p. 228; see also Blythe, 'The Interplay of Chinese Secret Societies and Political Societies in Malaya', Blythe Papers, RHO and Short, 'Communism and the Emergency', in Wang, ed., *Malaysia*, p. 152.

78 Chin, *The Communist Party of Malaya*, p. 30.

79 O'Ballance, *Malaya*, pp. 80–81.

80 Blythe, 'The Interplay of Chinese Secret Societies and Political Societies in Malaya', Blythe Papers, RHO; Clutterbuck, *Conflict and Violence in Singapore and Malaysia*, p. 170.

81 See 'Strategic Problems of the Malayan Revolutionary War', December 1948, in Hanrahan, *The Communist Struggle in Malaya*, pp. 170–197. Also 'Supplementary Views of the Central Political Bureau of the Malayan Communist Party', 12 Nov 1949; Short, 'Communism and the Emergency', in Wang, ed., *Malaysia*, p. 153.

82 Clutterbuck, *Conflict and Violence in Singapore and Malaysia*, p. 172; O'Ballance, *Malaya*, p. 89; 'Tan Chin Siong' to Dato Tan Cheng Lock, 18 May 1950, TCL.11.5, TCLP-ISEAS. See also Lieutenant-General Roger Bower, Director of Operations, Federation of Malaya, 'Report of Emergency in Malaya June 1948- Aug 1957', 12 Sep 57, WO 106/5990. Hereafter Bower Report.

83 'Supplementary Views of the Central Political Bureau of the Malayan Communist Party', 12 Nov 1949.

84 Fitzgerald, *Fire in the Lake*, pp. 215–216.

85 Short, *Communist Insurrection in Malaya*, p. 207; Clutterbuck, *Conflict and Violence in Singapore and Malaysia*, p. 174.

86 See Lt-General Sir Hugh Stockwell, 'Appreciation of the Situation in Malaya', 15 October 1953, Appendix B: 'Vital Areas'. Found in the papers of Maj-General Dennis Edmund Blaquiere Talbot, LHCMA. Talbot commanded the 18th Infantry Brigade and the 99 Gurkha Infantry Brigade in Malaya between 1953–1955.

87 Mackay, *The Malayan Emergency*, p. 109.

88 See Miller, *Menace in Malaya*, pp. 153–156; Brimmell, *Communism in Southeast Asia*, p. 326; Eliot Watrous, 'This is Communism', transcript of Radio Malaya broadcast, 6 Sep 1951, CO 537/7291.

89 Watrous, 'This is Communism', CO 537/7291; Brimmell, *Communism in Southeast Asia*, p. 326; Short, *Communist Insurrection in Malaya*, p. 313.

90 Adapted from the similar definition provided by Thornton. See Thornton, 'Terror as a Weapon of Political Agitation', in Eckstein, ed., *Internal War*, p. 73.

91 Schmid and de Graaf, *Violence as Communication*, p. 14.

92 Thornton, 'Terror as a Weapon of Political Agitation', in Eckstein, ed., *Internal War*, p. 75.

93 Schmid and de Graaf, *Violence as Communication*, p. 14.

94 Thornton, 'Terror as a Weapon of Political Agitation', in Eckstein, ed., *Internal War*, pp. 75–76.

95 See Schmid and de Graaf, *Violence as Communication*, pp. 12–13; Conor Gearty, *Terror* (London: Faber and Faber, 1991), pp. 23 25; Wardlaw, *Political Terrorism*, p. 19.

96 Harold J. Laski, *Communism* (London: Thornton Butterworth, 1928), p. 140. See also John Pustay, *Counterinsurgency Warfare* (New York: Free Press, 1965), p. 26.

97 Gearty, *Terror*, p. 31; Wardlaw, *Political Terrorism*, p. 43.

98 See Mao, *Selected Military Writings*, p. 260.

99 'Strategic Problems of the Revolutionary War', December 1948.

100 *Ibid.*

101 De Cruz, *Politics and Everyman Today*, p. 17.

102 *Communist Banditry in Malaya: the Emergency June 1948-Dec 1949* (Kuala Lumpur: Department of Public Relations, 1950), pp. 59–60.

103 'Talking Points for H.E.'s Farewell Visits on 29th and 30th April 1954', 7410-29-1, National Army Museum (hereafter NAM).

104 McHugh, 'Psychological, or Political Warfare', Part II, p. 84.

105 See the Reuters report dated 1 Nov 1951 in CO 1022/43.

106 McHugh, *Anatomy of Communist Propaganda*, p. 41.

107 'Strategic Problems of the Malayan Revolutionary War', December 1948.

108 Liew Thian Choy, 'Second Further Statement', 7 Oct 1949, B.P. Walker-Taylor Papers, MSS.Ind.Ocn.s.257, RHO.

109 Judith Strauch, *Chinese Village Politics in the Malaysian State* (Cambridge, Massachusetts, and London: Harvard University Press, 1981), p. 65; Gray, 'The Chinese Problem in the Federation of Malaya', Watts Papers, RHO.

110 *Straits Budget*, 9 Feb 1950. See also Operations Information Branch, Federal Police Headquarters, 'Short History of the Emergency', 21 Oct 1952, Young Papers, Box 1, RHO.

111 Cited in *Listener*, 31 July 1969.

112 Cited in McHugh, *Anatomy of Communist Propaganda*, p. 41.

113 Brimmell, *Communism in Southeast Asia*, p. 329.

114 William R. Andrews, *The Village War: Vietnamese Communist Revolutionary Activities in Dinh Tuong Province 1960–64* (Columbia, Missouri: University of Missouri Press, 1973), p. 54; Fitzgerald, *Fire in the Lake*, pp. 232–233.

115 Too US Lecture, PP.

116 Brimmell, *Communism in Southeast Asia*, p. 326.

117 This was promulgated in May 1950 by Lieutenant-General Harold Briggs, the newly-appointed Director of Operations. In a bid to break the logistics supply pipeline between the Min Yuen and the MRLA, the Plan called for the speeding up of the resettlement of squatters away from the vulnerable jungle fringe and into compact defended Resettlement Areas. It also called for more reliance on Army

patrols of the jungle fringe so as to ambush terrorists seeking to reconstruct the supply link. More details, and the argument that the Plan sought fundamentally to win rural Chinese confidence, are found in Chapter Four.

118 Extract from 'PMR 12/1951', CO 1022/187.
119 See Federal Government Press Statement, 20 Oct 1950, CO 537/6015.
120 *Ibid.*
121 *Ibid.*
122 R.B. Smith, 'China and Southeast Asia: the Revolutionary Perspective, 1951', *Journal of Southeast Asian Studies*, Vol. 19, No. 1 (March 1988), p. 109; Brimmell, *Communism in Southeast Asia*, p. 327.
123 C.C. Too, 'The Communist Party of Malaya', PP.
124 A total of seven documents were transmitted to Lyttelton. See Federation Director of Intelligence John Morton to Lyttelton, 31 Dec 1952, CO 1022/187.
125 *Times*, 1 Dec 1952. This article was written by *Times* correspondent Louis Heren, who had been shown a copy of the October 1951 Directives in confidence by a senior Government official. For his unauthorised 'scoop', Heren earned the ire of the new High Commissioner Gerald Templer, and was subsequently vilified as 'typical of all communist muck'. Templer even tried to get Heren recalled from Malaya. Carruthers, *Winning Hearts and Minds*, pp. 86–87, 120, n. 74.
126 *Times*, 1 Dec 1952.
127 *Ibid.*
128 *Ibid.*
129 See 'Functional Directive of the Central Politbureau on Carrying Out The Party's Tasks', 1 Oct 1951, CO 1022/187.
130 *Ibid.*
131 *Times*, 1 Dec 1952.
132 'Functional Directive', CO 1022/187.
133 *Ibid.*
134 Short, *Communist Insurrection in Malaya*, p. 320.
135 See 'Maintaining Party Discipline of MCP Cadres', 1 Oct 1951, CO 1022/187.
136 *The Communist Threat to the Federation of Malaya* (Kuala Lumpur: Government Printer, 1959), p. 19.
137 *Ibid.*, p. 17.
138 Chin, *The Communist Party of Malaya*, pp. 31–32, 42–43.
139 *Ibid.*, p. 55.
140 Crozier, *The Rebels*, p. 168.
141 Hugh Stockwell, 'Appreciation of the Situation in Malaya', Talbot Papers, LHCMA; Pye, *Guerrilla Communism in Malaya*, pp. 105–106.
142 D.F. Bayly Pike, 'Statistics of the Malayan Emergency', Part II, Operations Research Unit Far East, Technical Note 1/56, June 1956, WO 291/1719. See also Crozier, *The Rebels*, p. 168.
143 See P.B. Humphrey, 'An Investigation into Communist Terrorist Recruitment and Losses in Malaya, 1951–53', 29 Sep 1954, WO 291/1782. See also Robert Asprey, *War in the Shadows*, rev. edn. (London: Little, Brown and Co., 1994), p. 573.
144 Pye, *Guerrilla Communism in Malaya*, p. 106; Crozier, *The Rebels*, pp. 166–168.
145 Sunderland, *Winning the Hearts and Minds of the People*, p. 31.
146 Too, 'The Communist Party of Malaya', PP.
147 Cited in Pye, *Guerrilla Communism in Malaya*, p. 336. Perry Robinson, *Transformation in Malaya*, pp. 155–159.
148 Hack, 'Screwing Down the People', in Antlov and Tonnesson, eds., *Imperial Policy and South East Asian Nationalism*, p. 93.
149 *The Communist Threat to the Federation of Malaya*, pp. 19–30.

150 Director of Operations, Malaya, 'Review of the Emergency Situation in Malaya at the end of 1956', 12 Feb 1957, CO 1030/10. Hereafter *DOR 1956*.

CHAPTER THREE

1 [European business interests in Malaya]: notes by W.G. Sullivan of a meeting between the CO and a delegation representing European business interests on Malayan lawlessness and Sir E Gent's counter-measures, CO 717/172/52849/9/1948, No. 15, 22 Jun 1948. Reproduced in Stockwell, ed., *BDEEP, Malaya: The Communist Insurrection*, Doc. 149.

2 On 4 July, as Gent's aircraft approached London, it collided with another and he was killed. Short, *Communist Insurrection in Malaya*, p. 119.

3 'The Situation in Malaya': Cabinet Memorandum by Secretary of State for the Colonies, Mr Creech Jones, CAB 128/28, CP (48)171, 1 July 1948, in Stockwell, ed., *BDEEP, Malaya: The Communist Insurrection*, Doc. 153. See also *Communist Banditry in Malaya*, p. 2; Rhoderick D. Renick, Jr., 'The Emergency Regulations of Malaya: Causes and Effect', *Journal of Southeast Asian History*, Vol. 6, No. 2 (Sep 1965), pp. 1–39.

4 Bower Report, WO 106/5990.

5 *Communist Banditry in Malaya*, p. 3.

6 *Ibid*. See also Perry Robinson, *Transformation in Malaya*, pp. 127–128.

7 Stubbs, *Hearts and Minds in Guerrilla Warfare*, pp. 70–71; Stockwell, ed., *BDEEP, Malaya: The Communist Insurrection*, Doc. 153.

8 Bower Report, WO 106/5990.

9 Stubbs, *Hearts and Minds in Guerrilla Warfare*, p. 70.

10 'The Situation in Malaya': cabinet memorandum by Mr. Creech Jones, PREM 8/1406, CP (48) 190, 19 July 1948, in Stockwell, ed., *BDEEP, Malaya: The Communist Insurrection*, Doc. 159. The Gurkha Brigade arrived from Hong Kong in August 1948, one month after the arrival of the Inniskillings. See Robinson, *Transformation in Malaya*, p. 128.

11 [Appointment of Sir H Gurney as high commissioner]: inward telegram no 1067 from Mr MJ MacDonald to Mr Creech Jones about Malay criticisms, CO 537/3687, no 51, 31 Aug 1948, in Stockwell, ed., *BDEEP, Malaya,: The Communist Insurrection*, Doc. 165.

12 Heussler, *Completing a Stewardship*, pp. 183–184.

13 Tracey, *A Variety of Lives*, p. 134.

14 Heussler, *Completing a Stewardship*, p. 173.

15 J.M. Gullick to Heussler, 13 March 1982, Heussler Papers, MSS.Brit.Emp.s.480, Box 13, RHO.

16 Heussler, *Completing a Stewardship*, p. 174.

17 See Inward Telegram No. 1636 from High Commissioner Federation of Malaya to Secretary of State for the Colonies, 19 Dec 1948, CO 537/4242.

18 This was the opinion of Sjovald Cunyngham-Brown, Gurney's Principal Assistant Secretary, cited in Heussler, *Completing a Stewardship*, p. 174.

19 [Disorders and ways of enlisting Chinese support]: letter (reply) from Sir H Gurney to Sir T Lloyd. CO 537/3758, No. 19, in Stockwell, ed., *BDEEP, Malaya: The Communist Insurrection*, Doc. 168.

20 This was apparently the consensus of not only Gurney but also Gray and Boucher. The latter two officers prepared an appreciation of the situation in Malaya in April 1949. See the 'Present Attitude of the Chinese Population', Federation of Malaya, Despatch No. 4, 11 April 1949, CO 537/4751. Gurney endorsed the paper.

21 Inward Telegram No. 1636, 19 Dec 1948, CO 537/4242; Gurney to Sir Thomas Lloyd, 20 Dec 1948, CO 537/3758.

22 Inward Telegram No. 282 from High Commissioner Federation of Malaya to J.J. Paskin, 1 March 1949, CO 537/4242.

23 See the enclosure to Doc. 168 of Stockwell, ed., *BDEEP, Malaya: The Communist Insurrection*. Gurney identified four broad Chinese groups: local-born Chinese of at least two generations of residence in Malaya, whose fathers were local-born; local-born and English-speaking Chinese of the first generation whose fathers were immigrants; local-born and non-English-speaking Chinese of the first generation whose fathers were immigrants; and China-born newcomers to Malaya.

24 Brewer, *The Chinese Problem in the Federation of Malaya*, pp. 7–8.

25 Sjovald Cunyngham-Brown in Heussler, *Completing a Stewardship*, p. 174. See also H.A.L. Luckham to Heussler, 22 Oct 1979, Heussler Papers, Box 16, RHO. Resettlement, the large scale relocation of the rural Chinese into closely guarded compact communities, will be discussed in the next chapter.

26 Cunyngham-Brown to Heussler, 12 May 1969, Heussler Papers, Box 11, RHO.

27 Granada interview with Hugh Humphrey, n.d., EEP, RHO. Humphrey was Secretary of Internal Defence and Security, 1953–1957.

28 Granada interviews with Sir Michael Hogan, n.d., and Guy Madoc, Aug 1981, EEP; I.L. Phillips' interview with W.C.S. Corry, n.d., MSS.Ind. Ocn.s.215; I.L. Phillips' interview with Malcolm MacDonald, 15 Dec 1972, MSS.Brit.Emp.s.533, RHO. Hogan was Attorney-General Malaya (1950–1955); Madoc Head Special Branch (1950–1954) and Director of Intelligence (1954–1957); Corry was British Adviser Malacca (1949–1953).

29 MacDonald, son of pre-war Labour Prime Minister Ramsay MacDonald, had served between 1935 and 1940 as Colonial Secretary and Dominions Secretary. From 1941 to 1946 he was High Commissioner to Canada, then Governor-General of Malaya and Singapore between April 1946 to April 1948, and Commissioner-General in Southeast Asia from April 1948 to May 1955. From 1955 to 1960 he was High Commissioner to India.

30 Short, 'Communism and the Emergency', in Wang, ed., *Malaysia*, p. 154; Clyde Sanger, *Malcolm MacDonald: Bringing an End to Empire* (Liverpool: Liverpool University Press, 1995), p. 295; Granada interview with G. Perumal, Indian rubber factory supervisor, n.d., EEP, RHO.

31 Stockwell, 'British Imperial Policy and Decolonisation', p. 76.

32 A.J. Stockwell, 'Review of H.S. Barlow, *Swettenham* (Kuala Lumpur: Southdene, 1995) and Clyde Sanger, *Malcolm MacDonald: Bringing and End to Empire* (Montreal and Kingston: McGill-Queen's University Press and Liverpool: Liverpool University Press, 1995)', *Journal of Imperial and Commonwealth History*, Vol. 24, No. 3 (Sep 1996), p. 494.

33 For an account of the events leading up to this, see the MacDonald interview, 15 Dec 1972, RHO; Sanger, *Malcolm MacDonald*, p. 297.

34 'Political Developments in Malaya', CO brief for Mr Rees-Williams for his tour of Hong Kong, Singapore and Malaya, Oct-Nov 1949, communalism and nation-building', Oct 1949, CO 967/84, in Stockwell, ed., *BDEEP, Malaya: The Communist Insurrection*, Doc. 195.

35 Stockwell, 'Review', p. 495.

36 I.L. Phillips' interview with Malcolm MacDonald, 18 Dec 1972, Tape 2, MSS.Brit.Emp.s.533, RHO.

37 Author's interview with J.L.M. Gorrie, 16 Jan 1998, Singapore. Gorrie was an MCS officer who served in Selangor during resettlement; Pamela Ong Siew Im, *Blood and the Soil: A Portrait of Dr Ong Chong Keng* (Singapore and Kuala Lumpur: Times Books International, 1995), pp. 160–161; Gullick to H.P. Bryson, 4 Jan 1970, Heussler Papers, Box 13; Sanger, *Malcolm MacDonald*, Chapter 30.

38 MacDonald interview, 18 Dec 1972, Tape 2, RHO.
39 Brewer, 'The Chinese Protectorate', Brewer Papers, Box 1; Gray, 'The Chinese Problem in the Federation of Malaya', Watts Papers, RHO.
40 Note by Blythe on why the Colonial Office was not being kept informed of Chinese community developments, 12 Sep 1948, Heussler Papers, Box 9, RHO.
41 Purcell, *The Chinese in Malaya*, pp. 151–152. See Broome, 'Notes for the Proposed History of the MCS', 12 March 1970, Heussler Papers, Box 10, RHO.
42 Frank Brewer, 'Peculiar People', Address delivered at Penang Rotary Club, 1952, Brewer Papers, Box 1, RHO. Brewer was Federal SCA (1956–1957) and Secretary for Defence at *Merdeka*.
43 Gray, 'The Chinese Problem in the Federation of Malaya', Watts Papers, RHO. The pre-war Chinese Advisory Boards were fora which permitted Protectors to discuss proposed legislation affecting the Chinese community with selected Chinese leaders. The latter were appointed by the Governor and carried prestige. Blythe to Heussler, 26 Nov 1970, Heussler Papers, Box 9, RHO.
44 H.A.L. Luckham, who was DO Kinta in 1949, claims that Victor Purcell was instrumental in getting the Chinese Protectorate abolished and its functions absorbed by the Labour Department. Luckham to Heussler, 10 Aug 1980; Blythe Note, 12 Sep 1948, Heussler Papers, Boxes 16, 9, RHO. See also the report prepared by T.P.F. McNeice (Secretary for Social Welfare, Singapore), G.C.S Adkins (SCA Singapore) and G.W. Webb (Secretary for Internal Affairs, Singapore) annexed to [Disorder and ways of enlisting Chinese support]: letter (reply) from Sir F. Gimson to Sir T. Lloyd, 8 Dec 1948, in Stockwell, ed., *BDEEP, Malaya: The Communist Insurrection*, Doc. 170.
45 Purcell, *The Chinese in Malaya*, p. 153; Blythe to Heussler, 26 Nov 1970 and Blythe Note, 12 Sep 1948, Heussler Papers, Box 9; Brewer, 'The Chinese Protectorate', Brewer Papers, Box 1, RHO. Blythe was in fact SCA Malayan Union (1946–1948), and Colonial Secretary, Singapore (1950–1953).
46 The Chinese Consuls in Malaya looked after Kuomintang interests until January 1950. That month the British Government recognised the new Communist government in China, so the old Nationalist Consuls had to be withdrawn. This development led to fears that Communist Chinese Consuls would fill the vacuum, and act as the CCP's Trojan horse and a source of material assistance to the MCP. Note by Blythe, 12 Sep 1948, Heussler Papers, Box 9; Brewer, 'The Chinese Protectorate', Brewer Papers, Box 1, RHO. See also 'Note on tour of South-East Asia October 1949': report by Field Marshal Sir W Slim on the importance of civil action in counterinsurgency, CO 537/4374, no 5, Nov 1949, and 'Chinese consuls in Malaya': joint Cabinet memorandum by Mr Griffiths and Mr Younger, CAB 129/39, CP (50) 75, 21 Apr 1950, in Stockwell, ed., *BDEEP, Malaya: The Communist Insurrection*, Docs. 199, 213.
47 Pye, *Guerrilla Communism in Malaya*, p. 202.
48 Gurney to Paskin, 2 June 1949, CO 537/4751.
49 Heng Pek Koon, *Chinese Politics in Malaysia: A History of the Malaysian Chinese Association* (Singapore: Oxford University Press, 1988), p. 129; T.N. Harper, 'The Colonial Inheritance: State and Society in Colonial Malaya 1945–57', Unpublished PhD Dissertation, Cambridge University, 1991, p. 202.
50 Gray to Watts, 17 Dec 1951, Watts Papers, RHO. See also B.T.W. (Brian) Stewart, SCA Malacca during the Templer years. 'Winning in Malaya: An Intelligence Success Story', *Intelligence and National Security*, Vol. 14, No. 4 (Winter 1999), p. 273; John Weldon Humphrey, 'Population Resettlement in Malaya', Unpublished PhD Dissertation, Northwestern University, 1971, p. 237.
51 See Blythe Note, 12 Sep 1948, and Blythe to Heussler, 26 Nov 1970, Heussler Papers, Box 9, RHO.

52 A.W.D. James, Acting Federal SCA, to Federation Establishment Officer, 31 July 1956, 'Department of Chinese Affairs, Federation of Malaya, Miscellaneous Years', File no. 1648, Arkib Negara Malaysia (ANM); Brewer, 'The Chinese Protectorate'; *idem*, 'Chinese Advisory Boards', n.d., Brewer Papers, Box 1, RHO; [Enlisting Chinese Support]: letter from Sir H Gurney to Sir T Lloyd on the problems and methods of winning Chinese support, 20 Dec 1948, CO 537/3758; 'Political Developments in Malaya', Oct 1949, CO 967/84, in Stockwell, ed., *BDEEP, Malaya: The Communist Insurrection*, Docs. 172, 195. See also Stewart, 'Winning in Malaya', p. 270.

53 Blythe Note, 12 Sep 1948, Heussler Papers, Box 9, RHO.

54 Too US Lecture, PP.

55 *Ibid.*

56 F.A. Fielding, 'The Malayan Police Service – Post War', n.d., F.A. Fielding Papers, MSS.Ind.Ocn.s.298, RHO.

57 *Report of the Police Mission to Malaya, March 1950* (Kuala Lumpur: Government Printer, 1950), pp. 15–16.

58 See W.C. Johnson to Gurney, 18 Oct 1949, CO 537/5434. Johnson was the Inspector-General of Colonial Police, who was in Malaya from 11 August to 27 August 1949 to assess the level of professionalism of the Malayan Police.

59 Liew Thian Choy, 'Second Further Statement', 7 Oct 1949, Walker-Taylor Papers, RHO. Liew was a surrendered terrorist.

60 C.E. Howe, 'A Few Memories of My 2½ years as DO in Jelebu, Negri Sembilan, Central Malaya, May 1948-Nov 1950', Heussler Papers, Box 15, RHO.

61 'General Sir Neil Ritchie, 'Report on Operations in Malaya, June 48-July 49', WO 106/5884. Hereafter Ritchie Report.

62 Between 1 Jan 1949 and 31 May 1950, 4 500 National Servicemen were called up under the 1948 National Service Act and sent to Malaya. See *H.C. Debs*, 18 July 1950, Cols. 2007–2008.

63 Allen, *Savage Wars of Peace*, pp. 3–4.

64 'Weekly Situation Report', No. 57, 24 Feb – 2 March 1950, CO 717/201/2. Because of a lack of intelligence on terrorist whereabouts, early air strikes were mainly confined to area rather than precise targets. Mellersh, 'The Campaign against the Terrorists in Malaya', p. 410.

65 Inward Telegram No. 431 from High Commissioner Federation of Malaya to Secretary of State for the Colonies, 10 April 1949, CO 717/173.

66 'Weekly Situation Report', No. 57, 24 Feb–2 March 1950, CO 717/201/2.

67 *Report of the Police Mission to Malaya*, p. 21; 'Weekly Situation Report', No. 64, 14–20 April 1950, CO 717/201/2.

68 'Third Further Statement of Liew Thian Choy, Surrendered Bandit', 10 Oct 1949, Walker-Taylor Papers, RHO.

69 I.S. Gibb, 'A Walk in the Forest', n.d., Imperial War Museum (IWM). Newsinger has also commented on the dehumanising of the terrorists by British troops. See 'The Military Memoir in British Imperial Culture: The Case of Malaya', *Race and Class*, Vol. 35, No. 3 (1994), pp. 57–58.

70 'Present Attitude of the Chinese Population', 11 April 1949, CO 537/4751; Harper, 'The Colonial Inheritance', p. 187.

71 Blythe, 'The Significance of Chinese Triad Societies in Malaya', 16 March 1949; Blythe, 'Commentary on Purcell, *The Chinese in Malaya* (Oxford University Press)', 1949, Blythe Papers; Note by Blythe, 12 Sep 1948, Heussler Papers, Box 9, RHO.

72 Gray to Watts, 17 Dec 1951, Watts Papers, RHO.

73 1981 Granada interview with Mrs. Ching Yoong and Mrs Wong Foo Moi, who were villagers at Batang Kali at the time. Found in EEP, RHO. See also Stubbs, *Hearts and Minds in Guerrilla Warfare*, p. 74. Batang Kali is in Selangor State.

74 See below.
75 *Sunday Graphic*, 7 May 1950; Adrian Hayter, *The Second Step* (London: Hodder and Stoughton, 1962), pp. 208–209, 213. See also Perry Robinson, *Transformation in Malaya*, p. 79. See also Trevor Royle, *The Best Years of their Lives: the National Service Experience 1945–1963* (London: John Murray, 1997), pp. 180–181.
76 Hayter, *The Second Step*, pp. 208–209, 214–215.
77 Gray, 'The Chinese Problem in the Federation of Malaya', Watts Papers, RHO.
78 'Tan Chin Siong' to Dato Tan Cheng Lock, 18 May 1950, TCL.11.5, TCLP-ISEAS.
79 *Ibid.*
80 *Ibid.*
81 P. B. Humphrey, 'A Study of the Reasons for Entering the Jungle within a Group of Surrendered Chinese Communist Terrorists in Malaya', ORS (PW) Memorandum No. 8/54, 17 June 1954, WO 291/1781.
82 K.S. Sandhu and Zakaria Haji Ahmad, 'The Malayan Emergency: Event Writ Large', in *Melaka: The Transformation of a Malay Capital c. 1400–1980*, Vol 1, ed by Paul Wheatley and K.S. Sandhu (Singapore: Oxford University Press, 1983), p. 414.
83 Stubbs, *Hearts and Minds in Guerrilla Warfare*, pp. 69–77. See also Stubbs, 'The Malayan Emergency and the Development of the Malaysian State', in *The Counterinsurgent State: Guerrilla Warfare and State-Building in the 20th Century*, ed. by Paul B. Rich and Richard Stubbs (London: Macmillan, 1997), pp. 50–71. Stubbs argues that it was only when Government switched from a 'military' to a 'political' approach that the tide was turned.
84 Hack, 'Screwing Down the People', in Antlov and Tonnesson, eds., *Imperial Policy and South East Asian Nationalism*, pp. 83–90.
85 *H.C. Debs.*, 8 July 48, Cols. 701–702.
86 'Brief by Mr Anthony Gann for Secretary of State's Kenya Debate', 13 Dec 1952, CO 1022/132.
87 Short considers ER 17C as 'one of the three measures that would probably qualify without reservation for those of a police state'. See Short, *Communist Insurrection in Malaya*, p. 141, n. 40.
88 *Detention and Deportation during the Emergency in the Federation of Malaya* (Kuala Lumpur: Government Press, 1953), p. 8. Copy in CO 1022/132.
89 Inward Savingram No. 55 from High Commissioner Federation of Malaya to Secretary of State for the Colonies, 2 Dec 1948, CO 537/4240.
90 Gray, 'The Chinese Problem in the Federation of Malaya', Watts Papers, RHO.
91 Short, *Communist Insurrection in Malaya*, p. 124, n.16. A good illustration of the dubious, entirely subjective value of the Callus Index as a means of identifying a terrorist or Min Yuen worker, is found in the memoirs of a Police Lieutenant who served in Malaya between 1948 and 1953, J.W.G. Moran. See his *Spearhead in Malaya* (London: Peter Davies, 1959), pp. 79–80.
92 Brewer, 'Malaya: Administration of Chinese Affairs, 1945–57', 8 March 1982, Heussler Papers, Box 9, RHO.
93 Gray, 'The Chinese Problem in the Federation of Malaya', and W.J. Watts to Secretary for Chinese Affairs, Federation of Malaya, 7 Jan 1952, Watts Papers, RHO.
94 Stubbs, *Hearts and Minds in Guerrilla Warfare*, pp. 74–75.
95 'Weekly Situation Report', No. 68, 12–18 May 1950, CO 717/201/2.
96 Perry Robinson, *Transformation in Malaya*, p. 80. Ritchie however reported that it was only in December 1948 that the strategic importance of the squatters was recognised. Ritchie Report, WO 106/5884.
97 Extract from 'Federation of Malaya Savingram No. 645, 11 April 1953, CO 1022/132; *Detention and Deportation during the Emergency*, p. 9.

98 'Brief by Mr Anthony Gann for Secretary of State's Kenya Debate', 13 Dec 1952, CO 1022/132. On 10 October 1949, ER 17D was amended to allow for both selective as well as collective detention orders. *Detention and Deportation during the Emergency*, p. 10. See also Renick, 'The Emergency Regulations of Malaya', pp. 19–21.

99 *Detention and Deportation during the Emergency*, p. 9.

100 Inward Telegram No. 64 from High Commissioner Federation of Malaya to Secretary of State for the Colonies, 16 Jan 1949, CO 717/173.

101 *Detention and Deportation during the Emergency*, p. 9.

102 'The Squatter Problem in the Federation of Malaya in 1950', 17 Feb 1950, CO 717/201/1.

103 Inward Telegrams Nos. 275 and 276 from High Commissioner Federation of Malaya to Secretary of State for the Colonies, 26 and 27 Feb 1949, CO 717/173.

104 Inward Telegram No. 65 from High Commissioner, Federation of Malaya to Secretary of State for the Colonies, 16 Jan 1949, CO 717/173.

105 Cited in Short, *Communist Insurrection in Malaya*, p. 190.

106 *Ibid.*, p. 191.

107 John Gullick, correspondence with the author, 3 July 1997.

108 Liew Thian Choy, 'Second Further Statement', 7 Oct 1949, Walker-Taylor Papers, RHO.

109 'Tan Chin Siong' to Dato Tan Cheng Lock, 18 May 1950, TCL.11.5, TCLP-ISEAS.

110 *Detention and Deportation during the Emergency*, pp. 14–15.

111 David Watherston to A.R. Macintosh, 9 Dec 1951, CO 1022/163.

112 Inward Telegram No. 1173 from High Commissioner Federation of Malaya to Secretary of State for the Colonies, 15 Oct 1949, CO 717/173.

113 There were no 17D operations in 1950 and only two in 1951. *Detention and Deportation during the Emergency*, p. 9.

114 K.J. Henderson, 'The Experiment at the Taiping Rehabilitation Camp', July 1950, Heussler Papers, Box 14, RHO.

115 *Ibid.*

116 *Ibid.*

117 Gray to Chief Secretary, Federation of Malaya, 21 Oct 1950, CO 537/5973.

118 *Report of the Police Mission to Malaya*, pp. 16–21.

119 Sanger, *Malcolm MacDonald*, p. 297.

120 Perry Robinson, *Transformation in Malaya*, pp. 162–163.

121 Stubbs, *Hearts and Minds in Guerrilla Warfare*, p. 71.

122 Ritchie Report, WO 106/5884; Barber, *War of the Running Dogs*, p. 74.

123 Tim Jones, 'The British Army, and Counter-Guerrilla Warfare', p. 284.

124 Ritchie Report, WO 106/5884.

125 'Quarterly Historical Report', and Appendices, 1st Bn, 2nd Regiment, Gurkha Rifles, 31 Dec 1949. Cited in Riley Sunderland, *Army Operations in Malaya: 1947–1960* (Santa Monica: Rand Corporation, 1964), pp. 129–130.

126 'Report on the Royal Air Force Operations in Malaya, June 1948-March 1949', 9 May 1949, AIR 23/8699.

127 Ritchie Report, WO 106/5884.

128 'Interview with Lam Swee, ex-MCP, by Tom Driberg, M.P. at Criminal Investigation Division, Singapore', 1 Nov 1950, CO 537/6015.

129 F.H. Lakin, 'An Investigation into the Psychological Effects of Security Force Activities', ORS (PW) Memorandum No. 5/53, n.d., WO 291/1767.

130 *Ibid.*

131 *Ibid.*; 'The Role of the Air Force in the Present Emergency', 30 Jan 1953, AIR 23/8619.

132 MTP 51 was entitled *Preparation for Warfare in the Far East* (1945) and MTP 52 was called *Warfare in the Far East* (1944). The British Army in Malaya soon had to relearn the lessons of Burma: see Allen, *Savage Wars of Peace*, p. 4. Walker was a Gurkha officer who had served in Waziristan on the North West Frontier in India. He later commanded the 4/8 Gurkha Rifles in Burma during the war and the 1/6 Gurkhas between 1951 and 1954. Between 1954 and 1957 he served as a staff officer in Headquarters Eastern Command and then returned to Malaya as commander of the 99 Gurkha Infantry Brigade until the end of 1962, when he was appointed Director of all British and Commonwealth Forces in Borneo during the Brunei revolt. He was then appointed Director of Borneo Operations in response to the Indonesian Confrontation against Malaysia. He remained in this post until March 1965.

133 Broome to Heussler, 27 Aug 1981, Heussler Papers, Box 10, RHO. See Perry Robinson, *Transformation in Malaya*, pp. 131–137; Tom Pocock, *Fighting General: The Public and Private Campaigns of General Sir Walter Walker* (London: Collins, 1973), p. 86.

134 Mackay feels that the Force was disbanded 'for reasons that no-one to this day can plausibly explain'. Mackay, *The Malayan Emergency*, pp. 44–45. On the other hand, Gregorian suggests that the Force was disbanded because General Ritchie, the Commander-in-Chief FARELF felt that it would become redundant as regular Army units were gradually jungle-trained. Raffi Gregorian, '"Jungle Bashing" in Malaya: Towards a Formal Tactical Doctrine', *Small Wars and Insurgencies*, Vol. 5, No. 3 (Winter 1994), p. 346.

135 Broome to Heussler, 27 Aug 1981, Heussler Papers, Box 10, RHO; Paul Melshen, 'Pseudo-Operations: The Use by British and American Armed Forces of Deception in Counterinsurgency 1945–1973', Unpublished PhD Dissertation, Cambridge University, 1996, pp. 52–53.

136 See Gregorian, '"Jungle Bashing" in Malaya"', p. 356, n. 47; Liew Thian Choy, 'Second Further Statement', 7 Oct 1949, Walker-Taylor Papers, RHO.

137 Extract from 'Federation of Malaya Police Operational Intelligence Summary', No. 86, 9 March 1950, CO 717/201/1.

138 Ritchie Report, WO 106/5884.

139 Gregorian, '"Jungle Bashing" in Malaya', pp. 346–347. See also General Sir Walter Walker, *Fighting On* (London: New Millennium, 1997), pp. 112–113.

140 Jones, 'The British Army, and Counter-Guerrilla Warfare', p. 287.

141 Urquhart, who had served in India between 1938 and 1940, and during the war in North Africa and Europe, had replaced Boucher in February 1950. 'Weekly Situation Report', No. 57, 24 Feb–2 March 1950, CO 717/201/2.

142 Jones, 'The British Army, and counter-insurgency', pp. 288–289.

143 [Insurgency and counter-insurgency]: despatch No. 5 from Sir H. Gurney to Mr. Creech Jones, 30 May 1949, CO 537/4773, No. 3, in Stockwell, ed., *BDEEP, Malaya: The Communist Insurrection*, Doc. 189. See also C.C. Too, 'Defeating Communism in Malaya', *Military Review*, Vol. 47, No. 8 (Aug 1967), p. 87.

144 Too, 'Defeating Communism in Malaya', p. 87.

145 For example, 280 identity cards were stolen in Pahang, Perak, Johore and Selangor in April 1949. See Inward Telegram No. 481 from High Commissioner Federation of Malaya to Secretary of State for the Colonies, 23 April 1949, CO 717/173.

146 McHugh, *Anatomy of Communist Propaganda*, p. 46.

147 *Ibid.*, p. 47.

148 Dato Mubin Sheppard, *Taman Budiman: Memoirs of an Unorthodox Civil Servant* (Kuala Lumpur: Heinemann Educational Publications, 1979), p. 144; Dato J.N. McHugh, 'Psychological Warfare in Malaya (1942–46)', *Journal of the Historical Society*, reprint, Vol. 4 (1965/66), pp. 50–51.

149 Purcell, *The Memoirs of a Malayan Official*, pp. 312–315.
150 Sheppard, *Taman Budiman*, p. 144; McHugh, 'Psychological Warfare in Malaya (1942–46)', pp. 51–52. McHugh had worked in the Malayan Public Works Department as an engineer for 10 years until 1942. He had escaped the fall of Singapore by only 48 hours. He had then worked as a Malay specialist in the Far Eastern Bureau of the MOI in New Delhi prior to setting up the Malaya Section of PWD/SACSEA.
151 McHugh, 'Psychological Warfare in Malaya (1942–46)', pp. 61–62.
152 *Ibid.*, p. 62; Mohd. Kaus Hj. Salleh, 'Government Public Relations', in *Public Relations: The Malaysian Experience*, ed. by Benedict Morais and Hamdan Adnan (Kuala Lumpur: Institute of Public Relations Malaysia, 1986), p. 78; Sheppard, *Taman Budiman*, p. 144.
153 Sheppard, *Taman Budiman*, pp. 143–144; McHugh, 'Psychological Warfare in Malaya (1942–46)', pp. 61–62; *idem*, 'Psychological, or Political Warfare in Malaya', Part II, p. 77; Dato Ahmad Nordin bin Hj. Mohd. Zain, 'Public Relations Practice in Malaysia: An Overview', in Morais and Adnan, eds., *Public Relations*, p. 4, n.1; Mohd. Kaus Salleh, 'Government Public Relations', in Morais and Adnan, eds., *Public Relations*, p. 80.
154 Sheppard, *Taman Budiman*, pp. 148–150.
155 See *Federation of Malaya Annual Report 1948* (Kuala Lumpur: Government Printer, 1949), p. 190, and *Federation of Malaya Annual Report 1950* (Kuala Lumpur: Government Printer 1951), p. 141; *Communist Banditry in Malaya*, p. 59.
156 'Publicity and Propaganda Lines', 14 April and 11 May 1950, CO 537/6579.
157 Hugh Carleton Greene, 'Report on Emergency Information Services, September 1950 – September 1951', 14 Sep 1951, CO 537/7255. Hereafter Greene Report.
158 McHugh, 'Psychological, or Political Warfare in Malaya', Part II, p. 77.
159 Purcell, *Memoirs of a Malayan Official*, pp. 314–315.
160 *Annual Report 1948*, p. 190.
161 Greene Report, CO 537/7255.
162 'Third Further Statement of Liew Thian Choy, Surrendered Bandit', 10 Oct 1949, Walker-Taylor Papers, RHO. See also 'Weekly Report on Malaya for Period 27 Jan 1950 – 2 Feb 1950', No. 53, FO 371/84475.
163 *Annual Report 1948*, p. 113.
164 Sheppard, *Taman Budiman*, pp. 145; McHugh, 'Psychological, or Political Warfare in Malaya', Part II, p. 77; 'Department of Information Weekly News Summary' (*WNS*), week ending 1 Dec 1956.
165 Carruthers, *Winning Hearts and Minds*, p. 94.
166 *Federation of Malaya Annual Report 1951* (Kuala Lumpur: Government Printer, 1952), p. 184.
167 'Publicity and Propaganda Lines', 11 May 1950, CO 537/6579; *Annual Report 1950*, p. 144.
168 *Annual Report 1950*, p. 144; Carruthers, *Winning Hearts and Minds*, p. 94.
169 'Note by V.E. Dawson: New Premises for MFU', 15 July 1953, 'Department of Information, Federation of Malaya, 1953–1954', File No. 1333/53, Part 1, ANM.
170 Greene Report, CO 537/7255.
171 Norton Ginsburg and Chester F. Roberts, *Malaya* (Seattle: University of Washington Press, 1958), p. 176. See also 'Draft for Memorandum to Executive Council', 1957, 'Malaya' Papers, MSS.Ind.Ocn.s.216, RHO and Tripat Kaur Santokh, 'Broadcast Development in Malaysia: Communal Structures and National Aspirations', Unpublished PhD Dissertation, Northwestern University, 1979, pp. 42–44.
172 The Penang, Malacca and Seremban stations had been set up by the Japanese during the war. See 'Draft Memorandum', 'Malaya 'Papers, RHO. See also Ronny

Adhikarya *et al.*, *Broadcasting in Peninsular Malaysia* (London, Henley and Boston: Routledge and Kegan Paul, 1977), p. 29; Kaur, 'Broadcast Development in Malaysia', p. 43.

173 'History of the Two 10 K.W. Medium Wave and One 5 K.W. Short Wave Transmitters Ordered for Kajang', undated note in CO 875/39/1.

174 Inward Savingram No. 1211 from High Commissioner Federation of Malaya to Secretary of State for the Colonies, 18 Dec 1948, CO 875/39/1.

175 *Straits Times*, 8 Sep 1949.

176 *Annual Report 1950*, p. 143.

177 *Colonial Annual Report: Malayan Union 1947* (London: HMSO, 1949), p. 100.

178 *Annual Report 1950*, p. 143.

179 'Broadcasting in Malaya: Community and Domestic Receivers, their Cost, Availability and Respective Characteristics', Annex A to Memorandum from Secretary of State for the Colonies to Governor of Singapore and High Commissioner Federation of Malaya, 26 Jan 1949, CO 875/39/1.

180 *Annual Report 1947*, p. 101.

181 Ralph Glyn, M.P., 'Broadcasting and Wireless Stations in the Colonial Empire', 6 May 1948, PREM 8/1145.

182 Cabinet Conclusions, 22 July 1948, CAB 134/37.

183 Memorandum from Secretary of State for the Colonies to Governor of Singapore and High Commissioner Federation of Malaya, 26 Jan 1949; Memorandum from W.S. Morgan to Mr Gidden and Mr Armitage-Smith, 12 Oct 1949, CO 875/39/1.

184 Inward Savingram No. 1250 from High Commissioner Federation of Malaya to Secretary of State for the Colonies, 31 Oct 1949, CO 875/39/1.

185 'Weekly Situation Report', No. 58, 3–9 March 1950, CO 717/201/2.

186 Minutes of the 1st JIPC Meeting, 10 Feb 1950, CO 537/6579.

187 Inward Savingram No. 1250, 31 Oct 1949, CO 875/39/1.

188 Minutes of 10th JIPC Meeting, 7 July 1950, CO 537/6579.

189 Greene Report, CO 537/7255.

190 *Annual Report 1948*, p. 189.

191 Thomson, a Scotsman and former history lecturer, was to become, following the victory of the People's Action Party (PAP) in the 1959 general elections in Singapore, the head of the political study centre for senior government servants.

192 Blackburne to Thomson, 27 Oct 1948, CO 875/39/1.

193 Thomson called these the meetings of the 'Heads of Departments', but it stands to reason that he was referring to the Emergency Publicity Committee. See Thomson to Blackburne, 12 Nov 1948, CO 875/39/1.

194 Minutes of the 1st JIPC Meeting, 10 Feb 1950, CO 537/6579.

195 'Publicity and Propaganda Lines', 14 April 1950, CO 537/6579.

196 Minutes of the 3rd JIPC Meeting, 10 March 1950, CO537/6579.

197 *Ibid.*

198 Minutes of the 1st JIPC Meeting, 10 Feb 1950, CO 537/6579.

199 'Attitude to be adopted in publicity towards communism in Malaya and China': joint CO-FO note, Dec 1949, CO 537/6089, No. 17, in Stockwell, ed., *BDEEP, Malaya: The Communist Insurrection*, Doc. 202; Carruthers, *Winning Hearts and Minds*, pp. 81–82; Barber, *War of the Running Dogs*, p. 11.

200 Greene Report, CO 537/7255.

201 Copies of the cited Government propaganda leaflets can be found in CO 875/71/6. See also 'Publicity and Propaganda Lines', 27 April 1950, CO 537/6579.

202 Too US Lecture, PP.

203 'Weekly Situation Reports', No. 56, 17–23 Feb 1950 and No. 62, 31 March–6 April 1950, CO 717/201/2.

204 Short, *Communist Insurrection in Malaya*, p. 216.
205 'Weekly Situation Report', No. 56, 17–23 Feb 1950, CO 717/201/2.
206 *Annual Report 1950*, p. 141.
207 *Ibid*, p. 143. See also 'Weekly Situation Report', No. 52, 20–26 Jan 1950, CO 717/201/2.
208 *Annual Report 1950*, p. 144. See 'Publicity and Propaganda Lines', 8 June 1950, CO 537/6579.
209 *Annual Report 1950*, p. 8.
210 'Weekly Situation Report', No. 52, 20–26 Jan 1950, CO 717/201/2.
211 'Weekly Situation Report', No. 57, 24 Feb–2 March 1950, CO 717/201/2.
212 'Weekly Situation Report', No. 58, 3–9 March 1950, CO 717/201/2.
213 Stubbs, *Hearts and Minds in Guerrilla Warfare*, p. 86; Short, *Communist Insurrection in Malaya*, pp. 217–218; Mackay, *The Malayan Emergency*, pp. 91–92.
214 McHugh, 'Psychological, or Political Warfare in Malaya', Part II, p. 84.
215 Discussed in Chapter Six.
216 Minutes of 3rd Joint Information and Propaganda Committee (JIPC) Meeting, 10 March 1950, CO 537/6579. See also 'Weekly Situation Report', No. 62, 31 March–6 April 1950, CO 717/201/2.
217 Greene Report, CO 537/7255. See Stubbs, *Hearts and Minds in Guerrilla Warfare*, p. 85.
218 McHugh, 'Psychological Warfare in Malaya (1942–46)', p. 50.
219 Greene Report, CO 537/7255.
220 Too US Lecture, PP.
221 Copy in CO 875/71/6.
222 *Ibid*.
223 Too interview, Tape 1, EEP, RHO.
224 Copy in CO 875/71/6.
225 'Political Intelligence Report from Commissioner-General's Office', 16 Sep 1949, CO 537/4868; Bower Report, WO 106/5990; 1949 Amnesty leaflet in C.H. F. Blake Papers, MSS.Ind.Ocn.s. 276; 'Surrender Policy', March 1953, Young Papers, Box 1, RHO.
226 Inward Telegrams No. 1059 and 1085 from High Commissioner Federation of Malaya to Secretary of State for the Colonies, 17 and 24 Sep 1949, CO 717/173.
227 Short, *Communist Insurrection in Malaya*, p. 221, n. 14; Greene Report, CO 537/7255.
228 'Surrender Policy', Young Papers, Box 1, RHO. See also Lakin, 'Psychological Warfare Research', WO 291/1509.
229 Inward Telegram No. 1193 from High Commissioner Federation of Malaya to Secretary of State for the Colonies, 22 Oct 1949, CO 717/173.
230 Greene Report, CO 537/7255.
231 McHugh, 'Psychological, or Political Warfare in Malaya', Part II, p. 89; September 1949 Amnesty leaflet, Blake Papers; 'Third Further Statement of Liew Thian Choy, Surrendered Bandit', 10 Oct 1949, Walker-Taylor Papers, RHO.
232 '[Malay politics]: letter from Sir H. Gurney to J.J. Paskin on a variety of recent developments', CO 537/4741, No. 78, 2 Dec 1949, in Stockwell, ed., *BDEEP, Malaya: The Communist Insurrection*, Doc. 203.
233 'Tan' to Tan Cheng Lock, 18 May 1950, TCL.11.5, TCLP-ISEAS.
234 Lakin, 'Psychological Warfare Research', WO 291/1509.
235 Greene Report, CO 537/7255.
236 'China: recognition of Chinese communist government': Cabinet conclusions on the basis of UK policy in the region', CAB 128/16, CM 62 (49) 7, 27 Oct 1949, in Stockwell, ed., *BDEEP, Malaya: The Communist Insurrection*, Doc. 197.

237 'Attitude to be adopted in Publicity toward Communism in Malaya and China', Nov 1949, CO 537/6089; 'Note of Tour of South-East Asia October 1949': Report by Field Marshal Sir William Slim on the Importance of Civil Action in Counterinsurgency, November 1949, CO 537/4374, in Stockwell, ed., *BDEEP, Malaya: The Communist Insurrection*, Docs. 202, 199.
238 'Broadcast by Mr. Malcolm MacDonald, Commissioner-General Southeast Asia, on 6 Jan 1950', CO 875/72/1.
239 See for instance, Leaflet No. 358, April 1950, in CO 875/71/6.
240 Gray, 'The Chinese Problem in the Federation of Malaya', Watts Papers, RHO; Yap Mau Tatt, 'Emergency and Chinese Co-operation', n.d., TCL.24.4h, TCLP-ISEAS.
241 Loy Hean Heong with Andrew Croft, *Against All Odds: The Making of a Billionaire* (Singapore: Times Books International, 1997), p. 20. Loy's parents had been squatters during the Japanese Occupation. See also the Corry interview, RHO.
242 Pye, *Guerrilla Communism in Malaya*, pp. 286–287.
243 McHugh, *Anatomy of Communist Propaganda*, p. 4.
244 Ibid.
245 Ibid., p. 6.
246 Federal Government Press Release, Kuala Lumpur, 3 March 1949, CO 717/173.
247 McLane, *Soviet Strategies in Southeast Asia*, p. 393.

CHAPTER FOUR

1 See below.
2 See minute from Mr Shinwell to Mr Attlee, 27 March 1950, CAB 21/2510; and Attlee's reply, personal minute no. M. 47/50 to Shinwell, 1 Apr 1950, CAB 21/2510, in Stockwell, ed., *BDEEP, Malaya: The Communist Insurrection*, Docs. 209–210.
3 Inward Telegram No. 151 from High Commissioner Federation of Malaya to Secretary of State for the Colonies, 23 Feb 1950, CO 537/5994.
4 Ibid. See also Short, *Communist Insurrection in Malaya*, p. 234.
5 Inward Telegram No. 151, 23 Feb 1950, CO 537/5994.
6 The Colonial Secretary was James Griffiths and the Secretary of State for War was John Strachey. Griffiths had replaced Creech Jones in February 1950.
7 'Weekly Situation Report', No. 69, 19–25 May 1950, CO 717/201/2; Mackay, *The Malayan Emergency*, p. 86; *Straits Budget*, 30 Oct 1952.
8 *Daily Telegraph*, 22 March 1950; Stubbs, *Hearts and Minds in Guerrilla Warfare*, p. 98; Jones, 'The British Army, and Counter-Guerrilla Warfare', p. 289.
9 Short, *Communist Insurrection in Malaya*, pp. 235–237; 'Federation plan for the elimination of the communist organisation and armed forces in Malaya (the Briggs plan): report by COS for Cabinet Malaya Committee, CAB 21/1681, MAL C (50) 23, Appendix, 24 May 1950, in Stockwell, ed., *BDEEP, Malaya: The Communist Insurrection*, Doc. 216.
10 Short, 'Communism and the Emergency', in Wang, ed., *Malaysia*, p. 155.
11 Briggs Plan, in Stockwell, ed., *BDEEP, Malaya: The Communist Insurrection*, Doc. 216.
12 Miller, *Jungle War in Malaya*, p. 70; Mackay, *The Malayan Emergency*, p. 89; Stubbs, *Hearts and Minds in Guerrilla Warfare*, p. 100.
13 Briggs Plan, in Stockwell, ed., *BDEEP, Malaya: The Communist Insurrection*, Doc. 216.
14 Ibid.
15 Stubbs, *Hearts and Minds in Guerrilla Warfare*, pp. 98, 127, n.5.
16 Briggs was given this nickname by the *Evening News*, 10 April 1950. 'Ike' referred to General Dwight David Eisenhower, who had been Supreme Commander Allied Expeditionary Forces during the cross-channel invasion of Europe in June 1944.

17 See Corry interview, RHO; also Paul M.A. Linebarger, 'They Call 'Em Bandits in Malaya', in *Modern Guerrilla Warfare*, ed. by Franklin Mark Osanka (New York: Free Press, 1962), p. 296.

18 Corry interview; J.D.H. Neill to H.P. Bryson, 11 June 1969, Heussler Papers, Box 17, RHO.

19 Inward Telegram No. 191 from Gurney to Secretary of State for the Colonies, 9 March 1950, CO 537/5994; [Director of operations]: minute by Mr Shinwell to Mr Attlee recommending the appointment of General Briggs, PREM 8/1406/2, 7 March 1950, in Stockwell, ed., *BDEEP, Malaya,: The Communist Insurrection*, Doc. 206.

20 J.D. Higham to A.J. Newling, Ministry of Defence, 3 April 1950, CO 537/5994.

21 Inward Telegram No. 151, 23 Feb 1950, CO 537/5994.

22 *Scotsman*, 31 March 1950.

23 Briggs, 'Police Command', 25 Oct 1950, CO 537/5973.

24 Foster Sutton to Gurney, 3 Nov and 17 Nov 1950, CO 537/5973; See Secret and Personal Note by W.C. Johnson, Inspector-General of Colonial Police, to High Commissioner Federation of Malaya, 18 Oct 1949, CO 537/5434; John Gullick to Heussler, 13 March 1982, Heussler Papers, Box 13, RHO.

25 Madoc interview, EEP, RHO.

26 Short, *Communist Insurrection in Malaya*, p. 335; Stubbs, *Hearts and Minds in Guerrilla Warfare*, p. 138.

27 See 'Organisation for Dealing with Emergency Matters', Nov 1951, in CO 1022/7.

28 Inward Telegrams Nos. 1052 and 1054 from Officer Administering the Government, Federation of Malaya, to Secretary of State for the Colonies, 1 Nov 1951, CO 1022/7.

29 Following the Conservative victory in October 1951, Prime Minister Churchill sent his Colonial Secretary Oliver Lyttelton to Malaya to study the situation. One of the things Lyttelton did was to dismiss Gray. Mackay, *The Malayan Emergency*, p. 119. Stubbs, *Hearts and Minds in Guerrilla Warfare*, p. 138 and p. 152, n.13.

30 Bower Report, WO 106/5990.

31 In the Settlements of Penang and Malacca, the place of the *Mentri Besar* was taken by the Resident Commissioner. See 'Organisation for Dealing with Emergency Matters', Nov 1951, in CO 1022/7; Short, *Communist Insurrection in Malaya*, p. 245.

32 H.A.L. Luckham, 'The Malayan Emergency 1948–60: The Role of the MCS and the Resettlement of Squatters', 1982, and Luckham to Heussler, 30 Sep 1974, Heussler Papers, Box 16, RHO. Luckham was DO Kinta from 1949 to 1951.

33 Hugh Fraser, 'Papers on the Emergency in Malaya', 16 Jan 1952, CO 1022/22.

34 *Ibid.*

35 H.A.L. Luckham, 'The Malayan Emergency', and Luckham to Heussler, 30 Sep 1974 and 11 May 1977, Heussler Papers, Box 16, RHO.

36 Summary of Meeting between Attlee, Gurney and Briggs, 27 Nov 1950, CAB 130/65.

37 *Ibid.*; Bower Report, WO 106/5990.

38 [Briggs Plan]: Cabinet Office summary of a further meeting at 10 Downing Street on 8 Mar called by Mr. Attlee to consider the plan's slow progress', PREM 8/1406/2 GEN 345/7, 9 March 1951; [Gurney offers to resign]: letter from Sir H. Gurney to Sir T. Lloyd, CO 967/145, 19 March 1951; [Gurney's offer of resignation]: letter (reply) from Sir T. Lloyd to Sir H. Gurney, CO 967/145, 5 April 1951, in Stockwell, ed., *BDEEP, Malaya: The Communist Insurrection*, Docs. 233, 235–236.

39 Stockwell, ed., *BDEEP, Malaya: The Communist Insurrection*, Doc. 233.

40 Bower Report, WO 106/5990. Briggs' replacement was General Rob Lockhart, who was the brother of Sir Robert Bruce Lockhart, head of the wartime Political Warfare Executive. See *Daily Telegraph*, 1 Nov 1951; *Times*, 2 Nov 1951 and *Straits Times*, 22 Dec 1951.

41 Oliver Lyttelton, 'Malaya', 21 Dec 1951, CAB 129/48, C (51) 59, in Stockwell, ed., *BDEEP, Malaya: The Communist Insurrection,* Doc. 257. See also Oliver Lyttelton, *The Memoirs of Lord Chandos* (London: Bodley Head, 1964), pp. 366–367.

42 The observer was a friend of Viscountess Davidson. Davidson to Oliver Lyttelton, 1 Nov 1951, CO 1022/1.

43 *Ibid.*

44 Minute by T.C. Jerrom, 26 Oct 1951, CO 1022/1.

45 *Straits Budget,* 30 Oct 1952; Clausewitz, *On War,* ed. by Paret and Howard, pp. 104–105.

46 *Malaya,* Nov 1952, p. 16; *Straits Budget,* 30 Oct 1952.

47 Stubbs, *Hearts and Minds in Guerrilla Warfare,* p. 138. Briggs passed away in Cyprus in October 1952.

48 Dennis Duncanson to Heussler, 31 Oct 1981, Box 12, Heussler Papers, RHO.

49 Luckham to Heussler, 22 Oct 1979, Heussler Papers, Box 16, RHO.

50 'The Squatter Problem in the Federation of Malaya in 1950', 17 Feb 1950, CO 717/201/1. It should be noted that although the mass – 86 percent – of rural squatters to be resettled were Chinese, some Malays and Indians were resettled too. Sandhu and Zakaria, 'The Malayan Emergency' in Sandhu and Wheatley, eds., *Melaka,* Vol. 1, p. 395.

51 'The Squatter Problem', CO 717/201/1; Renick, 'The Emergency Regulations of Malaya', pp. 6–7.

52 Minute from Ms. Gaved to Mr. Gidden, 2 Nov 1950, CO 717/201/1.

53 Extract from 'Report of Proceedings of Rulers' Conference, 24 May 1950', CO 717/201/1.

54 Perry Robinson, *Transformation in Malaya,* p. 81; 'Publicity and Propaganda Lines', 3 July 1950, CO 537/6579.

55 Short, *Communist Insurrection in Malaya,* p. 201.

56 *Resettlement and the Development of New Villages in the Federation of Malaya* (Kuala Lumpur: Government Press, 1952), p. 2. Copy in CO 1022/29.

57 'Weekly Situation Report' No. 54, 3–9 February 1950, CO 717/201/2.

58 Extract from 'Federation of Malaya Telegram No. 921, 21 Sep 1950', CO 717/201/1.

59 Extract from 'Federation of Malaya Monthly Newsletter No. 22, 16 Oct–15 Nov 1950', CO 717/201/1.

60 Frank Brewer, 'The Malayan Emergency', Feb 1982, Heussler Papers, Box 9, RHO.

61 Sandhu and Zakaria, 'The Malayan Emergency', in Sandhu and Wheatley, eds, *Melaka,* Vol. 1, pp. 397–398. See also undated report by Mr S.R. Dawson, who was a Resettlement Officer in the Segamat District of Johore, from December 1950 till April 1952. Found in CO 1022/29. Hereafter Dawson Report. See also Max Lear Webber, Chief Resettlement Officer, Selangor to Chairman, Selangor SWEC, 12 April 1951, Max Lear Webber Papers, MSS.Ind.Ocn.s.88, RHO. Webber reported on the apparently well-organised Bukit Sepat Resettlement Area in Segamat, Johore. 4,200 families had been resettled on schedule. Also John C. Litton, 'After Resettlement', address to the Rotary Club, Malacca, 25 June 1951, John C. Litton Papers, MSS.Ind.Ocn.s.113, RHO. Litton was a Chinese Affairs officer who in January 1949 raised and ran a so-called Chinese Assault Team whose members masqueraded as MCP terrorists on patrol. The 'CATs' had some success, but like Ferret Force, was short-lived, folding in April 1949.

62 Granada interview with John Davis, Aug 1981, EEP, RHO. Davis was an ex-Force 136 officer who was appointed New Village Liaison Officer (1951–1954). Briggs set up the Home Guard in June 1950. Extract from 'Federation of Malaya Political Report for June 1950', CO 537/6003. By the end of 1951 every Resettlement Area was required to form a Home Guard to relieve the Police as far as possible of 'static

commitments' such as food checking and the defence of watch towers and strong points. The Home Guard was also to assist the Police in patrolling within the Resettlement Area. *Resettlement and the Development of New Villages*, p. 6.
63 Frank Brewer to H. Clemente, 6 Feb 1982, Heussler Papers, Box 9, RHO.
64 *Resettlement and the Development of New Villages*, p. 4.
65 Short, *Communist Insurrection in Malaya*, p. 249. Regrouping continued into 1951, however. Director of Operations, 'Progress Report on Situation in Malaya', 15 Feb 1951 (hereafter Briggs Report 1951), CAB 130/65.
66 Stubbs, *Hearts and Minds in Guerrilla Warfare*, p. 113.
67 *Ibid.*; Litton, Circular Letter, 12 Sep 1950, Litton Papers, RHO.
68 Stubbs, *Hearts and Minds in Guerrilla Warfare*, p. 113.
69 'The Squatter Problem', CO 717/201/1.
70 Inward Savingram No. 119 from the High Commissioner Federation of Malaya to the Secretary of State for the Colonies, 19 December 1950, CO 717/201/1.
71 Humphrey, 'Population Resettlement', p. 231.
72 Gray, 'The Chinese Problem in the Federation of Malaya', Watts Papers; Brewer, 'The Malayan Emergency', Heussler Papers, Box 9, RHO.
73 Briggs had pointed out the shortage of building materials like roofing and cement for squatter and labour resettlement in his progress report of February 1951. Briggs Report 1951, CAB 130/65.
74 Dato Tan Cheng Lock to *Mentri Besar*, Johore, 30 Oct 1951, CO 1022/29.
75 *Daily Telegraph*, 31 Oct 1951.
76 Tan to *Mentri Besar*, Johore, 30 Oct 1951, CO 1022/29.
77 *Ibid.*
78 Correspondence with W.P. Coughlan, 9 Dec 1998. Coughlan was a National Serviceman in Malaya in 1950.
79 Litton, Circular Letter, 30 Nov 1951, Litton Papers, RHO.
80 Gray to Watts, 17 Dec 1951, Watts Papers, RHO.
81 Tan Cheng Lock to George Maxwell, 18 Dec 1951, TCL.5.232, TCLP-ISEAS.
82 The propaganda fallout from Mawai was so bad that it was mentioned in the House of Commons. Woodrow Wyatt, M.P. argued that Mawai had been attacked because of inadequate security, and Lennox-Boyd admitted that large-scale resettlement in a short time meant that adequate protection was not always achievable. But this begged the question of why resettle in the first place. *H.C. Debs*, 5 Dec 1951, Cols. 2381–2382.
83 Briggs Plan, in Stockwell, ed., *BDEEP, Malaya: The Communist Insurrection*, Doc. 216.
84 Brewer, 'The Malayan Emergency', and 'Malaya: Administration of Chinese Affairs', Heussler Papers, Box 9, RHO. See also Acting Chief Secretary to all *Mentri Besars* and Resident Commissioners, 8 March 1952, 'Department of Chinese Affairs', File No. 1648, ANM.
85 Brewer, 'The Chinese Protectorate', Brewer Papers, Box 1, RHO.
86 Gray to Watts, 17 Dec 1951, Watts Papers, RHO; 'Memo on Home Guards and Chinese Affairs Department', n.d., TCL.15.13, TCLP-ISEAS.
87 R.P. Bingham, 'Suggestions for the Improvement of the Administration of the Chinese Rural Population', 3 Nov 1951, TCL.24.3g, TCLP-ISEAS.
88 Watts to Federal SCA, 7 Jan 1952, Watts Papers, RHO.
89 Dawson Report, CO 1022/29.
90 'Duties of CAOs attached to DOs', n.d., TCL.24.3i, TCLP-ISEAS.
91 The military situation in Malaya': memorandum from Mr Strachey for Cabinet Malaya Committee, CAB 21/1681, MAL C (50) 21, 17 June 1950; 'Malaya', Cabinet Conclusions on Reports by Mr Griffiths and Mr Strachey following their visits to

Malaya, CAB 128/17, CM 37 (50) 1, 19 June 1950, in Stockwell, ed., *BDEEP, Malaya: The Communist Insurrection,* Docs. 220–221.

92 'The Civil Situation in Malaya': Cabinet Malaya Committee Minutes, CAB 21/1681, MAL C 6 (50)1, 19 June 1950, in Stockwell, ed, *BDEEP, Malaya: The Communist Insurrection,* Doc. 222.

93 *Detention and Deportation during the Emergency,* p. 14; Briggs Report 1951, CAB 130/65.

94 Stockwell, ed., *BDEEP, Malaya: The Communist Insurrection,* Doc. 222.

95 Notes of meeting between a deputation of leading members of commercial interests in Malaya and His Excellency the High Commissioner at King's House at 1500 hours on 11 Jan 1951, CO 537/7262.

96 W.A. Muller to H. Fraser, 22 Dec 1951, CO 1022/165; Lyttelton Report, in Stockwell, ed., *BDEEP, Malaya: The Communist Insurrection,* Doc. 257.

97 Memorandum to the Right Honourable Oliver Lyttelton, Secretary of State for the Colonies, by an MCA delegation headed by Dato Tan Cheng Lock at King's House, Kuala Lumpur, 2 Dec 1951, TCL.3.271, TCLP-ISEAS.

98 Litton, Circular Letter, 30 Nov 1951, Litton Papers, RHO.

99 *Ibid.*

100 Inward Telegram from High Commissioner Federation of Malaya to Secretary of State for the Colonies, 25 Feb 1951, CO 537/7280.

101 'Collective Punishment in Malaya, 1950–51', note for Secretary of State brief, Kenya debate, 16 Dec 1952, CO 1022/56.

102 *Ibid.*

103 Gray to Watts, 17 Dec 1951; Gray, 'The Chinese Problem in the Federation of Malaya', Watts Papers, RHO.

104 Yap Mau Tatt, Secretary MCA Negri Sembilan Branch, to Tan Cheng Lock, 26 Oct 1950, TCL.3.266, TCLP-ISEAS.

105 Federal Government Press Statement, 19 Dec 1950, CO 537/6007; Renick, 'The Emergency Regulations of Malaya', pp. 26–27.

106 Cited in 'Collective Punishment in Malaya, 1950–51', CO 1022/56.

107 Inward Telegram from High Commissioner, Federation of Malaya, 25 Feb 1951, CO 537/7280.

108 Yap Mau Tatt, Secretary MCA Negri Sembilan Branch, to Tan Cheng Lock, 26 Oct 1950, TCL.3.266, TCLP-ISEAS.

109 *Singapore Standard,* 20 Feb 1951.

110 Griffiths to Lloyd, n.d., CO 537/6007.

111 Gray to Watts, 17 Dec 1951, Watts Papers, RHO. Japanese collective punishment methods were actually far more brutal. See Chapman, *The Jungle is Neutral,* pp. 85, 99.

112 *Scotsman,* 3 Feb 1951.

113 Extract from 'Monthly Review of Chinese Affairs for Feb 51', CO 537/7280.

114 Litton, Circular Letter, 12 Sep 1950, Litton Papers, RHO.

115 Gray to Watts, 17 Dec 1951; Gray, 'The Chinese Problem in the Federation of Malaya', Watts Papers, MSS.Ind.ocn.s.320, RHO.

116 Extract from 'Monthly Review of Chinese Affairs for Feb 51', CO 537/7280.

117 Lyttelton Report, in Stockwell, ed., *BDEEP, Malaya: The Communist Insurrection,* Doc. 257; Muller to Fraser, 22 Dec 1951, CO 1022/165.

118 Litton, Circular Letter, 30 Nov 1951, Litton Papers, RHO.

119 Outward Telegram from Commonwealth Relations Office to UK High Commissioner in Australia, 20 May 1950, FO 371/84506.

120 See Federal Government Press Statement, 19 Dec 1950, CO 537/6007. The directive required males between 17 and 45 years of age to serve with Government bodies like

the Police, for a period of three years or the duration of the Emergency, whichever was less.

121 The Deputy Comptroller of Manpower, 'Manpower and National Service', Appendix F to Agenda dated 10 Nov 1951, TCL.24.3j, TCLP-ISEAS. Although by November 1951 45,600 men had been registered, only 4,100 men had actually been directed into the Police, of which a mere 1,825 were Chinese.

122 Muller to Fraser, 22 Dec 1951, CO 1022/165.

123 Before this School was set up, the practice had been to send MCS and Police officers to China for up to two years of language training. This had stopped with the Communist victory in October 1949, and for a time Macao and Hong Kong were the centres for instruction in Cantonese instead of Canton, and Taiwan replaced Amoy as a centre of Hokkien teaching. But it was found that these arrangements were simply not suitable to meet Emergency requirements. See Brewer, 'Malaya: Administration of Chinese Affairs', Heussler Papers, Box 9, RHO. See also 'Chinese Language School for Government Officers', Executive Council Paper No. 9/4/53, 26 Feb 1953, CO 1022/343.

124 Brewer, 'Malaya: Administration of Chinese Affairs', Heussler Papers, Box 9, RHO.

125 'Appendix VIII: Language Training', n.d., CO 1022/343.

126 'The Co-operation of the Peoples of Malaya against Communism: Federation Policy', Appendix A to Agenda dated 10 Nov 1951, TCL.24.3, TCLP-ISEAS.

127 Watts to Federal SCA, 7 Jan 1952, Watts Papers, RHO.

128 John Litton agreed with Victor Purcell that soldiers and Police, in dealing with the Chinese and unable to tell friend from foe, treated them as foes. See Purcell's letter in *Times*, 14 Nov 1951. Litton quoted the entire letter in his Circular Letter of 30 Nov 1951. See also Litton's Circular Letter of 12 Sep 1950, Litton Papers, RHO.

129 George Maxwell to Tan Cheng Lock, 8 Dec 1951, TCL.5.228, TCLP-ISEAS; Litton, Circular Letter, 30 Nov 1951, Litton Papers, RHO.

130 Litton, Circular Letter, 3 June 1951, in Litton Papers, RHO. Charles Townshend goes so far as to charge that the authorities camouflaged a 'high level of casual violence by both troops and police'. However, he provides no evidence for this claim. Townshend, *Britain's Civil Wars: Counterinsurgency in the Twentieth Century* (London: Faber and Faber, 1986), p. 165.

131 Litton, Circular Letter, 30 Nov 1951, Litton Papers, RHO.

132 Extract from 'Legislative Council Meeting, 30 Jan 1952', CO 1022/29; *Scotsman*, 2 Nov 1951.

133 'Report on the Royal Air Force Operations in Malaya, April 1949-Dec 1950', 8 Jan 1951, AIR 23/8699. The RAF actually chafed at the restrictions placed on its operations, principally the need to secure Police clearance before any attack. The argument was that as the Police were evacuating civilians the MRLA also took the hint and dispersed as well. It was held that this 'kid-gloved' kind of war was detrimental to the 'effective use of aircraft'. See 'Third Report on the Royal Air Force Operations in Malaya, Jan-Aug 1951', 30 Nov 1951, AIR 23/8699. See also H.C. Debs., 25 Oct 1950, Col. 2772; 18 Oct 1950, Cols. 2026–2027.

134 Litton, Circular Letter, 30 Nov 1951, RHO.

135 MCA Memorandum to Lyttelton, 2 Dec 1951, TCL.3.271, TCLP-ISEAS.

136 *Ibid*.

137 Briggs Plan, in Stockwell, ed., *BDEEP, Malaya: The Communist Insurrection*, Doc. 216.

138 Appreciation of situation in Malaya by Briggs for Gurney, 10 April 1950, cited in Short, *Communist Insurrection in Malaya*, pp. 235–237.

139 Briggs Report 1951, CAB 130/65.

140 Lieutenant-General Briggs' Final Press Statement, Kuala Lumpur, 27 Nov 1951, CO 1022/1.

141 Briggs Report 1951, CAB 130/65.

142 Extract from 'Federation of Malaya Police Operational Intelligence Summary, No. 86, 9 March 1950', CO 717/201/1.

143 Luckham, 'The Malayan Emergency', Heussler Papers, Box 16, RHO.

144 240,000 people had been resettled by this time, mainly in southern Malaya, enabling Briggs to implement food control measures. 'Federation of Malaya – combined appreciation of the emergency situation': joint memorandum by Sir H Gurney and Lieutenant-General Sir H Briggs, CO 537/7263, no 38A, 4 June 1951, in Stockwell, ed., *BDEEP, Malaya: The Communist Insurrection*, Doc. 239.

145 Director of Operations, Malaya, Directive No. 14, 'Offensive to Prevent Leakage of Supplies to Communist Elements', 22 May 1951. This came into effect on 16 June 1951. See CO 537/7262.

146 However, some perishable foodstuffs had, and were allowed, to be transported from point to point at night: fresh fish, poultry, fresh fruit, eggs, shell fish, crabs and prawns for instance. *Ibid*.

147 *Ibid*.

148 Stubbs, *Hearts and Minds in Guerrilla Warfare*, p. 123.

149 Federal Government Press Statement, 28 Aug 1951, CO 537/7262.

150 Stubbs, *Hearts and Minds in Guerrilla Warfare*, p. 123; Extract from 'Federation of Malaya Political Report for Dec 1950', CO 537/7270.

151 Stubbs, *Hearts and Minds in Guerrilla Warfare*, p. 124; Bower Report, WO 106/5990.

152 Miller, *Jungle War in Malaya*, p. 80.

153 'Summary of a Meeting with Director of Operations, Malaya', 4 Dec 1950, CAB 130/65.

154 Statement of Perak SEP Liew Kow. See 'Weekly Intelligence Summary (*WINSUM*)', No. 82, week ending 29 Nov 1951, CO 1022/13.

155 Calvert had served with and was influenced by Wingate in Burma. See Tony Geraghty, *Who Dares Wins: the Story of the SAS, 1950–1992* (London: Warner Books, 1993), pp. 327–333; Royle, *Orde Wingate*, p. 232.

156 Briggs Plan, *BDEEP, Malaya: The Communist Insurrection*, Doc. 216.

157 Briggs Report 1951, CAB 130/65; Jones, 'The British Army, and Counter-Guerrilla Warfare', pp. 290–292.

158 Jones, 'The British Army, and Counter-Guerrilla Warfare', p. 292.

159 Stockwell, ed., *BDEEP, Malaya: The Communist Insurrection*, Doc. 239.

160 Briggs Report 1951, CAB 130/65.

161 *Ibid*.

162 Bower Report, WO 106/5990.

163 Briggs used this term to describe large-scale operations mounted in response to terrorist incidents. See Miller, *Jungle War in Malaya*, p. 60.

164 Sunderland, *Army Operations in Malaya*, p. 133.

165 Briggs Plan, in Stockwell, ed., *BDEEP, Malaya: The Communist Insurrection*, Doc. 216.

166 Extract from 'Minutes of the 15th Commisioner-General's Conference at Bukit Serene, 7 June 1950', CO 537/6011; Carruthers, *Winning Hearts and Minds*, p. 91.

167 Greene Report, CO 537/7255. This was the 'propaganda expert' referred to in the Briggs Plan. Briggs Plan, in Stockwell, ed., *BDEEP, Malaya,: The Communist Insurrection*, Doc. 216.

168 Litton, Circular Letter, 30 Nov 1951, Litton Papers, RHO.

169 Secret and Personal from C.J. Jeffries to Sir Ian Jacob, 18 May 1950, CO 537/6579; *H.C. Debs.*, 12 March 1952, cols. 1363–1364.

170 Greene Report, CO 537/7255.

171 Minutes of 8th JIPC Meeting, 9 June 1950, CO 537/6579.

172 Greene Report, CO 537/7255.

173 Minutes of 8th JIPC Meeting, 9 June 1950, CO 537/6579.

174 Tracey, *A Variety of Lives*, p. 127; Litton, Circular Letter, 30 Nov 1951, Litton Papers, RHO.

175 Extract of 'Minutes of 15th Commissioner-General's Conference at Bukit Serene, 7 June 1950', CO 537/6011.

176 'Malaya', Cabinet Conclusions on Reports by Mr Griffiths and Mr Strachey following their visits to Malaya, CAB 128/17, CM 37 (50) 1, 19 June 1950.

177 'Weekly Situation Report', No. 81, 11–17 Aug 1950, CO 717/201/2.

178 *Times*, 21 Feb 1987; Tracey, *A Variety of Lives*, pp. 68–71.

179 *Listener*, 31 July 1969.

180 Tracey, *A Variety of Lives*, pp. 81–83, 87–88.

181 *Ibid.*, p. 79.

182 Minutes of 15th JIPC Meeting, 15 Sep 1950, CO 537/6579.

183 Tracey, *A Variety of Lives*, pp. 127–128.

184 Greene Report, CO 537/7255.

185 *Ibid.*; Federal Government Press Statement 4 Feb 1953, 'Department of Information, Trengganu, 1946–1961', File No. 102/52, ANM; Tracey, *A Variety of Lives*, p. 128.

186 'Weekly Situation Report', No. 98, 8–14 Dec 1950, CO 717/201/2; Greene Report, CO 537/7255.

187 Barber, *War of the Running Dogs*, p. 139; H.C. Greene to C.C. Too, 22 Feb 1951, 'Department of Information, Federation of Malaya', File No. 401/53, ANM.

188 Too, 'Curriculum Vitae', PP; Lee Kam Hing and Chow Mun Seong, *Biographical Dictionary of the Chinese in Malaysia* (Petaling Jaya: Pelanduk Publications, 1997), pp. 171–172. I am indebted to Prof Dato Khoo Kay Kim for information on Too's dialect group.

189 Too, 'Curriculum Vitae', PP; Stubbs, *Hearts and Minds in Guerrilla Warfare*, p. 46. Despite some accounts suggesting that Chin Peng went to the Victory Parade, Chin Peng himself confirmed that he never attended as he had been 'too busy'. *Far Eastern Economic Review*, 3 Sep 1987; Group Discussion with Chin Peng, 18 June 1998.

190 Too, 'Curriculum Vitae', PP; C.C. Too to R.G.K. Thompson, 27 Nov 1950, 'Department of Information, Federation of Malaya', File No. 401/53, ANM.

191 Too, 'Curriculum Vitae', PP; Too interview, Tape 1, EEP, RHO; Too to Thompson, 27 Nov 1950, 'Department of Information, Federation of Malaya', File No. 401/53, ANM.

192 Granada Interviews with Too, Tapes 1 and 2, EEP, RHO.

193 Greene Report, CO 537/7255; Driberg interview with Lam Swee, CO 537/6015; Too, 'The Communist Party of Malaya', PP; McHugh, 'Psychological, or Political Warfare', Part II, p. 89.

194 Granada Interview with Too, Tape 1, EEP, RHO.

195 Too US Lecture, PP.

196 Greene Report, CO 537/7255. In this context, Zarougui is surely incorrect in asserting that it was Peterson who was responsible for ensuring 'close co-ordination' with the intelligence services. Greene had done this earlier. See Zarougui, 'Propaganda and Psychological Warfare in Guerrilla and Counter-Guerrilla Warfare', p. 280.

197 Crossman, 'Supplementary Essay', in Lerner, *Psychological Warfare against Nazi Germany*, p. 339; *idem*, 'Psychological Warfare III', p. 529.

198 Greene Report, CO 537/7255.

199 *Ibid.*; Tracey, *A Variety of Lives*, p. 133.

200 Gurney actually tried to extend Greene's tenure, but the BBC was not keen. Gurney to Griffiths, 24 Aug 1951, CO 537/7255.

201 Greene Report, CO 537/7255.

202 Bower Report, WO 106/5990.

203 Dawson Report, CO 1022/29.

204 Greene Report, CO 537/7255. 50,000 copies were produced in its first run.

205 'Weekly Situation Report', No. 53, 27 Jan–2 Feb 1950, CO 717/201/2.

206 Extract from 'Federation of Malaya Police Operational Intelligence Summary, No. 82, 2 Feb 1950', CO 717/201/1.

207 Cited in Pye, *Guerrilla Communism in Malaya*, p. 178.

208 Minutes of 3rd JIPC Meeting, 10 March 1950, CO 537/6579. See also 'Weekly Situation Report', No. 62, 31 March–6 April 1950, CO 717/201/2.

209 See below.

210 Greene Report, CO 537/7255.

211 *Ibid.*

212 Extract from 'PMR Nov 1950', CO 537/6011.

213 Greene Report, CO 537/7255.

214 *Ibid.* See also Extract from 'Weekly Intelligence Summary, n.d.', in CO 537/7262.

215 *WINSUM*, No. 83, week ending 6 Dec 1951, CO 1022/13.

216 Perry Robinson, *Transformation in Malaya*, p. 48.

217 Greene Report, CO 537/7255.

218 Extract of 'Minutes of 15th Commissioner-General's Conference at Bukit Serene, 7 June 1950', CO 537/6011.

219 Greene Report, CO 537/7255.

220 *Ibid.*

221 *Federation of Malaya Annual Report 1951* (Kuala Lumpur: Government Printer, 1952), pp. 183–184.

222 Greene Report, CO 537/7255.

223 *Ibid.*

224 *Ibid.*; Ginsburg and Roberts, *Malaya*, p. 185.

225 Greene Report, CO 537/7255; Perry Robinson, *Transformation in Malaya*, p. 61; Carruthers, *Winning Hearts and Minds*, p. 111.

226 Greene Report, CO 537/7255.

227 *Straits Budget*, 24 Aug 1950.

228 Inward Savingram No. 1038 from Governor of Singapore to Secretary of State for the Colonies, 18 Sep 1950, CO 537/6582.

229 Extract of '17th JIPC Meeting, 20 Oct 1950', CO 537/6582.

230 Stubbs, *Hearts and Minds in Guerrilla Warfare*, p. 181.

231 Ginsburg and Roberts, *Malaya*, p. 182. These private radios were also to be found in clubs, kongsis, associations in rural areas, apart from the urban centres. 'Government to People through Radio Malaya's Broadcasts for Rural Audiences', Dec 1951, 'Department of Information, Federation of Malaya', File No. 810/53, ANM.

232 Greene Report, CO 537/7255; 'Government to People', File No. 810/53, ANM. The contract between Government and the GEC was signed on 27 September 1950. See 'Contract between GEC of England and the Government of the Federation of Malaya for Community Listening Sets', 27 Sep 1950, 'Department of Information, Johore, 1948–1955', File No. 6/54, ANM.

233 *Annual Report 1951*, pp. 181–182; 'Government to People', File No. 810/53, ANM.

234 Minutes of 1st JIPC Meeting, 10 Feb 1950, CO 537/6579; J.S. Dumeresque to D.C. Watherston, 16 Aug 1950, CO 537/6579.

235 Minutes of 14th JIPC Meeting, 1 Sep 1950, CO 537/6579; *Straits Budget*, 24 Aug 1950; Minutes of 15th JIPC Meeting, 15 Sep 1950, CO 537/6579.

236 Greene Report, CO 537/7255; Tracey, *A Variety of Lives*, p. 132. Dumeresque was eventually replaced as Director Radio Malaya by H.W. Jackson in 1951. See 'Extracts from Donor's Letter, 8 Oct 1985', Jackson Papers, MSS.Brit.Emp.s.500, RHO.

237 Minutes of 19th JIPC Meeting, 17 Nov 1950, CO 537/6579; Greene Report, CO 537/7255.

238 Greene Report, CO 537/7255.

239 'Government to People', File No. 810/53, ANM.

240 *Ibid.*

241 Greene Report, CO 53/7/255.

242 *Ibid.*; Extract from 'PMR Nov 1950', CO 537/6011.

243 Carruthers, *Winning Hearts and Minds*, p. 84. In December 1951, Mr. Frederick Gough M.P. asked why the Federal Government still persisted in calling the Communist terrorists 'bandits'. In reply, Mr. Lennox-Boyd, speaking on behalf of the Colonial Secretary, assured Gough that the Government in Malaya was not unaware that the MCP was behind the banditry. Lennox-Boyd added that 'personally' he himself preferred the term 'terrorist'. See *H.C. Debs.*, 5 Dec 1951, Cols. 2379–2380.

244 Too interview, Tape 2, EEP, RHO.

245 Too interview, Tape 1, EEP, RHO.

246 Minutes of 8th JIPC Meeting, 9 June 1950, CO 537/6579.

247 Stockwell, ed., *BDEEP, Malaya: The Communist Insurrection*, Doc. 221.

248 Driberg interview with Lam Swee, CO 537/6015.

249 Minutes of 9th JIPC Meeting, 23 June 1950, CO 537/6579.

250 Minutes of 10th JIPC Meeting, 7 July 1950, CO 537/6579.

251 See Greene Report, CO 537/7255. See also Inward Telegram No. 593 from High Commissioner Federation of Malaya to Secretary of State for the Colonies, 12 May 1952, CO 1022/49.

252 Greene Report, CO 537/7255.

253 Inward Telegram No. 593, 12 May 1952, CO 1022/49.

254 Too interview, Tape 1, EEP, RHO.

255 See 'Publicity and Propaganda Lines', 3 July 1950, CO 537/6579.

256 Greene Report, CO 537/7255.

257 *Ibid.*; Too interview, Tape 1, EEP, RHO; Barber, *War of the Running Dogs*, p. 140.

258 Greene Report, CO 537/7255.

259 See the attack on Lam Swee by Chan Lo, Secretary of the PMFTU, in *Freedom News*, No. 29, 15 Sep 1952, CO 1022/46; Stubbs, *Hearts and Minds in Guerrilla Warfare*, p. 148.

260 See Minutes of 10th JIPC Meeting, 7 July 1950, CO 537/6579.

261 Bum-Joon Lee Park, 'The British Experience of Counterinsurgency in Malaya: The Emergency, 1948–1960', Unpublished PhD Dissertation, American University, January 1965, p. 187.

262 *WINSUM*, No. 79, week ending 8 Nov 1951, CO 1022/13.

263 Too interview, Tape 1, EEP, RHO.

264 Greene Report, CO 537/7255.

265 A.D.C. Peterson, 'Report and Recommendations on the Organisation of Information Services in the Federation of Malaya', 20 Aug. 1952, hereafter Peterson Report, CO 967/181.

266 Extract from 'Weekly Intelligence Summary, No. 53, week ending 10 May 1951', CO 537/7291.
267 'Publicity and Propaganda Lines', No. 12, 19 July 1950, CO 537/6579.
268 Greene Report, CO 537/7255.
269 Federal Government Press Statement, 15 Dec 1950, CO 537/6015. The 'lowest rank and file' included ordinary Party members, MRLA combatants, members of Military Work Forces and Protection Corps. Members of the 'public', also included unpaid volunteers like the Auxiliary Police, Home Guard and Kampong Guard.
270 Federation of Malaya Press Releases Summary, 8 June 1951, CO 537/7291.
271 Ibid.; Greene Report, CO 537/7255.
272 Leaflet no. 459, December 1950, Extract from 'Federal Government Press Statement, Feb 1951', CO 537/7291; 'Memorandum by Secretary of Defence: Surrender Policy', 12 Aug 1954, CO 1030/22.
273 Federation of Malaya Press Releases Summary, 8 June 1951, CO 537/7291.
274 WINSUM, No. 87, week ending 3 Jan 1952, CO 1022/13.
275 Greene Report, CO 537/7255.
276 WINSUM, No. 79, week ending 8 Nov 1951, CO 1022/13.
277 Greene Report, CO 537/7255; Extract from 'Federation of Malaya Political Report for Dec 50', CO 537/7291.
278 WINSUM, No. 79, week ending 8 Nov 1951, CO 1022/13.
279 A.W.D. James to T.S. Tull, 30 Sep 1952, 'Department of Information, Federation of Malaya', File No. 944/53, ANM.
280 In order to give selected local members of the appointed Legislative Council the experience of executive responsibility, Gurney had introduced the Member system in April 1951. The first Members were Dato Onn bin Jaafar (Home Affairs), Tengku Yaacob bin Sultan Hamid (Agriculture and Forestry), Dato Mahmud bin Mat (Lands, Mines and Communications), Dato E.E. Thuraisingham (Education) and Dr Lee Tiang Keng.
281 Peterson Report, CO 967/181.
282 Director of Operations, Federation of Malaya, 'The Co-operation of the Peoples of Malaya against Communism: Federation Policy', Appendix A to the Agenda dated 10 Nov 1951, TCL.24.3, TCLP-ISEAS.
283 Times, 14 March 1951; Tan Cheng Lock to Pelgrave Simpson, 19 Feb 1951, TCL.5.36, TCLP-ISEAS.
284 WINSUM, No. 92, week ending 7 Feb 1952, CO 1022/14. See also Stubbs, Hearts and Minds in Guerrilla Warfare, pp. 133–134.
285 Lyttelton, Memoirs of Lord Chandos, pp. 361–362.
286 Goh Chee Yan to Malcolm MacDonald, 22 Nov 1951, TCL.24.5, TCLP-ISEAS.
287 Interview with J.L.M. Gorrie.
288 Field-Marshal Lord Montgomery to Field-Marshal Slim, 3 Dec 1951, PREM 11/121.

CHAPTER FIVE

1 Granada interview with Tan Sri Mubin Sheppard, n.d., EEP, RHO.
2 MacDonald interview, 15 Dec 1972, RHO.
3 Michael Carver, 'Montgomery', in Keegan, ed., Churchill's Generals, p. 158; Stephen Hart, 'Montgomery, Morale, Casualty Conservation and "Colossal Cracks": 21st Army Group's Operational Technique in North-West Europe, 1944–45', in Military Power: Land Warfare in Theory and Practice, ed. by Brian Holden Reid (London and Portland, Oregon: Frank Cass, 1997), pp. 134–135.

4 'Success in Malaya', note by Field Marshal Lord Montgomery (M/222, 2 Jan 1952), enclosed as part of [Appointment of Templer]: letter from Field Marshal Lord Montgomery to Mr Churchill, PREM 11/169, 2 Jan 1952, Stockwell, ed., *BDEEP, Malaya: The Communist Insurrection,* Doc. 260.

5 Other candidates considered for the post of High Commissioner included General Sir John Harding; Marshal of the RAF Sir Arthur Harris (wartime c-in-c Bomber Command); General Sir Brian Robertson (c-in-c Middle East Land Forces); the current Chief of the Imperial General Staff, Field Marshal Slim; Marshal of the RAF Lord Portal; Lieutenant-General Sir R. Scobie (GOC Greece 1944–1946), and Lieutenant General G.G. Bourne. Bourne actually became GOC Malaya at the end of May 1954. See [Appointment of Templer]: telegram no. T6/52 from Mr Lyttelton to Mr Churchill, PREM 11/639, 4 Jan 1952, in Stockwell, ed., *BDEEP, Malaya: The Communist Insurrection,* Doc. 259.

6 'Second draft of speech for the Alamein Reunion, 22 Oct 1954', 28 Sep 1954, 7410-29-3, NAM.

7 Stubbs, *Hearts and Minds in Guerrilla Warfare,* pp. 143–144; 'Proposed Dialogue Script for a Filmed Discussion with Field Marshal Sir Gerald Templer on the Anti-Terrorist Campaign in Malaya', 30 March 1977, 8011-132-2, NAM.

8 Stubbs, *Hearts and Minds in Guerrilla Warfare,* pp. 140–141.

9 'Proposed Dialogue Script', 8011-132-2, NAM; Cabinet Committee Minutes, 28 Dec 1951, CAB 130/74.

10 Cloake, *Templer: Tiger of Malaya,* pp. 211–212, 243–244; Mackay, *The Malayan Emergency,* pp. 119–120; Stubbs, *Hearts and Minds in Guerrilla Warfare,* pp. 142–143.

11 Montgomery of Alamein, *The Memoirs of Field Marshal the Viscount Montgomery* (London: Collins, 1958), pp. 81–87.

12 David Lloyd-Owen to Hankins, 15 April 1969, 8011-132, NAM.

13 *Ibid.*

14 Lloyd-Owen to Hankins, 15 April 1969, 8011-132, NAM.

15 Cloake, *Templer: Tiger of Malaya,* p. 241.

16 See 'The Machinery of Command for Planning', Aug 1952; and 'Courses for Members of DWECs – Joining Instructions', Aug 1952, Hugh Stockwell Papers, LHCMA; Cloake, *Templer: Tiger of Malaya,* p. 252.

17 Interview with J.L.M. Gorrie.

18 A. Kirk-Greene's interview with Sir Kerr Bovell, 12 June 1972, MSS.Brit.Emp.s.397, RHO.

19 Lloyd-Owen to Hankins 15 April 1969, 8011-132, NAM.

20 'Proposed Dialogue Script', 8011-132-2, NAM.

21 J.D.H. Neill to H.P. Bryson, 11 June 1969, Heussler Papers, Box 17, RHO.

22 Parkinson, *Templer in Malaya,* pp. 16–17.

23 Lapping, *End of Empire,* p. 220; Allen, *Savage Wars of Peace,* p. 37.

24 Madoc interview, EEP, RHO.

25 Interview with J.L.M. Gorrie.

26 Sheppard interview, EEP, RHO.

27 Cloake, *Templer: Tiger of Malaya,* p. 213.

28 Bovell interview, RHO.

29 Corry interview, RHO.

30 'Outline of C.P.'s Talk for America', n.d., Young Papers, Box 3, RHO.

31 John Loch, 'My First Alphabet', 1994, pp. 154–155. Copy of manuscript available in IWM.

32 Author's correspondence with O.W. Wolters, 27 Feb 1998.

33 Lieutenant-General Neville Brownjohn to Lloyd-Owen, 18 June 1952, 8301-6, NAM.

34 *Economist*, 12 July 1952.
35 Lloyd-Owen to Hankins, 15 April 1969, 8011-132, NAM
36 Interview with Peter Lucy, Aug 1981, EEP, RHO.
37 Lloyd Owen to Brownjohn, 9 June 1952, 8301-6, NAM.
38 *Times*, 7 Aug 1952; *Sunday Pictorial*, 29 June 1952; Inward Telegram No. 787 from High Commissioner Federation of Malaya to Secretary of State for the Colonies, 29 June 1952, CO 1022/464; Cloake, *Templer: Tiger of Malaya*, pp. 264–265.
39 'Speech by H.E. the High Commissioner to F.M.S. Chamber of Commerce', 25 April 1952, 7410-29-1, NAM.
40 'Address by H.E. the High Commissioner to Division III officers at the Selangor Badminton Hall, Kuala Lumpur', 30 Oct 1952, 7410-29-1, NAM.
41 'Proposed Dialogue Script', 8011-132-2, NAM.
42 Author's correspondence with C.M. Turnbull, 31 July 1997. Turnbull was one of the first female MCS officers, serving in Malaya from December 1952 to October 1955. An account of her time in Malaya during this period is found in C.M. Turnbull, 'The Post-War Decade in Malaya: The Settling Dust of Political Controversy', *Journal of the Malaysian Branch of the Royal Asiatic Society*, Vol. LX, Part 1 (June 1987), pp. 7–26.
43 Parkinson claims that Templer's travels enabled him to know the Malayan countryside better than Europeans who had been in the country for 20 years. Parkinson, *Templer in Malaya*, pp. 35–36.
44 *Straits Budget*, 17 July 1952; Stubbs, *Hearts and Minds in Guerrilla Warfare*, p. 146.
45 Neill to Bryson, 11 June 1969, Heussler Papers, Box 17, RHO.
46 Perry Robinson, *Transformation in Malaya*, p. 108.
47 *Straits Budget*, 11 Sep 1952.
48 *Ibid.*
49 Inward Savingram from High Commissioner Federation of Malaya to Secretary of State for the Colonies, 24 March 1952, CO 1022/29.
50 *Resettlement and Development of the New Villages*, pp. 2–5.
51 See for instance, Harper, 'The Colonial Inheritance', pp. 208–215; Stubbs, *Hearts and Minds in Guerrilla Warfare*, Chapter Four; Perry Robinson, *Transformation in Malaya*, Chapter Two; Cloake, *Templer: Tiger of Malaya*, pp. 274–276.
52 Davis interview, EEP, RHO.
53 *Daily Telegraph*, 23 June 1952. See also Note from Military Assistant to 'Y.E.', 17 April 1952, 8301-6, NAM, on the problem of the Special Constable protection of Paya Mengkuang New Village.
54 Kernial S. Sandhu, 'Emergency Resettlement in Malaya', *Journal of Tropical Geography*, Vol. 18 (1964), pp. 166–167.
55 In 1952, 361 of the New Villages had fences and 56 had double fences, but not all were adequate. *Resettlement and the Development of New Villages*, p. 6.
56 By April 1952, 161 of 486 New Villages had received perimeter lighting. This figure rose to 180 by December. Perimeter lighting was given to those Villages which had the highest number of incidents of villagers, perhaps Min Yuen, passing food over the fence to the terrorists. Extract from 'Federation of Malaya Administrative Report for January 1953', CO 1022/30. By March 1953, another 38 New Villages were given perimeter lighting. 'H.E.'s Speech opening the Connaught Bridge Power Station', 26 March 1953, 7410-29-1, NAM.
57 See 'Memorandum from the Secretary for Defence: Perimeter Fences', 28 April 1952, CO 1022/30. A new Emergency Regulation ER 19B, strengthened existing ER 17 EA provisions for food restricted areas by making it an offence to attempt to cross, to pass or to try to pass articles over the fence at all times. The Executive Council approved in principle the electrification of fences on 15 May.

58 Extract from 'Monthly Review of Chinese Affairs for January 1952', CO 1022/29.
59 Luckham, 'The Malayan Emergency', Heussler Papers, Box 16, RHO.
60 *Resettlement and the Development of New Villages*, p. 7. This New Village Liaison Officer was John Davis. Stubbs, *Hearts and Minds in Guerrilla Warfare*, p. 169.
61 Alamein Reunion Speech, 28 Sep 1954, 7410-29-3, NAM.
62 *Resettlement and the Development of New Villages*, p. 7; interview with J.L.M. Gorrie.
63 Extract from 'Federation of Malaya Savingram No. 101, 19 Sep 1953', CO 1022/29.
64 Extract from 'High Commissioner's Address to the Federation of Malaya Legislative Council, 19 November 1952'; Extract from 'Review of Chinese Affairs, July 1952', CO 1022/29.
65 Extract from 'Federation of Malaya Administrative Report, January 1953', CO 1022/29.
66 Frank Brewer, 'Resettlement', n.d., in Heussler Papers, Box 9, RIIO.
67 Extract from 'Federation of Malaya Savings No. 1623, 12 Aug 1952'; CO 1022/29.
68 Extract from 'Federation of Malaya Saving No. 470, 16 March 1953', CO 1022/29.
69 Extract from 'High Commissioner's Budget Speech to the Federation of Malaya Legislative Council, 25 Nov 1953', CO 1022/29.
70 Cited in Harper, 'The Colonial Inheritance', p. 245.
71 *Ibid.*, pp. 217–218.
72 Davis interview, EEP, RHO; Clutterbuck, *Conflict and Violence in Singapore and Malaysia*, pp. 246–247; Loh, *Beyond the Tin Mines*, pp. 152–154.
73 Granada interview with Sjovald Cunyngham-Brown, Aug 1981, EEP, RHO. Cunyngham-Brown, who had been Gurney's Principal Assistant Secretary, oversaw the setting up of 66 New Villages in Johore in 1952.
74 Extract from 'Federation of Malaya Savingram No. 645, 11 April 1953', CO 1022/29.
75 *Straits Budget*, 14 Aug 1952; Federal Government Press Statement, 30 March 1952, CO 1022/35; *Daily Mail*, 31 March 1952; Brewer, 'The Malayan Emergency', Heussler Papers, Box 9, RHO. See Extract from 'Malayan Federal Exco Minutes, 25 March 1952', CO 1022/35.
76 Brewer, 'The Malayan Emergency', Heussler Papers, Box 9, RHO. See also Strauch, *Chinese Village Politics*, pp. 70–72.
77 Davis interview, EEP, RHO.
78 Author's interview with Datin Jean Marshall, Singapore, 21 Jan 1998. Datin Marshall is the widow of Mr David Marshall, the first Chief Minister of Singapore.
79 Acting Chief Secretary to all *Mentri Besars* and Resident Commissioners, 8 March 1952, 'Department of Chinese Affairs', File No. 1648, ANM.
80 *Resettlement and the Development of New Villages*, p. 4; Extract from 'Federation of Malaya Savingram No. 645, 11 April 1953', CO 1022/29. R.H. Oakeley to Dato Tan Cheng Lock, 5 Jan 1953, TCL.10.4, TCLP-ISEAS; interview with J.L.M. Gorrie.
81 Loh, *Beyond the Tin Mines*, p. 156.
82 Interview with J.L.M. Gorrie; 'Notes of a meeting held at King's House', 2 Feb 1952, TCL.3.274a, TCLP-ISEAS.
83 This was related to the author by the Chinese boy – now a successful businessman – Christopher Gorrie, on 19 January 1998, in Singapore. For a further account of the work of State SCAs in New Villages, see Perry Robinson, *Transformation in Malaya*, pp. 94–95.
84 'H.C.'s Speech at the First Meeting of the 6th Session, Legislative Council, 18 March 1953', 7410-29-1, NAM; Brewer, 'The Chinese Protectorate', Brewer Papers, Box 1, RHO; A.W.D. James, Acting Secretary for Chinese Affairs, Federation of Malaya, to Federation Establishment Officer, 14 June 1955, 'Department of Chinese Affairs', File No. 1635, ANM.

85 Gray, 'The Chinese Problem in the Federation of Malaya', Watts Papers, RHO; 'Chinese Affairs Service Association, Federation of Malaya: Report on the Official Conference held on 27 April 1953', 'Department of Chinese Affairs', File No. 1635, ANM. Also Frank Brewer, 'Chinese Affairs Officers and Assistant Chinese Affairs Officers', 10 Sep 1953; and David Gray, 'The Chinese Affairs Officers' Conference held at Kuala Lumpur on Monday, 27th April 1953: Views of the Secretary for Chinese Affairs, Federation of Malaya', 25 July 1953, 'Department of Chinese Affairs', File No. 1648, ANM.

86 Harper, 'The Colonial Inheritance', pp. 245–246, 251–252, 255; Stubbs, *Hearts and Minds in Guerrilla Warfare*, p. 204; Loh, *Beyond the Tin Mines*, p. 138. See also Gray to Watts, 17 Dec 1951, Watts Papers, RHO.

87 Harper, 'The Colonial Inheritance', pp. 249–252.

88 Author's interview with Datin Marshall.

89 Too US lecture, PP.

90 Muller to Fraser, 22 Dec 1951, CO 1022/165. See also A.J. Stockwell, 'Policing during the Malayan Emergency: Communism, Communalism and Decolonisation', in Anderson and Killingray, eds., *Policing and Decolonisation*, pp. 110–114.

91 *Federation of Malaya Annual Report 1953* (London: HMSO, 1954), p. 227; *Federation of Malaya Annual Report 1954* (London: HMSO, 1955), p. 410.

92 Gray, 'The Chinese Problem in the Federation of Malaya', Watts Papers, RHO. On European and Malay Police antipathy toward the Chinese, see Stockwell, 'Policing during the Malayan Emergency', in Anderson and Killingray, eds., *Policing and Decolonisation*, p. 117.

93 Muller to Fraser, 22 Dec 1951, CO 1022/165. By the end of 1951, 6,250 full-time Police had been stationed in New Villages, housed in buildings costing $6,390,000. *Resettlement and the Development of New Villages*, p. 5.

94 *WINSUM*, No. 101, week ending 10 April 1952, CO 1022/14.

95 'Broadcast on Operation Service by H.E.', 26 Jan 1953, 7410-29-1, NAM.

96 Arthur Young, 'Malaya', May 1967; Letter from Home Secretary to Lord Mayor, City of London, 16 Jan 1952, Young Papers, Box 3, RHO.

97 Bovell interview, RHO.

98 Separate departments were created to look after administration, operations, supplies, transport and signals. Young also appointed two Deputy Police Commissioners, 16 Senior Assistant Commissioners, eight Assistant Commissioners and 45 Superintendents. Locally recruited officers were brought in to fill permanent posts. A staff officer was also appointed to deal with resettlement issues while a supplies officer was stationed in London. Extract from '*Malayan Bulletin*, No. 65, 25 May 1952', CO 1022/165.

99 Young, 'The Duties of the Police', n.d., Young Papers, Box 3, RHO.

100 Young. 'Malaya', Young Papers, Box 3, RHO.

101 Young, 'The Duties of the Police', Young Papers, Box 3, RHO.

102 *Ibid.*

103 *New York Herald Tribune*, 3 June 1953. In fact, Government planned not only to stop the Police from getting bigger, it wanted it to get much smaller. Basically the idea was to save money and in particular, to demobilise the Specials so as to let them return to normal life. As at 30 Oct 1952, the Specials numbered 39,128. The aim was to have a smaller establishment of 23,570 by 1 Jan 1955. See Extract from 'Federation of Malaya Savingram 1601, 19 Sep 1953'; Extract from 'Federation of Malaya Savingram 2455, 12 Dec 1952', CO 1022/169; Young, 'The World Today', transcript of broadcast 19 May 1953, and 'The Federation Police in 1952', Young Papers, Box 3, RHO.

104 'Police Training Progress Report up to and including 31 July 1952', CO 1022/168.

105 'Progress Report Training – 1 June 1953–31 July 1953', CO 1022/168; *Straits Budget*, 17 April 1952.
106 Extract from 'Federation of Malaya Savingram No. 1377, 10 July 1952', CO 1022/168; Young, 'The Federation Police in 1952', Young Papers, Box 3, RHO.
107 See Federal Government Press Statements, 31 March 1952 and 13 April 1952 and Extracts from 'Monthly Review of Chinese Affairs', July and Aug 1952, CO 1022/149.
108 'Progress Report Training up to and including 30 Nov 1952', 'Progress Report – Training 1 Feb 1953 – 4 April 1953', CO 1022/168.
109 'Supplementary Memorandum from Secretary of Defence· Recruitment into the Rank and File of the Police Force, Supplement to Exco Paper No. 49/3/53, 5 Dec 1953', CO 1022/169.
110 Outward Savingram No. 1101 from Secretary of State for the Colonies to High Commissioner Federation of Malaya, 1 May 1952; Inward Savingram No. 1070 from High Commissioner Federation of Malaya to Secretary of State for the Colonies, 28 May 1952, CO 1022/343.
111 Extract from 'Federation of Malaya Saving No. 1377, 10 July 1952', CO 1022/168.
112 *Ibid.*; 'Progress Report Training – 1 Feb 1953–4 April 1953', CO 1022/168; Brewer, 'Malaya – Administration of Chinese Affairs', Heussler Papers, Box 9, RHO; *Straits Budget*, 24 July 1952.
113 'The World Today', transcript of broadcast, 19 May 1953, Young Papers, Box 3, RHO.
114 Young, 'Malaya', Young Papers, Box 3, RHO.
115 *Federation of Malaya Annual Report 1952* (London: HMSO, 1953), p. 6.
116 'The World Today', transcript of broadcast, 19 May 1953, Young Papers, Box 3, RHO.
117 Young, 'Malaya', Box 3, *idem*, 'Talk to Rotary Club, Kuala Lumpur', Feb 1953, Young Papers, Box 2, RHO.
118 Draft of article for *New York Herald Tribune*, 6 May 1953, in Young Papers, Box 2, RHO.
119 'Broadcast on Operation Service by H.E.', 26 Jan 1953, 7410-29-1, NAM.
120 'H.C.'s Speech at the First Meeting of the 6th Session, Legislative Council, 18 March 1953', 7410-29-1, NAM.
121 Correspondence with the author, 3 July 1997. See also *Yorkshire Post*, 19 May 1953.
122 Professor Max Beloff's interview with Oliver Lyttelton, 27 Feb 1970, MSS.Brit. Emp.s.525, RHO.
123 Humphrey, 'A Study of Reasons for Entering the Jungle', WO 291/1781.
124 Lieutenant-Colonel Walter Walker, CO 1/6th Gurkha Rifles, to Colonel C. Graham, CO Gurkha Brigade, 12 July 1952, Hugh Stockwell Papers, LHCMA.
125 Peterson Report, CO 967/181.
126 'Address by H.E. the High Commissioner to Division III officers at the Selangor Badminton Hall, Kuala Lumpur', 30 Oct 1952, 7410-29-1, NAM.
127 'A New Year Message from the HC to all Public Servants, 1 Jan 1953', 7410-29-1, NAM.
128 'H.E. the High Commissioner's Address to the Annual General Meeting of the European Civil Servants Association of Malaya', 13 Feb 1953, in 7410-29-1, NAM.
129 'H.C.'s Speech at the First Meeting of the 6th Session, Legislative Council, 18 March 1953', 7410-29-1, NAM.
130 Alamein Reunion Speech, 28 Sep 1954, 7410-29-3, NAM. See also Cloake, *Templer: Tiger of Malaya*, p. 251; K.R. Brazier-Creagh, 'Malaya', *RUSI Journal*, Vol. XCIX, No. 594 (May 1954), pp. 183–184.

131 'Report on the Role of the Army in the Cold War in Malaya', n.d., 7410-29-2, NAM.
132 Harper, 'The Colonial Inheritance', pp. 227–228.
133 Victor Purcell, 'General Templer', *Twentieth Century*, Vol. CLV, No. 923 (Feb 1954), pp. 124–125. See also Arthur Campbell, *Jungle Green* (London: George Allen and Unwin, 1953).
134 See note entitled '20th Century', Feb 1954, 7410-29-2, NAM.
135 Templer to Lyttelton, 19 Aug 1953, 7410-29-5, NAM.
136 Purcell had earned Templer's ire by producing, ostensibly in his capacity as the MCA's Honorary Adviser in the United Kingdom – something which the MCA denied – a series of articles in late 1952 and early 1953 in the *Times*, *Daily Telegraph* and the *New Statesman and Nation* criticising Government's New Village policy and accusing Templer himself of being anti Chinese. This had resulted in Government pressure being exerted on the MCA to disassociate itself from Purcell. See for instance, Tan Hong Thye, Executive Secretary MCA to DGIS (Director-General Information Services), 29 Dec 1952; R.H Oakeley to Tan Cheng Lock, 5 Jan 1953; Tan Cheng Lock to Purcell, 26 Jan 1953; B.T.W. Stewart to Tan Cheng Lock, 26 Jan 1953 and 6 Feb 1953; Oakeley to Tan Cheng Lock, 9 Feb 1953; Purcell to Tan Cheng Lock, 8 Feb and 12 Feb 1953; Tan Cheng Lock to Templer, 11 Feb 1953; Templer to Tan Cheng Lock, 25 Feb 1953, all in TCL.10, TCLP-ISEAS.
137 The *Spectator* noted that even if Templer was indeed 'autocratic', 'tactless', lacking in 'humanity', and had a 'thin-lipped tigerish sneer', it was a pity that Purcell had not 'found it possible to write more objectively of a man whom he clearly very much dislikes'. *Spectator*, 5 Feb 1954.
138 Letters to the Editor, *Spectator*, 12 March and 26 March 1954.
139 Letter to the Editor, *Spectator*, 19 March 1954.
140 M. Harvey, 'Malaya – Time for a Change', *Army Quarterly*, Vol. LXX, No. 1 (April 1955), p. 42.
141 'An Appreciation of Police Affairs', 5 Feb 1953, Young Papers, Box 2, RHO.
142 *Ibid.*
143 Correspondence with Turnbull, 31 July 1997. Also Sandhu and Zakaria, 'The Malayan Emergency', in Sandhu and Wheatley, eds., *Melaka*, Vol. 1, p. 414; Renick, 'The Emergency Regulations of Malaya', p. 17.
144 Lyttelton Report, in Stockwell, ed. *BDEEP, Malaya: The Communist Insurrections*, Doc. 257.
145 Extract from 'Minutes of Federal Legislative Council Meeting, 30 Jan 1952', CO 1022/132.
146 Extract from 'Federation of Malaya Monthly Newsletter No. 36 for the period 16 Dec 1951- 15 Jan 1952', CO 1022/132.
147 Most Chinese detainees (2,737) were in Ipoh Detention Centre. Extract from 'Proceedings of Malayan Legislative Council 19 March 1952', and Extract from 'Federation of Malaya Monthly Newsletter No. 39 for the period 16 March 1952 to 15 April 1952', CO 1022/132.
148 'Minutes of Meeting of MCA Representatives held at Federal Executive Council meeting room, 21 April 1952', TCL.3.274, TCLP-ISEAS.
149 *Detention and Deportation during the Emergency*, p. 8.
150 Extract from 'Federation Saving No. 1751, 17 Oct 1953', and Extract from 'Federation of Malaya Saving No. 79, 18 Jan 1954', CO 1022/132.
151 Extract from 'Federation of Malaya Saving No. 79, 18 Jan 1954', Extract from 'Federation of Malaya Administrative Report for January 1953', CO 1022/132.
152 Inward Telegram No. 256 from High Commissioner Federation of Malaya to Secretary of State for the Colonies, 13 March 1953, CO 1022/132; Extract from 'FM Savings No. 645, 11 April 1953', CO 1022/132.

153 Gann to Jerrom, 14 March 1953, CO 1022/132.
154 'Proposed Dialogue Script', 8011-132-2, NAM.
155 Stubbs, *Hearts and Minds in Guerrilla Warfare*, p. 165; Short, *Communist Insurrection in Malaya*, pp. 340–341; Inward Telegram No. 441 from High Commissioner Federation of Malaya to Secretary of State for the Colonies, 2 April 1952, CO 1022/54.
156 For instance, see Barber, *War of the Running Dogs*, p. 185.
157 Madoc interview, EEP, RHO; Mackay, *The Malayan Emergency*, pp. 125–127; Peterson letter to the *Listener*, 14 Aug 1969.
158 The curfew was lifted and the rice ration returned to normal after more than a week, after information was received from the people. Stubbs, *Hearts and Minds in Guerrilla Warfare*, p. 165; Barber, *War of the Running Dogs*, pp. 185–187.
159 'Minutes of Meeting of MCA Representatives', TCL.3.274, TCLP ISEAS.
160 *Straits Budget*, 17 July 1952, 4 Sep 1952. The Yong Peng Operation Question was conducted in May 1953. See C.R.D. Danby to Robert Heussler, 16 March 1982, Heussler Papers, Box 11, RHO.
161 Director of Operations Staff, 'Permatang Tinggi: Action taken against the village under ER 17D in August 1952', 9 Oct 1952, CO 1022/56. The operation was conducted under both ER 17D and 17 DA, actually. Under the latter the villagers were fined $4,650, while the village was demolished under 17D when information eventually obtained led to the detention of 62 persons. See also 'Notice to the Peoples of Malaya', 27 August 1952, CO 1022/56 and Cloake, *Templer: Tiger of Malaya*, pp. 272–273.
162 Inward Savingram No. 2376 from High Commissioner Federation of Malaya to Secretary of State for the Colonies, 27 Nov 1952, CO 1022/56.
163 For instance, Lord Listowel's letter to the *Times*, 28 Aug 1952; W.J. Field M.P. to Lennox-Boyd, *H.C. Debs.*, 23 April 1952, Cols. 394–395. See also the Commons debate on collective punishment in Malaya, *H.C. Debs.*, 30 April 1952, Cols. 1453–1455.
164 See note by Jerrom, 10 Nov 1951, CO 1022/58.
165 'High Commissioner's Press Conference: Replies to Written Questions', 26 May 1954, 7410-29-2, NAM.
166 Extract from 'High Commissioner's Budget Speech to Federation of Malaya Legislative Council, 25 Nov 1953', CO 1022/58.
167 'An Appreciation of Police Affairs', Young Papers, Box 2, RHO.
168 'Surrender Policy', Young Papers, Box 1, RHO.
169 Inward Telegram No. 880 from High Commissioner Federation of Malaya to Secretary of State for the Colonies, 26 Aug 1953, and Inward Savingram No. 1480 From High Commissioner Federation of Malaya to Secretary of State for the Colonies, 28 Aug 1953, CO 1022/58.
170 *Liverpool Post*, 4 Sep 1953.
171 Inward Savingram No. 1480, 28 Aug 1953, CO 1022/58; Stewart, 'Winning in Malaya', p. 277.
172 *Times*, 4 Sep 1953; Federal Government Press Statement, 3 Sep 1953, CO 1022/58.
173 Federal Government Press Statement, 3 Sep 1953, CO 1022/58.
174 *Ibid.* Voice Aircraft broadcast the following message over the White Area: 'General Templer congratulates the people of Malacca's White Area for driving out the Communist terrorists; keep them out, and see that they never come back'.
175 Correspondence with Turnbull, 31 July 1997; M.C.A. Henniker, *Red Shadow over Malaya* (London: William Blackwood and Sons, 1955), p. 290.
176 Hugh Stockwell, 'Appreciation of the Situation in Malaya',Talbot Papers, LHCMA. See also Barber, *War of the Running Dogs*, p. 235.

177 Extract from 'High Commissioner's Budget Speech to Federation of Malaya Legislative Council, 25 Nov 1953', CO 1022/58.

178 'H.E.'s Address to State Councillors and Heads of Departments of the Johore State Government', 13 May 1954, 7410-29-1, NAM; Federal Government Press Statement, 29 April 1954, CO 1030/1.

179 Madoc interview, EEP, RHO.

180 Federal Government Press Statement, 29 April 1954, CO 1030/1.

181 Perry Robinson, *Transformation in Malaya*, pp. 49–50.

182 Stewart, 'Winning in Malaya', pp. 275–276.

183 D.C. Watherston to Tan Cheng Lock, 29 Feb 1952, TCL.5.259a, TCLP-ISEAS.

184 Morton had been in charge of regional security matters in the Commissioner-General's Office in Singapore. Cloake, *Templer: Tiger of Malaya*, pp. 228–229.

185 'Meeting with General Sir Gerald Templer', 31 Jan 1952, 'Charter for the Federation Intelligence Committee and Combined Intelligence Staff', n.d., CO 1022/51.

186 Extract from 'Malayan Bulletin No. 65, 25 May 1952', CO 1022/165.

187 Madoc turned Jenkin's CID Training School into a Special Branch Training School and worked out the curriculum. Claude Fenner was the first Commandant. Madoc interview, EEP, RHO; Extract from 'Federation of Malaya Savingram No. 1377, 10 July 1952', CO 1022/168. For an account of what the Special Branch course was like, see R.A. Ruegg, 'The Wind of Change in Malaya and North Borneo: A Junior Police Officer's Story', Part I, MSS.Ind.Ocn.s.290, RHO.

188 Melshen, 'Pseudo-Operations', pp. 64–65.

189 Hugh Stockwell, 'Appreciation of the Situation in Malaya', Talbot Papers, LHCMA; Extract from 'Malayan Bulletin No. 65, 25 May 1952', CO 1022/165.

190 Hugh Stockwell, 'Appreciation of the Situation in Malaya', Talbot Papers, LHCMA.

191 *WINSUM*, No. 123, week ending 11 Sep 1952 and *WINSUM*, No. 130, week ending 30 Oct 1952, CO 1022/16; AVM G.H. Mills, 'Fifth Report on the Royal Air Force Operations in Malaya, Feb-Dec 1952', 31 Dec 1952, AIR 23/8696. Hereafter Mills Report; *WINSUM*, No. 169, week ending 30 July 1953, CO 1022/18. See also *Scotsman*, 19 May 1953.

192 Madoc interview, EEP, RHO; Brazier-Creagh, 'Malaya', p. 183.

193 Cloake, *Templer: Tiger of Malaya*, p. 241; Lloyd-Owen to Brigadier J.R.C. Hamilton, 19 Sep 1952, 8301-6, NAM.

194 Mills Report, AIR 23/8696; *WINSUM*, No. 186, week ending 26 Nov 1953; *WINSUM*, No. 185, week ending 19 Nov 1953, CO 1022/19.

195 *WINSUM*, No. 176, week ending 17 Sep 1953, CO 1022/18; *WINSUM*, No. 182, week ending 29 Oct 1953, CO 1022/18.

196 Gregorian, 'Jungle Bashing in Malaya', pp. 349–350; *Annual Report 1952*, pp. 4–5.

197 K. Pennycuick, Lieutenant-Colonel R.S. Hawkins, 'Standards of Shooting in Malaya 1952–53', n.d., WO 291/1736.

198 Extract from 'Federation of Malaya Savingram No. 995, 17 June 1953', CO 1022/50; *Yorkshire Post*, 19 May 1953.

199 Melshen, 'Pseudo-Operations', pp. 60–64.

200 *WINSUM*, No. 185, week ending 19 Nov 1953, CO 1022/19. See also Henniker, *Red Shadow over Malaya*, pp. 270–271.

201 Air Officer Commanding (AOC) Malaya to C-in-C Far East Air Force, 4 March 1953; Director of Operations to Advanced Air Headquarters, 'Comments on AOC's Directive for Officers appointed as RAF Representative at SWECs and at Security Force Headquarters in the Field', 26 March 1953, AIR 23/8619.

202 See *WINSUM*, No. 188, week ending 10 Dec 1953, CO 1022/19.

203 See *WINSUM*, No. 186, week ending 26 Nov 1953, CO 1022/19.

204 'Policy Concerning the Use of Air Forces in a Support and/or Independent Role', 27 May 1953, AIR 23/8619.

205 Air Vice Marshall F.R.W. Scherger, 'Employment of the RAF in the Emergency', and 'Summary of Conclusions', 10 Dec 1953, AIR 23/8619. Communication flying referred to the transport of commanders around their units' area of operations.

206 Lakin, 'An Investigation into the Psychological Effects of Security Force Activities', WO 291/1767.

207 *Ibid.* Security Force patrols until late in the Emergency were equipped mainly with Enfield rifles. In addition, the lead scout was usually equipped with an automatic shotgun, a couple of soldiers would carry a carbine or a submachine gun, and one would carry the Bren for 'a blast of firepower'. See Sunderland, *Army Operations in Malaya*, p. 41.

208 *WINSUM*, No. 122, week ending 4 Sep 1952, CO 1022/16.

209 See the note from Lau Cheng, SCM Selangor to Liew Kon Kim, 10 June 1952, *WINSUM*, No. 129, week ending 23 Oct 1952, CO 1022/16.

210 *WINSUM*, No. 168, week ending 23 July 1953, CO 1022/18.

211 P.B. Humphrey, 'Some Items of Psychological Warfare Intelligence as Obtained from Surrendered Communist Terrorist Terrorists in Malaya', ORS (PW) Memorandum No. 8/53, 5 Oct 1953, WO 291/1770. See also *WINSUM*, No. 162, week ending 11 June 1953, CO 1022/17.

212 F.H. Lakin, 'A Further Study of Surrender Behaviour among Chinese Communist Terrorists in Malaya', ORS (PW) Memorandum No. 4/53, n.d., WO 291/1766; Lakin and Humphrey, 'A Study of Surrenders in Malaya', WO 291/1783.

213 These were the observations of the MCP Johore State Secretariat. *WINSUM*, No. 168, week ending 23 July 1953, CO 1022/18.

214 Lakin, 'A Further Study of Surrender Behaviour', WO 291/1766.

215 'H.C.'s Speech at the First Meeting of the Sixth Session, Legislative Council', 18 March 1953, 7410-29-1, NAM.

216 Sheppard interview, EEP, RHO.

217 Greene Report, CO 537/7255; Peterson Report, CO 967/181.

218 *Glasgow Herald*, 5 March 1952; *WINSUM*, week ending 7 Feb 1952, CO 1022/14.

219 *WINSUM*, No. 105, week ending 8 May 1952, CO 1022/15; C.R.D. Danby to Heussler, 16 March 1982, Heussler Papers, Box 11, RHO; *WINSUM*, No. 96, week ending 6 March 1952, CO 1022/14.

220 M. Noor Ismail, Information Officer Trengganu, to Director of Information Services, Kuala Lumpur, 26 Feb 1952, W. Fernando to Information Officer, Trengganu, 18 July 1952, 'Department of Information, Trengganu', File No. 3/52, ANM.

221 *Glasgow Herald*, 5 March 1952; *WINSUM*, No. 96, week ending 6 March 1952, CO 1022/14.

222 Too interview, Tape 2, EEP, RHO.

223 *WINSUM*, No. 100, week ending 3 April 1952, CO 1022/14.

224 *Annual Report 1952*, p. 283.

225 Cloake, *Templer: Tiger of Malaya*, p. 236; *Malaya: The Journal of the British Association of Malaya*, November 1952, p. 47.

226 Cloake, *Templer: Tiger of Malaya*, pp. 236–237. See also notes of a meeting on Information Services in London, 20 June 1952, CO 1022/492.

227 Peterson Report, CO 967/181; A.D.C. Peterson, Letter to the Editor, *Listener*, 14 Aug 1969.

228 Peterson Report, CO 967/181.

229 *Ibid.*

230 *Ibid.*

231 'Re-organisation of Information Services', 10 Nov 1952; Federal Government Press Statement, 4 Feb 1953, 'Department of Information, Trengganu', File No. 102/52, ANM.

232 See James to T.S. Tull, 30 Sep 1952, and J.A. Cradock, for Acting Malayan Establishment Officer, to James, 1 Oct 1952, 'Department of Information, Federation of Malaya', File No. 944/53, ANM.

233 It is unclear exactly when Isaac joined EIS, as he is not mentioned in the Greene Report which was written in September 1951. He must have joined between September 1951 and the inauguration of Information Services. Major R.J. Isaac, HPWS, Director of Operations Staff, to Director of Museums, Federation of Malaya, 14 Aug 1954, 'Department of Information, Federation of Malaya', File No. 401/53; 'Re-organisation of Information Services', 'Department of Information, Trengganu', File No. 102/52, ANM.

234 'Re-organisation of Information Services', 'Department of Information, Trengganu', File No. 102/52, ANM; Annual Report 1952, p. 292; Cloake, Templer: Tiger of Malaya, p. 237; Peterson, Letter to Editor, Listener, 14 Aug 1969; Straits Budget, 7 Aug 1952.

235 Annual Report 1952, p. 283; Templer's speech at the opening of the new offices of the Department of Information Services, 21 Nov 1952, 7410-29-1, NAM; 'Re-organisation of Information Services', Federal Government Press Statement: Statement to the Press by Mr. A.D.C. Peterson, 21 Nov 1952, 'Department of Information, Trengganu', File No. 102/52, ANM.

236 Annual Report 1952, p. 7; Peterson Report, CO 967/181; Malay Mail, 22 Nov 1952.

237 Peterson Report, CO 967/181.

238 Annual Report 1953, p. 314; P. Egerton to A.D.C. Peterson, 13 March 1953, 'Department of Information, Trengganu', File No. 37/53, ANM.

239 'H.C's Speech at the Fifth Meeting of the Sixth Session, Legislative Council, 25 Nov 1953', 7410-29-1, NAM; Cloake, Templer:Tiger of Malaya, p. 290.

240 Sunderland, Winning the Hearts and Minds of the People, p. 31; Malay Mail, 22 Nov 1952. So important did Peterson consider the mobile units that he later lobbied the Colonial Office to 'maintain a fully trained and equipped corps of mobile information units, which could be used to strengthen the local services of territories where political tension was likely to develop'. Peterson to C.Y. Carstairs, 14 May 1960 and 3 June 1960, CO 1027/421.

241 Annual Report 1953, p. 313.

242 Annual Report 1954, pp. 378, 403; 'Probable Off-the Record Questions', 12 May 1954, 7410-29-2, NAM.

243 Sunderland, Winning the Hearts and Minds of the People, p. 51. It must be remembered that Greene, not Peterson, had introduced SEPs to the propaganda effort.

244 Hodge to all SIOs, 20 July 1953; Peterson to Head Films Division, Training Officer, all State and District Information Officers, 23 April 1953, 'Department of Information, Federation of Malaya, 1953–54', File No. 566/53, ANM.

245 Annual Report 1954, p. 373. This was made up of 10 Division I, 5 Division II, 44 Division III and 62 Division IV staff.

246 Templer's Budget Speech, 19 Nov 1952, 7410-29-1, NAM; Peterson to Head Films Division, Training Officer, all State and District Information Officers, 23 April 1953, 'Department of Information, Federation of Malaya', File No. 566/53, ANM.

247 Annual Report 1953, pp. 319–320; Annual Report 1954, p. 379.

248 'P.A. and Cinema Shows, April 1953', May 1953, 'Department of Information, Federation of Malaya', File No. 566/53, ANM.

249 Peterson Report, CO 967/181.
250 *Ibid*. Cloake, *Templer: Tiger of Malaya*, p. 237.
251 See Lloyd Williams, 'Radio Malaya Takes Stock'; *idem*, 'Radio Malaya', 18 Dec 1955, Jackson Papers, RHO; *Annual Report 1954*, p. 383.
252 Peterson Report, CO 967/181.
253 *Annual Report 1952*, p. 289.
254 *Annual Report 1953*, p. 322. See also 'Talks and Features in Various Chinese Dialects Broadcast from October 18 – October 24th 53', n.d., and 'Talks and Features in Various Chinese Dialects Broadcast from August 9 – 15th 53, n.d., 'Department of Information, Federation of Malaya', File No. 225/53, ANM.
255 *Annual Report 1954*, p. 383.
256 *Ibid*., p. 376; *Annual Report 1953*, p. 315.
257 *Annual Report 1953*, p. 315.
258 *Ibid*., p. 316.
259 Lloyd Williams, 'Radio Malaya Takes Stock', Jackson Papers, RHO; *Annual Report 1953*, p. 317. See 'Talks and Features in Various Chinese Dialects Broadcast from February 1st – 7th', n.d., 'Department of Information, Federation of Malaya', File No. 225/53, ANM.
260 Lloyd Williams, 'Radio Malaya Takes Stock', Jackson Papers, RHO. 'Talks and Features in Various Chinese Dialects Broadcast from February 1st – 7th', n.d., and 'Talks and Feature in Various Chinese Dialects Broadcast from October 18 – October 24th 53', n.d., 'Department of Information, Federation of Malaya', File No. 225/53, ANM.
261 'Requirements of Department of Broadcasting to Improve Broadcasting Information Services', 23 Sep 1952, 'Draft for Memo to Executive Council: Department of Broadcasting', n.d., 'Malaya' Papers, RHO.
262 Watts to Peterson, 24 March 1953, Watts Papers, RHO; Walker to Col. Graham, 12 July 1952, Hugh Stockwell Papers, LHCMA.
263 K.J. Henderson, 'Civics Courses and Community Development', 25 Nov 1953, Heussler Papers, Box 14, RHO; 'H.C's Speech at the Fifth Meeting of the Sixth Session, Legislative Council, 25 Nov 1953', 7410-29-1, NAM.
264 Henderson, 'Civics Courses', Heussler Papers, Box 14, RHO.
265 'H.C's Speech at the Fifth Meeting of the Sixth Session, Legislative Council, 25 Nov 1953', 7410-29-1, NAM.
266 Henderson, 'Civics Courses', Heussler Papers, RHO; *Annual Report 1953*, p. 317.
267 *Annual Report 1953*, p. 317.
268 'DGIS Impressions', n.d., Heussler Papers, Box 14, RHO.
269 *Ibid*.; *Annual Report 1954*, p. 375.
270 Lucien Pye to Adam Watson of the British Embassy, Washington, D.C., 20 Jan 1953, CO 1022/28.
271 Pye, *Guerrilla Communism in Malaya*, pp. 185–186.
272 G.N.H. Morris, SIO Pahang to all Field Officers, 24 July 1953, 'Department of Information, Federation of Malaya', File No. 566/53, ANM.
273 Perry Robinson, *Transformation in Malaya*, p. 67.
274 Sunderland, *Winning the Hearts and Minds of the People*, p. 51.
275 Peterson Report, CO 967/181.
276 Peterson Letter to the *Listener*, 14 Aug 1969.
277 See Morris to Hodge, 24 July 1953; Morris to Assistant Director (Field), Information Services, 3 Aug 1953; Mortlock to DGIS, 7 Aug 1953, Hodge to Mortlock, 11 Aug 1953, Mortlock to Hodge, 17 Aug 1953, 'Department of Information, Federation of Malaya', File No. 566/53, ANM.
278 Peterson Report, CO 967/181.

264 NOTES

279 Too to Deputy Chief Secretary, Federation of Malaya, 26 Jan 1952; A.W.D. James to Chief Secretary (Service Branch), 18 July 1952; G. de G. Sieveking, for Acting Director Museums, Federation of Malaya, to DGIS, 6 Aug 1954, 'Department of Information, Federation of Malaya', File No. 401/53, ANM; Too interview, Tape 2, EEP, RHO.

280 Too interview, Tape 2, EEP, RHO.

281 *Ibid.*; *New Straits Times*, 4 Dec 1989; Correspondence with Professor Richard Stubbs, 27 Dec 1996; Too to DGIS, 29 Nov 1952, 'Department of Information, Federation of Malaya', File No. 401/53, ANM; Too, 'Curriculum Vitae', PP.

282 Too interview, Tape 2, EEP, RHO.

283 F.H. Lakin, 'A Study of Surrender Behaviour among Chinese Communist Terrorists in Malaya', ORS (PW) Memorandum No. 1/53, May 1953, WO 291/1763.

284 Extract from 'Minutes of Federal Executive Council Meeting 20 May 1952', CO 1022/48. The formal name of the Min Yuen was also changed to 'Communist Terrorist Organisation'.

285 *Annual Report 1953*, p. 341. Strategic leaflets put across a general theme while tactical leaflets provided news of specific Security Force successes and MCP losses.

286 Lakin, 'A Study of Surrender Behaviour', WO 291/1763; Lakin, 'A Further Study of Surrender Behaviour', WO 291/1766.

287 Cloake, *Templer, Tiger of Malaya*, p. 238.

288 Lakin, 'A Further Study of Surrender Behaviour', WO 291/1766.

289 *Daily Telegraph*, 27 March 1954; Haynes to Templer, 27 March 1954, 7410-29-5, NAM.

290 SEPs were defined as 'enemy personnel who willingly surrender to the forces of law and order at a time when they could otherwise without difficulty have made good their escape'. CEPs were defined as 'enemy personnel who come into our hands otherwise than an SEP'. Young made it clear that SEPs were the responsibility of Special Branch. See 'Commissioner's Instruction No. 3: The Treatment of Surrendered Enemy Personnel (SEP) and Captured Enemy Personnel (CEP)', n.d., CO 1022/49.

291 Lakin and G.J. Humphrey, 'A Study of Surrenders in Malaya', WO 291/1783. Data from 343 SEPs had been analysed. See also *WINSUM*, No. 92, week ending 7 Feb 1952, CO 1022/14.

292 Lakin, 'A Study of Surrender Behaviour', WO 291/1763.

293 *Ibid.* See also Lakin's 'A Further Study of Surrender Behaviour', WO 291/1766.

294 Inward Telegram No. 593 from High Commissioner Federation of Malaya to Secretary of State for the Colonies, 12 May 1952, CO 1022/49; *Daily Telegraph*, 23 June 1952; *Scotsman*, 7 Jan 1953.

295 See note, 24 Jan 1952, with respect to Information Meeting on 28 Jan 1952, CO 537/7255.

296 Inward Telegram No. 593, 12 May 1952, CO 1022/49. See also *Daily Telegraph*, 30 Jan 1953.

297 Extract of 'Answers to Questions, Federation of Malaya Legislative Council Meeting, 7 May 1952', CO 1022/49.

298 Inward Telegram No. 593, 12 May 1952, CO 1022/49; *Daily Telegraph*, 30 Jan 1953.

299 In July 1952 David Gray, Federal Secretary for Chinese Affairs, had argued that detainees who were found to be unsuitable for rehabilitation at Taiping ought to be given work, encouraged to grow their own food, and to build and repair their own accommodation. They should also be given agricultural training and taught a trade so as to make them think that Government was seeing them as 'unfortunates' rather than 'delinquents'. Gray, 'The Chinese Problem in the Federation of Malaya', Watts

Papers, RHO. On 1 March 1954, Templer opened Kemendore Agricultural Settlement so that SEPs who could not join the SOVF, or were no longer required to assist the Security Forces and not deemed suitable for rehabilitation, could be employed and trained in producing poultry, pigs and vegetables. Once Kemendore SEPs had performed satisfactorily, they were to be released as free men. 'H.E. the High Commissioner's Speech at 5th Meeting of 6th Session, 25 Nov 1953', 7410-29-1, NAM; *Federation of Malaya Annual Report 1956* (London: HMSO, 1957), p. 451.

300 Inward Savingram No. 1687 from High Commissioner Federation of Malaya to Secretary of State for the Colonies, 20 Aug 1952, CO 1022/49; A. Gann to J. Higham, 1 Sep 1952, CO 1022/49; 'Memorandum by Secretary of Defence – Surrender Policy', 12 Aug 1954, CO 1030/22; 'Surrender Policy', Young Papers, Box 1, RHO.

301 Lakin, 'A Study of Surrender Behaviour', WO 291/1763.

302 The public reward of $500 for assisting terrorists in the act of surrender had been introduced earlier in 1953. *Annual Report 1953*, p. 341.

303 P.B. Humphrey, G.J. Humphrey and J. Gunn, 'An Estimate of the Effectiveness of Operation 'Bison' as a means of bringing about Group Surrenders', ORS (PW) Memorandum No. 12/54, 18 Aug 1954, WO 291/1784.

304 *Ibid.*

305 *WINSUM*, No. 189, week ending 17 Dec 1953, CO 1022/19; Inward Telegram No. 645 from High Commissioner Federation of Malaya to Secretary of State for the Colonies, 18 June 1953, CO 1022/49.

306 Inward Savingram No. 1226 from High Commissioner Federation of Malaya to Secretary of State for the Colonies, 20 June 1952, CO 1022/152. Between February and June 1952, a sum of $204,530 was paid out for information leading to the capture or killing of terrorist leaders, and $409,946 in the case of rank and file terrorists.

307 *Times*, 1 May 1952. The rewards offered for District Committee Secretaries and below remained unchanged.

308 Exco Paper No. 2/13/53, 8 January 1953, CO 1022/152; Inward Telegram No. 762 from High Commissioner Federation of Malaya to Secretary of State for the Colonies, 29 Oct 1954, CO 1030/23.

309 'Information Obtained from SEP Interrogations', ORS (PW), Technical Note No. 2/53, n.d., WO 291/1793; P.B. Humphrey, 'Some Further Items of Psychological Warfare Intelligence as obtained from Surrendered Communist Terrorists in Malaya', ORS (PW) Memorandum No. 9/53, 5 Oct 1953, WO 291/1771. Cloake claims that *New Path News* was a black (unattributable) paper, but cites no source to back this up. Cloake, *Templer: Tiger of Malaya*, p. 238. Greene certainly did not identify it as such in his report. If it really was black propaganda to the terrorists, then it certainly was unsuccessful.

310 F.H. Lakin, 'An Investigation into the Value of Ground Loudspeaker Equipment in Anti-Terrorist Operations in Malaya', n.d., ORS (PW) Memorandum No. 7/53, WO 291/1769.

311 In fact the Chiefs of Staff Committee in London had been enthused for some time about the apparent success of American 'psywar' units in Korea, but did not wish to 'slavishly adopt American ideas on this subject'. Lieutenant-General Sir Neville Brownjohn to Vice-Chief Naval Staff and Deputy Chief Air Staff, 12 Sep 1951, WO 216/425.

312 See the telex correspondence in Air Headquarters between 8 September and 1 November 1952, AIR 23/8558. Henniker had experimented with 'voice balloons'. *Red Shadow over Malaya*, pp. 48–49.

313 F.H. Lakin, 'Experiments in the Use of Airborne Loudspeakers: Operation Hailer', ORS(PW) Memorandum No. 2, n.d., AIR 23/8558.
314 Liew had been District Committee Chairman and a ruthless and unscrupulous MRLA company commander in Selangor until his elimination by Security Forces. *Ibid.* See Appendix D.
315 *Ibid.*
316 Mills Report, AIR 23/8696; F.H. Lakin and Mrs A.D.C. Peterson, 'A Further Study of Surrender Behaviour among Chinese Communist Terrorists in Malaya', ORS (PW) Memorandum No. 10/53, n.d., WO 291/1772.
317 *WINSUM*, No. 188, week ending 10 Dec 1953 and *WINSUM*, No. 189, week ending 17 Dec 1953, CO 1022/19.
318 Mrs. A.D.C. Peterson, 'Immediate Interrogation of SEP', n.d., ORS (PW) Memorandum No. 4/53, WO 291/1795. See also her Memorandum No. 7/53, WO 291/1798.
319 F.H. Lakin, 'A Voice Aircraft Trial carried out on 11 Sep 1953 in Malaya', ORS (PW) Memorandum No. 6/53, n.d., WO 291/1768; ORS (PW) Technical Note No. 3/53, n.d., WO 291/1794. See also 'Some Observations on Voice Aircraft', ORS (PW) Memorandum No. 5/53, 28 Aug 1953, WO 291/1796.
320 Captain J.O. Williams, 'A Report on Voice Aircraft Trials carried out on 15 January 1954 using a Dakota Aircraft', 30 Jan 1954, ORS (PW) Memorandum No. 3/54, WO 291/1776; Malcolm Postgate, *Operation Firedog: Air Support in the Malayan Emergency,1948–1960* (London: HMSO, 1992), p. 115.
321 Postgate, *Operation Firedog*, p. 115.
322 Captain J.O. Williams, 'An Auster Voice Aircraft Trial carried out on 4 Jan 1954 in Malaya', ORS (PW) Memorandum No. 2/54, 22 Jan 1954, WO 291/1775.
323 Scherger, 'Employment of the RAF in the Emergency', AIR 23/8619; Postgate, *Operation Firedog*, p. 115.
324 *Annual Report 1954*, p. 403.

CHAPTER SIX

1 Director of Operations, 'Review of the Emergency Situation in Malaya at the end of 1954', 10 Jan 1955, CO 1030/10. Hereafter *DOR 1954*.
2 Inward Telegram No. 717 from High Commissioner Federation of Malaya to Secretary of State for the Colonies, 6 Oct 1954, CO 1030/20.
3 See 'Federation of Malaya: the Chinese Schools': despatch no. 232 from Sir D. MacGillivray to Mr Lennox-Boyd, 2 March 1955, CO 1030/51, No. 69, in *BDEEP, Series B, Vol. 3, Malaya, Part III: The Alliance Route to Independence, 1953–1957*, ed. by A.J. Stockwell (London: HMSO, 1995), Doc. 345. 'Department of Information Weekly News Summary', week ending 19 Feb 1955. Hereafter *WNS*.
4 *DOR 1954*, CO 1030/10.
5 Interview with J.L.M. Gorrie.
6 Lloyd-Owen to Hankins, 15 April 1969, 8011-132, NAM.
7 While Tunku's Alliance Party had wanted Federal elections in November 1954 for 60 elected seats or a three-fifths elected majority to the Legislative Council, incoming High Commissioner MacGillivray had quietly agreed with the Rulers that elections would be held in 1955 and a bare majority of 52 out of 99 seats would be elected. Incensed, Tunku had tried to reverse this decision by flying to London in April 1954 to meet Lyttelton, but was unsuccessful, whereupon he returned to Malaya and launched a nation-wide boycott of the Federal elections and public service. At this 'unpropitious moment' MacGillivray assumed power. Fortunately, on 2 July aboard HMS *Alert*, MacGillivray and Tunku agreed that after the elections, the former would

consult with the leader of the party with the most elected seats on the new Council before filling the nominated seats. 'Introduction', in Stockwell, ed., *BDEEP, Series B, Vol. 3, Malaya, Part I: The Malayan Union Experiment* (London: HMSO, 1995), p. lxxiii. See also [Federal Elections]: telegram from Tunku Abdul Rahman and Tan Cheng Lock to Mr Lyttelton protesting against the recommendations and requesting a meeting in London with the secretary of state, CO 1030/309, no 23, 1 April 1954, in *BDEEP, Malaya: The Alliance Route to Independence,* Doc. 313. Also Tunku Abdul Rahman Putra Al-Haj, *Looking Back: Monday Musings and Memories* (Kuala Lumpur: Pustaka Antara, 1977), pp. 29–30.

8 For accounts of MacGillivray's activities in Senai New Village in Johore and Kampong Lalang New Village in Kedah, see *WNS*, week ending 12 March 1955; *WNS*, week ending 21 May 1955.

9 Lloyd-Owen to Hankins, 15 April 1969, 8011-132, NAM.

10 Corry interview, RHO.

11 For example, in June 1955 MacGillivray addressed the Malayan Planting Industries Employers Association in Kuala Lumpur. *WNS*, week ending 11 June 1955.

12 *Annual Report 1954*, p. 401. Lieutenant-General Hugh Stockwell relinquished his GOC Malaya appointment in April 1954. *Malaya*, Jan 1954, p. 26.

13 Between 1943 and 1946 Bourne had served in numerous capacities: as commanding officer of the 21st Anti-Tank Regiment of the Guards Armoured Division; on the staff of the Supreme Allied Commander Southeast Asia; as commanding officer 152 Field Regiment in Italy; on the staff of the 1st Airborne Corps, and then the 5th Indian Division in Java. Between September 1947 and December 1948 moreover he headed the British Services Mission to Burma and was promoted Maj-General. Between January 1949 and November 1951 he was GOC British Troops, Berlin, and then the commanding officer 16th Airborne Division (Territorial Army). During his Berlin appointment Bourne had met and subsequently maintained contact with his American counterpart General Maxwell Taylor. Taylor visited Malaya in March 1955. See *Malaya*, Jan 1954, p. 26; *WNS*, week ending 12 March 1955.

14 Loch, 'My First Alphabet', pp. 124–125.

15 *WNS*, weeks ending 12 February and 12 March 1955.

16 *WNS*, weeks ending 8 Jan 1955, 22 Jan 1955 and 12 Feb 1955.

17 *DOR* 1954, CO 1030/10.

18 Loch reports that Bourne had lost his arm bob-sleighing as a young man. Loch, 'My First Alphabet', pp. 124–125. It must be noted that other sources claim that Bourne lost the arm as a young officer. *WNS*, week ending 14 May 1955.

19 *WNS*, weeks ending 21 May 1955 and 9 July 1955.

20 The Alliance won 51 out of the 52 available seats in the newly reconstituted Federal legislature, winning 818,013 out of the 1,027,211 votes cast. Tunku, *Looking Back*, pp. 49–50.

21 See 'Malaya': Cabinet conclusions on agreement reached at the constitutional conference, 8 Feb 1956, CAB 128/30/1, CM 9 (56) 7; 'Federation of Malaya': Cabinet memorandum by Mr Lennox-Boyd on the constitutional conference, 21 Feb 1956, CAB 129/79, CP (56) 47, Annex C, in Stockwell, ed., *BDEEP, Malaya: The Alliance Route to Independence* Docs. 404–405.

22 'Broadcast by High Commissioner', 20 Oct 1954, and Inward Telegram No. 717 from High Commissioner Federation of Malaya to Secretary of State for the Colonies, 6 Oct 1954, CO 1030/20. *Times*, 11 Aug 1955. Until the Federal elections at the end of July 1955, Dato Onn bin Jaafar and V.M.N. Menon had been on the Director of Operations Committee. They were replaced by Razak and Sambanthan following the Alliance victory.

23 *WNS*, week ending 3 March 1956; *DOR* 1956, CO 1030/10.

24 *DOR* 1954, CO 1030/10.
25 [Emergency operations]: letter from Sir D MacGillivray to E Melville on the continuing role of British troops after independence, 28 July 1956, DEFE 7/501, No. 15, in Stockwell, ed., *BDEEP, Malaya: The Alliance Route to Independence,* Doc. 422.
26 *Ibid.* Also [The role of British troops in Malaya]: letter from Sir D MacGillivray to Sir J Martin on their role in the periods before and after independence, 7 May 1956, DEFE 7/501, No. 4, in *BDEEP, Malaya: The Alliance Route to Independence,* Doc. 413. See also Minute by John Hennings of the Colonial Office, 25 March 1957, CO 1030/10.
27 'Federation of Malaya': Cabinet memorandum by Mr Lennox-Boyd on the constitutional conference, Annex C, 21 Feb 1956, in Stockwell, ed., *BDEEP, Malaya: The Alliance Route to Independence,* Doc. 405.
28 Bower had been Director of Military Training in Germany, and had also served in Palestine and Greece. Bourne was appointed Commander-in-Chief Middle East Land Forces in October. *WNS*, weeks ending 21 April 1956 and 19 May 1956; *Straits Budget,* 17 May 1956.
29 Templer had begun recruiting local Malayans for a multiracial Federation Regiment as part of his commitment to building a multiracial Malaya, in August 1952. The GOC was Maj-General F.H. Brooke, who had been a former Deputy Director of Military Training at the War Office and had commanded the 1st Malay Infantry Brigade in 1953–54. *Malaya,* Aug 1956, p. 47; *Straits Budget,* 21 Aug 1952.
30 'Use of Commonwealth forces on emergency operations in the Federation of Malaya after independence': joint note by the CO and the Ministry of Defence for the Chief of Staff Committee, 14 Dec 1956, DEFE 7/501, COS (56) 437, in Stockwell, ed., *BDEEP, Malaya: The Alliance Route to Independence,* Doc. 437. See *Federation of Malaya Annual Report 1957* (Kuala Lumpur: Government Printer 1958), p. 469; *Straits Budget,* 18 July 1957, 18 Sep 1957 and 25 Sep 1957. Cassells' immediately prior appointment had been Director-General of Military Training at the War Office, a post he had held since 1954. Prior to this he had been commander of the 51st Highland Division in 1945, the 6th Airborne Division in Palestine in 1946, the 1st Corps in Germany and the 1st British Commonwealth Division in Korea (1951–52). He had also been the Director of Land-Air Warfare between 1948 and 1949.
31 Harry Miller, *Prince and Premier: A Biography of Tunku Abdul Rahman Putra Al-haj, First Prime Minister of the Federation of Malaya* (London: George G. Harrap, 1959), pp. 106–109; Khong Kim Hoong, *Merdeka! British Rule and the Struggle for Independence in Malaya 1945–57* (Kuala Lumpur: Institute for Social Analysis, 1984), p. 170; Lapping, *End of Empire,* p. 230.
32 'Introduction', in Stockwell, ed., *BDEEP, Malaya: The Malayan Union Experiment,* p. lxxi. On 16 October 1954, the UMNO General Assembly approved the creation of an Alliance Supreme Council to plan for elections and chart out the Alliance electoral platform. 15 representatives each from UMNO and the MCA sat on the Council. Frank Brewer, 'Political Parties in Malaya, 1954', n.d., Brewer Papers, Box 1, RHO.
33 Lapping, *End of Empire,* pp. 231–233.
34 W.C.S. Corry, *Malaya Today* (London: Longmans, Green and Co., 1955), pp. 37–38.
35 MacDonald later argued that Dato Onn was the real father of the Malayan nation, who through persuasion and leadership first introduced to the Malay elites the idea of political accommodation with the non-Malays. He added that Onn's big mistake was his timing in launching the Independence of Malaya Party (IMP), as the Malay elites were not ready for political integration with the non-Malays in a non-communal party. With the IMP's defeat as early as the February 1952 Kuala Lumpur municipal

elections, Onn became marginalised. Onn's political demise became complete when he formed Party Negara in 1954, whose Malay communal line was rejected by voters in the July 1955 Federal election. MacDonald interview, 15 Dec 1972, also John Gullick to Heussler, 14 Sep 1982, Heussler Papers, Box 13, RHO. Also Brewer, 'Political Parties in Malaya, 1954', n.d., Brewer Papers, Box 1, RHO.

36 Corry, *Malaya Today*, p. 38.
37 MacDonald interview, 18 Dec 1972, RHO.
38 Lyttelton interview, RHO.
39 Miller, *Prince and Premier*, pp. 41–42; Lapping, *End of Empire*, p. 230.
40 Miller, *Prince and Premier*, p. 93.
41 This observer was Ivan Lloyd Phillips, who had served as Secretary to the Member for Home Affairs, and then as Secretary to the Chief Minister when Home Affairs was subsumed under his portfolio. Letters from Ivan Lloyd Phillips to the Rev. A. Lloyd Phillips, 22 Sep 1957 and 13 Oct 1957, MSS.Brit.Emp.s.499, RHO.
42 Miller, *Prince and Premier*, p. 180.
43 John Gullick to Heussler, 10 Oct 1981, Heussler Papers, Box 13, RHO; 'Malayanisation of the public service in the Federation of Malaya': CO brief for Mr Lennox-Boyd [July 1955], CO 1030/230, No. 11, in Stockwell, ed., *BDEEP, Malaya: The Alliance Route to Independence*, Doc. 354. See also Anthony Kirk-Greene, *On Crown Service: A History of HM Colonial and Overseas Civil Services, 1837–1997* (London: I.B. Tauris, 1999), Chapter Four.
44 Gullick to Heussler, 10 Oct 1981, Heussler Papers, Box 13, and Gullick, 'My Time in Malaya', June 1970, p. 56, Heussler Papers, Box 13, RHO.
45 The Committee on Malayanisation consisted of Tunku, Alliance Ministers Razak, Col. H.S. Lee, V.T. Sambanthan, and Abdul Aziz, Chief Secretary David Watherston and the Federal Establishment Officer, Mr Gracie. The Committee met once a week between September 1955 and September 1956. Gullick, 'My Time in Malaya', pp. 57–59.
46 The 'Report on the Malayanisation of Public Service' was written in 1956 by Gullick himself. Gullick to Heussler, 10 Oct 1981, Heussler Papers, Box 13, RHO.
47 *WNS*, week ending 10 Nov 1956.
48 *DOR 56*, CO 1030/10. Expatriate abolition terms involved a formula of three, five or seven years of guaranteed post-independence service. The Alliance Government was not prepared to offer these terms to every expatriate because there were some it had blacklisted. Gullick, 'My Time in Malaya', p. 59; Letter to Heussler, 10 Oct 1981, Heussler Papers, Box 13, RHO.
49 The Baling Talks will be discussed later in this chapter.
50 Gullick, 'My Time in Malaya', p. 57; J.C.S. Mackie to Heussler, 12 Sep 1979, Heussler Papers, Box 16, RHO.
51 *WNS*, week ending 24 March 1956.
52 *WNS*, week ending 14 April 1956. In July 1957, in Bahau, Negri Sembilan, moreover, Tunku personally congratulated Lieutenant Low Lai Fook and his men of the 1st Battalion Federation Regiment for eliminating two terrorists. *Straits Budget*, 25 July 1957.
53 Sheppard interview, EEP, RHO.
54 Ivan Lloyd Phillips to Heussler, 17 Feb 1980, Heussler Papers, Box 15, RHO.
55 Gullick to Heussler, 10 Oct 1981, Heussler Papers, Box 13, RHO.
56 *Straits Budget*, 11 Sep 1957. By *Merdeka*, 232 Federal Police officers were eligible for departure under Malayanisation terms. The corresponding figures for Public Works, for instance was 129 and for the Medical Department, 107.
57 MacDonald interview, 18 Dec 1972, RHO.
58 Miller, *Prince and Premier*, p. 47.

59 *Ibid.*, pp. 56, 63.
60 Gullick to Heussler, 10 Oct 1981, Heussler Papers, Box 13, RHO.
61 Correspondence with Gullick, 3 July 1997.
62 Corry interview, RHO.
63 Lapping, *End of Empire*, p. 233.
64 *WNS*, week ending 10 March 1956.
65 *WNS*, week ending 7 July 1956.
66 Bower Report, WO 106/5990.
67 Cited in Miller, *Prince and Premier*, pp. 173–174.
68 Lloyd Phillips to Heussler, 17 Feb 1980, Heussler Papers, Box 15, RHO.
69 W.C.S. Corry, *A General Survey of the New Villages* (Kuala Lumpur: Government Printer, 1954), p. 16.
70 Sandhu, 'Emergency Resettlement in Malaya', pp. 164–165.
71 Corry, *General Survey of New Villages*, p. 22.
72 Stubbs, *Hearts and Minds in Guerrilla Warfare*, pp. 232.–233.
73 Humphrey, 'Population Resettlement', pp. 229–230; 251–253.
74 Stubbs, *Hearts and Minds in Guerrilla Warfare*, p. 234.
75 C.H.F. Blake, 'Notes on New Villages in Batang Padang District', 1954, Blake Papers, MSS.Ind.Ocn.s.276, RHO.
76 Stubbs, *Hearts and Minds in Guerrilla Warfare*, pp. 234–235; Loh, *Beyond the Tin Mines*, pp. 146–149; Harper, 'The Colonial Inheritance', pp. 214–215.
77 *WNS*, week ending 12 March 1955.
78 Strauch, *Chinese Village Politics*, p. 71; Loh, *Beyond the Tin Mines*, p. 223.
79 Corry, *General Survey of New Villages*, pp. 38–40.
80 See for instance *WNS*, week ending 4 June 1955. See also Inspector-General E.B. de Fonblanque's assessment of the Malay Home Guards in *WNS*, week ending 30 June 1956.
81 Brewer, 'The Malayan Emergency', Heussler Papers, Box 9, RHO.
82 Home Guard training had to pass through three broad phases: in Phase I, New Villagers were gradually introduced to the idea of helping with village defence by the Police, and arms were not issued initially. Gradually as Home Guard units were formed however, the Police started training the villagers in the use of shotguns. In Phase II, the nascent Home Guard patrolled the New Village with the Police and carried weapons. In Phase III, the Police withdrew and the Home Guard kept its weapons and assumed responsibility for village defence. Brewer, 'The Malayan Emergency', in Heussler Papers, Box 9, RHO.
83 *WNS*, week ending 5 March 1955.
84 Director of Operations, 'Review of the Emergency Situation in Malaya at the end of 1955', January 1956, CO 1030/10. Hereafter *DOR 1955*.
85 *Ibid.*
86 *WNS*, week ending 30 June 1956; *DOR 1956*, CO 1030/10; Short, *Communist Insurrection in Malaya*, p. 415.
87 *WNS*, week ending 20 Oct 1956.
88 *DOR 1956*, CO 1030/10. The Home Guard as a whole was reduced in strength from 152,000 in 1955 to 68,000 in 1958 with the improvement in the overall security situation. *Straits Budget*, 2 Oct 1957.
89 C.B. Ormerod to Colonel A.E. Young, 16 June 1953, Young Papers, Box 3, RHO.
90 Brewer to all State Secretaries of Chinese Affairs, 21 Feb 1955, Watts Papers, RHO.
91 Watts to Secretary of Chinese Affairs, Federation of Malaya, 7 Feb 1952, Watts Papers, RHO.
92 Watts to A.D.C. Peterson, 24 March 1953, Watts Papers, RHO.

93 Broome, 'Notes on the Proposed History of the MCS', 12 March 1970, Heussler Papers, Box 10, RHO.
94 Extract from 'Malaya Savingram No. 775, 17 April 1952'; Federal Government Press Statement, 23 April 1952, CO 1022/35.
95 Watts to Secretary of Chinese Affairs, Federation of Malaya, 7 Feb 1952, Watts Papers, RHO.
96 The teams also ministered to 132,000 Malays and 13,000 Tamils. *WNS*, week ending 5 March 1955.
97 Watts, 'An Appreciation of the Present Political Endeavour and Organisation Among the Chinese in the Federation', February 1956, Watts Papers, RHO.
98 A.W.D. James, Acting Federal SCA to Federation Establishment Officer, 14 June 1955, 'Department of Chinese Affairs', File no. 1635. Also 'Duties and Functions of Assistant Chinese Affairs Officers in Districts', 11 Oct 1955; C.G. Ferguson, DO Upper Perak to Federal SCA, 9 Sep 1955; A.W.D. James, Federal SCA to C.G. Ferguson, 30 Sep 1955, 'Department of Chinese Affairs', File no. 1603/12; V.I. Galletly, Acting Federal SCA to Federation Establishment Officer, 3 May 1956, enclosure on 'Duties and Functions of CAOs in Districts', 'Department of Chinese Affairs', File no. 1603/13, ANM.
99 Tan Tuan Boon, President, Chinese Affairs Officers Service Association to SCA Federation of Malaya, 6 Jan 1955, 'Department of Chinese Affairs', File no. 1635, ANM.
100 Brewer, 'Malaya: Administration of Chinese Affairs', Heussler Papers, Box 9; 'Handing Over Notes', 3 April 1962, Phillips Papers, RHO; N.L. Alexander to Federal SCA, 14 March 1956; W.I. Galletly, SCA Johore to Federal SCA, 17 July 1956, 'Department of Chinese Affairs,' File no. 1709. See also H.R.M. Storey for Federal SCA to Secretary, Public Service Commission (Designate), 15 Aug 1957; B.L. Drake for Principal Establishment Officer to Secretary, Public Service Commission, 23 Nov 1957, 'Department of Chinese Affairs', File no. 1603/13, ANM.
101 W.I. Galletly, SCA Johore, to Federal SCA, 9 March 1957, 'Department of Chinese Affairs', File no. 1438, Part II, ANM.
102 Humphrey, 'Population Resettlement', pp. 236–237; 275–276.
103 Muller to High Commissioner Federation of Malaya, 5 July 1955, CO 1030/168.
104 The number of European Police officers fell from 425 in 1955 to 376 in 1956, while the number of Asian officers rose from 143 to 191 in the same period. Meanwhile the contracts of European Police Lieutenants were allowed to lapse without renewal. Hence 95 contracts expired in 1957 and 239 in 1958. *DOR* 1956, CO 1030/10.
105 *Federation of Malaya Annual Report 1955* (Kuala Lumpur: Government Press, 1956), p. 293.
106 *Annual Report 1957*, p. 316.
107 See 'Ceremonial Parade for His Majesty *Yang Di-Pertuan Agong* to Confer Title "Royal" on the Federation of Malaya Police', 24 July 1958, Brewer Papers, Box 3, RHO.
108 *Annual Report 1955*, p. 293.
109 'Ceremonial Parade', Brewer Papers, Box 3, RHO.
110 Muller to High Commissioner Federation of Malaya, 5 July 1955, CO 1030/168. J.S. Bennett of the Colonial Office fretted that Muller had painted a picture of an 'over-militarised' Force. See *DOR* 1956, CO 1030/10; Stockwell, 'Policing during the Malayan Emergency', in Anderson and Killingray, eds., *Policing and Decolonisation*, p. 119.
111 Muller to High Commissioner Federation of Malaya, 5 July 1955, CO 1030/168.

112 *Ibid.*
113 Officer Administering the Government to Secretary of State for the Colonies, 16 Jan 1956, CO 1030/168.
114 *Annual Report 1957*, p. 318.
115 See MacGillivray's Christmas message to the Malayan Police. *WNS*, week ending 22 Dec 1956. See also Resident Commissioner H.G. Hammett's message to police officers on a Civics Course in Malacca. *Straits Budget*, 30 May 1957.
116 Muller to High Commissioner Federation of Malaya, 5 July 1955, CO 1030/168; Stockwell, 'Policing during the Malayan Emergency', in Anderson and Killingray, eds., *Policing and Decolonisation*, p. 118.
117 *Annual Report 1957*, p. 317.
118 Frank Brewer to Chief Secretary, Service Branch, Federation of Malaya, 4 June 1954, 'Department of Chinese Affairs', File no. 1200/94, ANM.
119 See Margaret Symes, Government Officers' Language School to Acting SCA, Federation of Malaya, 4 June 1954, 'Department of Chinese Affairs', File no. 1200/94, ANM.
120 *Ibid.*
121 Robert Bruce, 'A Note on the Usefulness of Chinese to Non-Chinese Members of the Public Service', n.d., in 'Department of Chinese Affairs', File no. 1200/94, ANM.
122 *WNS*, week ending 24 Dec 1955.
123 'Johore SWEC General Operational Instruction No. 13: The Employment of British Troops in Villages', 19 May 1955, Talbot Papers, LHCMA.
124 Richard Miers, 'Miers on Malaya', *Counterinsurgency Case History: Malaya, 1948–60* (Fort Leavenworth, Kansas: US Army Command and General Staff College, 1965), p. 59.
125 Loy, *Against All Odds,* pp. 62–63.
126 *Report on the Conduct of Food Searches at Semenyih in the Kajang District of the State of Selangor* (Kuala Lumpur: Government Printer, 1956), p. 4. Copy in CO 1030/33.
127 *Ibid.*, p. 6.
128 *Ibid.*, pp. 8–9.
129 Ominously, 'Kachau' or 'kacau' in Malay means to annoy or to harass!
130 *Report on the Conduct of Food Searches at Semenyih*, pp. 9–13.
131 *Ibid.*, pp. 15–21.
132 *Ibid.*, p. 22. Short, *Communist Insurrection in Malaya*, p. 410.
133 *Report on the Conduct of Food Searches at Semenyih*, p. 13; 'Government Press Statement', May 1956, CO 1030/33; *WNS*, weeks ending 14 Jan 1956 and 12 May 1956.
134 *Straits Budget*, 17 May 1956.
135 Watts to Peterson, 24 March 1953, Watts Papers, RHO.
136 *Annual Report 1955*, p. 435.
137 *Federation of Malaya Annual Report 1956* (London: HMSO, 1957), p. 451. From the beginning of the Emergency till September 1957, 33,992 detention orders had been issued. Bower Report, WO 106/5990.
138 *Annual Report 1956*, p. 451.
139 *WNS*, week ending 31 December 1955; Bower Report, WO 106/5990.
140 *Annual Report 1955*, p. 435.
141 *Annual Report 1956*, p. 451.
142 *Straits Budget*, 22 Aug 1957. From the beginning of the Emergency till September 1957, a total of 12 190 persons had been deported and another 2 717 repatriated at their own request. Bower Report, WO 106/5990.
143 Melshen, 'Pseudo Operations', pp. 67–68.

144 *WNS*, weeks ending 26 March 1955 and 16 April 1955.

145 *WNS*, week ending 1 Dec 1956.

146 *Ibid.* For instance the CEPS asked the Perak SWEC to study the Tartan Rock model. 'Minutes of the 237th Formal Meeting of the Operations Sub-Committee of Perak SWEC, held in the Combined Operations Room, Ipoh, on Tuesday, 30th July 1957, at 10.00 a.m.', Blake Papers, RHO.

147 Federal Government Press Statement, 7 July 1954, CO 1030/1.

148 Federal Government Press Statement, 27 April 1956, CO 1030/1.

149 AVM V.E. Hancock, 'Ninth Report of the Royal Air Force Operations in Malaya: 1 Jan 1957 to 31 Dec 1957', n.d., AIR 23/8697. Hereafter Hancock Report 1957.

150 *Straits Budget*, 9 May 1957.

151 'Notes on Psychological Warfare', 21 May 1955, Talbot Papers, LHCMA. See also *WNS*, week ending 25 June 1955.

152 'Paper by the Combined Intelligence Staff: White Areas', 2 June 1955. It was considered by the Executive Council on 7 June. CO 1030/1.

153 *Ibid.*

154 Extract from 'Minutes of Exco Meeting, 5 July 1955', CO 1030/1; *DOR* 1956, CO 1030/10; *WNS*, week ending 19 May 1956.

155 *WNS*, week ending 19 Feb 1955, 9 June 1956. See also Sheppard, 'Rice-less Reds', *Malaya*, (Jan 1957), pp. 25–27; *idem, Taman Budiman*, pp. 202–203, 212. Sheppard interview, EEP, RHO.

156 *DOR* 1956; Sheppard interview, EEP, RHO. See also Sheppard, 'Rice-less Reds', pp. 25–27.

157 Sheppard, *Taman Budiman*, p. 203; *idem*, 'Rice-less Reds', pp. 25–27.

158 Sheppard, *Taman Budiman*, pp. 218–221.

159 *DOR* 1956, CO 1030/10.

160 Alabaster, 'Note on the Notebook', Adrian G.A. Alabaster Papers, MSS.Ind.Ocn.r.19, RHO. Alabaster was Executive Secretary of Perak SWEC between October 1957 and June 1958. He was also a Chinese Affairs officer.

161 *Ibid.* See also 'Minutes of the 237th Formal Meeting of the Operations Sub-Committee of Perak SWEC, held in the Combined Operations Room, Ipoh, on Tuesday, 30th July 1957, at 10.00 a.m.', and 'Minutes of the 264th Meeting of Perak SWEC, held in the Combined Ops Room, Ipoh, on Tuesday, 20th Aug 1957, at 10.00 a.m.', Blake Papers, RHO.

162 *DOR* 1954, CO 1030/10.

163 *Ibid.* See also 'HQ 18 Infantry Brigade Operational Instruction No.4: Conduct of 'Domination' Operation (New Tactical Concept)', 2 Oct 1954, Talbot Papers, LHCMA.

164 *DOR* 1955, CO 1030/10; *WNS* week ending 14 Jan 1956.

165 *DOR* 1956, CO 1030/10; Hancock Report 1957, AIR 23/8697.

166 Federation Army headquarters had by this time assumed operational responsibility for all indigenous Army units: the seven Malay Regiment battalions, the single battalion of the Federation Regiment, the Federation Armoured Car squadron, the Federal Military College and the Malay Regiment Depot. The core of the Federation Army were the 1st and 2nd Federal Infantry Brigades consisting of 9000 officers and men. See *DOR* 1956, CO 1030/10. Also AVM V.E. Hancock, 'Tenth Report on the Royal Air Force Operations in Malaya, 1 January to 31 December 1958', n.d., AIR 23/8698. Hereafter Hancock Report 1958; Hancock Report 1957, AIR 23/8697. *Annual Report 1957*, p. 4; *Straits Budget*, 6 June 1957; *WNS*, week ending 11 Aug 1956.

167 Sheppard interview, EEP, RHO; Sheppard, 'Rice-less Reds', pp. 25–27.

168 *WNS*, week ending 7 May 1955.

169 *WNS*, week ending 15 January 1955.

170 Sheppard interview, EEP, RHO; C.H.F. Blake to Robert Heussler, 16 May 1982, Heussler Papers, Box 9, RHO.

171 Group discussion with Chin Peng, 18 June 1998.

172 F.H. Lakin, 'A Review of Recent Trends in Surrender Behaviour', ORS (PW) Memorandum No. 6/55, 17 March 1955, WO 291/1792. See also Lakin and Mrs. G.J. Humphrey, 'A Study of Surrenders', WO 291/1783; Major Wynford, 'Review of Surrender Behaviour from 1951 to February 1955, with particular reference to the period July 1954 to February 1955', 4 May 1955, CO 1030/22.

173 D.F. Bayly Pike, 'Surrender Rate', Operations Unit Far East, Technical Note No. 3/55, 1 Nov 1955, WO 291/1718; F.H. Lakin and G.J. Humphrey, 'A Study of Surrenders Amongst Communist Terrorists in Malaya, June to November 1954', ORS (PW) Memorandum No. 15/54, 18 Nov 1954, WO 291/1786.

174 Bayly Pike, 'Interrogation of 112 Surrendered Terrorists', WO 291/1699.

175 *WNS*, weeks ending 19 Feb 1955, 26 Feb 1955 and 30 April 1955.

176 Bayly Pike, 'Interrogation of 112 Surrendered Terrorists', WO 291/1699.

177 *Ibid*. A view captured succinctly by Ming Lee, the Communist leader and arch villain of Richard Miers' excellent memoir *Shoot to Kill*, who when asked why he had suddenly surrendered, simply replied that the British were winning. Miers, *Shoot to Kill* (London: Faber and Faber, 1959), pp. 208–209.

178 F.H. Lakin, 'Some Effects of International Affairs on Communist Terrorists in Malaya', ORS (PW) Memorandum No. 17/54, 7 Dec 1954, WO 291/1788. See also 'Introduction', in Stockwell, ed., *BDEEP, Malaya: The Malayan Union Experiment*, p. lxxiii.

179 *DOR 1956*, CO 1030/10.

180 Director-General Information Services.

181 'Re-organisation of Headquarters', 25 June 1954, 'Department of Information, Trengganu', File No. 102/52, ANM. The 'General' suffix was dropped. Similarly, the Deputy DGIS was now referred to as Deputy DIS.

182 *Straits Budget*, 9 May 1957.

183 Federal Government Press Statement, 4 Feb 1953, 'Department of Information, Trengganu', File No. 102/52, ANM. Correspondence with Gullick, 3 July 1997. Perry Robinson considered Yaacob 'one of the most able and imposing Malays in the country'. *Transformation in Malaya*, p. 64.

184 For instance, see *WNS*, weeks ending 4 Feb 1956, 7 July 1956, 22 Sep 1956. See also *Straits Budget*, 9 May 1957. *WNS*, weeks ending 26 March 1955, 2 April 1955.

185 C.H.W. Goult (Production), Soon Cheng Hor (Administration) and Syed Zainal Abidin (Field).

186 'Re-organisation of Headquarters', 'Department of Information, Trengganu', File No. 102/52, ANM.

187 *Annual Report 1954*, p. 402.

188 'Annual Report 1954: Information Services', 'Department of Information, Trengganu', File No. S.I.O. TR 70/55, ANM.

189 The work of the VAC will be discussed below.

190 'Re-organisation of Headquarters', 'Department of Information, Trengganu', File No. 102/52, ANM.

191 'Annual Report 1954: Information Services', 'Department of Information, Trengganu', File No. S.I.O. TR 70/55, ANM.

192 *Ibid*.

193 *Annual Report 1957*, pp. 426–427.

194 *Annual Report 1955*, pp. 394–395; *Annual Report 1956*, p. 403.

195 *WNS*, week ending 2 July 1955; *Annual Report 1956*, p. 403.

196 'Annual Report 1954: Information Services', 'Department of Information, Trengganu', File No. S.I.O. TR 70/55, ANM; *Annual Report 1957*, pp. 426–427.
197 *Annual Report 1957*, p. 427.
198 Dense undergrowth associated with secondary jungle.
199 *WNS*, week ending 30 April 1955.
200 'Annual Report 1954: Information Services', 'Department of Information, Trengganu', File No. S.I.O. TR 70/55, ANM; *Annual Report 1957*, pp. 431–432.
201 *Annual Report 1954*, p. 378; *Annual Report 1955*, p. 393; *Annual Report 1957*, p. 431.
202 *Annual Report 1957*, p. 431.
203 *Annual Report 1955*, p. 395; *Annual Report 1956*, p. 401.
204 In larger States, the AIO acted as the link between the SIO and the FOs in several Districts. The *Conduct of Anti-Terrorist Operations in Malaya*, 3rd edn. (Kuala Lumpur: Government Printer, 1958), Chapter III, p. 17.
205 'Weekly Report by CFO Kemaman', week ending 8 Oct 1958 in 'Department of Information, Trengganu', File No. TR 268, ANM.
206 Ahmad bin Zain, 'Report on Refresher Courses for AIOs and FOs held at Seginting, Port Dickson, from November 3 1958 to March 7, 1959', 12 Oct 1959, 'Department of Information, Trengganu', File No. 37/53, ANM. Hereafter Nordin Report.
207 *Ibid.*
208 *Ibid.*; F.W. Bustin to All SIOs and Deputy SIO, Perlis, 29 Sep 1958, in 'Department of Information, Trengganu', File No. 37/53, ANM.
209 Nordin Report, 'Department of Information, Trengganu', File No. 37/53, ANM.
210 *WNS*, week ending 19 Feb 1955.
211 *WNS*, week ending 1 Dec 1956.
212 *Annual Report 1956*, p. 404; *Annual Report 1957*, p. 433.
213 *Annual Report 1956*, p. 404.
214 'Returns of Attendance of P/A and Cinema Shows for October 1955', enclosed as part of SIO Trengganu to DIS, 7 Nov 1955, 'Department of Information, Trengganu', File No. S.I.O. TR 11, ANM.
215 Peterson, letter to the *Listener*, 14 Aug 1969.
216 Nordin Report, 'Department of Information, Trengganu', File No. 37/53, ANM.
217 *WNS*, week ending 30 June 1956.
218 *Straits Budget*, 13 June 1957.
219 In 1955, Ow had won a scholarship to Britain where he had spent five months working with documentary film makers. *Annual Report 1955*, p. 400.
220 *Straits Budget*, 13 June 1957. It was agreed that Information Services headquarters would look after MFU financial and establishment matters as well as keep an eye on 'general policy'.
221 Yaacob Latiff to Secretary to the Minister for Interior and Justice, 19 Sep 1957, 'Department of Information, Federation of Malaya', File No. 1333/53, Pt. 1, ANM.
222 Ow Kheng Law, 'Memorandum Dealing with the Special Urgent Need for New Buildings by the MFU', 10 Sep 1958, 'Department of Information, Federation of Malaya', File No. 1333/53, Pt. 1, ANM.
223 It would take up too much space to chart in detail the tortuous route the MFU had to traverse from Jalan Bungsar to Jalan Utara. See, for instance, Ow Kheng Law, 'Development Estimates 1961', n.d.; W.F.G. Pentadbir le Bailly to Head MFU, 16 July 1959; Ow to Secretary to the Treasury, 2 May 1961; Ow to Secretary, Ministry of Interior and Justice, 9 July 1959; W.J. Watts, Deputy Secretary, Ministry of the Interior to the Honourable State Secretary, Selangor, 13 July 1959, 'Department of Information, Federation of Malaya', File No. 1333/53, Pt. 1, ANM.

224 *Annual Report 1956*, p. 406, *Annual Report 1957*, p. 434.
225 *Annual Report 1955*, p. 401; *Annual Report 1956*, p. 408; *Annual Report 1957*, p. 438.
226 District Officer, Klang to SIO Selangor, 15 Sep 1958, 'Department of Information, Kuala Lumpur, 1946–1963', File No. 123/555, ANM.
227 *Straits Budget*, 30 May 1957.
228 *Straits Times*, 6 Nov 1958; *Straits Budget*, 18 Dec 1957.
229 *Straits Budget*, 30 May 1957, 20 June 1957.
230 *Straits Times*, 6 Nov 1958.
231 'Text of Broadcast by Acting Deputy Prime Minister Dato Abdul Razak bin Hussein', 4 Jan 1959, DIS 30/59, National Archives of Singapore (hereafter NAS).
232 *Ibid. Straits Times*, 26 Nov 1958.
233 *Straits Budget*, 29 Aug 1957; *Straits Times*, 25 Nov 1958.
234 *Straits Times*, 25 Nov 1958
235 'Text of Broadcast by Razak', DIS 30/59, NAS.
236 'Draft for Memo to Executive Council: Department of Broadcasting', n.d., Malaya Papers, RHO.
237 Syed Zainal Abidin to All Honourable State/Settlement Secretaries, 17 November 1954; Syed Othman bin Ali to All State/Settlement Information Officers, 22 Aug 1956, 'Department of Information, Kuala Lumpur', File No. 123/555, ANM.
238 *Annual Report 1955*, pp. 395–396; *Annual Report 1957*, p. 428.
239 'Notes of Meeting on Rural Broadcasts in the Office of the Director of Broadcasting', 29 Jan 1957, Malaya Papers, RHO.
240 *Ibid.* Standing in for Yaacob Latiff (on long leave) at this meeting was the Acting Director of Information Services, Dennis J. Duncanson. Duncanson, a Chinese Affairs officer, had been Assistant Federal Secretary for Chinese Affairs in Kuala Lumpur (1949–50); Federal Secretary for Chinese Affairs (1950–1951); Assistant Secretary for Chinese Affairs, Singapore (1951–54); Private Secretary to the Governor of Singapore (1954–56); Acting Commissioner for Labour (1956) and Acting Director of Information Services in 1957. Duncanson then entered the Hong Kong Government Information Services (1957–61), before joining R.G.K. Thompson in the British Advisory Mission to Vietnam (1961–65).
241 H.H. Beamish, Acting Deputy Director of Broadcasting, Singapore, 'Rural Broadcasts, Singapore', 25 Jan 1957, DIS 52/57, NAS.
242 *DOR 1954*, CO 1030/10. On another occasion, Bourne told 200 Selangor Chinese students in Kuala Lumpur that the shooting war was only one-quarter of the campaign. The other part was 'persuading the people to help the government'. *WNS*, week ending 7 May 1955.
243 *WNS*, week ending 26 March 1955.
244 *WNS*, week ending 9 April 1955.
245 *WNS*, week ending 16 April 1955.
246 *WNS*, week ending 25 June 1955.
247 *Ibid.*
248 *WNS*, week ending 2 July 1955.
249 *WNS*, week ending 26 Nov 1955.
250 *DOR 1955*, CO 1030/10.
251 *WNS*, week ending 24 March 1956.
252 Major R.J. Isaac to Director of Museums, Federation of Malaya, Taiping, 14 Aug 1954, 'Department of Information, Federation of Malaya', File No. 401/53, ANM; Interview with Too, Tape 2, EEP, RHO.
253 Wolters to SIO Johore, 13 April 1955, 'Department of Information, Federation of Malaya', File No. 401/53, ANM.

254 $870 a month. See Yaacob Latiff to Federal Establishment Officer, 30 March 1955, 'Department of Information, Federation of Malaya', File No. 401/53, ANM; Too interview, Tape 2, EEP, RHO.

255 Too interview, Tape 2, EEP, RHO.

256 W.H.F. Lucas for Federal Establishment Office to DIS, 6 May 1955; W. Fernando for FEO to DIS, 22 June 1956,'Department of Information, Federation of Malaya', File No. 401/53, ANM.

257 Too and the PSC had locked horns over the intention of the latter to downgrade the post of HPWS from Superscale H to Superscale J. Too wanted to know why this needed to be done since as a local, he was already being paid less than what an expatriate like Wolters had received in the same appointment at Superscale H. As HPWS from February 1958, Too was paid a salary of $929.16 a month, a Cost of Living Allowance of $19.17 and a housing allowance of $100. See Yeap Kee Aik for Federal Establishment Officer to HPWS, Director of Operations Staff, 6 May 1955; Too to Secretary for Defence and Internal Security, through PSO, Director of Operations Staff, 12 Sep 1957; P.S. Bolshaw for PSC to DIS and Principal Establishment Officer, Malaya, 22 January 1958; Yaacob Latiff to Secretary, PSC, 10 Feb 1958; C. Nagalingam for Secretary of Defence to HPWS, 24 Jan 1958; Gazette Notification No. 481 of 6 Feb 1958 reproduced in INF. 232/58/9, Journal Voucher dated 4 March 1958, 'Department of Information, Federation of Malaya', File No. 401/53, ANM.

258 Wynford, 'Review of Surrender Behaviour', CO 1030/22. 430 SEPs were in this sample.

259 *WNS*, week ending 17 Sep 1955.

260 *WNS*, week ending 21 Jan 1956.

261 *Straits Budget*, 18 Sep 1957. Unfortunately, a promising file on 'Magnavoxes and Loud Hailers' in the ANM has been retained: 'Department of Information, Negri Sembilan, 1946–65', File No. S.I.S.N.S. 36/56, ANM.

262 Wynford, 'Review of Surrender Behaviour', CO 1030/22.

263 P.B. Humphrey, 'Differences in the use of Psychological Warfare between Six Malayan States, Part B: Differences in the Techniques of Disseminating Propaganda by Voice Aircraft Broadcasts', ORS (PW) Memorandum No. 4/55, 7 April 1955, WO 291/1790.

264 *Ibid.*

265 Miers, 'Miers on Malaya', *Counterinsurgency Case History*, p. 62.

266 Humphrey, 'Differences in the use of Psychological Warfare between Six Malayan States', WO 291/1790.

267 Miers, 'Miers on Malaya', *Counterinsurgency Case History*, p. 61.

268 Inward Telegram No. 762 from High Commissioner Federation of Malaya to Secretary of State for the Colonies, 29 Oct 1954, CO 1030/23.

269 *WNS*, week ending 12 March 1955.

270 *Ibid.*; Inward Savingram No. 186 from High Commissioner Federation of Malaya to Secretary of State for the Colonies, 17 Feb 1955, CO 1030/23.

271 *DOR* 1955, CO 1030/10.

272 Inward Telegram No. 17 from High Commissioner Federation of Malaya to Secretary of State for the Colonies, 7 Jan 1955; Reuters report, 6 Jan 1955, CO 1030/22.

273 Minute by R.L. Baxter, 10 Jan 1955, CO 1030/22.

274 Inward Telegram No. 31 from High Commissioner Federation of Malaya to Secretary of State for the Colonies, 13 Jan 1955, CO 1030/22.

275 Inward Telegram No. 37 from High Commissioner Federation of Malaya to Secretary of State for the Colonies, 17 Jan 1955, CO 1030/22.

276 'Memorandum by Secretary of Defence: Surrender Policy', 12 Aug 1954; 'Memorandum for the Attorney-General: Surrender Offer to Communist Terrorists', 13 March 1956; CO 1030/22.
277 WNS, week ending 12 March 1955; Scotsman, 7 March 1955. Despite this, however, the Alliance electoral manifesto still proclaimed that if it won the Federal elections it would 'propose a general amnesty for all Communist terrorists'. 'The elections in the Federation of Malaya': FO circular intelligence telegram no 147 to selected HM representatives overseas reporting and commenting on the results, CO 1030/225, no 7, 15 Aug 1955, in Stockwell, ed., BDEEP, Malaya: The Alliance Route to Independence, Doc. 362.
278 'Surrender Policy', 12 Aug 1954, CO 1030/22, Kemendore eventually closed on 30 September 1956. 255 SEPs had passed through this camp. Annual Report 1956, p. 451.
279 See the text of a Radio Malaya talk by Yaacob Latiff, in WNS, week ending 4 Feb 1956.
280 Too interview, Tape 2, EEP, RHO.
281 This change of strategy was outlined in a document called 'Guidance Instruction' found in December 1955 in a terrorist camp overrun by the Royal Hampshire Regiment. The same document was also found in camp evacuated by Yeong Kwo, the Deputy Secretary-General of the MCP. See WNS, week ending 12 May 1956.
282 WNS, week ending 25 June 1955.
283 Ibid.; 'Report by the Chief Minister of the Federation of Malaya on the Baling Talks', n.d., Exco Paper No. 386/17/56, CO 1030/30.
284 WNS, week ending 2 July 1955.
285 WNS, week ending 4 Feb 1956.
286 'Considerations Concerning a Declaration of Amnesty', 25 Aug 1955, Talbot Papers, LHCMA.
287 'The Question of Offering an Amnesty to the Communist Terrorists in Malaya', 30 July 1955, FO 371/116940.
288 DOR 1955, CO 1030/10.
289 Ibid.
290 Inward Telegram No. 378 from High Commissioner Federation of Malaya to Secretary of State for the Colonies, 30 June 1955, FO 371/116939.
291 Ibid.
292 Inward Telegram No. 497 from High Commissioner Federation of Malaya to Secretary of State for the Colonies, 24 Aug 1955; H. Macmillan to Prime Minister, 23 Aug 1955, FO 371/116940.
293 Inward Telegram No. 539 from High Commissioner Federation of Malaya to Secretary of State for the Colonies, 6 Sep 1955, FO 371/116940.
294 Inward Telegram No. 497, 24 Aug 1955, FO 371/116940.
295 WNS, week ending 27 Aug 1955.
296 Lieutenant-General Geoffrey Bourne, Director of Operations on behalf of High Commissioner Federation of Malaya, 'Declaration of Amnesty', 9 Sep 1955, Talbot Papers, LHCMA.
297 Inward Telegram No. 539, 6 Sep 1955, FO 371/116940.
298 WNS, week ending 10 Sep 1955; 'Government's Amnesty Declaration: Instructions', 25 Aug 1955, Talbot Papers, LHCMA.
299 WNS, week ending 3 Sep 1955.
300 WNS, week ending 24 Sep 1955.
301 Too, 'The Communist Party of Malaya', PP; Too interviews, EEP, RHO.
302 Too interview, Tape 2, EEP, RHO.

303 Secret 'Note', n.d.; Inward Savingram No. 1545 from High Commissioner Federation of Malaya to Secretary of State for the Colonies, 20 Dec 1955, CO 1030/27; 'Report by Chief Minister of the Federation of Malaya on the Baling Talks', n.d., Exco Paper No. 386/17/56, CO 1030/30.

304 [Amnesty talks with the communists]: inward telegram no 646 from Sir D MacGillivray to Mr Lennox-Boyd on the risks involved in a meeting between Tunku Abdul Rahman and Chin Peng, 20 Oct 1955, FO 371/116941, no 67/9, in Stockwell, ed., *BDEEP, Malaya: The Alliance Route to Independence*, Doc. 371.

305 [Amnesty and talks with the communists]: inward telegram no 140 from Sir R Scott to Sir A Eden assessing the risks, 23 Oct 1955, CO 1030/27, no 1, and [Amnesty and talks with the communists]: inward telegram (reply) no 654 from Sir D MacGillivray to Mr Lennox-Boyd, 24 Oct 1955, FO 371/116941, no 69/A, in Stockwell, ed., *BDEEP, Malaya: The Alliance Route to Independence*, Docs. 374, 377. Scott had replaced MacDonald as Commissioner-General for the United Kingdom in Southeast Asia in September 1955. *WNS*, week ending 18 June 1955.

306 PSO to the Director of Operations Staff.

307 *New Straits Times*, 4 Dec 1989. Years later, Too revealed that the idea for the dress rehearsal had been Lindsay's, and Too, to his annoyance, had been given short notice to prepare for it. Granada interviews with Too, EEP, RHO.

308 Outward Telegram No. 142 from Secretary of State for the Colonies to Governor Singapore, 27 Oct 1955, CO 1030/27.

309 [Meeting between Tunku Abdul Rahman and Chin Peng]: inward telegram no. 659 from Sir D MacGillivray to Mr Lennox-Boyd suggesting that self-government precede the end of the emergency, 25 Oct 1955, FO 371/116941, no 72, and 'Federation of Malaya': minute no PM (55) 78 by Mr Lennox-Boyd to Sir A Eden on the forthcoming talks between Tunku Abdul Rahman and Chin Peng, 31 Oct 1955, FO 371/116941, no 77, in Stockwell, ed., *BDEEP, Malaya: The Alliance Route to Independence*, Docs. 378, 381; Inward Telegram No. 669 from High Commissioner Federation of Malaya to Secretary of State for the Colonies, 29 Oct 1955; MacGillivray to Sir John Martin, 1 Dec 1955; Inward Telegram No. 778 from High Commissioner Federation of Malaya to Secretary of State for the Colonies, 9 Dec 1955, CO 1030/27.

310 *DOR 1955*, CO 1030/10.

311 *Annual Report 1955*, p. 424.

312 *Ibid.*, p. 421. The proximate cause of the revocation of the safe areas was a terrorist attack on a New Village in the Cameron Highlands. 'Secret Note', n.d., CO 1030/27.

313 'Report by the chief minister of the Federation of Malaya on the Baling talks': draft summary by Tunku Abdul Rahman on the verbatim record, CO 1030/30, ff 3–16, 29 Dec 1955, Stockwell, ed., *BDEEP,Malaya: The Alliance Route to Independence*, Doc. 391.

314 *WNS*, week ending 31 Dec 1955.

315 In July 1957, for instance Tunku emphasised that the MCP was soon going to be fighting an independent Malayan Government and asked how it intended to justify that. Just before *Merdeka*, moreover, Tunku reminded Chin Peng of his promise to lay down weapons and leave the jungle once Malaya was independent. *Straits Budget*, 18 July 1957, 11 Sep 1957.

316 *WNS*, week ending 11 Feb 1956.

317 *DOR 1956*, CO 1030/10.

318 Inward Telegram No. 190 from High Commissioner Federation of Malaya to Secretary of State for the Colonies, 15 March 1956, CO 1030/22; *WNS*, week ending 17 March 1956.

319 *DOR 1956*, CO 1030/10.

320 *Ibid.*; *Annual Report 1956*, pp. 439–440.
321 *DOR* 1954, CO 1030/10.
322 Too US lecture, PP.
323 *DOR* 1956, CO 1030/10.
324 Author's correspondence with Clutterbuck, 22 July 1997. Clutterbuck served in Malaya between 1956 and 1958.
325 *DOR* 1956; Bower Report, WO 106/5990.
326 *WNS*, week ending 7 April 1956; Inward Telegram No. 161 from High Commissioner Federation of Malaya to Secretary of State for the Colonies, 18 March 1957, CO 1030/412.
327 Inward Telegram No. 161 from High Commissioner Federation of Malaya to Secretary of State for the Colonies, 18 March 1957, CO 1030/412; *WNS*, week ending 17 Nov 1956. Operation Iceland involved RAF Valettas dropping 10 million leaflets
328 Inward Telegram No. 177 from High Commissioner Federation of Malaya to Secretary of State for the Colonies, 23 March 1957; Federal Government Press Statement, 23 March 1957, CO 1030/412.
329 *Straits Budget*, 18 July 1957. In September, Tunku rather optimistically revised this projected end-date to 31 August 1958. *Straits Budget*, 25 Sep 1957.
330 *Straits Budget*, 4 July 1957.
331 *Straits Budget*, 1 Aug 1957.
332 *Straits Budget*, 4 Sep 1957.
333 *Straits Budget*, 11 Sep 1957 and 18 Sep 1957; *Annual Report 1957*, p. 470. A copy of the *Merdeka* Amnesty leaflet is available in DIS 176/58, NAS.
334 *Straits Budget*, 11 Sep 1957 and 18 Sep 1957.
335 *Annual Report 1957*, p. 473.
336 *Straits Budget*, 18 Sep 1957.
337 *Ibid.*
338 'Information Services Monthly Reports', June and November 1957, DIS 116/57, NAS; *Straits Budget*, 29 Aug 1957.
339 *Straits Budget*, 2 Oct 1957.
340 *Ibid.*
341 Inward Telegram No. 271 from High Commissioner Federation of Malaya to Commonwealth Relations Office, 5 Oct 1957, CO 1030/412.
342 Inward Telegram No. 268 to Commonwealth Relations Office, 5 Oct 1957, CO 1030/412.
343 *Straits Budget*, 30 Oct 1957.
344 Inward Telegram No. 398 from High Commissioner Federation of Malaya to Commonwealth Relations Office, 14 Nov 1957, CO 1030/412.
345 *Straits Budget*, 13 Nov 1957.
346 *Straits Budget*, 4 Dec 1957.
347 Hancock Report 1957, AIR 23/8697.
348 *Straits Budget*, 18 Dec 1957.
349 *Straits Budget*, 25 Dec 1957.
350 *Ibid.*; Hancock Report 1957, AIR 23/8697.
351 *Annual Report 1957*, p. 473.
352 Hancock Report 1957, AIR 23/8697.
353 'Psychological Warfare Section Monthly Report', January 1958, DIS 176/58, NAS.
354 *Straits Times*, 7 Nov 1958 and 14 Nov 1958. An account of Ah Ann's elimination is provided by Walter Walker, who commanded the 99 Gurkha Infantry Brigade Group which was in south Johore at the time as part of Operation Tiger. Walker, *Fighting On*, pp. 131–138.

355 'Psychological Warfare Section Monthly Report', March 1958, DIS 176/58, NAS.
356 *Annual Report 1957*, p. 471.
357 See text of Operation Greenland III leaflet, appended at back of 'Psychological Warfare Section Monthly Report', March 1958, DIS 176/58, NAS; *Straits Times*, 10 July 1958. Dato Razak announced in early July 1958 that after the end of the *Merdeka* Amnesty on 31 July, Government would revert to the old policy of 'fair treatment' and avoidance of promises of non-prosecution.
358 Hancock Report 1958, AIR 23/8698.
359 *Malaya*, Aug 1958, pp. 16–18; *Straits Times*, 10 July 1958. HPWS publicised the MCP collapse in south Perak via Operation Elba – a mass drop of seven million leaflets. Hancock Report 1958, AIR 23/8698.
360 *Straits Times*, 17 Jan 1959.
361 Hancock Report 1958, AIR 23/8698. HPWS mounted Operation St. Helena (8.5 million leaflets) to publicise the MCP collapse in north Johore.
362 *Ibid.*, Hancock Report 1957, AIR 23/8697.
363 Short, 'Communism and the Emergency', in Wang ed., *Malaysia*, p. 160.
364 Group discussion with Chin Peng, 18 June 1998; Chin, *The Communist Party of Malaya*, pp. 50–51. In 1959 the demobilisation policy was modified to allow retiring MRLA combatants to retain Party membership, on application and subject to certain conditions.
365 Group Discussion with Chin Peng, 18 June 1998; 'Federation Affairs', *Malaya* (Sep 1958), pp. 15–16.

CONCLUSION

1 Cecil. B. Currey, *Edward Lansdale: The Unquiet American* (London and Washington: Brassey's, 1998), p. 281.
2 Fitzgerald, *Fire in the Lake*, p. 395; Andrew F. Krepinevich, Jr., *The Army and Vietnam* (Baltimore and London: Johns Hopkins Press, 1990), p. 209.
3 Michael Maclear, *Vietnam: The Ten Thousand Day War* (London: Thames Mandarin, 1989), p. 374.
4 Napoleon D. Valeriano and Charles T.R. Bohannan, *Counterguerrilla Operations: The Philippine Experience* (London: Pall Mall Press, 1962), pp. 200–228.
5 Correspondence with Turnbull, 31 July 1997.
6 Correspondence with Clutterbuck, 22 July 1997.
7 Fitzgerald, *Fire in the Lake*, p. 142; William Colby, *Lost Victory: A Firsthand Account of America's Sixteen-year Involvement in Vietnam* (Chicago and New York: Contemporary Books, 1989), p. 211; Report by Brigadier R.L. Clutterbuck on a confidential seminar on Vietnam, held at the Centre for Strategic Studies, Georgetown University, 20–21 May 1968, Liddell Hart Papers, 1/176, LHCMA.
8 We part ways here with Hack, who downplays Templer's impact. Hack, 'Screwing Down the People', in Antlov and Tonneson, eds., *Imperial Policy and Southeast Asian Nationalism*, p. 90.
9 Jose V. Abueva, *Ramon Magsaysay: A Political Biography* (Manila: Solidaridad Publishing House, 1971), pp. 253–254. See also Douglas S. Blaufarb, *The Counterinsurgency Era: US Doctrine and Performance 1950 to the Present* (New York: Free Press, 1977), pp. 29–30.
10 Fitzgerald, *Fire in the Lake*, pp. 301–302.
11 Maclear, *Vietnam,*, pp. 213–214; Fitzgerald, *Fire in the Lake*, p. 405. See also Clutterbuck, *The Long, Long War*, pp. 161–162.

12 Maclear, *Vietnam*, p. 229; Colby, *Lost Victory*, pp. 178–179; Thompson, *No Exit from Vietnam* (London: Chatto and Windus, 1969), p. 136.
13 The Editors, 'PSYOP in Vietnam: A Many Splintered Thing', in De McLaurin *et al.*, eds., *The Art and Science of Psychological Operations*, Vol.1, pp. 225–228.
14 Clutterbuck, *Conflict and Violence in Singapore and Malaysia*, p. 192.

Bibliography

UNPUBLISHED SOURCES

Public Record Office, London

Colonial Office Papers

CO 717   Federated Malay States, Original Correspondence
CO 537   General Supplementary
CO 875   Public Relations and Information, Original Correspondence
CO 967   Private Office Papers of the Secretary of State
CO 1022   South East Asia Department, Original Correspondence
CO 1027   Information Department, Original Correspondence
CO 1030   Far Eastern Department, Original Correspondence

War Office Papers

WO 106   Military Operations and Intelligence Records
WO 216   Chief of Imperial General Staff Papers
WO 219   Supreme Headquarters Allied Expeditionary Forces
WO 291   Military Operational Research

Cabinet Office Papers

CAB 128   Cabinet Conclusions, 1945–61
CAB 130   Cabinet Committees, *ad hoc* Committees, 1945–61
CAB 134   Cabinet Committees, 1945–61

Prime Minister's Office Papers

PREM 8   Correspondence and Papers, 1945–51
PREM 11   Correspondence and Papers, 1951–64

Foreign Office Files

FO 371   General Political Correspondence
FO 898   Political Warfare Executive Files

Air Ministry Files

AIR 9   Directorate of Operations and Plans
AIR 23   RAF Overseas Commands: Reports

Arkib Negara Malaysia (*National Archives of Malaysia*)

Department of Information Files:
Negri Sembilan 1946–65
Johore 1948–55
Trengganu 1946–61
Kuala Lumpur 1946–63
Federal 1953–54
Department of Chinese Affairs, Malaysia, Miscellaneous Years

National Archives of Singapore

Department of Information Services Files 1955–59

PRIVATE PAPERS

Rhodes House Library, Oxford

Adrian G.A. Alabaster
C.H.F. Blake
Conrad S.K. Bovell
Frank Brewer
W.C.S. Corry
John C. Litton
Malaya Papers (on Radio Malaya)
R.A. Ruegg
B.P. Walker-Taylor
W.J. Watts
Max Lear Webber
'End of Empire' Granada interview transcripts
Frank A. Fielding
Robert Heussler
Harold W. Jackson
Ivan Lloyd Phillips
Oliver Lyttelton
Malcolm MacDonald
Arthur E. Young

Liddell Hart Centre for Military Archives, King's College London

Sir Basil Liddell Hart
Maj-General Dennis Edmund Blaquiere Talbot
General Sir Hugh Charles Stockwell

National Army Museum, London

General Sir Gerald Templer 7410–29, 8011–132
Major David Lloyd-Owen 8301–6

Imperial War Museum, London

John Loch
I.S. Gibb

Institute of Southeast Asian Studies, Singapore

Tan Cheng Lock Papers

In Author's Possession

C.C. Too Private Papers

UNPUBLISHED THESES

Hack, Karl A. 'British Strategy and South East Asia, 1941–1957', Unpublished PhD Dissertation, Oxford University, 1995.

Harper, T.N. 'The Colonial Inheritance: State and Society in Colonial Malaya 1945–57', Unpublished PhD Dissertation, Cambridge University, 1991.

Humphrey, John Weldon, 'Population Resettlement in Malaya', Unpublished PhD Dissertation, Northwestern University, 1971.

Melshen, Paul, 'Pseudo-Operations: The Use by British and American Armed Forces of Deception in Counterinsurgency 1945–1973', Unpublished PhD Dissertation, Cambridge University, 1996.

Park, Bum-Joon Lee, 'The British Experience of Counterinsurgency in Malaya: The Emergency, 1948–1960', Unpublished PhD Dissertation, American University, January 1965.

Santokh, Tripat Kaur, 'Broadcast Development in Malaysia: Communal Structures and National Aspirations', Unpublished PhD Dissertation, Northwestern University, 1979.

Zarougui, M. 'Propaganda and Psychological Warfare in Guerrilla and Counter-Guerrilla Warfare: The Malayan Emergency 1948–1960', Unpublished PhD Dissertation, Reading University, 1992.

PUBLISHED SOURCES

Official Publications

Brewer, Frank, *The Chinese Problem in the Federation of Malaya* (Kuala Lumpur: Government Printer, 1955).

Corry, W.C.S. *A General Survey of the New Villages* (Kuala Lumpur: Government Printer, 1954).
Colonial Annual Report: Malayan Union 1947 (London: HMSO, 1949).
Communist Banditry in Malaya: the Emergency June 1948-Dec 1949 (Kuala Lumpur: Department of Public Relations, 1950).
Counterinsurgency Case History: Malaya, 1948–60 (Fort Leavenworth, Kansas: US Army Command and General Staff College, 1965).
De Cruz, Gerald, *Politics and Everyman Today* (Kuching, Sarawak: Government Printer, 1963).
Department of Information Weekly News Summaries (Kuala Lumpur: 1955–56).
Detention and Deportation during the Emergency in the Federation of Malaya (Kuala Lumpur Government Press, 1953)
Federation of Malaya Annual Report 1948 (Kuala Lumpur: Government Printer, 1949).
Federation of Malaya Annual Report 1950 (Kuala Lumpur: Government Printer, 1951).
Federation of Malaya Annual Report 1951 (Kuala Lumpur: Government Printer, 1952).
Federation of Malaya Annual Report 1952 (London: HMSO, 1953).
Federation of Malaya Annual Report 1953 (London: HMSO, 1954).
Federation of Malaya Annual Report 1954 (London: HMSO, 1955).
Federation of Malaya Annual Report 1955 (Kuala Lumpur: Government Press, 1956).
Federation of Malaya Annual Report 1956 (London: HMSO, 1957).
Federation of Malaya Annual Report 1957 (Kuala Lumpur: Government Printer, 1958).
McHugh, J.N. *Anatomy of Communist Propaganda* (Kuala Lumpur: Department of Public Relations, 1949).
Parliamentary Debates, Official Report, 5th Series (Commons) 1948–54.
Report on the Conduct of Food Searches at Semenyih in the Kajang District of the State of Selangor (Kuala Lumpur: Government Printer, 1956).
Report of the Police Mission to Malaya, March 1950 (Kuala Lumpur: Government Printer, 1950).
Resettlement and the Development of New Villages in the Federation of Malaya (Kuala Lumpur: Government Press, 1952).
The Communist Threat to the Federation of Malaya (Kuala Lumpur: Government Printer, 1959).
The Conduct of Anti-Terrorist Operations in Malaya, 3rd edn. (Kuala Lumpur: Government Printer, 1958).

Books and Articles

Abueva, Jose V. *Ramon Magsaysay: A Political Biography* (Manila: Solidaridad Publishing House, 1971).
Adams, David K. and Cornelis A. Van Minnen, eds. *Aspects of War in American History* (Keele: Keele University Press, 1997).
Adams, Thomas K. 'LIC (Low-Intensity Clausewitz)', *Small Wars and Insurgencies*, Vol. 1, No. 3 (Dec 1990), pp. 266–275.
Adhikarya *et al.* Ronny, *Broadcasting in Peninsular Malaysia* (London, Henley and Boston: Routledge and Kegan Paul, 1977).
Ali, S. Husin, *Malay Peasant Society and Leadership* (London: Oxford University Press, 1975).

Allen, Charles, *The Savage Wars of Peace: Soldiers' Voices 1945–1989* (London and Sydney: Futura, 1991).

Allen, James de V. *The Malayan Union* (Connecticut: Yale University Press, 1967).

Andrews, William R. *The Village War: Vietnamese Communist Revolutionary Activities in Dinh Tuong Province 1960–64* (Columbia, Missouri: University of Missouri Press, 1973).

Anderson, David M. and David Killingray, eds. *Policing and Decolonisation: Nationalism, Politics and the Police 1917–65* (Manchester: Manchester University Press, 1992).

Antlov, Hans, and Stein Tonnesson, eds. *Imperial Policy and South East Asian Nationalism* (Surrey: Curzon Press, 1995).

Arasaratnam, Sinnapah, *Indians In Malaysia and Singapore* (Bombay and Kuala Lumpur: Oxford University Press, 1970).

Asprey, Robert B. *War in the Shadows,* rev. edn. (London: Little, Brown and Co., 1994).

Balfour, Michael, *Propaganda in War, 1939–1945: Organisations, Policies and Publics in Britain and Germany* (London, Boston and Henley: Routledge and Kegan Paul, 1979).

Barber, Noel, *War of the Running Dogs: Malaya 1948–1960* (London: Arrow, 1989).

Beckett, Ian F.W. 'The Study of Counterinsurgency: A British Perspective', *Small Wars and Insurgencies*, Vol. 1, No. 1 (1990), pp. 47–53.

——, 'Robert Thompson and the British Advisory Mission to South Vietnam, 1961–1965', *Small Wars and Insurgencies*, Vol. 8, No. 3 (Oct 1997), pp. 41–63.

Beckett, Ian F.W. and John Pimlott, eds. *Armed Forces and Modern Counter-insurgency* (London and Sydney: Croom Helm, 1985).

Belfield, Eversley, *The Boer War* (London: Leo Cooper, 1993).

Blaufarb, Douglas S. *The Counterinsurgency Era: US Doctrine and Performance 1950 to the Present* (New York: Free Press, 1977).

Blythe, Wilfred, *The Impact of Chinese Secret Societies in Malaya: A Historical Study* (London: Oxford University Press, 1969).

Bowden, Tom, *The Breakdown of Public Security: The Case of Ireland 1919–1921 and Palestine 1936–1939* (London and Beverly Hills: SAGE Publications, 1977).

Brazier-Creagh, K.R. 'Malaya', *RUSI Journal*, Vol. XCIX, No. 594 (May 1954), pp. 175–190.

Brimmell, J.H. *Communism in South East Asia: A Political Analysis* (London: Oxford University Press, 1959).

Campbell, Arthur, *Jungle Green* (London: George Allen and Unwin, 1953).

Carruthers, Susan L. *Winning Hearts and Minds: British Governments, the Media and Colonial Counterinsurgency, 1944–1960* (London: Leicester University Press, 1995).

Chapman, F. Spencer, *The Jungle is Neutral* (Singapore and Kuala Lumpur: Times Books International, 1997).

Cheah, Boon Kheng, *The Masked Comrades: A Study of the Communist United Front in Malaya, 1945–48* (Singapore: Times Books International, 1979).

——, *Red Star over Malaya: Resistance and Social Conflict During and After the Japanese Occupation 1941–1946* (Singapore: Singapore University Press, 1983).

——, ed. *From PKI to the Comintern, 1924–1941: The Apprenticeship of the Malayan Communist Party* (Ithaca: Cornell University Press, 1992).

Chin, Aloysius, *The Communist Party of Malaya: The Inside Story* (Kuala Lumpur: Vinpress, 1995).

Clausewitz, Carl von, *On War*, ed. by Anatol Rapoport (London: Penguin, 1982).

——, *On War*, ed. by Michael Howard and Peter Paret (Princeton: Princeton University Press, 1989).

Cloake, John, *Templer: Tiger of Malaya* (London: Harrap, 1985).

Clutterbuck, Richard, *The Long, Long War: The Emergency in Malaya 1948–1960* (London: Cassell, 1967).

——, *Riot and Revolution in Singapore and Malaya 1945–1963* (London: Faber and Faber, 1973).

——, *Conflict and Violence in Singapore and Malaysia 1945–1983*, rev., updtd. and enlgd. edn. (Singapore: Graham Brash, 1985).

Coates, John, *Suppressing Insurgency: An Analysis of the Malayan Emergency* (Boulder: Westview Press, 1992).

Colby, William, *Lost Victory: A Firsthand Account of America's Sixteen-year Involvement in Vietnam* (Chicago and New York: Contemporary Books, 1989).

Comber, Leon, *13 May 1969: A Historical Survey of Sino-Malay Relations* (Singapore: Graham Brash, 1988).

——, '"The Weather has been Horrible": Malayan Communist Communications during "The Emergency" (1948–60)', *Asian Studies Review*, Vol. 19, No. 2 (Nov 1995), pp. 37–57.

Corry, W.C.S. *Malaya Today* (London: Longmans, Green and Co., 1955).

Cowan, C.D. *Nineteenth-Century Malaya* (London: Clarendon Press, 1961).

Crossman, Richard H.S. 'Psychological Warfare', *RUSI Journal*, Vol. XCVII, No. 587 (Aug 1952), pp. 319–332.

——, 'Psychological Warfare', *RUSI Journal*, Vol. XCVIII, No. 591 (Aug 1953), pp. 351–361.

——, 'Psychological Warfare', *RUSI Journal*, Vol. XCVIII (Nov 1953), pp. 528–539.

Crozier, Brian, *The Rebels: a Study of Post-War Insurrections* (Boston: Beacon Press, 1964).

——, *Southeast Asia in Turmoil* (Harmondsworth, Middlesex: Pelican, 1966).

Cruickshank, Charles, *The Fourth Arm: Psychological Warfare 1938–45* (London: Davis-Poynter, 1977).

Currey, Cecil B. *Edward Lansdale: The Unquiet American* (London and Washington: Brassey's, 1998).

Dalyell, Tam, *Dick Crossman: A Portrait* (London: Weidenfeld and Nicolson, 1989).

Daugherty, William E. and Morris Janowitz, eds. *Psychological Warfare Casebook* (Baltimore, Maryland: Johns Hopkins Press, 1958).

de Cruz, Gerald, *Rojak Rebel: Memoirs of a Singapore Maverick* (Singapore and Kuala Lumpur: Times Books International, 1993).

De McLaurin, Ronald, *et al.* eds. *The Art and Science of Psychological Operations: Case Studies of Military Application,* Vol. 1 (Washington, D.C.: American Institutes for Research, 1976).

Drabble, J.H. *Rubber in Malaya 1876–1922: The Genesis of the Industry* (London: Oxford University Press, 1973).

Eckstein, Harry, ed. *Internal War* (New York: Free Press, 1964).

Fairbairn, Geoffrey, *Revolutionary Guerrilla Warfare: The Countryside Version* (Middlesex: Penguin, 1974).

Fein, Helen, *Imperial Crime and Punishment: The Massacre at Jallianwala Bagh and British Judgement 1919–1920* (Honolulu: University of Hawaii Press, 1977).

Fitzgerald, Frances, *Fire in the Lake: The Vietnamese and the Americans in Vietnam* (New York: Vintage Books, 1973).

Fraser, George MacDonald, *Quartered Safe Out Here: A Recollection of the War in Burma* (London: HarperCollins, 1995).

Furedi, Frank, *Colonial Wars and the Politics of Third World Nationalism* (London: I.B. Tauris, 1994).

Gearty, Conor, *Terror* (London: Faber and Faber, 1991).

Geraghty, Tony, *Who Dares Wins: the Story of the SAS, 1950–1992* (London: Warner Books, 1993).

Ginsburg, Norton, and Chester F. Roberts, *Malaya* (Seattle: University of Washington Press, 1958).

Glass, Leslie, *The Changing of Kings: Memories of Burma 1934–49* (London: Peter Davies, 1985).

Greene, Graham, *Ways of Escape* (London: Penguin Books, 1981).

Gregorian, Raffi, '"Jungle Bashing" in Malaya: Towards a Formal Tactical Doctrine', *Small Wars and Insurgencies*, Vol. 5, No. 3 (Winter 1994), pp. 338–359.

Hack, Karl, 'Corpses, Prisoners of War and Captured Documents: British and Communist Narratives of the Malayan Emergency, and the Dynamics of Intelligence Transformation', *Intelligence and National Security*, Vol. 14, No. 4 (Winter 1999), pp. 211–241.

Hall, D.G.E. *A History of Southeast Asia*, 4th edn. (London: Macmillan, 1988).

Hamilton, Nigel, *Monty: The Making of a General 1887–1942* (London: Hamish Hamilton, 1981).

Hanrahan, Gene Z. *The Communist Struggle in Malaya* (Kuala Lumpur: University of Malaya Press, 1971).

Harper, T.N. *The End of Empire and the Making of Malaya* (Cambridge: Cambridge University Press, 1999).

Harvey, M. 'Malaya – Time for a Change', *Army Quarterly*, Vol. LXX, No. 1 (April 1955), pp. 38–43.

Haycock, Ronald, ed. *Regular Armies and Insurgency* (London: Croom Helm, 1979).

Hayter, Adrian, *The Second Step* (London: Hodder and Stoughton, 1962).

Haythornthwaite, Philip J. *Colonial Wars Sourcebook* (London: Arms and Armour Press, 1995).

Hearden, Patrick J. ed. *Vietnam: Four American Perspectives* (West Lafayette, Indiana: Purdue University Press, 1991).

Heng, Pek Koon, *Chinese Politics in Malaysia: A History of the Malaysian Chinese Association* (Singapore: Oxford University Press, 1988).

Henniker, M.C.A. *Red Shadow over Malaya* (London: William Blackwood and Sons, 1955).

Heussler, Robert, *British Rule in Malaya: The Malayan Civil Service and its Predecessors, 1867–1942* (Oxford: Clio Press, 1981).

——, *Completing a Stewardship: The Malayan Civil Service, 1942–1957* (Westport: Greenwood Press, 1983).

Hibbert, Christopher, *The Great Mutiny, India 1857* (London: Penguin, 1988).

Hoffman, Bruce, *The Failure of British Military Strategy within Palestine 1939–1947* (Jerusalem: Bar-Ilan University Press, 1983).

Howard, Michael, *Clausewitz* (Oxford and New York: Oxford University Press, 1983).

Howe, Irving, *Trotsky* (Glasgow: Fontana, 1978).

Hyam, Ronald, *Britain's Imperial Century, 1815–1914: A Study of Empire and Expansion*, 2nd edn. (London: Macmillan, 1993).

James, Lawrence, *The Rise and Fall of the British Empire* (London: Abacus Books, 1997).

Jeffery, Keith, *The British Army and the Crisis of Empire* (Manchester: Manchester University Press, 1984).

Jones, Tim, 'The British Army, and Counter-Guerrilla Warfare in Transition, 1944–1952', *Small Wars and Insurgencies*, Vol. 7, No. 3 (Winter 1996), pp. 265–307.

Keegan, John, ed. *Churchill's Generals* (London: Warner, 1995).

Khong, Kim Hoong, *Merdeka! British Rule and the Struggle for Independence in Malaya 1945–57* (Kuala Lumpur: Institute for Social Analysis, 1984).

Kiernan, V.G. *The Lords of Human Kind: European Attitudes to the Outside World in the Imperial Age* (Middlesex: Pelican, 1972).

Kirk-Greene, Anthony, *On Crown Service: A History of HM Colonial and Overseas Civil Services, 1837–1997* (London: I.B. Tauris, 1999).

Knei-Paz, Baruch, *The Social and Political Thought of Leon Trotsky* (Oxford: Clarendon Press, 1978).

Komer, Robert W. *The Malayan Emergency in Retrospect: Organisation of a Successful Counterinsurgency Effort* (Santa Monica: Rand, 1972).

Kratoska, Paul H. *The Japanese Occupation of Malaya 1941–1945* (St Leonards, New South Wales: Allen and Unwin, 1998).

Krepinevich, Jr. Andrew, *The Army and Vietnam* (Baltimore and London: Johns Hopkins Press, 1990).

Lapping, Brian, *End of Empire* (London: Paladin, 1989).

Laqueur, Walter, ed. *The Guerrilla Reader: a Historical Anthology* (London: Wildwood House, 1978).

Lau, Albert, *The Malayan Union Controversy 1942–1948* (Singapore: Oxford University Press, 1991).

Laski, Harold J. *Communism* (London: Thornton Butterworth, 1928).

Lasswell, Harold D. *Propaganda Technique in the World War* (London: Kegan Paul, Trench, Trubner and Co., 1938).

Lee, Kam Hing and Chow Mun Seong, *Biographical Dictionary of the Chinese in Malaysia* (Petaling Jaya: Pelanduk Publications, 1997).

Lerner, Daniel, *Psychological Warfare against Nazi Germany: The Sykewar Campaign, D-Day to VE-Day* (Cambridge, Massachusetts: The MIT Press, 1971).

Linebarger, Paul M.A. *Psychological Warfare*, 2nd edn. (New York: Duell, Sloan and Pearce, 1954).

Lockhart, Sir Robert H. Bruce, 'Political Warfare', *RUSI Journal*, Vol. XCV, No. 577 (1950), pp. 193–206.

Loh, Kok Wah Francis, *Beyond the Tin Mines: Coolies, Squatters and New Villagers in the Kinta Valley, Malaysia c. 1880–1980* (Singapore: Oxford University Press, 1988).

Loy, Hean Heong, with Andrew Crofts, *Against All Odds: The Making of a Billionaire* (Singapore and Kuala Lumpur: Times Books International, 1997).

Lyttelton, Oliver, *The Memoirs of Lord Chandos* (London: Bodley Head, 1964).

Mackay, Donald, *The Malayan Emergency 1948–60: The Domino that Stood* (London and Washington: Brassey's, 1997).

Maclear, Michael, *Vietnam: The Ten Thousand Day War* (London: Thames Mandarin, 1989).

Mao, Tse-Tung, *The Selected Works of Mao Tse-Tung*, Vol. 2 (Peking: Foreign Languages Press, 1965).

——, *The Selected Works of Mao Tse-Tung*, Vol. 4 (Peking: Foreign Languages Press, 1969).

——, *Selected Military Writings of Mao Tse-Tung*, 2nd edn. (Peking: Foreign Languages Press, 1966).

——, *Selected Readings from the Works of Mao Tse-Tung* (Peking: Foreign Languages Press, 1967).

Masters, John, *Bugles and a Tiger* (London: Four Square, 1967).
McHugh, J.N. 'Psychological Warfare in Malaya (1942–46)', *Journal of the Historical Society University of Malaya*, reprint, Vol. 4 (1965/66), pp. 48–64.
——, 'Psychological, or Political Warfare in Malaya', Part II, *Journal of the Historical Society University of Malaya*, Vol. 5 (1966/67), pp. 75–94.
McLane, Charles B. *Soviet Strategies in Southeast Asia: an Explanation of Eastern Policy under Lenin and Stalin* (New Jersey: Princeton University Press, 1966).
Mellersh, AVM Sir Francis, 'The Campaign against the Terrorists in Malaya', *RUSI Journal*, Vol. XCVI (1951), pp. 401–415.
Miers, Richard, *Shoot to Kill* (London: Faber and Faber, 1959).
Miller, Harry, *Menace in Malaya* (London: Harrap, 1954).
——, *Jungle War in Malaya: The Campaign against Communism 1948–60* (London: Arthur Barker, 1972).
——, *Prince and Premier: A Biography of Tunku Abdul Rahman Putra Al-Haj, First Prime Minister of the Federation of Malaya* (London: Harrap, 1959).
Mockaitis, Thomas R. *British Counterinsurgency, 1919–60* (London: Macmillan, 1990).
——, 'Low-Intensity Conflict: The British Experience', *Conflict Quarterly*, Vol. 13, No. 1 (Winter 1993), pp. 7–16.
——, 'The Origins of British Counter-Insurgency', *Small Wars and Insurgencies*, Vol. 1, No. 3 (Dec 1990), pp. 209–225.
Montgomery, Field Marshal the Viscount, *The Memoirs of Field Marshal Montgomery* (London: Collins, 1958).
Morais, Benedict, and Hamdan Adnan, eds. *Public Relations: The Malaysian Experience* (Kuala Lumpur: Institute of Public Relations Malaysia, 1986).
Moran, J.W.G. *Spearhead in Malaya* (London: Peter Davies, 1959).
Newsinger, John, 'The Military Memoir in British Imperial Culture: The Case of Malaya', *Race and Class*, Vol. 35, No. 3 (1994), pp. 47–62.
——, '"Pox Britannica": Orwell and Empire', *Race and Class*, Vol. 38, No. 2 (1996), pp. 33–49.
Nicolson, Nigel, *Alex: The Life of Field Marshal Earl Alexander of Tunis* (London: Weidenfeld and Nicolson, 1973).
Nyce, Ray, *Chinese New Villages in Malaya: A Community Study* (Kuala Lumpur: Malaysian Sociological Research Institute, 1973).
O'Ballance, Edgar, *Malaya: The Communist Insurgent War, 1948–60* (Hamden, Connecticut: Archon Books, 1966).
Omissi, David E. *Air Power and Colonial Control: The Royal Air Force 1919–1939* (Manchester: Manchester University Press, 1990).
Ong, Siew Im Pamela, *Blood and the Soil: A Portrait of Dr Ong Chong Keng* (Singapore and Kuala Lumpur: Times Books International, 1995).
Orwell, George, *The Road to Wigan Pier* (London: Penguin, 1989).
Orwell, Sonia and Ian Angus, eds. *The Collected Essays, Journalism and Letters of George Orwell, Vol. 1: An Age Like This, 1920–1940* (London: Secker and Warburg, 1969).
Osanka, Franklin Mark, ed. *Modern Guerrilla Warfare* (New York: Free Press, 1962).
Owen, David, *Battle of Wits: A History of Psychology and Deception in Modern Warfare* (London: Leo Cooper, 1978).
Paget, Julian, *Counter-Insurgency Campaigning* (London: Faber and Faber, 1967).
Pakenham, Thomas, *The Boer War* (London: Abacus, 1996).
Paret, Peter and John W. Shy, *Guerrillas in the 1960s* (London and Dunmow: Pall Mall Press, 1962).

Paret, Peter, ed. *Makers of Modern Strategy: From Machiavelli to the Nuclear Age* (Oxford: Clarendon Press, 1991).

Parkinson, C. Northcote, *Templer in Malaya* (Singapore: Donald Moore, 1954).

——, *British Intervention in Malaya 1867–1877* (Singapore: University of Malaya Press, 1960).

Perry Robinson, J.B. *Transformation in Malaya* (London: Secker and Warburg, 1956).

Pocock, Tom, *Fighting General: The Public and Private Campaigns of General Sir Walter Walker* (London: Collins, 1973).

Porter, Bernard, *The Lion's Share: A Short History of British Imperialism 1850–1995*, 3rd edn. (London and New York: Longman, 1996).

Postgate, Malcolm, *Operation Firedog: Air Support in the Malayan Emergency, 1948–1960* (London: HMSO, 1992).

Pustay, John, *Counterinsurgency Warfare* (New York: Free Press, 1965).

Purcell, Victor, 'General Templer', *Twentieth Century*, Vol. CLV, No. 923 (Feb 1954), pp. 118–129.

——, *The Chinese in Malaya* (London: Oxford University Press, 1967).

——, *The Memoirs of a Malayan Official* (London: Cassell, 1965).

Pye, Lucien W. *Guerrilla Communism in Malaya: its Social and Political Meaning* (New Jersey: Princeton University Press, 1956).

Rahman, Tunku Abdul Putra Al-Haj, *Looking Back: Monday Musings and Memories* (Kuala Lumpur: Pustaka Antara, 1977).

Reid, Brian Holden, ed. *Military Power: Land Warfare in Theory and Practice* (London and Portland, Oregon: Frank Cass, 1997).

Renick, Jr. Rhoderick D. 'The Emergency Regulations of Malaya: Causes and Effect', *Journal of Southeast Asian History*, Vol. 6, No. 2 (Sep 1965), pp. 1–39.

Roetter, Charles, *Psychological Warfare* (London: B.T. Batsford, 1974).

Royle, Trevor, *The Best Years of their Lives: The National Service Experience 1945–1963* (London: John Murray, 1997).

——, *Orde Wingate – Irregular Soldier* (London: Weidenfeld and Nicolson, 1995).

Sadka, Emily, *The Protected Malay States, 1874–1895* (Kuala Lumpur: University of Malaya Press, 1970).

Sandhu, K.S. 'Emergency Resettlement in Malaya', *Journal of Tropical Geography*, Vol. 18 (1964), pp. 157–183.

——, *Indians in Malaya: Some Aspects of their Immigration and Settlement, 1786–1957* (London: Cambridge University Press, 1969).

Sandhu, K.S. and Paul Wheatley, eds. *Melaka: The Transformation of a Malay Capital, c. 1400–1980*, Vols. 1–2 (Singapore: Oxford University Press, 1983).

Sanger, Clyde, *Malcolm MacDonald: Bringing an End to Empire* (Liverpool: Liverpool University Press, 1995).

Saunders, Kay, '"An Instrument of Strategy": Propaganda, Public Policy and the Media in Australia during the Second World War', *War and Society*, Vol. 15, No. 2 (Oct 1997), pp. 75–90.

Schmid, Alex P. and Jaany de Graaf, *Violence as Communication: Insurgent Terrorism and the Western News Media* (London: SAGE Publications, 1982).

Sheppard, Dato Mubin, *Taman Budiman: Memoirs of an Unorthodox Civil Servant* (Kuala Lumpur: Heinemann Educational Publications, 1979).

Short, Anthony, *The Communist Insurrection in Malaya 1948–60* (London: Frederick Mueller, 1975).

Simpson, Christopher, *Science of Coercion: Communication Research and Psychological Warfare 1945–1960* (Oxford and New York: Oxford University Press, 1996).

Simson, H.J. *British Rule, and Rebellion* (London and Edinburgh: William Blackwood, 1937).

Slim, Field Marshal Sir William, *Defeat into Victory* (London: Cassell, 1956).

Smith, R.B. 'China and Southeast Asia: the Revolutionary Perspective, 1951', *Journal of Southeast Asian Studies*, Vol. 19, No. 1 (March 1988), pp. 97–110.

Smyth, Rosaleen, 'Britain's African Colonies and British Propaganda during the Second World War', *Journal of Imperial and Commonwealth History*, Vol. 14, No. 1 (Oct 1985), pp. 65–82.

Stenson, M.R. *Industrial Conflict in Malaya: Prelude to the Communist Revolt of 1948* (London: Oxford University Press, 1970).

——, *The 1948 Communist Revolt In Malaya: A Note on Historical Sources and Interpretation; A Reply by Gerald de Cruz* (Singapore: Institute of Southeast Asian Studies, 1971).

Stevenson, Rex, 'Cinemas and Censorship in Colonial Malaya', *Journal of Southeast Asian Studies*, Vol. 5, No. 2 (Sep 1974), pp. 209–224.

Stewart, Brian, 'Winning in Malaya: An Intelligence Success Story', *Intelligence and National Security*, Vol. 14, No. 4 (Winter 1999), pp. 267–283.

Stockwell, A.J. 'British Imperial Policy and Decolonisation in Malaya, 1942–52', *Journal of Imperial and Commonwealth History*, Vol. 13, No. 1 (Oct 1984), pp. 68–87.

——, 'The White Man's Burden and Brown Humanity: Colonialism and Ethnicity in British Malaya', *Southeast Asian Journal of Social Science*, Vol. 10, No. 1 (1982), pp. 44–68.

——, *British Policy and Malay Politics during the Malayan Union Experiment, 1942–1948* (Kuala Lumpur: Malayan Branch of the Royal Asiatic Society, 1979).

——, '"A Widespread and long-concocted plot to overthrow the government in Malaya"? The Origins of the Malayan Emergency', *Journal of Imperial and Commonwealth History*, Vol. 21, No. 3 (Sep 1993), pp. 66–88.

——, 'Review of H.S. Barlow, *Swettenham* (Kuala Lumpur: Southdene, 1995) and Clyde Sanger, *Malcolm MacDonald: Bringing and End to Empire* (Montreal and Kingston: McGill-Queen's University Press and Liverpool: Liverpool University Press, 1995)', *Journal of Imperial and Commonwealth History*, Vol. 24, No. 3 (Sep 1996), pp. 491–495.

——, ed. *British Documents on the End of Empire, Series B, Vol. 3, Malaya, Part I: The Malayan Union Experiment 1942–1948* (London: HMSO,1995).

——, *British Documents on the End of Empire, Series B, Vol. 3, Malaya, Part II: The Communist Insurrection 1948–1953* (London: HMSO,1995).

——, *British Documents on the End of Empire, Series B, Vol. 3, Malaya, Part III: The Alliance Route to Independence 1953–1957* (London: HMSO, 1995).

Strauch, Judith, *Chinese Village Politics in the Malaysian State* (Cambridge, Massachusetts, and London: Harvard University Press, 1981).

Stubbs, Richard, *Hearts and Minds in Guerrilla Warfare: The Malayan Emergency 1948–1960* (Singapore: Oxford University Press, 1993).

Stubbs, Richard, and Paul B. Rich, eds. *The Counterinsurgent State: Guerrilla Warfare and State-Building in the 20th Century* (London: Macmillan, 1997).

Sunderland, Riley, *Winning the Hearts and Minds of the People: Malaya, 1948–1960* (Santa Monica: Rand, 1964).

——, *Army Operations in Malaya: 1947–1960* (Santa Monica: Rand, 1964).

Taber, Robert, *The War of the Flea: A Study of Guerrilla Warfare Theory and Practice* (London: Paladin, 1970).

Tarling, Nicholas, *British Policy in the Malay Peninsula and Archipelago 1824–1871* (London: Oxford University Press, 1969).

Taylor, Philip M. *Munitions of the Mind: War Propaganda from the Ancient World to the Nuclear Age* (Wellingborough, Northamptonshire: Patrick Stephens, 1990).

Thio, Eunice, *British Policy in the Malay Peninsula 1880–1910, Vol. 1: The Southern and Central States* (Kuala Lumpur and Singapore: University of Malaya Press, 1969).

Thompson, Robert, *Defeating Communist Insurgency: Experiences from Malaya and Vietnam* (London: Chatto and Windus, 1966).

——, *No Exit from Vietnam* (London: Chatto and Windus, 1969).

Tilman, Robert O. 'The Non-Lessons of the Malayan Emergency', *Asian Survey*, Vol. 6, No. 8 (August 1966), pp. 407–419.

Too, C.C. 'Defeating Communism in Malaya', *Military Review*, Vol. 47, No. 8 (Aug 1967), pp. 82–92.

Towle, Philip, *Pilots and Rebels: The Use of Aircraft in Unconventional Warfare 1918–1988* (London: Brasseys, 1989).

Townshend, Charles, *The British Campaign in Ireland 1919–1921: The Development of Political and Military Policies* (London: Oxford University Press, 1975).

——, *Britain's Civil Wars: Counterinsurgency in the Twentieth Century* (London: Faber and Faber, 1986).

Tracey, Michael, *A Variety of Lives: A Biography of Sir Hugh Greene* (London: Bodley Head, 1983).

Turnbull, C.M. 'The Post-War Decade in Malaya: The Settling Dust of Political Controversy', *Journal of the Malaysian Branch of the Royal Asiatic Society*, Vol. LX, Part 1 (June 1987), pp. 7–26.

Valeriano, Napoleon D. and Charles T.R. Bohannan, *Counterguerrilla Operations: The Philippine Experience* (London: Pall Mall Press, 1962).

Walker, General Sir Walter, *Fighting On* (London: New Millennium, 1997).

Wang Gung Wu, ed. *Malaysia: A Survey* (London and Dunmow: Pall Mall Press, 1964).

Wardlaw, Grant, *Political Terrorism: Theory, Tactics and Counter-Measures*, 2nd edn. (Cambridge: Cambridge University Press, 1989).

Winstedt, Richard, *The Malays: A Cultural History* (London: Routledge and Kegan Paul, 1961).

Wong, Lin Ken, *The Malayan Tin Industry to 1914: with Special Reference to the States of Perak, Selangor, Negri Sembilan and Pahang* (Tucson, Arizona: University of Arizona Press, 1965).

Yong, C.F. *The Origins of Malayan Communism* (Singapore: South Seas Society, 1997).

Newspapers and Periodicals

Daily Mail
Daily Telegraph
Economist
Evening News
Far Eastern Economic Review
Glasgow Herald
Listener
Liverpool Post
Malay Mail
Malaya: The Journal of the British Association of Malaya
New Straits Times

New York Herald Tribune
Scotsman
Singapore Standard
Spectator
Straits Budget
Straits Times
Sunday Graphic
Sunday Pictorial
Times
Yorkshire Post

CORRESPONDENCE

Richard Clutterbuck, 22 July 1997.
W.P. Coughlan, 9 Dec 1998.
John Gullick, 3 July 1997.
Richard Stubbs, 27 Dec 1996.
C.M. Turnbull, 31 July 1997.
O.W. Wolters, 27 Feb 1998.

INTERVIEWS/DISCUSSIONS

Chin Peng (with Dr. Anthony Short, Prof. A.J. Stockwell, Prof. R.B. Smith and
    Mr. Robert Lemkin), 18 June 1998, London.
J.L.M. Gorrie, 16 Jan 1998, Singapore.
Christopher Gorrie, 19 Jan 1998, Singapore.
Datin Jean Marshall, 21 Jan 1998, Singapore.

Index

aborigines 45, 143
ACAO *see* Chinese Affairs Officers, Assistant Chinese Affairs Officers
Adams, Thomas K. 11
Adventures of Yaacob, The see propaganda, mobile units
AEBUS *see* Anti-Enemy Backing Up Society
Agency for International Development 14
AIO *see* Area Information Officers
Alexander, Harold 21
Alexander, Noel 130
Aliens Ordinance 6
Alliance *see* Alliance Party
Alliance Amnesty *see* surrender policies
Alliance Party 160, 162, 164–166, 190–191, 194, 198
All India Radio 76
All-Malayan Council for Joint Action 10
AMCJA *see* All-Malayan Council for Joint Action
amnesty *see* surrender policies
Anti-Bandit Month 79–80, 82, 84, 109, 212
Anti-Enemy Backing Up Society 8, 28
Anti-Terrorist Operations Manual 142, 149
Area Information Officers 182
Area Security Units *see* Security Forces
Army *see* Security Forces
ARO *see* Resettlement Officers, Assistant Resettlement Officers

Askenasy, Alexander 14, 16
assassination *see* Henry Gurney *and* propaganda
Assistant Chinese Affairs Officers *see* Chinese Affairs Officers
Assistant District Officers *see* District Officers
ATOM see Anti-Terrorist Operations Manual
Austers *see* propaganda, Voice Aircraft
Auxiliary Police *see* Security Forces

Babas see Chinese
Baling Peace Talks 160, 165, 194–198, 202, 215
banishment *see* propaganda, deportation
Banishment Ordinance *see* propaganda, deportation
Banting 175, 186–187, 214
base areas 1, 40, 42
BBC *see* British Broadcasting Corporation
Berita Melayu see propaganda, news
Blackburne, Kenneth 76
BMA *see* British Military Administration
Boer guerillas 17, 24–25
Boer War 24, 207
Boucher, C.H. 55, 63, 70–72
Bourne, Geoffrey 162–163, 165, 178, 186–187, 189–190, 192–193, 209

Bower, Roger 163, 167
Brett, J.G.H. 92
Brewer, Frank 59–60, 66, 163, 169
Briggs, Harold 12, 87–92, 94, 97–98,
    102–106, 118–120, 122, 124,
    127, 140, 155, 162–163, 177,
    204, 206–207, 209
Briggs Plan 17, 87 89, 91 92, 94, 97,
    102, 104, 119, 121, 159
British Advisers see British Residents
British Army (general) 21, 24, 121, 135
British Broadcasting Corporation 18,
    75, 105
    East European Service 105
    European Service 20, 106
    German Service 19, 105–106
British East India Company 4
British forces see Security Forces
British Military Administration 9, 28,
    33, 73, 75, 107
    Department of Publicity and Printing
    73
British Residents 5
    British Advisers 5, 90–91, 121–122,
    124–125, 176–177
British troops see Security Forces
Broga 125, 137, 176–177, 199
Broome, Richard 32, 59, 70, 114, 169
Broome, R.N. see Richard Broome
Brousse, Paule 13
Buffaloes are Ploughing see
    propaganda, mobile units
Burma 10, 12, 18–19, 23, 70, 74, 88,
    104, 183
Burma Revolt 24

Calcutta 10
Calvert, Mike 104
Campbell, Arthur 135
Can I Help You? see propaganda, radio
CAO see Chinese Affairs Officers
Cassells, James 163
Carruthers, Susan L. 2
central cooking 174, 176–179, 202,
    207, 210
Chen Tien 156, 194, 197–198
China 5–6, 8, 31, 34, 41, 59, 61, 132
    Communist 26, 34, 85, 113–114
    Communist, British Government
    recognition of 85, 107
    repatriation to 66–67, 83, 98, 174,
    193, 196, 198

Republican 28, 85
Chinese
    Home Guard 94, 129, 168–169
    immigration 5–7, 27, 59
    rural 2–4, 6–7, 16, 21, 24–31, 34,
    38–43, 45, 47, 49, 51–54,
    57–58, 60–65, 67–68, 72–74,
    76, 78–80, 84–85, 87, 89, 92,
    94–98, 100–102, 109,
    112–113, 118–120, 124–132,
    134–136, 140, 144, 147–151,
    159–162, 167–172, 174,
    176–177, 181, 186–187,
    196–197, 201–202, 204–208,
    211–212
    squatters 7–8, 10, 26, 29, 45, 57–58,
    60, 62–63, 65–67, 71, 73, 79,
    89, 93–96, 101–104, 112, 127,
    169–170, 204
    Straits (Babas) 5
    urban 7, 16, 28, 58, 60, 85, 112
Chinese Affairs Officers 87, 97,
    129–130, 140, 170, 208
    Assistant Chinese Affairs Officers
    130, 170, 208
Chinese Affairs Service 30, 59, 61, 67,
    97–98, 100–101, 105, 108,
    123–124, 138, 169–170, 187
Chinese Women's Association 9
Ching Kien 38–39
Chin Peng 10, 31–34, 36, 41, 48, 51,
    107, 117, 156–157, 160, 179,
    188, 190–191, 194–200, 202
Churchill, Winston 21, 121, 123
civic action see propaganda
Civics Courses see propaganda
Civic Talk see propaganda, radio
civil-military co-operation 3
Clausewitz, Carl von 11–13, 205
Cloake, John 2
Clutterbuck, Richard 15
collective punishment see propaganda
Colonial Film Committee 17
Colonial Film Unit 17
Colonial Office 4, 48, 55, 60, 76–77,
    83, 88, 92–93, 136, 138, 145,
    162, 190
Comforts from Uganda see
    propaganda, mobile units
Comintern 7, 31–32
Communist Extortion Methods see
    propaganda, mobile units

Communist terror *see* Malayan
    Communist Party
Community Listening *see* propaganda,
    radio
confidence 4, 11–12, 14–17, 21, 24–25,
    27, 35–36, 38–40, 52, 54–57,
    61–62, 64, 67–68, 70–72,
    83–87, 89, 92, 94, 97–98,
    102–103, 106, 109, 114,
    118–120, 124–127, 130–131,
    134–136, 140, 150–151, 156,
    159–161, 167–169, 171–172,
    174, 179, 186, 190–191, 197,
    201–202, 204–205, 208–209,
    211, 213, 215
Corry, W.C.S. 124, 164, 167–168
counterinsurgency 3, 11, 14, 24, 88–89,
    204–205
Crossman, Richard H.S. 18–20, 106,
    113–114, 116, 184, 212

Dakotas *see* propaganda, Voice
    Aircraft
d'Astugues, A.R. 146, 181
Davis, John 128–129, 208
Darkest Africa, The see propaganda,
    mobile units
Dawson, S.R. 97, 109
de Cruz, Gerald 33
de Fonblanque, E.B. 168–169
DEIO *see* District Emergency
    Information Officers
Delmer, Sefton 19
Department of Information Services 15,
    120, 138–139, 146, 148–149,
    151, 153–154, 156, 159–160,
    175, 180–182, 184, 197, 202,
    210–214
    Operations Section *or* Division 146,
        152, 181, 212, 213
Department of Public Relations 73,
    105, 180, 210–212
deportation *see* propaganda
detention *see* propaganda
DGIS *see* A.D.C. Peterson
Director-General Information Services
    see A.D.C. Peterson
Director of Information Services *see*
    Yaacob Latiff
DIS *see* Yaacob Latiff
District Emergency Information
    Officers 108

District Officers 61, 90, 97, 108, 122,
    129–130, 165–166, 168, 170,
    177, 182
    Assistant District Officers 137
District War Executive Committees 90,
    92, 103, 106, 108, 118,
    122–123, 138, 162–163, 165,
    177
DO *see* District Officers
documentaries *see* propaganda
DPR *see* Department of Public
    Relations
Dumeresque, J.S. 75–77, 112
DWEC *see* District War Executive
    Committees

EIS *see* Emergency Information Services
elections 16, 170, 182
    Federal 2, 160, 162, 164–166, 181,
        190, 192–193
    municipal 164
    New Village 2, 16, 129, 168–170
    State 2
Emergency
    military aspects 1–3, 11, 14, 16, 26,
        31–32, 44, 52–53, 57, 69, 71,
        90, 101, 121–122, 162, 179,
        186, 191, 202, 204–205, 210,
        214
    origins 9–10
    political aspects 1–2, 7–10, 12,
        14–15, 18, 27, 30–32, 34–36,
        40–41, 43–46, 49–53, 56–59,
        84–85, 89, 91–92, 102, 107,
        110, 121, 124, 161, 163–164,
        166, 169–170, 186, 191–192,
        194, 197, 199, 201–205, 208,
        213, 215
    psychological aspects 3, 11–16, 18,
        23–26, 43–44, 53, 70, 102,
        115–116, 133, 135, 139–141,
        143, 152, 159, 177–180, 186,
        188, 200, 204–205, 207, 214
    Regulations 54–55, 58, 64–68, 73,
        84, 87, 93–94, 97–100, 120,
        128, 136, 138, 159, 174, 194,
        196, 207
Emergency Food Denial Organisation
    176–177
Emergency Information Services 69,
    106–109, 115, 118, 144–146,
    154, 211–212

entertainment *see* propaganda
Ex-Servicemen's Association 9
Extortion see propaganda, mobile units

face-to-face propaganda *see*
    propaganda, speech
fair treatment policy *see* surrender policies
Family Resettled, A see propaganda,
    mobile units
Farmers' News see propaganda, news
Farming Talk see propaganda, radio
FEB *see* Ministry of Information, Far
    Eastern Bureau
Federal Military College 183
Federal Priority operations 178
Federated Malay States 5–7, 59
Federation Agreement 9–10
Federation Army 163, 172, 178
Ferret Force 63, 70–71, 104, 142, 209
Field Officers (mobile units) 74, 110,
    145–148, 151–152, 180, 182,
    213–214, 182–183, 210
film *see* propaganda, mobile units
FMS *see* Federated Malay States
FO *see* Field Officers (mobile units)
food control *see* propaganda
food denial *see* propaganda
Frezza, Daria 12

GCC *see* Good Citizens' Committees
Gent, Edward 55, 166
Gimson, F. 76, 123
Glass, Leslie 18
Good Citizens' Committees 80, 160,
    186–187, 190, 197, 199, 202,
    204, 211, 214
Gorrie, J.L.M. 123, 129–130
Gray, David 68
Gray, W.N. 55–56, 63, 88–90, 119, 122
Greene, Hugh Carleton 3–4, 19, 56,
    81–84, 87, 105–119, 144–145,
    147, 152, 155, 183–184, 186,
    210–214
Griffiths, James 99, 105–106
Gullick, J.M. *see* John Gullick
Gullick, John 67, 134, 166
Gurney Amnesty *see* surrender policies
Gurney, Henry 12, 56–58, 60–61, 65,
    68–69, 74–76, 79, 83, 88–89,
    91, 93–95, 97, 99, 101, 105,
    110, 114–115, 155, 207, 212
    assassination of 91, 98

Hack, Karl A. 2–3, 53, 64
Hackett, Jack 186, 214
Hassan's Homecoming see propaganda,
    mobile units
Hayter, A.G. 63
Head Emergency Information Services
    see Hugh Carleton Greene,
    A.W.D. James *and* Eliot
    Watrous
Head Psychological Warfare Section *see*
    R.J. Isaac, C.C. Too *and* O.W.
    Wolters
Health Talk see propaganda, radio
hearts and minds 1–4, 11–12, 24-25,
    39, 43, 57, 140, 162, 179, 201,
    204–205
Henderson, K.J. 68, 150
Ho Chi Minh 209
Hodge, Tom 146–147, 152, 181,
    183–184, 210, 214
Honorary Information Officers 182
Humphrey, P.B. 153

Immigration Restriction Ordinance 6
independence 1–2, 160–161, 163–196,
    198
    Merdeka 1–2, 125, 160, 163,
        166–167, 170, 177–178, 182,
        184, 195–196, 198–200, 204
Indian Empire 4
Indian Mutiny 21, 205
Indians 5, 7, 22, 43, 136, 171
Indonesia 9–10, 193
Infant Care and Feeding
    see propaganda, mobile units
intelligence 1, 3, 18, 21, 66, 68–70,
    81–82, 104, 108, 132,
    140–141, 146, 152, 159, 177,
    194, 204, 209, 212–213
    Combined Intelligence Staff 176
    Special Military Intelligence Staff
        141, 177
    Weekly Intelligence Summaries 142
Isaac, R.J. 146, 152, 181, 187, 212

Jackson, R.N. 108
Jackson, W.H. 76
James, A.W.D. 144, 146, 108, 152,
    211
Japanese Occupation 6–8, 28, 30–32,
    41, 107, 166, 184
Japanese surrender 8, 19, 28, 88

Jenderam 96, 98
Jenkin, William 90, 104, 108, 119
Jerrom, T.C. 92, 138
Josey, Alex 105–106, 112
Jungle Green 135

Katsina Tank see propaganda, mobile
    units
Katz, Phillip 15
Kropotkin, Peter 15

Lai Tek 10, 32
Lakin, E.H. 84, 153
Lam Swee 69–70, 107–110, 115–117,
    119, 152, 179, 212
Lasswell, Harold 11, 13
Lau Lee 32, 36, 156
leaflets *see* propaganda
lectures *see* propaganda, speech
Lee Dai Soh 113, 149, 210
Lee, H.S. 162–163
Linebarger, Paul M.A. 13
Litton, John C. 98, 101, 105, 108
live shows *see* propaganda,
    entertainment
Lloyd Owen, David 124
Loch, John 124
Lockhart, Robert Bruce 18–19, 122
Loose Nut see propaganda, mobile
    units
Love in the Jungle see propaganda,
    mobile units
Lucy, Peter 124
Luttwak, Edward 14
Lyttelton, Oliver 90, 119, 122, 134,
    136, 155, 164, 213

MacDonald, Malcolm 58, 61, 68, 74,
    85, 91, 121, 164, 166
MacGillivray, Donald 122, 162–163,
    187, 190, 192–195, 206, 209
Madoc, Guy 139
Magsaysay, Ramon 209
Malacca 4–5, 8, 43, 59, 67, 75, 98, 101,
    108, 110, 117, 138–139, 142,
    147–148, 150, 153, 157, 170,
    184–185
Malayan Administrative Service 7,
    180
Malayan Chinese Association 2, 49, 56,
    58, 60, 64, 68, 97–98, 128,
    130, 132, 164, 191

Malayan Civil Service 7, 56, 61, 67–68,
    73, 101, 121–122, 124, 161, 177
Malayan Communist Party 1–2, 4,
    7–10, 12, 16, 25–34, 36–55,
    57–58, 62–65, 67–68, 72–73,
    78–86, 89, 94, 99, 102, 107,
    110, 113–115, 117, 119, 130,
    135, 137, 141–144, 147,
    152–155, 160, 170, 176,
    178–180, 187–188, 191–192,
    194–199, 201–202, 204–207,
    212–215
    Central Committee 27, 32–34,
        36–53, 72, 82, 85–86, 103,
        115, 117, 144, 156, 159–160,
        189, 191–192, 194–199,
        201–202, 205, 214–215
    Communist terror 16, 26–27, 42–49,
        51–53, 57, 78–79, 103, 122,
        125, 176, 196, 204, 208
    demobilisation 4, 202–203, 214–215
    intelligence 31, 66, 146
    leadership 26, 29, 31–34, 38–39, 42,
        44, 47, 50, 52, 82, 106–107,
        116, 143, 147, 155–157, 180,
        189, 191–192, 198, 205
    mass surrenders of 1958 4, 84, 160,
        200–202, 214
    Min Yuen 30–31, 47, 95, 102, 106,
        115, 141, 143, 175, 186, 204
    October 1951 Directives 31, 41, 46,
        48, 50–51, 53, 205
    propaganda 4, 25, 36–37, 39, 41,
        44–46, 67, 72–73, 76–79, 86,
        108–109, 115, 146, 151–153,
        156, 159, 189, 191–192, 194,
        196, 205
    People's Awakening News 110
    People's Comments, The 119
    rank and file 3–4, 26–27, 29–31, 34,
        36, 38–40, 44, 47, 49–54, 72,
        82–83, 85–86, 104, 106, 115,
        117, 143, 147, 153, 156–157,
        160, 178–180, 192, 195, 200,
        201– 202, 205, 209–210, 215
    terrorists 1, 3–4, 12, 21, 24–27,
        29–31, 38–39, 42, 44–45,
        47–55, 57, 62–64, 66, 68–72,
        77–87, 89, 91, 94–96, 98–105,
        108–109, 111, 113–120,
        125–126, 128, 130–132, 135,
        137–147, 153–161, 163,

167–169, 172–182, 186–202, 204–206, 208–215
Malayan Democratic Union 9–10
Malayan Film Unit 74, 77, 80, 84, 110–111, 118–119, 144–146, 148, 152, 159, 181, 183–184, 202, 210–211, 213–214
Malayan News see propaganda, news
Malayan People's Anti-Japanese Army 8–10, 28–29, 31, 107
Malayan People's Anti-Japanese Union 8
Malayan Scouts see Special Air Service
Malayan Union 8–9, 73–74, 166
Malay College 7
Malay Nationalist Party 9
Malay Rulers 5, 7–9, 56, 93
Malays 2, 5–10, 26, 34, 43, 56, 58, 62, 73, 76, 93, 102, 111–112, 134, 136, 138, 146, 151, 164, 166–167, 171, 180, 182
    Home Guard 168
Malay States 5–6, 8–9, 30–31, 59, 61, 64, 69, 73–74, 76, 87, 90–93, 97, 104, 108, 110, 11, 118, 122–123, 127, 129–130, 134, 138, 145–147, 149–150, 165, 171, 176, 178, 181–182, 185, 189, 211
Marshall, David 195
Marshall, Jean 129
Mawai 95–96, 118, 207
Maxwell Police Mission 62
MCA see Malayan Chinese Association
McHugh, J.N. 73, 77, 81, 106, 118, 144, 146, 180, 210–213
MCP see Malayan Communist Party
MCS see Malayan Civil Service
MDU see Malayan Democratic Union
Merdeka see independence
Merdeka Amnesty see surrender policies
MFU see Malayan Film Unit
Miers, R.C.H. see Richard Miers
Miers, Richard 172, 189
Ministry of Information 17, 72
    Far Eastern Bureau 18, 72–73
    Political Warfare Division 73
Min Yuen see
    Malayan Communist Party
mobile cinema vans see propaganda, mobile units
Mockaitis, Thomas R. 2, 204
MOI see Ministry of Information

Montgomery, Bernard 21, 119, 121–123, 208
Morton, Jack 141
Moscow 10
Most, Johannes 15
MPAJA see Malayan People's Anti-Japanese Army
MPAJU see Malayan People's Anti-Japanese Union
music see propaganda, entertainment

national registration see propaganda
New Democratic Youth League 9, 28
New Villages see propaganda, resettlement
news, newsletters, newspapers, newsreels or newssheets see propaganda
New Life: Resettlement in Johore, The see propaganda, mobile units
New Malayan Gazette see propaganda, news
New Path News see propaganda, news
News of Malaya see propaganda, news

October 1951 Directives see Malayan Communist Party
Onn bin Jaafar 8, 164–166
Operation Bison see psychological warfare
Operations Greenland, Greenland II and Greenland III see surrender policies, Merdeka Amnesty
Operation Habitual see propaganda, food denial
Operation Hammer see propaganda, food denial
Operation Hammer II see propaganda, food denial
Operation Hive see propaganda, food denial
Operation Iceland 197
Operation Letter Box 140
Operation Question 137
Operations Section or Division see Department of Information Services
Operation Service see propaganda, Security Force behaviour towards public
Operation Sting see propaganda, food denial

Operation Tartan Rock 175, 207
Osman China 33, 52
Ow Kheng Law 184

pamphlets *see* propaganda
Pan-Malayan Federation of Trade
    Unions 9–10, 69, 107
Pan-Malayan General Labour Union 9
Pekan Jabi 137
Penang 4, 6, 8, 27–28, 42, 58–59, 67,
    75, 80, 100, 127, 145, 148, 154,
    170–171, 184–185
Permatang Tinggi 137
Peterson, A.D.C. 3–4, 51, 120, 134,
    145–153, 159–161, 180, 183,
    187, 206, 210–214
Philippines, the 206, 209
Phillips, Ivan Lloyd 165–166
Pisacane, Carlo 13, 15
plays, *see* propaganda, entertainment
PMFTU *see* Pan-Malayan Federation of
    Trade Unions
PMGLU *see* Pan-Malayan General
    Labour Union
Poland 10
Police *see* Security Forces
Police Field Forces *see* Security Forces
Police Special Squads *see* Security
    Forces
political warfare 12
Political Warfare Executive 19, 72
propaganda 2–4, 7, 11–17, 19–21, 25,
    27, 40, 47, 52–54, 56, 61, 64,
    66–67, 72, 74, 77–82, 84, 87,
    97, 104–106, 108–111,
    113–115, 117–118, 120,
    125–126, 128–129, 134,
    138–139, 142, 144–147,
    149–155, 159, 166–167, 175,
    178, 181–183, 186–188,
    191–193, 200, 202, 205–207,
    210–215
    assassination 13, 44, 119–121, 208
    British wartime philosophy of 3–4,
        18–21, 25, 80, 106, 114, 119,
        152, 212, 214
    civic action 14
    Civics Courses 3, 120, 149–151, 159,
        181–182, 202, 210
    collective punishment 22–23, 66,
        99–100, 118–119, 136–139,
        174, 207

definition of 12–17, 205
deportation 1, 57, 65–68, 83, 93, 98,
    136, 174, 194, 202, 207
    banishment 10, 134
    Banishment Ordinance 59
detention 1, 22, 55, 63, 65–68, 93,
    97–98, 100–101, 108, 118,
    136, 174, 177, 191, 193–195,
    202, 207
documentaries 17, 74
entertainment 17, 19, 21, 77, 111–113,
    150, 183–184, 213–214
    live shows 144, 147, 151–152, 210
    music/songs 17, 19, 37
    plays 113, 146, 151
    sketches 113, 144, 150–151, 182
    Bloody Revenge 144
mobile units 17, 19, 73, 110–111,
    118–119, 137, 144, 146–147,
    149, 151, 159, 175, 182–183,
    197, 202, 210–211, 214
    film shows 3, 13–14, 74, 77,
        110–111, 117, 144–148, 152,
        176, 210, 214
    Adventures of Yaacob, The 111
    Buffaloes are Ploughing 183
    Comforts from Uganda 17
    Communist Extortion Methods
        111
    Darkest Africa, The 144
    Extortion 148
    Family Resettled, A 111
    Hassan's Homecoming 183
    Infant Care and Feeding 148
    Katsina Tank 17
    Loose Nut 148
    Love in the Jungle 111
    *New Life: Resettlement in Johore,
        The* 111
    Rewards for Information 111
    Rohani Steps Out 183
    Serve to Lead 183
    Shame of Pusing, The 111
    Use of Shotgun 148
food control 1, 3, 87, 103–104, 113,
    118, 120, 138, 141, 143, 156,
    173, 196, 209
food denial 3, 21, 24, 141–142,
    172, 176–180, 190, 205,
    209–210
    Operation Habitual 141
    Operation Hammer 158

Operation Hammer II 141
Operation Hive 141
Operation Sting 141
ground-hailing equipment 157
 Magnavox 188, 211
 Stentor 188, 211
 Thunderer 188, 211
leadership, propaganda implications
 of 12, 21, 54, 68, 118–119,
 135, 208–209
 Bourne, Geoffrey 161–162
 Briggs, Harold 89, 92, 119, 123,
 208
 Gurney, Henry 56–57, 84, 98,
 125, 161, 208
 MacDonald, Malcolm 57–58, 208
 MacGillivray, Donald **161**
 Rahman, Tunku Abdul 164–167,
 201–202, 208
 Templer, Gerald 21, 119,
 123–126, 131, 137, 140, 159,
 161–162, 165, 208
leaflets/pamphlets 3, 13–15, 17,
 19–21, 38, 73–74, 77–84, 102,
 108–109, 113–117, 128, 139,
 144–145, 152–156, 158–159,
 175, 182, 188, 190, 192–193,
 197, 199–201, 210–212
national registration 25, 47, 71–72,
 209
news/newsletters/newspapers/
 newsreels/newssheets 17, 19,
 21, 72–74, 109, 113, 115, 139,
 148–149, 155, 180, 185, 189,
 210, 213
 Berita Melayu 74
 Farmers' News 73, 157
 Malayan News 111
 New Malayan Gazette 148
 New Path News 109, 152, 157
 News of Malaya 111
posters 3, 73, 80, 82
radio 13–14, 17, 19–20, 75–76, 80,
 95, 105, 111–113, 133,
 147–149, 184–186, 210, 212
 Community Listening 17, 76,
 112–113, 119, 127, 144, 149,
 159, 184–186, 210, 212–213
 Can I Help You? 113, 149
 Civic Talk 149
 Farming Talk 186
 Health Talk 149

*Six Golden Rules for the Home
 Guard* 149
Spotlight on the Emergency 113,
 149
*Surveys of Market Prices for Local
 Produce* 186
This is Communism 113
Village Gossip 186
Visit to Cheras New Village, A 149
Youth Talk 149
resettlement 1, 3, 24–26, 57, 66,
 79–80, 87, 89, 92–97, 99–100,
 102–103, 113, 118, 126–128,
 136, 207, 209
 New Villages 1, 16, 120, 125–132,
 134–137, 139–141, 147,
 149–150, 159–162, 167–170,
 172–173, 175–176, 178,
 180–185, 187, 194, 199, 202,
 206–208, 214
 Resettlement Areas *or* Camps 16,
 47, 76, 93–97, 99, 102–104,
 110–112, 115, 126–127, 144,
 207–208, 210
rewards 3, 17, 77, 116–117, 119,
 156–157, 189–190, 193,
 210–211
Security Force behaviour towards
 public 14, 21, 29, 47, 54,
 61–64, 68, 84–85, 87,
 100–102, 114, 118, 131–132,
 135–136, 172–174, 202,
 205–207
 Operation Service 120, 133–136,
 140, 149–150, 159, 171,
 206–207, 213
Security Force pressure on terrorists
 3, 69–71, 103–104, 141–143,
 177–179, 202, 209–210
Selected Areas 176
speech (spoken/lectures/talks/
 word-of-mouth/face-to-face) 3–4, 13,
 15, 18, 36, 39, 41, 54, 56, 63,
 72, 74, 76–80, 84, 87, 97, 106,
 109–111, 113, 117, 128, 139,
 144, 147, 149–151, 155, 167,
 171, 176, 181–182, 210
Voice Aircraft 120, 139, 157–159,
 188–190, 210
 Austers 158, 175, 182, 188–189
 Dakotas 157–158, 182, 188
 Valettas 158

Voice Aircraft broadcasts 3, 139, 143, 154, 175
Voice Aircraft Committee 181, 188–189
White Areas 120, 138–140, 159, 174–178, 187, 194, 201–202, 207
propaganda of the deed 4, 13–16, 25–27, 35–36, 38–39, 43–44, 52, 54, 68, 79, 86–87, 118, 120, 128, 135, 143–144, 151, 158–159, 179, 186, 201–202, 205, 207, 209, 212, 215
propaganda of the word 4, 12–16, 18–21, 25, 35–36, 39, 41, 44, 54, 72, 76–78, 84, 86–87, 105, 116, 118, 143–145, 151, 158, 186, 202, 205, 211, 214–215
psychological moment 20–21, 80, 84, 116, 144, 155, 158, 188–189, 192, 200, 213, 215
psychological warfare 12, 29, 104, 113–114, 117, 119–120, 124, 153, 157–160, 181–182, 187, 189–190, 196, 198, 212, 215
Operation Bison 155–156
Psychological Warfare Divisions (Europe) 20, 108
Psychological Warfare Division see Supreme Allied Commander Southeast Asia
Psychological Warfare Interrogation Centre 153, 155–156
Psychological Warfare Section, Director of Operations Staff 114, 153, 180–181, 188–190, 194, 196–197, 200, 202, 210, 212
4th PSYOP Group 211
Purcell, Victor 72, 135, 154
Pusing 100, 103, 199, 207
PUTERA 10
PWIC see Psychological Warfare Interrogation Centre
PWS see Psychological Warfare Section, Director of Operations Staff

radio see propaganda
Radio Malaya 75–77, 80, 84, 105, 111–112, 118, 139, 145, 148–150, 157, 159, 162, 180–181, 184–186, 189, 202, 210–212

Radio Singapore 185, 212
RAF see Royal Air Force
Rahman, Tunku Abdul 159–167, 174, 184, 190–202, 205, 207–209, 215
Razak, Abdul 162–163
Rees-Williams, David 64
resettlement see propaganda
Resettlement Areas or Camps see propaganda, resettlement
Resettlement Officers or Supervisors 97, 100, 108–109, 129, 140, 150
Assistant Resettlement Officers 97, 129–130, 137, 140, 150, 170, 176, 208
Resettlement Supervisors see Resettlement Officers
rewards see propaganda
Rewards for Information see propaganda, mobile units
Ritchie, Neil 56
Robinson, Perry J.B. 69, 126, 151
Rohani Steps Out see propaganda, mobile units
Royal Air Force 17, 23, 56, 62, 69–70, 101–102, 104–105, 107, 135, 142– 143, 157–158, 175, 188, 209
rubber 5–7, 28–29, 41, 44–45, 48, 51, 95, 102, 105, 107, 112, 125, 128, 139, 143, 149, 167–168, 172, 176, 204
Rundquist, E.A. 12

SACSEA see Supreme Allied Commander Southeast Asia
Sambanthan, V.T. 162–163
SAS see Special Air Service
Saunders, Kay 13
SCA see Secretary for Chinese Affairs
Second Congress of the Communist Party of India 10
Secretary for Chinese Affairs 59–61, 67, 73, 97–98, 125, 129–130, 138, 140, 144, 149–150, 163, 170, 208
Security Forces 1, 3, 8, 21, 26, 29, 42, 45, 48–49, 51, 53,, 58, 62–63, 67–72, 77, 79, 81–82, 84–85, 88–89, 99, 102, 104, 115–116, 117–118, 123, 125, 131, 138, 140, 163, 187

Area Security Units 131
Army 1, 43, 55, 61–63, 69. 72, 90, 162, 172–173, 175, 177–178
Police 1, 5, 7, 10, 30, 43, 45, 49, 55, 58, 61 69, 71, 73, 81, 83, 88, 90, 92, 94–95, 98–101, 106, 108, 110–111, 117, 121–123, 125, 129–132, 134–137, 141–142, 146, 150, 153–155, 157, 159, 162–163, 169, 171–179, 181, 187–188, 190, 199, 206, 213
Auxiliary 55, 77
Field Forces 131
Special Branch 32, 101, 104, 141–142, 150, 175–177, 182, 186, 189, 191, 194, 200–201, 207
Special Constables 24, 55, 57, 62–64, 95–96, 100–101, 123, 125–126, 128–129, 131–132, 171, 173, 206
Special Squads 131, 171
Semenyih 172–174, 177, 199, 202, 206
SEP see Surrendered Enemy Personnel
September 1949 Amnesty see surrender policies
September 1955 Amnesty see surrender policies
September 1957 Amnesty see surrender policies
SEIO see State Emergency Information Officers
Selected Areas see propaganda
Serve to Lead see propaganda, mobile units
Shame of Pusing, The see propaganda, mobile units
Sheppard, Mervyn 73–74, 120–121, 123, 176, 209
Short, Anthony 11, 31, 33, 88, 93
Siew Lau 43, 49, 117
Singapore 4, 8–9, 27–28, 59, 72–73, 75–76, 106–107, 118, 123, 139, 148, 184–185, 195
Singapore Federation of Trade Unions 9
Sino-Malay clashes 8
SIO see State Information Officers
Six Golden Rules for the Home Guard see propaganda, radio
sketches see propaganda
Sletto, R.F. 12

Slim, William 12, 88
songs see propaganda, entertainment
sook ching campaign 7
Sookoo Ling Nam 46
Southeast Asian Youth Conference 10
SOVF see Special Operations Volunteer Force
Special Air Service 104
Malayan Scouts 104
Special Constables see Security Forces
Special Operations Volunteer Force 142, 156, 191
Spotlight on the Emergency see propaganda, radio
Squatter Committee 207
squatters see Chinese
State Emergency Information Officers 107–110, 114–116, 118–119, 144–145, 147, 150, 152, 212
State Information Officers 146–147, 150–152, 181–183, 186, 188, 199, 213–214
State War Executive Committees 90–92, 106, 108, 122–123, 129, 138, 143, 146–147, 163, 165, 172, 176–177, 188, 190
Stewart, Brian 138, 140
Stockwell, Hugh 122, 142
Straits of Malacca 4
Straits Settlements 4, 8, 59, 91, 108, 113, 138
Stubbs, Richard 2, 64, 204
Sungei Siput 10, 177
Supreme Allied Commander Southeast Asia 72, 75, 145
Psychological Warfare Division 73
Burma section 18, 74
Malaya section 73
Surrendered Enemy Personnel 3, 29–30, 36–39, 41, 45, 60, 63–64, 67, 70–71, 74, 80, 82–84, 102, 107–111, 113–117, 119, 138, 142–145, 147, 149, 151–156, 158, 178–180, 182, 188–191, 193, 195–196, 198–200, 209–210, 212–213
surrender policies 3, 12, 82–84
Alliance/September 1955 Amnesty 192–196, 198–199
amnesty 17, 84, 114, 116, 154–155, 159, 190–192, 213, 215

fair treatment policy 12, 114–115, 144, 153–155, 179, 191–192, 196, 213
Gurney/September 1949
   Amnesty 82–84, 86, 114, 155, 191, 193, 212
March 1956 surrender terms 196
Merdeka/(September) 1957–8
   Amnesty 160, 198–201, 214–215
   Operation Greenland 199
   Operation Greenland II 200
   Operation Greenland III 201
Surveys of Market Prices for Local Produce, see propaganda, radio
SWEC *see* State War Executive Committees

talks *see* propaganda, speech
Tan Cheng Lock 58, 60, 64, 96, 98, 102
Tanjong Malim 102, 137, 140, 199
Taylor, Philip M. 13
Templer, Gerald 3, 21, 51, 56, 87, 120–129, 131–140, 142–146, 150, 152–159, 161–162, 174, 177, 206–209, 211, 213
Temporary Occupation Licences 6–7
terrorists *see* Malayan Communist Party
This is Communism see propaganda, radio
Thompson, Robert G.K. 15, 107–108, 204
Thomson, G.G. 76–77
tin 5–7, 27–29, 41, 48, 51, 59, 95, 100–101, 129, 168, 176, 204
TOLs *see* Temporary Occupation Licences
Too, C.C. 3–4, 29, 33–34, 38, 50–51, 61, 69, 79, 81–82, 106–109, 114–116, 119–120, 130, 144–146, 152, 159–160, 187–188, 190, 194–198, 202, 212–214
Tras 96, 98, 119
Trinity of War concept 11–14

UMNO *see* United Malays National Organisation

Unfederated Malay States 5
United Malays National Organisation 2, 8–9, 164, 191
Use of Shotgun see propaganda, mobile units

V Campaign 20, 80
Valettas *see* propaganda, Voice Aircraft
Vietcong 14, 210
Vietminh 156, 179–180
Vietnam 179
   South Vietnam 14, 26, 40, 42, 183, 208–209, 211
Village Gossip see propaganda, radio
Visit to Cheras New Village, A see propaganda, radio
Voice Aircraft *see* propaganda
Voice Aircraft broadcasts *see* propaganda
Voice Aircraft Committee *see* propaganda

Walker, Walter 70–71, 142, 149
Watrous, Eliot 106, 144, 211
Watson, Francis M. 14
Watts, W.J. 97, 108, 149–150, 169
Weekly Intelligence Summaries *see* intelligence
White Areas *see* propaganda
Wingate, Orde 24
Wolters, O.W. 68, 124, 187–188, 194, 212
word of mouth propaganda *see* propaganda, speech

Yaacob Latiff 3–4, 146, 160, 180–181, 183–184, 187–188, 202, 211–212, 214
Yeong Kwo 32, 197
Yong Peng 137, 177
Young, Arthur 122, 124, 131–133, 135–136, 138, 150, 159, 169
Younghusband, George 22
Youth Talk see propaganda, radio

Zhdanov, Andrei 10
Zhdanov line 10